# SAP® CRM Web Client—Customizing and Development

 PRESS

SAP PRESS is a joint initiative of SAP and Galileo Press. The know-how offered by SAP specialists combined with the expertise of the Galileo Press publishing house offers the reader expert books in the field. SAP PRESS features first-hand information and expert advice, and provides useful skills for professional decision-making.

SAP PRESS offers a variety of books on technical and business related topics for the SAP user. For further information, please visit our website: *www.sap-press.com*.

Markus Kirchler, Dirk Manhart, Jörg Unger
Service with SAP CRM
2009, 382 pp.
978-1-59229-206-6

John Burton
Maximizing Your SAP CRM Interaction Center
2008, 463 pp.
978-1-59229-197-7

Srini Katta
Discover SAP CRM
2008, 406 pp.
978-1-59229-173-1

Thorsten Franz, Tobias Trapp
ABAP Objects: Application Development from Scratch
2008, 505 pp.
978-1-59229-211-0

Michael Füchsle, Matthias E. Zierke

# SAP® CRM Web Client — Customizing and Development

Galileo Press

Bonn • Boston

Galileo Press is named after the Italian physicist, mathematician and philosopher Galileo Galilei (1564–1642). He is known as one of the founders of modern science and an advocate of our contemporary, heliocentric worldview. His words *Eppur se muove* (And yet it moves) have become legendary. The Galileo Press logo depicts Jupiter orbited by the four Galilean moons, which were discovered by Galileo in 1610.

**Editors** Florian Zimniak, Maike Lübbers
**English Edition Editor** Justin Lowry
**Translation** Lemoine International, Inc., Salt Lake City, UT
**Copyeditor** Lori Newhouse
**Cover Design** Jill Winitzer
**Photo Credit** Getty Images/Mark Harwood
**Layout Design** Vera Brauner
**Production Editor** Kelly O'Callaghan
**Assistant Production Editor** Graham Geary
**Typesetting** Publishers' Design and Production Services, Inc.
**Printed and bound in** Canada

**ISBN 978-1-59229-297-4**

© 2010 by Galileo Press Inc., Boston (MA)
1st Edition 2010
1st German edition published 2009 by Galileo Press, Bonn, Germany

**Library of Congress Cataloging-in-Publication Data**
F|chsle, Michael.
  SAP CRM web client : customizing and development / Michael Fuchsle, Matthias E. Zierke. -- 1st ed.
    p. cm.
  Includes bibliographical references and index.
  ISBN-13: 978-1-59229-297-4 (alk. paper)
  ISBN-10: 1-59229-297-6
  1. SAP CRM. 2. Customer relations--Management--Computer programs. 3. Management information systems. 4. Client/server computing. I. Zierke, Matthias E. II. Title.
  HF5415.5F86 2010
  658.8'120285676--dc22
                        2009028103

# Contents at a Glance

# Contents

## 7  Integrating Office Applications ................... 173

## 8  Web Client UI Framework ........................... 187

## 9  UI Component Architecture ......................... 209

## 15 Tips and Tricks ....................................................... 359

## 16 Practical Examples ................................................ 371

# Preface

SAP Customer Relationship Management (SAP CRM) is a comprehensive solution for managing customer relationships. It supports all customer-oriented business areas from marketing to sales to services, and customer interaction channels such as the Interaction Center, the Internet, and mobile devices. SAP AG makes a large number of innovative and additional functions for customer relationship management available with SAP CRM 2007, and this software solution is presented with a modern, browser-based user interface.

The goal of this book is to introduce the new browser-based CRM Web Client user interface and to help you understand how to use it. Its objective is to explain, in detail, the most important issues from real-life scenarios for real-life scenarios. This book supports you in your daily work as a *sales employee, user, application consultant,* or *technology consultant* using the SAP CRM 2007 product. Whether you are a beginner or an experienced user of SAP CRM solutions, the structure of this book ensures that you will always find questions from different perspectives and fields of experience addressed in one area. Many chapters also include selected practical examples.

> **Note**
>
> The book was written based on SAP CRM 2007 (SAP CRM UIF 600, SP 3). For the most part, however, the explanations about the Web Client UI framework also apply to SAP CRM 7.0. Differences between the two releases are summarized in Chapter 17, Outlook for CRM 7.0.

Because this is a very new topic and because we do not expect that all of our intended broad audience will have the same level of knowledge, we have chosen explanations and practical examples that are clear and easy to understand even for readers without detailed SAP technical knowledge. Nevertheless, we must assume that our readers have a basic understanding of SAP NetWeaver and, where technically-oriented chapters are concerned, are familiar with the ABAP programming language. Experience with integration or application knowledge of earlier SAP CRM solutions can be an advantage, but is not an essential prerequisite for understanding the content of this book.

Due to the complexity of the topics, we needed to limit coverage of closely-related CRM topics. Therefore, the book does not present the mapping of customer-based CRM business processes in SAP CRM 2007. For the process-oriented mapping of CRM contained in the kernel of the CRM solution, we recommend the book, *Service with SAP CRM* [Kirchler, Manhart, Unger, SAP PRESS 2009].

Our book instead focuses on the structure and options available for adjusting the user interface and the system we always refer to is the standard system. Industry-specific CRM solutions from SAP could not be taken into account and would far exceed the scope of this book. We also had to exclude CRM on-demand solutions and Interaction Center (IC) scenarios. The user interface for IC agents is originally based on the Web Client framework and SAP PRESS provides the book, *Maximizing Your SAP CRM Interaction Center*, [John Burton, SAP PRESS 2009] for the IC business scenario.

> **Note**
>
> In this book, we use the terms *user interface*, *CRM Web Client*, and *Web Client* synonymously.

We will now briefly introduce the content of the book's chapters. The application-oriented Chapters 1–7 were written by Matthias E. Zierke, and the technical Chapters 8–16 were written by Michael Füchsle.

Are you already familiar with the new browser-based user interface or have you yet to experience it? To address both situations, we have divided **Chapter 1** into two focus areas. If already know the user interface you can refresh your knowledge in a short and concisely summarized section—Overview of the User Interface. Or if you do not yet have any experience with the new CRM Web Client you can read the the detailed section — Detailed Analysis of the User Interface.

The role concept is the topic we focus on in **Chapter 2**, where we discuss how to utilize the new user interface correctly. The role concept is used to control the interface after the user logs on to the CRM Web Client. If you are not an expert in using the CRM role concept, be sure to read the first part of Chapter 2, in which we first describe a general business scenario in the CRM environment and then demonstrate a practical implementation in the system. If you are already familiar with the role concept, we recommend the Technical Description of the Role Concept section of Chapter 2. Here, you will learn how the business role is set up and the way in which changes to the Customizing of the business role affect the CRM Web Client.

**Chapter 3** centers on the configuration of the navigation bar that is part of the new user interface. In this chapter, we show you how to create links to connect CRM and non-CRM applications and how to define and assign work center pages. You will delve deeply into the related Customizing and learn how to set up and adjust your own navigation bar after you have completed this chapter. We will also introduce the transaction launcher — an integrated modeling tool for adjusting the user interface without requiring development knowledge. We will use selected examples such as integrating a BOR transaction to describe the advantages and disadvantages of the transaction launcher, and we will close this very important and complex chapter with two practical examples.

Another important area of the CRM Web Client is the header area. **Chapter 4** explains the adjustments you can make in this area without having any development knowledge. The key topics include defining the navigation frame and adjusting the layout components. The fourth chapter concludes with the topic of integrating the central search function, a function you can use to comprehensively search for business objects.

**In Chapter 5**, we will discuss how to redesign and restructure the user interface without development knowledge. At the core of the chapter, we describe the most important modeling tools such as the UI Configuration Tool and the Easy Enhancement Workbench (EEWB). You can use the UI Configuration Tool to redesign selected screen elements, and we will show you how to set up and use this tool correctly, including an explanation of the tool's limitations. If you need a new project-related input or output field on a CRM business object and subsequently want to present it in the user interface, the EEWB and UI Configuration Tool help facilitate this implementation. In this chapter, we also provide you with an in-depth discussion of the design layer for adjusting field descriptions, and you will find several practical tasks contained in this chapter.

**Chapter 6** covers the authorization concept for the CRM Web Client, the integration of Business Warehouse reports, and the inclusion of the CRM Web Client in the SAP NetWeaver Portal. For the Portal integration (optional for the CRM Web Client), we will illustrate the configuration steps required in the CRM Web Client. Chapter 6 also forms the foundation for the technically-oriented chapters. Basic technical knowledge is required starting with Chapter 7.

In addition to a software solution for customer relationship management, many users also require documents for their daily work. **Chapter 7** concentrates on the integration of web services and document templates for

Microsoft Word and PDF documents. Aside from the web service tool, which you can use to create model-driven web services, we will also show you how to create document templates using the Template Designer.

In **Chapter 8**, you will learn the basics of the Web Client UI framework and the functions of the Component Workbench, which is the work tool application developers use for creating UI components.

**Chapter 9** provides an introduction to the architecture of a UI component and explains the individual components of views, windows, and controllers. In addition to a brief introduction to programming BSP views, we will also introduce you to subject areas such as context binding, model integration, and navigation.

In **Chapter 10,** you will learn how to create form views, table views, and tree views. In this chapter, we will also show you how to create special page types such as overview pages, work center pages, and search pages. This chapter requires basic BSP programming knowledge.

**Chapter 11** explains the concept for enhancing UI components without having to make modifications. You will learn how to use enhancement sets as containers for enhancements and you will find useful information on enhancing UI components.

**Chapter 12** describes the components of an object model with GenIL objects along with the relationships they have with each other. After a brief description of the analysis tools, we will draw your attention to the ways in which you can enhance object models for business partners and business transactions. We will conclude the chapter with an explanation of the Web Service Consumption Tool (WSCT), which you can use to make GenIL objects available based on web services.

In **Chapter 13,** we will describe how to use the business object layer (BOL) on an object model of the GenIL. You will learn how to define a BOL entity and what the meaning of collections is. In this chapter, we will also explain traversing through an object model, and conclude with an explanation of the functions to process BOL entities.

**Chapter 14** provides details of cross-component services for designing the Web Client user interface. Specifically, we will explain how to create messages in the message bar, create breadcrumbs in the page history, and how to display dialogs.

**Chapter 15** contains many hints and tips about analyzing runtime errors. In addition to an explanation of the VIEW HIERARCHY dialog, in this chapter you will find helpful information on using limited breakpoints or reasonable entry points for debugging CRM applications.

In **Chapter 16**, you put the knowledge you have acquired into practice. Step by step, you will create your own UI component, which will encompass a search page and an overview page. We conclude the chapter by showing you how to integrate your UI component into the user interface.

In **Chapter 17**, we will give you a brief overview of the latest additional developments in CRM 7.0, divided into application-oriented and technical parts.

We hope that you enjoy reading this book and applying the knowledge you will gain.

## Acknowledgments

We would like to thank our publishing company for its great cooperation. In particular, we thank Maike Lübbers and Florian Zimniak for an outstanding job in editing and proofreading the manuscript.

Many of our SAP colleagues participated in the writing of this specialist book without whose help this could not have been achieved. Our thanks go to *Christian Altmoos, Dr. Silke Arians, Tim Back, Marek Barwicki, Katharina Bonitz, Thomas Buske, Gernot Conrad, Oliver Gräff, Daniel Grimm, Peter Hahn, Dominik Mark, Pascal Rössel, Volker Schwanenhorst* and *Felix Wente* for their expert cross-checking. We received valuable feedback and contributions on technical matters from *Uwe Reimitz*, who also acted as a co-author with a forward look to the upcoming CRM 7.0 release. We thank him sincerely for his commitment and contributions, which played a large role in improving the book.

Finally, I would to thank my wife, Silke, and my son, Valentin, for their understanding and constant encouragement and liters of coffee provided, and for spending time without me for many weekends and evenings, almost without complaint. I dedicate this book to you, my most beloved ones.

**Michael Füchsle, Landau**

It took many more days off than I had planned, many more weekends than I had thought, and many more evenings than I had imagined — and most of the time I felt as though a weight was hanging over my head. During this time, you always supported me and gave up so much: My most heartfelt thanks to my girlfriend, Caroline Lemonnier, to whom I dedicate this book.

**Matthias E. Zierke, Kelsterbach**

*The new SAP CRM 2007 is an integrated browser-based plat-form for handling all customer processes uniformly. Amid a pictogram-controlled interface, the user-friendly application builds an invisible bridge between all of the different types of task and knowledge areas in your company.*

# 1 Structure of the CRM Web Client User Interface

With SAP CRM 2007, SAP AG provides an enhancement of the SAP CRM product, a key application of the SAP Business Suite. This powerful software was developed together with customers and partners to make managing customer relationships even more effective and easier. During the redesigning of the CRM applications, great emphasis was placed on the graphical user interface. The challenge when redeveloping this product was creating a standard user interface for all CRM applications that can also be operated easily and intuitively. This goal has been achieved and implemented with the development of SAP CRM 2007's new graphical user interface, hereafter referred to as the *CRM Web Client*.

The browser-based interface not only increases acceptance among users, it also increases productivity for users working with CRM applications. Clear and structured classifications of the work area and navigation were implemented consistently for all application areas and levels. This ensures that data is processed faster through the user interface, which in turn makes it significantly easier for end users to analyze and enter information.

**Standardized user interface**

Despite the focus on a standardized user interface, the CRM Web Client offers a scope for personalizing the user interface that never existed before, and graphical elements can be readjusted and compiled based on the wishes of each user. The personalized user interface does not, however, affect other users or the functions of CRM applications and makes it easier for each user to carry out his daily work with any data processing system.

**Personalized user interface**

In addition to standardization and personalization, quick adjustments to the user interface to meet customer requirements are another key part of the new CRM Web Client. Embedding corporate identity components such as a logo or company colors can be implemented quickly. The uncomplicated

**Adjustable user interface**

options for customizing the user interface without any programming knowledge whatsoever are unique. You can also use numerous redesigning and restructuring tools to customize subareas of the user interface individually at any time according to your requirements. Despite the support from tools, an application developer may at times be required to help with customizing the user interface. In this book you will learn which adjustments you can make to the CRM Web Client using tools, and when development work is necessary.

Role-based user interface
The daily work in companies is carried out by highly specialized employees and every employee has a specialized view of the value added in the company. During development, these universal views of tasks and issues were also incorporated into the CRM Web Client. This enables each employee to obtain his own view of daily tasks and requirements based on his role in the company. The new CRM Web Client provides different views of CRM applications for different employee roles in the standard system. These different views can be used for subsequent adjustments to company-specific processes and thereby simplify the Customizing and development effort required.

Supported user interfaces
We would also like to mention at this point that, in the future, SAP will no longer support previously familiar user interfaces such as the *People-Centric User Interface* (PCUI) for technical enhancement issues. Only administrative tasks for the CRM Web Client will still be performed using the SAP Graphical User Interface (SAP GUI). If you want to upgrade an existing SAP CRM 4.0 or 5.0 system to SAP CRM 2007, you cannot automatically transfer customer-specific user interfaces to the CRM Web Client. For more information, refer to SAP Note 1118231.

## 1.1    Overview of the User Interface

This section provides you with an overview of the structure of the CRM Web Client user interface. You will find a more thorough analysis and detailed description of the page types in Section 1.2. If you already have some experience with the CRM Web Client, this section will be sufficient to refresh your knowledge.

Range of functions
The purpose of the CRM Web Client user interface is to support an employee in fulfilling all of the important day-to-day tasks that his role entails. For employees from the marketing department, this involves segmenting target groups or creating marketing campaigns; sales employees can create new orders; and service employees can worry about necessary repairs. Consequently, the user interface in the standard system is already preconfigured for special task areas in the company. CRM applications not relevant for indi-

vidual task areas of employees are hidden or displayed using the role concept of the CRM Web Client (see Chapter 2). For example, service employees will not need access to CRM applications for creating and executing campaigns, and sales employees will not have access to the CRM service applications for resource planning and service confirmations.

Figure 1.1 shows the range of functions of the CRM Web Client. The structure of the user interface is the same for all users and roles.

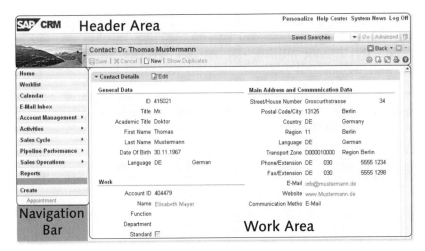

**Figure 1.1** Range of Functions of the CRM Web Client

The user interface is divided into three large and self-contained areas:

▶ Navigation bar

▶ Header area

▶ Work area

The layout of the navigation bar and header area is also referred to as an *L shape*. The L shape consists of the header (top) and navigation (left). The work area appears in the center of the user interface. It is also known as the "flexible component" of the user interface due to its customizability.

*Breakdown of the user interface areas*

We will first provide you with an initial overview of the layout of the individual areas on the user interface and their tasks, and then give you a more detailed description of the individual areas in the next section.

The *navigation bar* supports you in the intuitive interaction between individual CRM applications that you call in the work area. The structure of the navigation bar depends on the navigation bar profile (Chapter 3) that is used to call

*Navigation bar*

the CRM Web Client. In addition to calling CRM applications, every user can also manage his appointments (CALENDAR), daily tasks (WORKLIST), and the creation and sending of e-mails (E-MAIL INBOX) using the navigation bar.

Header area

Components of the *header area* include starting search queries (saved searches) or navigating to pages that have already been visited (page history). The header area also contains system links. Work area titles and toolbars relate to the information displayed in the work area but are assigned to the header area (Chapter 4).

Work area

In the *work area,* all page types (see Section 1.2.3) of the CRM Web Client are displayed with the corresponding information (the types of pages displayed can vary). The navigation bar and header area create the framework for accurate navigation.

Displaying subject matter in the work area

Following this very brief overview of the range of functions of the CRM Web Client, we will focus on the flexible component of the user interface, the work area. As the owner of a role, you can perform different tasks in the work area of the user interface. Entering a sales order or searching for a contact person are just two task areas you'll encounter in your daily work using a CRM application. Different page types are required to be able to fulfill these tasks. Page types are always displayed in the work area of the user interface and they use different interfaces customized to the corresponding tasks. For example, the layout of a search page differs significantly from that of a page for processing a business partner. While specifically defined properties such as name, address, or telephone number are of primary importance on an edit page for business partners, the main area of interest on a search page (aside from the result list) is the input of search criteria. Due to these very different requirements, several page types are available for the CRM Web Client. Table 1.1 shows an overview of the different page types you can call in the work area and briefly describes the properties of the pages.

In addition to the previously-mentioned pages, we also differentiate other supporting pages *(dialogs)*. These are windows for entering search and value help and for personalizing the user interface.

Breakdown of page types

| Page Types | Short Description |
| --- | --- |
| Home page | The home page is always displayed after you start the CRM Web Client. The most important information about the daily work is presented in collapsed format, and you can directly access frequently used applications. |

**Table 1.1** Breakdown of Page Types

| Page Types | Short Description |
|---|---|
| Work center page | The layout of the work center page corresponds to the business role and the page contains links to important applications. The links for calling applications are grouped according to tasks. |
| Search page | The search page provides users with comprehensive search capabilities for every CRM component. You call a search page through the second level of the navigation bar, via the work center page or home page. |
| Overview page | The overview page displays all information about a business object. Relationships to other business objects are also shown here. From here, you can navigate to subordinate overview pages. In certain business objects, the details are displayed as a hierarchy. The overview page is used in two modes: Display mode (you can view all data) and edit mode (you can change business object data as well as the data in most assignment blocks). |
| Edit page | You use the edit page to adjust business objects and relationships to other objects. The data is displayed either as simple forms or as lists for processing. |
| Assignment blocks | The overview page contains assignment blocks that you can use to display the most important data for a business object. From here, you can also navigate to edit pages. |
| Reports page | Links for starting reports are stored on the reports page. You can start the page from the first level of the navigation bar. |
| Calendar | The calendar can be accessed through the first level of the navigation bar and displays all of the user's appointments and tasks. |
| E-mail inbox | The e-mail inbox gives you access to your groupware solution (Microsoft Outlook or Lotus Notes) to ensure that e-mails from the CRM application can be sent and received. |

**Table 1.1** Breakdown of Page Types (Cont.)

## 1.2 Detailed Analysis of the User Interface

We recommend reading this section if you do not have any experience with the CRM Web Client. In this section, in addition to a detailed description of all areas of the user interface, we explain the individual page types fully. All page types are displayed in the work area of the user interface, and the CRM Web Client UI framework makes different page types available based on the assigned task. For example, a summary of all of the important information for your daily work is displayed on the home page, while the search page has been optimized for identifying business objects quickly.

> **Note**
>
> Due to the wide range of possible applications involved when working with the CRM Web Client, we can only illustrate selected examples. For practical examples, we primarily use the standard sales role (SALESPRO). For describing the page types and their properties, we use the CONTACT DETAILS and ACCOUNT business objects as examples. There may be differences compared with other CRM applications.

### 1.2.1 Navigation Bar

The navigation bar is located on the left side of the user interface and you cannot change its position (see Figure 1.2). Together with the header area, it forms the *L shape*. You can call CRM applications using the navigation bar and if you do, they are always displayed in the work area. You can also display external applications such as web pages in a separate browser window (see Chapter 3). In addition to the role-based CRM applications, the *home*, *e-mail inbox*, *calendar,* and *worklist* pages can also be called via the navigation bar in the standard system to record the daily tasks for each user. Now let's take a look at the exact structure of the navigation bar and then discuss the differences in structure depending on the user role.

**Structure of the navigation bar**

The navigation bar of the CRM Web Client is divided into three strictly defined areas:

▶ First level navigation

▶ Second level navigation

▶ Direct links (Create area)

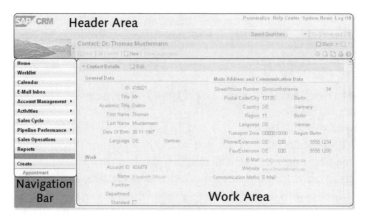

**Figure 1.2** Layout of the Navigation Bar

The first level navigation is always located in the upper part of the navigation bar and contains the main menu options (❶ in Figure 1.3). We recommend that the first level navigation you build contains no more than ten menu options. Any more entries will quickly become confusing for the user. You should also pay attention to the sequence of the menu options because this makes it easier for users to use the CRM Web Client.

First level navigation

We recommend the following sequence for menu options:

1. Home
2. Worklist
3. Calendar
4. E-mail Inbox
5. Role-based menu options
6. Reports

With the exception of the HOME menu option, you can customize all of the other entries of the navigation bar. After you have selected a menu option, the relevant CRM application is called in the work area. We will describe the individual page types in detail when we discuss the work area (see Section 1.2.3). We also recommend that you use no more than 18 characters when selecting names for the menu options. Longer names will automatically result in a line break.

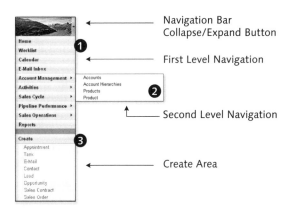

**Figure 1.3** Navigation Bar for Sales Employees

Figure 1.3 shows the navigation bar of the CRM Web Client in the role of a sales employee. It also shows the context menu for the ACCOUNT MANAGE-MENT (❷) CRM application next to the first level navigation. The context menu enables you to navigate to the second level. Not every menu option

Context navigation

of the first level navigation has supporting navigation. Menu options with a context menu can be identified by an arrow in the right-hand area of the menu button. You can use the context menu to open a search page in the work area. The search page called is displayed in a predefined format based on the selected business object, for example, CONTACT. If you click on the triangle a second time, the context menu collapses again.

When subsequently customizing the navigation bar, you should ensure that the links of the context menu form a subset of the menu option for the first level navigation. However, in addition to search pages for business objects, you can also store other CRM applications in the context menu.

Direct links
The direct links are grouped in the third area of the navigation bar (❸, see Figure 1.3). You can navigate directly to other CRM applications using the links stored here. You can also access web-based applications (e.g., web pages) and other SAP systems directly. The application you call using a direct link can be displayed in a new browser window or in the work area of the CRM Web Client. The APPOINTMENT, E-MAIL, TASK, and CONTACT direct links are by default maintained in the navigation bar for each role. Four other role-specific links are also stored here.

Hidden navigation
The navigation bar can be expanded or collapsed from its header (see Figure 1.3). If the user closes the navigation bar, the work area of the CRM Web Client is extended by space previously taken up by the navigation bar area. If the user expands the navigation bar again, the Web Client UI framework readjusts the size of the work area accordingly.

Role-based navigation
As already mentioned, the navigation bar depends on the role of the employee in the company. Corresponding navigation bars for standard roles (e.g., marketing, sales, or service employees) are already predefined in the standard system. Make sure that you use these default settings. They will make it easier for you to set up your own user interfaces. However, it is worth mentioning that you should only customize a copy of the standard role, not the actual standard role provided in the standard system. We will discuss this topic and the options for customizing the menu bar based on specific roles in more detail in Chapter 2.

### 1.2.2 Header Area

Aside from the navigation area, the header area of the CRM Web Client is the second area statically arranged on the user interface. You cannot change the position of the header area on the user interface; you can only change its size and content. You also cannot scroll in the header area. The navigation bar and header area create the framework for navigation.

Figure 1.4 shows the header area of the CRM Web Client, which is divided into several areas: **Structure of the header area**

▶ Logo area

▶ System links

▶ Saved searches

▶ Page history

▶ Work area title

▶ Work area toolbar

▶ Message bar

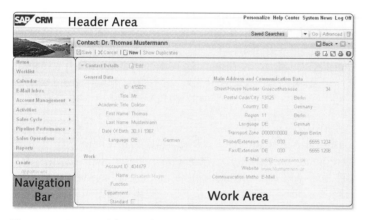

**Figure 1.4** Layout of the Header Area

In the header area, we differentiate between global functions and the context area. Global functions include the logo area, system links, the page history, and saved searches. These areas are global functions and do not depend on the CRM application displayed in the work area. The work area title, work area toolbar, and message bar are assigned to the context area. They relate to the CRM application displayed in the work area.

The logo area of the header is located in the upper left corner of the user interface. Here, you can store a company logo. The dimension of the logo in the standard system should be 111 x 42 pixels. If you want to store a bigger logo, we recommend that you change the size of the header in Customizing (see Section 4.2). The logo area is not shown in Figure 1.5 for space reasons. In Section 2.6.2, we will show an example of how you can change the logo in the header of the user interface. **Logo area**

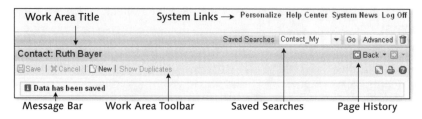

**Figure 1.5** Header Area of the CRM Web Client

**System links**   The system links are located in the upper right-hand area of the header. In the standard system, the four system links are arranged in the following sequence: (1) PERSONALIZE, (2) HELP CENTER, (3) SYSTEM NEWS and (4) LOG OFF. The sequence of the system links may differ for CRM on-demand solutions and for the user interface in the Interaction Center (IC) agent role. In the text that follows, we will look at the system links for the CRM Web Client and their properties in more detail. (We will not be discussing IC scenarios here. For more information on IC scenarios, you can refer to the book, *Maximizing Your SAP CRM Interaction Center*, by John Burton, which is also published by SAP PRESS.)

### 1. Personalize

**System link: Personalize**   You can design the user interface of the CRM Web Client according to your requirements. In addition to customizing the color of the background and text, you can also determine the size of the text itself. You can also use the personalization option to create shortcuts for applications. You store general information about the CRM Web Client user on the MY DATA tab. The settings you configure here have no effect on the CRM applications. Because personalization affects a large area in the CRM Web Client, we have dedicated a separate section to this topic. In Section 1.3, we describe—in detail—the areas of the user interface that you can personalize.

> **Note**
>
> You can store shortcuts for starting CRM applications using the PERSONALIZE (system links) function or the Customizing for business roles (see Section 2.2). These shortcuts should not overlap with commands for the browser.

### 2. Help Center

**System link: Help Center**   You use this link in the standard system to call the CRM online help, which gives you an initial overview of how to use the CRM Web Client. Detailed information about customer-specific adjustments to the user interface are not stored here. SAP Note 1038204 provides support in setting up the Help Center.

3. **System News**

This link provides you with additional, detailed system news, giving you information about any necessary additional steps. A distinction is made between news that relates to the work context (this news is displayed in the message bar) and news that refers to the system.

System link: System News

4. **Log Off**

Entering your user ID and password in the logon box takes you to the home page, which contains your most important personal information such as tasks and appointments. Click Log Off to end your work session. You can control or adjust which Web page is subsequently called. In the standard system, the SAP AG Web page is called (see Section 2.3.2).

System link: Log Off

In addition to system links, *saved searches* are also part of the global functions of the header area. Saved searches enable you to access a list of already saved search queries. They are stored under the system links in the header area of the CRM Web Client. You start search queries from the search page (see Section 1.2.3). You can also save search queries on the search page. Only the user who is logged on can subsequently call saved search queries through the Saved Searches field in the header area of the CRM Web Client. When the Saved Searches option is executed, the result list is always dynamically adjusted and updated.

Saved Searches

The work area title depends on the business object displayed in the work area and can therefore be defined in different ways. Aside from deriving the work area title from the displayed business object, you can also derive it from the transaction type or category name (e.g., activities management). When you call a search page, the type of business object is used for determining the title. Table 1.2 shows how the work area title is composed for the different page types.

Work area title

We recommend that you use this composition of titles when creating your own pages. An example of implementing an individual work area title is shown in Chapter 14, Section 14.7.2.

| Page Type | Composition of Work Area Title | Example |
|---|---|---|
| Work center page | <Description of work center page> | Activities |
| Search page | Search: <Object type (plural)> | Search: Contact person |

**Table 1.2** Composition of Work Area Title

| Page Type | Composition of Work Area Title | Example |
|---|---|---|
| Overview page | <Object type>: <Attribute> (maximum of three attributes) | Account: SAP AG, Walldorf |
| Edit page | <Object type>: <Attribute>, <Attribute> – title of assignment block | Contact: Max Mueller |
| Page for creating a new object | <Object type>: New | Contact: New |
| Saved searches | Search: <Name of search> | Search: My contact |

**Table 1.2**  Composition of Work Area Title (Cont.)

Page history  The page history (*history navigation*) is also located at the same level as the work area title in the header area of the user interface. Using the page history, you can access pages you've already visited. A selection list (see Figure 1.6) shows the history based on breadcrumbs. If you select one of the work area titles in the selection list, you are taken directly to the required page.

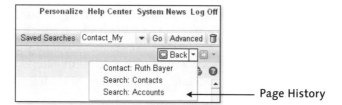

Page History

**Figure 1.6**  Page History in the Header Area

When you use the page history, you will always find the pages of your application in the same context in which you left them. For instance, all results and search terms will be displayed again for a search page.

The framework automatically controls the deletion of entries. Every work area title is only displayed once in the selection list even if you navigate to the same page twice. In Section 14.3, we describe how to use the navigation bar to perform actions.

You can also use the page history of the Internet browser, but in a limited way. SAP recommends that you do not navigate through the Internet browser at all because for the CRM Web Client, the page history functions have not been integrated fully to the Internet browser. Navigating through the Internet browser can also impair the performance of the CRM Web Client because different technical settings have to be defined. Refer to SAP Note 1002385 (for IC, SAP Note 884976) to find out the relevant settings.

The work area toolbar is located under the work area title. It contains all functions that are required to display or edit content in the work area. You can also use the work area toolbar to create a new business object, or it can provide support (e.g., buttons) for editing the displayed content (see Figure 1.7). The home and overview pages contain settings to personalize the page. For every overview page, on the right side of the user interface you will also find a button for personalizing and printing.

**Work area toolbar**

**Figure 1.7**  Work Area Toolbar and Message Bar

The message bar is situated below the work area toolbar in the header area of the CRM Web Client. The message bar displays information and warning and error messages that have occurred during the editing of content in the work area. Messages are triggered by stored plausibility checks when business objects are being edited. The messages in the message bar differ from the system news in the system links, and messages that refer to activities in the work area are not displayed through the system links. If additional information exists for the message text in the message bar, the DETAILS link appears before the message. By clicking on this link, you can display a detailed description of the error. If you want to create separate logic with separate messages, refer to Section 14.1.

**Message bar**

### 1.2.3    Work Area

The work area is in the center of the user interface (see Figure 1.8). Its flexibility lies in the fact that it allows parts of pages in the work area to be moved using drag-and-drop. For example, the user can move individual assignment blocks on the overview page or information blocks on the home page with the mouse, without any involvement in Customizing and without additional development. The framework saves the changes made to the layout by the user. They will be available again the next time the page is called and when the user logs on to the CRM Web Client again. Next, we will look in detail at the individual page types and their flexible components.

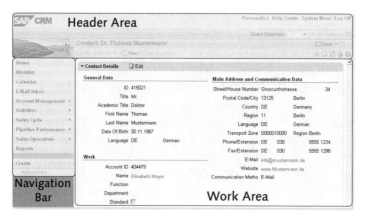

**Figure 1.8** Layout of the Work Area

Page types
The CRM Web Client uses different page types for maximum flexibility when displaying information. The following page types are available:

▶ Home

▶ Work center page

▶ Search page

▶ Overview page

▶ Edit page

▶ Reports page

▶ Calendar

▶ E-mail Inbox

Overview of the main pages
The home page, work center page, overview page, and pages for displaying reports are composite pages and are also known as the main pages of the CRM Web Client. You can use these main pages to display different content variably in information blocks. Main pages support 1 to n information blocks that can be arranged in two columns to get a better overview (see Figure 1.9). In terms of structure and size, the information blocks of the first column (left part of the screen) are independent and variable from those of the second column. An information block may also fill the entire work area.

Structure of information blocks
A defined information block typically consists of a title and a work area. You can navigate from the work area of the information block to other page types using links. The title should summarize the content of the information block. On the home page, graphics can also be displayed in addition to the title of information blocks.

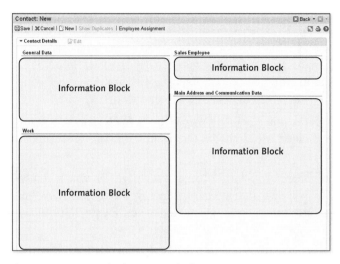

**Figure 1.9** Layout of Information Blocks on Page Types

Displaying data in information blocks can have different characteristics for main pages, as shown in Figure 1.10:

*Displaying data in information blocks*

▶ List

▶ Written description

▶ Form or edit mode

▶ Analytical content block

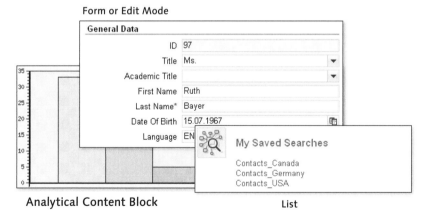

**Figure 1.10** Information Block Display

Lists enable you to organize a vast amount of information in rows. Each line can contain several fields or a freely defined text. Usually, a line is displayed

*Displaying lists in information blocks*

and through this line, the user can navigate to other information using a link. The link can also reference third-party applications outside of the CRM application. The list display in information blocks is used on the home page of the CRM Web Client in the standard SAP system (see Figure 1.11). Here, you can display daily appointments and tasks or important reports. You can then use the link to navigate directly to the selected appointment.

The contents of information blocks can also include a freely definable written description. User-defined text describes the application that can be opened by a stored link.

**Form or edit mode in information blocks**

You can also display data using forms. Some of the pages on which you will find forms include overview and edit pages. Here, you can create new business objects or service orders, or implement changes. Figure 1.10 shows a form from the CRM application for creating a contact.

**Analytical content block in information blocks**

You can also have an analytical content block in information blocks. In most cases, however, it makes sense to display these content blocks in the entire work area, not in an information block. Analytical content blocks require a greater share of system resources and should only be used if displaying content as a list, form, or written description is not feasible. Having looked at the primary components used across the pages, we will now describe the page types in detail.

**Home page**

The home page is the starting point for every user after they log on to the CRM Web Client, regardless of their role in the company. This page contains the most important tools and provides direct links to individual applications based on the business role (see Section 2.2).

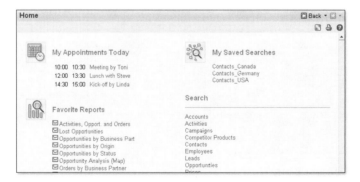

**Figure 1.11** Home Page

Figure 1.11 shows a section of the Home page. In this example, four information blocks are on the page. At a glance, you can find the open tasks and appointments for the current day. Important reports and saved searches are also displayed here. You can use the personalization function (see Section 1.3) of the page to define how many and which information blocks should be displayed. You can display a maximum of fourteen information blocks on the home page.

Among other things, the work center page is used as an entry point for all role-based menu options at the first level (first level navigation) in the navigation bar. The page is divided into several information blocks and contains data and links to pages that relate to the selected menu option of the navigation bar. Work center pages therefore provide a holistic overview of a subject area.

**Work center page**

In the standard system, the work center page for the ACCOUNT MANAGE-MENT example is made up of three information blocks (see Figure 1.12). This reflects the structure of most work center pages, although you will find some with a different structure. So we will take a closer look at the three different information blocks, SEARCH, REPORTS, and CREATE.

**Figure 1.12**  Work Center Page

▶ **Search**

The SEARCH information block (❶) shows all branches to possible search queries based on the stored role. You can add search queries to the information block and if you do, you should ensure that the search queries also relate to the selected menu option. When you select a search query, for example, ACCOUNT, a *Search page* page type opens.

**Work center page: Search**

▶ **Reports**

Reports relating to the work center page are displayed in the REPORT (❷) information block. Figure 1.12 shows two reports for Account Management. You can add more reports using Customizing options.

**Work center page: Reports**

► **Create**

In the CREATE (❸) information block, you can create new sales orders, individual accounts, or corporate accounts, depending on the page assignment. In the standard system, the menu option selected in the navigation bar determines the CRM applications to which this information block can branch; in this example, the sales role (SALESPRO, see Section 2.1.2) and the ACCOUNT MANAGEMENT menu option were selected in the navigation bar. The links can overlap with direct links in the navigation bar. In the standard system, the CREATE content block is always stored on the right side of the work center pages. In addition to being used when creating the work center page, information blocks are also used to display information when the reports page is being set up.

You can also call the reports page from the navigation bar. The reports page is the "hub" for all evaluation options. The selection of reports is based on roles; in other words, in the standard system, not all evaluation reports are available for every user.

Different information blocks that already divide reports into specific subject areas are provided in the standard system. Figure 1.13 shows a Reports page that has several information blocks and is assigned to a standard sales role (SALESPRO).

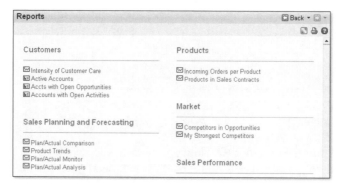

**Figure 1.13**   Reports Page

The names of the reports are displayed as hyperlinks in the assigned information blocks. Before you name a report, you can also create small pictograms for individual identification. When you follow the link, the report is started in a new browser window or in the work area of the user interface. In Chapter 6, Section 6.1, we will describe how you integrate reports into the work area of the CRM Web Client.

Now that you know where you can perform evaluations using reports, we will discuss the overview page next. This page contains an overview of all relevant data of a selected business object and of assigned business objects. The properties of the selected business object are displayed in the header area (details area) of the overview page. You can use the assignment blocks of the overview page to display the associated business objects. There are specific overview pages for different business objects (e.g., for business partners, business transactions, or campaigns) that, accordingly, have different structures.

Overview page

We will now look at the structure of the overview page using a contact example (see Figure 1.14). You will find a development example in Section 16.4. The overview page for displaying the contact consists of a title (❶), detailed description of the header data (❷), and information related to the business object, which is displayed as an assignment block (❸). In this case, 1 to n assignment blocks (e.g., business partner or opportunity) can be displayed on the overview page for the contact. If a very large number of assignment blocks are defined through Customizing or by personalizing the page, the user must scroll to display all assignment blocks.

Structure of the overview page

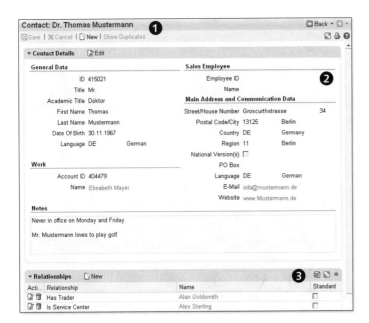

**Figure 1.14** Overview Page for a Contact

We will use the contact example to get a detailed picture of the three main characteristics of an overview page.

### Title and Work Area Toolbar

The title and work area toolbar (❶ in Figure 1.14) are elements of the header area of the CRM Web Client. The title of the overview page is meant to give the user a quick overview of the called business object. The title in this case consists of the type of business object (here, Contact) and additional descriptive object attributes. The title of all overview pages is structured as follows in the standard system:

<Object type>: <Attribute 1>, <Attribute 2 (optional)>, <Attribute 3 (optional)>

Figure 1.15 shows the composition of the overview page title for a corporate account.

**Figure 1.15** Title of an Overview Page

The object type of the title is always a written description of the business object in singular form. The CORPORATE ACCOUNT: MEGASTORE/DENVER CO 80224 business object is displayed in the example chosen here. The selected attributes (Name, Postal Code/City and State) of the business object are used for more precise description purposes. If the attribute descriptions are too long, a second line is added for the title. In this context, we recommend that you select a screen resolution of at least 1024 × 768 pixels for using the CRM Web Client so that a second line will not be needed for the title.

The work area toolbar of the overview page is situated under the title in the header area of the CRM Web Client. You can use the buttons of the work area toolbar to edit the selected business object. In the example, the SAVE and CANCEL functions for implemented changes and the NEW function for creating a new business object are available. In addition to a duplicate check, in the standard system the MORE function contains a *fact sheet* (PDF or online version) for the account.

## Details Area

The most important header information of the business object is displayed to view at a glance in the details area (❷ in Figure 1.14). To explain the details area of the overview page, we refer again to the illustrated CONTACT example. Each details area has a title. When you define the details area using the UI Configuration Tool (see Chapter 5, Section 5.1), you determine which titles and fields you want to be available in the details area as display and input fields. As you can see from the contact example, general data such as the name and title are displayed in the standard system. Next to this, you will find the main address and communication data, the business address, and the name of the sales employee responsible.

Overview page:
Details area

## Assignment Block

The information of dependent objects is displayed in assignment blocks (❸ in Figure 1.14). This is how you get detailed insight into the selected business object. You can navigate directly to the related business object from the entries in assignment blocks. You can personalize the sequence of assignment blocks using drag-and-drop.

Overview page:
Assignment blocks

Which of the assignment blocks should be displayed is already defined when you call the overview page. You define this by personalizing the overview page (see Section 1.3) and using the UI Configuration Tool. Figure 1.16 shows a selection of assignment blocks for the overview page of the account.

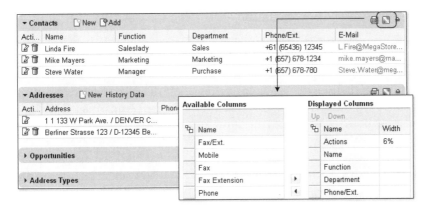

**Figure 1.16** Assignment Blocks of an Overview Page

First, the UI Configuration Tool is used to determine which assignment blocks are available for the selected overview page. Using the personalization function of the overview page, the user can then also choose whether certain assignment blocks should be displayed or hidden. The same model is used to define whether assignment blocks are already open or closed when the overview page is called. You can use the UI Configuration Tool to determine whether the assignment blocks are displayed in a *direct* (expanded) or *lazy* (closed) way. Using the personalization function of the overview page, the user can partially override the settings specified with the UI Configuration Tool. If too many assignment blocks are already open when the overview page is called, this can have a negative impact on performance.

Each assignment block can also be personalized. We will take up this topic again in Section 1.3.

Overview page: Maintaining data in assignment blocks

How can the user now edit the content of assignment blocks? There is a distinction between direct and indirect data maintenance when editing content in assignment blocks. If the content can be maintained in the assignment block without having to branch to a new page, this is *direct data maintenance*. *Indirect data maintenance*, on the contrary, involves navigation to a new page in the work area of the CRM Web Client. The new page is opened in change mode. Creating a new address for accounts (see Figure 1.16) is an example of indirect data maintenance in assignment blocks. When the adjustments have been made, the user can navigate back to the overview page. The page history in the header area of the user interface or the buttons in the work area toolbar should be used for navigating between pages. An assignment block remains in change mode until the user saves or cancels. A save or cancel event sets all assignment blocks from change mode into display mode. If you have implemented changes on the overview page and then cancel, the operation terminates directly without confirmation being issued in a dialog.

Overview page: Titles of assignment blocks

Now that you have an idea of how the assignment blocks of overview pages work, we will look in a little more detail at the individual components of the assignment block. Each assignment block has a title you can adjust according to the content using the UI Configuration Tool. The title enables the user to enter content quickly. If an assignment block describes information about a business object with a 1 to n relationship, you should consider a plural form when choosing the title. Let us take a look at the following example: The overview page for contacts contains an assignment block for assigned business addresses. Therefore, in this case, the plural form should be chosen for the title (see Figure 1.17) because more than one business address can be assigned.

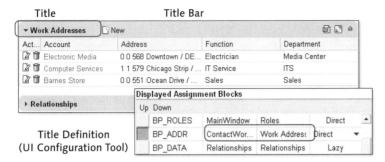

**Figure 1.17**  Title of Assignment Blocks

The functional area of the assignment block is situated to the right of the title. In addition to application-based buttons, this area can also contain customer-specific buttons. You will generally find the following buttons on the right side of the functional area:

*Overview page: Functional area of assignment blocks*

▶ **Export to Excel**
This selection displays only if the data in the assignment block is displayed as a table or tree structure. The displayed information is exported into the Excel document in the same column sequence.

▶ **Personalization**
This display is also only available to the user if the data in the assignment block is displayed as a table or tree structure. The user can decide which columns should be displayed or hidden (see Figure 1.16).

▶ **Back to Top**
This selection is available for every assignment block. Only in the detail view has this button been omitted.

As you might have already noticed in Figure 1.17, other buttons may be available in the left part of the functional area of assignment blocks. The selection of buttons displayed in the functional area differs depending on the content of the assignment block. You can also add your own buttons to the selection (see Section 14.6). The most important buttons and their tasks for assignment blocks are EDIT, EDIT LIST, NEW and ADD. Other buttons are available in addition to those shown within the framework of this book.

*Other buttons of the functional area*

Buttons can appear in different combinations, with the stored functions relating only to editing the lower-level assignment block. After introducing the individual buttons, we will discuss the combination options (for which we have made a selection here as well).

The EDIT button has a written description and pictogram (see Figure 1.18).

*Functional area: Edit*

**Figure 1.18**   Edit – Assignment Block

In the standard system, you will only find this button in assignment blocks that are based on forms and not on frequently used tables or tree structures. After you click the button, the assignment block switches to edit mode. This means that you can edit the content directly in the assignment block, or you are navigated to a separate *edit page* page type. One difference with the NEW button in the functional area of the assignment block is that the EDIT button is only active if the user is working in display mode.

Functional area:
Edit List

The EDIT LIST button in the functional area of the assignment block only has a written description in the standard system (see Figure 1.19). To find out how you can display pictograms for a button you have created yourself, refer to Section 14.6.

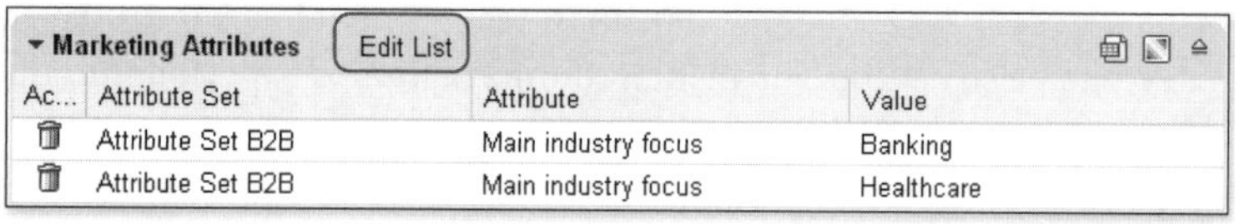

| ▼ Marketing Attributes | Edit List | | |
|---|---|---|---|
| Ac...  Attribute Set | | Attribute | Value |
| 🗑  Attribute Set B2B | | Main industry focus | Banking |
| 🗑  Attribute Set B2B | | Main industry focus | Healthcare |

**Figure 1.19**   Edit List – Assignment Block

You can only use the EDIT LIST button with assignment blocks that have tables or tree structures. After you click the button, the assignment block switches to edit mode. Changes are therefore not made in a separate window but in the assignment block itself. The button is only active if the assignment block is in display mode.

Functional area:
New

In the standard system, the NEW button in the functional area of the assignment block has a written description and pictogram (see Figure 1.20).

| ▼ Opportunities | New | | | |
|---|---|---|---|---|
| Ac...  Description | Account | Status | Closing Date | Sales Volu... |
| 📝🗑 Fair Munich | Electronic Media / DENVER CO 8... | new | 27.04.2009 | 1.000,00 |
| 📝🗑 Fair. Detroit | ATL PM / ATLANTA GA 30328 | new | 27.04.2009 | 200,00 |

**Figure 1.20**   New – Assignment Block

Like the EDIT LIST button, the NEW button is only used in applications of assignment blocks that display tables or tree structures. Unlike the EDIT LIST button, the user is always taken to a separate *edit page* page type after clicking the NEW button. The user can use the NEW button to create an opportunity, relationship, or activities, depending on the assignment block. Use the page history in the header area of the CRM Web Client to return to the starting point of its assignment block. The assignment block display is subsequently updated automatically. The new entry is always the last entry in the results table. In contrast to the EDIT LIST button, the NEW button is always active, irrespective of whether you are working in display or edit mode.

The ADD button has a written description and pictogram.

Functional area: Add

You also only use this function in assignment blocks with a table or tree structure. In the standard system, you will find an example of this button on the CONTACTS assignment block of the CORPORATE ACCOUNT overview page (see Figure 1.21). You can use this button to search for an existing contact and add this contact to the corporate account through the assignment block. You can create a new contact by clicking the NEW button.

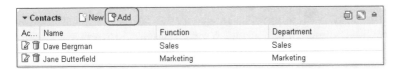

**Figure 1.21**  Add – Assignment Block

> **Note**
>
> You can make changes to assignment blocks using the illustrated functions. However, you cannot identify which changes a user has made to which assignment block.

A whole range of combination options has now been developed in the standard system from the buttons presented for functional areas of assignment blocks. These include NEW and EDIT LIST, ADD and EDIT LIST or ADD and NEW. If the button combinations provided by default are not sufficient, you can add other buttons and combination options you have developed yourself (see Chapter 14, Section 14.6).

Multifunction buttons also exist for some assignment blocks. One example is the ATTACHMENTS assignment block (Figure 1.22). Here, you can choose whether to create a folder or a new attachment from scratch or from a template, or whether you want to store a *Uniform Resource Locator* (URL). The ADVANCED button contains additional functions available through a context menu.

Functional area: Combination options

| ▾ Attachments | 📄 Attachment 📄 URL 📄 With Template │ Advanced | | | 🖾 🖾 ⏏ |
|---|---|---|---|---|
| Ac... Name | | Type | Created On | Language |
| Pr... Bonus | | MS Excel File | 28.03.2009 10:52 | EN |
| Pr... New York Times | | URL | 28.03.2009 10:51 | EN |
| Pr... SAP PRESS | | Simple Text | 28.03.2009 10:49 | EN |

**Figure 1.22** Combination – Assignment Block

### Note

You cannot customize or personalize any button on the user interface (neither on the work area toolbar, nor in the functional area of the assignment blocks, nor on views) with the UI Configuration Tool (Section 5.1). Development work is always required for customizing or creating new buttons (see Chapter 14, Section 14.6).

Search page

After having dealt with the overview page and its assignment blocks in detail, we can look more closely at the SEARCH PAGE. The search page is called through three different options in the standard system: through a work center page, saved searches in the header area of the CRM Web Client, or the context menu of the navigation bar (see Figure 1.23).

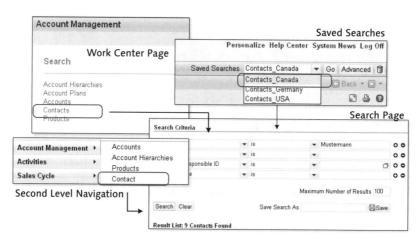

**Figure 1.23** Page History for Calling Search Pages

The search page is always displayed in the work area of the user interface. In accordance with the call, the search page for the relevant business objects (e.g., CONTACTS or also SALES CONTRACTS or SERVICE CONTRACTS) is already predefined based on specific business objects. Therefore, after you call the search page for contacts, you will not find any selection options for a marketing campaign.

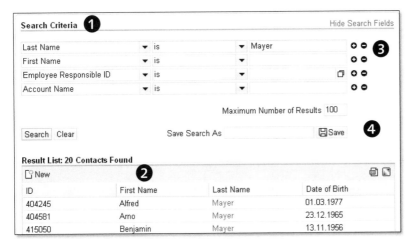

**Figure 1.24** Structure of a Search Page

The search page is roughly divided into two areas (see Figure 1.24). Search criteria for the search query (❶) are stored in the upper area. The result list of the search query appears in the lower part of the search page (❷).

The search page enables the user to perform a specific search for business objects—for example, using different combination options—and is based on the SELECT OPTIONS ABAP command. The search page in the standard system has four lines of predefined search attributes. Horizontally, the search is made up of three columns. The first column displays search attributes, the second shows the operator, and the third contains the search field. Combined, it looks as follows:

**Structure of search criteria**

```
<search attribute> <operator> <search field> [and <search
field>]
```

You can select the search attributes from a selection box with predefined values and you can expand or restrict search attributes. You can also define the sequence of search attributes in the selection box and the search attributes that should be displayed when a page is called. When selecting search attributes, make sure that the selection box is limited to seven entries. If you exceed this limit when storing search attributes, the Web Client UI framework automatically provides a scrollbar. You use the UI Configuration Tool to define search attributes that should be displayed in the selection box. Section 5.4.2 contains a practical example for customizing a search page.

**Search attributes**

**Operators** The user can influence the search results by the selection of operators. The operator here represents the relationship between the search attribute and the search field. The following operators can be used:

| Use with Search Attribute | Operator |
|---|---|
| Text field | is, is not, is empty, starts with, contains |
| Identification field | equals, does not equal, is greater than, is less than, is between, is empty, contains |
| Numeric fields | equals, does not equal, is greater than, is less than, is between, is empty, contains |
| Date fields | is, is not, is between, is earlier than, is later than |

**Table 1.3** Selection of Available Search Operators

The selection of operators also influences the structure of the search page and its search criteria. If you select the IS BETWEEN operator, the Web Client UI framework automatically sets up a second search field to enable a value range to be defined. If you select the IS EMPTY operator, the framework sets the search field to inactive.

The user can define the number of special search criteria using the (+) or (–) buttons (❸ in Figure 1.24). For example, (+) will add a new line under the first search criterion, MAYER, and the user can then also search for the first name, "Hans". The user can restrict the search up to at least one search query. However, customizing the search page (via the UI Configuration Tool) can restrict the extent to which the user can adjust the number of search criteria (in other words, how many maximum search criteria he can add).

**Result list** The search results are displayed in a tabular result list (❷). In the standard system, the maximum number of search results is limited to 100 hits. If the result list of entries found exceeds this limit, a warning message is displayed for the user in the message bar. A maximum of ten entries per page of the result list is displayed in the standard system. However, you can define the number of results per page using the personalization function of the result list.

For some result lists of search pages in the standard SAP system, you can make changes to the result objects directly in the result list. One example is the result list of search pages for ACTIVITIES. By marking several search results (activities), you can set the status of selected activities in the result list to Open, In process, or Completed.

Now that we have looked at the search criteria and result list of the search page, we want to save the search query (❹, see Figure 1.24). To save a search with the corresponding search criteria, enter a suitable name for the search in the SAVE SEARCH AS field (see Figure 1.25).

Saved searches

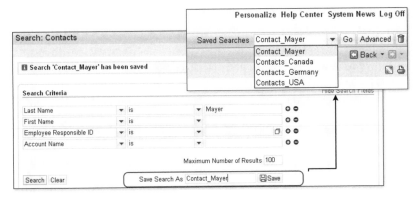

**Figure 1.25**  Saving the Search Query

Without providing a search criterion, 100 search results will be delivered in the standard system. Search results depend on the dynamic search object that is executed for a search (see Section 12.1.3). To save searches, however, you need to store at least one search criterion. After you save the search, it is immediately available as an entry under SAVED SEARCHES in the header area of the user interface. If you start the saved search from the header area of the user interface, the result list of the search is displayed in the work area of the user interface. With saved searches, only the search criteria is saved, not the result lists. For this reason, the result lists may differ after a certain amount of time. However, the user can change saved searches at any time. To do this, click the ADVANCED button in the header area of the user interface. You can then redefine the search criteria and save them under the same name or remove a saved search using the DELETE pictogram. We will show you how to customize a search page via Customizing in Chapter 5, Section 5.4.2 and we will use a practical example in Chapter 16, Section 16.3 to explain how to implement a search page.

> **Note**
>
> Saved searches are always specific to a user and system. Therefore, saved searches cannot be transported into a live system.

Archive search    You can search for archived business objects in the CRM Web Client. A button labeled ARCHIVE SEARCH then appears in the header area of the search page. The page type for the archive search is in turn a search page and is only differentiated by the selection of search attributes. An archive search is not available for all search pages. Examples of archive searches are available on the search page for activities and in the marketing role for archived campaigns. To return to the standard search, click BACK TO STANDARD SEARCH under the title of the search page.

Calendar    Before we look at types of supporting pages (*dialogs*), we need to describe the CALENDAR, E-MAIL INBOX, and WORKLIST. In the standard system, these pages are available in the navigation bar for every logged-on role. The CALENDAR page type provides a graphical interface that contains the daily tasks for the user. In addition to a daily view, you can also select a weekly or monthly view. You can also look at the calendars of your colleagues.

When you create daily tasks, you can choose between several event types, for example, MEETING, ACTIVITY, or CONTACT. Figure 1.26 shows a selection of differently maintained event types that you can process further. If you created a *business activity* as an event type in the calendar, you will also find this activity in your worklist.

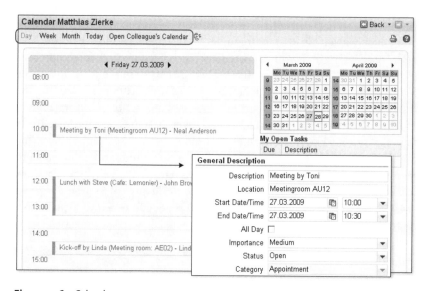

**Figure 1.26**   Calendar

Worklist    The WORKLIST page type in the standard SAP system is also available in the navigation bar for all users and all roles. The worklist gives the user an overview of the tasks that he must complete. Aside from activities, all tasks that derive from stored workflows for the user are also displayed here. The tasks in the worklist can also be prioritized for the user from SAP CRM using a warning system. This means that you can display high priority tasks directly on the home page of the user interface. Figure 1.27 shows the WORKLIST and E-MAIL INBOX pages.

The user can search for his tasks in the worklist. The user can also display the tasks of his assigned team. Additional assignment blocks are used to display workflow tasks and special warnings for the user.

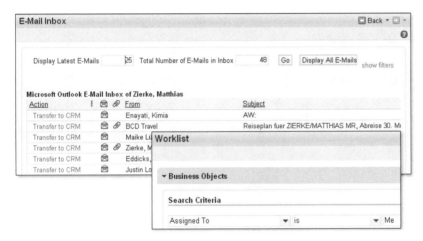

**Figure 1.27**  Worklist and E-Mail Inbox

In the standard system, the E-MAIL INBOX is available for all users, in addition to the CALENDAR and WORKLIST. The E-Mail Inbox shows the existing e-mails for the user from his e-mail program. E-mails are only replicated after the page is opened and can be suppressed at any time. If you allow e-mails to be transported to the CRM Web Client, a copy of the e-mails can be created from your Microsoft Outlook or Lotus Notes e-mail program. You can also define which e-mail messages you want to be copied.

E-Mail Inbox

Comprehensive filters are available for searching for copied e-mail messages.

| Note |
| --- |
| If you use Lotus Notes as your e-mail program, we recommend reading SAP Notes 1247072 and 1281387. |

Edit page    The EDIT PAGE (❶ in Figure 1.28) enables users to change existing or create new content. Edit pages are linked to an assignment block and this, in turn, is linked to the overview page. The edit page is displayed in a view similar to a form.

EDIT LIST PAGES are available in addition to the edit page. You can use edit lists (❷) to edit lists in a sequence.

**Figure 1.28**   Edit Page

Supporting Pages    In addition to the pages presented previously, an entire range of supporting pages exists. When searching for business objects, you will find these types of *dialogs* in the form of value help, as interactive dialog boxes, and for displaying additional information or notes. A distinction exists between simple and complex dialogs for dialogs that are used for value help. The Web Client UI framework displays *simple dialogs* for searching for countries or for defining the language for a contact (❶ in Figure 1.29).

Complex dialogs    You will encounter *complex dialogs* when you set up contact-partner relationships (❷, see Figure 1.29). In addition to supporting you in searches (value selection), dialogs are used as information and note dialogs in your daily work (❸). You will find other types of dialogs when personalizing your user interface. ❹ in Figure 1.29 shows a dialog you can use to customize columns for a table on an overview page. You will notice that the user is provided with additional information about this action in the header of the dialog. However, the Web Client UI framework only makes this support available for complex dialogs. In addition, the framework does not display a message bar for additional information for every type of dialog (❷). In Chapter 14, Section 14.4, we explain how you can implement your own dialogs.

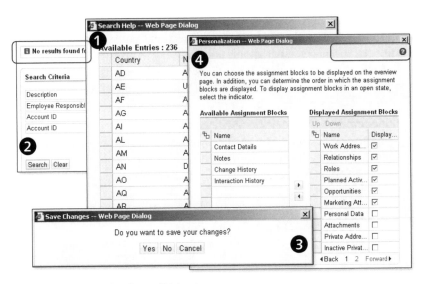

**Figure 1.29** Supporting Pages (Dialogs)

When you create your own dialogs, you should ensure that the window size corresponds to 50% of the main window. Tables and tree structures should be embedded without a necessity to scroll.

Tables and hierarchies or tree structures are frequently used to display objects for page types and dialogs. Tables are frequently used if an overview of a business object and its relationships should be displayed. A good example of this is the overview page. Both the detail area of the business object and related objects (assignment blocks) are mapped using tables. It is obvious that there is hardly any difference in the structure of the tables on the different page types. The following properties describe a table in the CRM Web Client:

*Tables and hierarchies*

▶ **Title**
The title briefly describes the content of the table or assignment block. The user must be able to quickly identify what the content of the table contains (❶ in Figure 1.30).

*Table title*

▶ **Table header**
The table header is where you store the column titles. Most tables also have a sort or filter function for each column. You can use the sort function to sort table entries in ascending as well as descending order (❷). You can also customize the table columns using drag-and-drop.

*Table header*

53

▶ **Selection column**

Selection column
You can use the selection column to select and edit several entries in a table (❸). However, you can only edit table entries by row, not by column. Not all table types have a selection column (❹) because the framework only provides a selection column if a common change to several table entries makes sense (e.g., in campaign management).

▶ **Table footer**

Table footer
Using the personalization function, you can define how many entries a table can display. If more entries exist, these are displayed in the table footer. The framework then makes navigation available for displaying all table entries (❶).

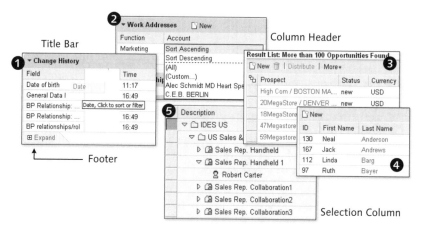

**Figure 1.30** Tables and Hierarchies

Tree structures
In addition to tables, Figure 1.30 also shows a hierarchical tree structure (❺). Tree structures are used to display a company's organizational model, to map customer installations (installed bases), or to plan marketing campaigns. The advantage of tree structures is that they display dependencies in a structured format. Dependencies cannot be displayed in a simple table format.

> **Note**
>
> Personalization functions for tables are summarized in Section 1.3. Chapter 10, Section 10.2 outlines the technical implementation of table views and Chapter 10, Section 10.3 details how to implement your own tree views.

### 1.2.4 Navigating in the User Interface

Now let's take a closer look at how you can navigate between the different page types in the user interface. There may be deviations from our description; therefore, it does not contain all navigation options in detail.

After you log on to the CRM Web Client, the home page appears where you will find your tasks and appointments. The home page is the entry point to the CRM Web Client for every user and cannot be removed for any role through Customizing. After you select a role-based menu option from the navigation bar (e.g., ACCOUNT MANAGEMENT, ACTIVITIES, SALES CYCLE), the relevant work center page opens (see Figure 1.31). It is divided into the SEARCH, CREATE, and REPORTS information blocks.

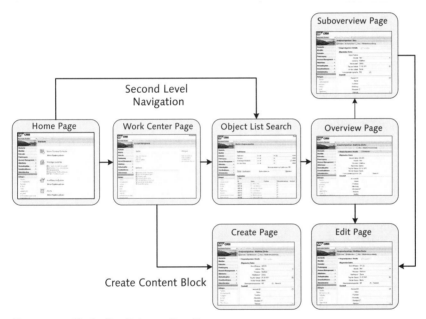

**Figure 1.31** Navigation Between Page Types

After you select a link from the SEARCH (work center page) information block, navigation occurs on the search page. You go from the result list of the search operation to the overview page of the selected business object. You can also navigate to lower-level pages from the overview page of the business object, and you can edit the selected object from the overview page. To do this, switch to the edit mode of the overview page (edit page).

**Navigation steps**

When you select CREATE from the information block of the work center page, you navigate directly to the page where you can create a new business object.

The page is immediately in input mode; therefore, you can create a new business object with the preselection properties.

By navigating the context (second level navigation) of the navigation bar, you go directly to the predefined search page of the selected business object (e.g., CONTACTS). In the standard system, you then select a business object from the result list of the search page and navigate to the overview page of the selected object. The most important information for the selected business object is then provided. If you click a link to another business object in the assignment block of the displayed business object, this business object will be displayed again on the overview page. Only information about the related business object will subsequently be displayed on the overview page. You can navigate to the original selection again from the page history in the header area of the user interface.

> **Note**
>
> The navigation between page types displayed in Figure 1.31 only shows one section. Other navigation paths are possible. For example, you can navigate from the home page directly to an overview page. The option to create your own pages means that you are free to make individual adjustments when navigating between pages.

## 1.3    Personalizing the User Interface

Providing a personalization function means giving the user the option to customize the interface of the application according to his requirements. Personalization is always driven by the user, whereas configuration in any form is always defined by administrators or project teams. Personalizing software therefore always affects a user individually, while configuration is always performed for a user group. Consequently, personalizing software is available for the user longer than for a just a single user session. In the configuration of the user interface, the settings defined by the user should be kept as minimal as possible. Personalization does not mean that the user can redesign his own user interface completely.

General personalization    The CRM Web Client uses a uniform standard layout for displaying all pages. You can adjust this standard layout for the entire user interface. You call the general personalization of the user interface using the PERSONALIZE system link in the header area of the user interface. Here, the five information blocks of MY DATA, SETTINGS, GROUPWARE INTEGRATION, LAYOUT, and SHORTCUTS are available for general personalization:

► **My Data**

You can use this information block to personalize or extend general user, communication, and organizational information. You can also use this information block to specify a new password for logging on to the CRM Web Client.

Personalization: My Data

► **Settings**

General screen settings, the mode for the screen reader program (SAP Note 1139953), and activating the configuration mode are the general personalization options of this information block. You can use the general screen settings to store the current time zone, date format, and decimal notation. The Web Client UI framework uses these settings in the entire system. Activating the mode for the screen reader program helps visually impaired users to interact with the user interface.

Personalization: Settings

Lastly, you can also enable the configuration mode (❶ in Figure 1.32). Two new buttons subsequently appear on the toolbar of the page types (e.g., *overview page*). You can use these buttons to enable the configuration mode for each page (❷).

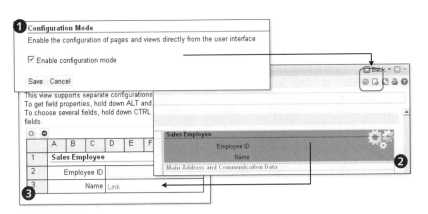

**Figure 1.32** Enabling the Configuration Mode

You can then select an information block on the page (colored dark gray) and get the technical description of the information block, or the UI Configuration Tool opens (❸). You can use the UI Configuration Tool (see Chapter 5, Section 5.1) to customize the information block by adding or deleting input or output fields. You can use the second button on the toolbar to determine the structure of assignment blocks.

► **Groupware Integration**

With this information block, you can define the exchange between SAP CRM 2007 and a groupware application used across the company. In this

Personalization: Groupware Integration

case, the client-based groupware integration for Microsoft Outlook and Lotus Notes is released. Not only can you store settings for synchronizing e-mails, you can also store them for CALENDAR, TASKS, and CONTACTS. If your users are provided with groupware integration, you should consider the option of general personalization.

▶ **Layout**

Personalization:
Layout

The fourth information block is divided into two subareas: PERSONALIZE LAYOUT and PERSONALIZE NAVIGATION BAR. In the PERSONALIZE LAYOUT area, you can adjust or enable the skin, text size, and performance mode for the CRM Web Client. After you enable the performance mode, some UI characteristics are disabled, which can lead to the user interface being uploaded more quickly. To increase the performance of the CRM Web Client further, also refer to SAP Notes 1162685 and 1114557. Different skins for customizing your layout are provided in the standard system (❶ in Figure 1.33). If a separate corporate identity is set up for the user interface (see Section 2.6), this can also be activated using the LAYOUT information block. Aside from skins being customized, the text size can also be changed for the entire user interface.

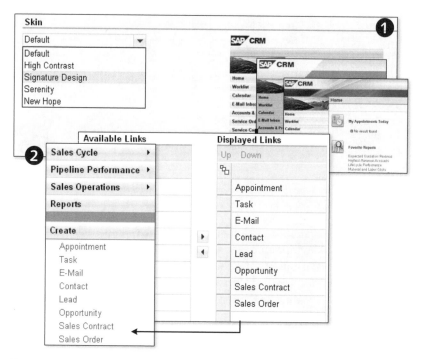

**Figure 1.33**  Layout of the User Interface

The user can also use the LAYOUT information block to personalize the navigation bar—he can influence which direct links should be displayed in the lower part of the navigation bar (❷). The user can also determine the sequence of direct links.

▶ **Shortcuts**

The fifth information block is a useful tool for users who prefer working with the keyboard. Here, you can create shortcuts for applications according to your requirements. You can store key combinations for focal purposes and for calling menu options from the navigation bar. However, make sure that you do not select key combinations that are already reserved for the operating system or the browser. For more information on this topic, refer to the HELP CENTER system link in the header area of the CRM Web Client.

Personalization: Shortcuts

After having looked at general personalization, we can now also personalize selected areas of the CRM Web Client using specific personalization. Unlike general personalization, the specific personalization of individual areas does not affect the entire user interface. Figure 1.34 shows examples of areas of the user interface that have been personalized.

Specific personalization

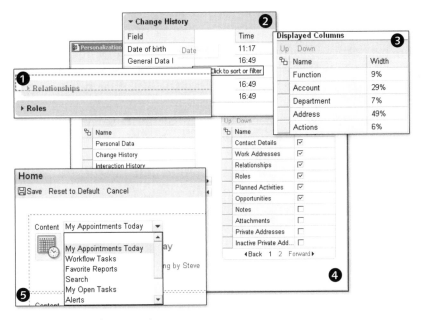

**Figure 1.34** Specific Personalization

You can move the assignment blocks of an overview page at any time using drag-and-drop and adjust their sequence according to your requirements (❶ in Figure 1.34). After the adjustment, the new sequence of assignment blocks is automatically saved for you, without you explicitly having to execute the Save command. In addition, the page setting you implemented is still available the next time you call the CRM Web Client. The same applies for adjusting table columns (❷). You can also adjust columns using drag-and-drop and use the mouse to specify the width of table columns. If you want to hide table columns, you do this by changing the personalization settings for the table. Every table offers these options. Item ❸ in Figure 1.34 shows the personalization options in the table header. This is where you define the visibility and width of the table columns.

Overview pages also have a personalization function for assignment blocks (see Section 1.2.3). You can therefore specify whether assignment blocks should already be expanded when you log on to the CRM Web Client. You can also hide assignment blocks (❹). If a page type has information blocks, you can adjust them accordingly. The Home page is shown under ❺ in Figure 1.34. You can personalize the position of existing information blocks entirely according to your requirements. All changes mentioned are specific personalizations of subareas of the user interface and do not affect the overall user interface.

**Deactivating personalization**
You can restrict general personalization as well as the personalization of assignment blocks for users. To do so, you use the PERSCV_PROFILE maintenance view (Transaction SM30) to deactivate one of the personalization options (❶, see Figure 1.35). You must then create and assign a new function profile for your business role (see Section 2.2) using the Personalize parameter (❷).

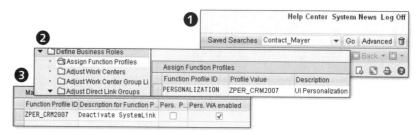

**Figure 1.35** Deactivating Personalization

Item ❸ in Figure 1.35 shows that only the PERSONALIZE system link was hidden; the user can still personalize the assignment blocks.

> **Note**
>
> To increase the performance of the CRM Web Client, enable the performance mode using the system links. For more information on increasing performance, refer to SAP Notes 1162685 and 1114557.

## 1.4 Logging On to the CRM Web Client

Now that we have looked at the structure and the personalization functions of the CRM Web Client user interface in detail, we will log on to the CRM Web Client. When you start the CRM Web Client for the first time through the SAP GUI, you must first specify some settings.

In the SAP Easy Access CRM interface, select the ADD OTHER OBJECTS entry from the selection list that displays when you right-click FAVORITES. Then, select BSP APPLICATION (*Business Server Pages*). The sequence of the configuration is displayed in Figure 1.36.

Logging on to the Web Client through the SAP GUI

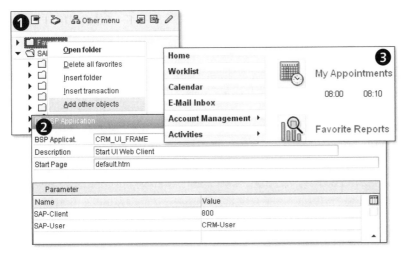

**Figure 1.36** Logging On to the CRM Web Client

Add the default component name, CRM_UI_FRAME, to the input fields of the BSP application and enter a meaningful description. This description will appear in your favorites, from where you start the CRM Web Client. Enter "default.htm" in the START PAGE input field. You can also specify parameters to log on to the CRM Web Client. For example, enter the logon client (SAP-CLIENT), logon language (SAP-LANGUAGE), user name (SAP-USER), or password (SAP-PASSWORD). After you have logged on to the CRM Web Client, the user interface of your assigned business role (Chapter 2) is called. If several business roles are assigned to you, an overview of the selectable business roles is displayed.

Make sure you log on to the CRM Web Client in the correct logon language. Adjustments to the user interface are often made in a language different from the one the user subsequently uses when logging on. The adjustments are then visible only to a certain extent.

**Logging on to the Web Client using Favorites**

Not only can you call the CRM Web Client through the SAP GUI, you can also save the starting URL in your favorites in the Internet browser. You can then call the CRM Web Client directly from there.

> **Note**
>
> If you face the problem of getting a blank screen after logging into the Web-Client UI, check your authorization in Transaction SU01. SAP Note 1144511 and 1244321 can help as well.

## 1.5 Prerequisites and Performance Optimization

You should now have an initial understanding of the general structure of the CRM Web Client, so let's discuss technical adjustment options. You can adjust the user interface technically using entries in Customizing or through development. Make sure that the following prerequisites are fulfilled to ensure that you can reproduce all of the practical examples and notes in the book. In the second part of this section, you will learn about the options for optimizing the performance of the CRM Web Client.

**Prerequisite: Authorization**

In the individual chapters of this book, we do not explicitly describe which authorization profiles you need as an application or development consultant to be able to perform the described practical examples, but assume that the SAP_ALL authorization profile has been assigned to your SAP logon user. To reproduce the practical examples, we also assume that you have unrestricted access to the SAP NetWeaver Portal, SAP NetWeaver Business Warehouse (BW), and the network drives of the SAP NetWeaver Application Server (AS).

**Prerequisite: Transport requests**

We also do not explicitly specify when the system requires transport requests for changes in Customizing or to development objects (Customizing or Workbench requests). All changes can be handled as local objects and (for test purposes) must not be transported.

The following paragraphs discuss the options that are available to you for adjusting the CRM Web Client in Customizing. The standard system contains a range of predefined settings and *business roles*, *navigation profiles,* and *views* are some of the keywords we will introduce to you during the course of this book. In the practical examples, we frequently use default settings that are already on hand and adjust existing Customizing entries for test purposes. We recommend that you do not change any original settings of the standard SAP system in Customizing. Always copy the default settings provided and then make the changes in Customizing. For example, you can copy existing roles, profiles, and views from the standard system if necessary and then make adjustments to the copies. In addition, existing settings are not overwritten by future system upgrades.

Prerequisite: Customizing

> **Note**
>
> The system we refer to in all of our explanations and practical examples is always the standard system (SAP CRM UIF 600, SP 3). We must highlight this point again specifically for entries in Customizing.

As of SAP CRM 2007, you can use Mozilla Firefox in addition to Microsoft Internet Explorer as your browser. Other browsers such as Apple Safari are not supported. You will find more information about this topic in the SAP Service Marketplace (*http://service.sap.com/PAM*) and for CRM2007 in SAP Note 1114557. For SAP CRM 7.0, you can consult SAP Note 1262304.

Prerequisite: Browser version

SAP also continues to support the ability of the CRM Web Client to run in `F11` full screen mode of the Internet browser. This enables you to display applications completely without having to scroll on the screen. The CRM Web Client was developed for working on a 17" monitor. The resolution should therefore be at least 1024 × 768 pixels.

In most cases, you can display the CRM Web Client in the browser without additional settings (e.g., ACTIVE X) and browser plug-ins. Exceptions are described in SAP Note 1018674.

> **Note**
>
> We performed all of the examples in this book using Internet Explorer Version 6.0 and the Windows XP Professional operating system.

You should be able to reproduce the examples presented in this book using the settings mentioned. In the text that follows, we will describe additional options that can positively affect the performance of the CRM Web Client. First, we will look at optimization options in the *frontend*. When creating

JavaScript, HTML, and CSS files, you should typically ensure that you keep the program code as simple as possible. This will enable the Internet browser to set up the created pages much more quickly. Although you do not need to exclude program blocks such as <input> or <br> explicitly in HTML 4.0, we nevertheless recommend that you do exclude them to optimize performance. In the following paragraphs, we structure other subject areas according to SAP Notes.

<table>
<tr><td>Performance:<br>Internet browser</td><td>Check whether SAP Notes 1171444, 1277476 and 1162685 have already been imported. Some of the tasks for which you use these notes include optimizing the browser caching time, activating compression for certain files, and suppressing the uploading of unnecessary files. By importing the SAP Notes, you can optimize the process of starting the CRM Web Client.</td></tr>
<tr><td>Performance: PAI<br>and table rows</td><td>In addition to increasing the performance of the browser, you can also increase the performance for tables that are displayed in the CRM Web Client. Check SAP Notes 1255130 and 1283980. After you change or choose a table row, one of the things these notes do is ensure that only this one line is updated.</td></tr>
</table>

Having looked primarily at optimizations in the frontend in the previous paragraphs, in the next paragraphs, you will find options for optimizing *backend* applications.

<table>
<tr><td>Performance:<br>Tables</td><td>If performance is unsatisfactory when you call views with configurable tables and trees, check whether SAP Note 1179315 has been imported. It improves the backend rendering time for large tables.</td></tr>
<tr><td>Performance:<br>Comprehensive<br>measurement</td><td>You can use the tool from SAP Note 1041556 to obtain general performance information. You use this tool with the Solution Manager Diagnostics to get a full breakdown of the end-to-end performance of a process. SAP Notes 1162605 and 1048388 contain other general suggestions for improving backend performance.</td></tr>
</table>

> **Note**
>
> Irrespective of performance, SAP Note 1244321 is useful for analyzing incorrect behavior of the CRM Web Client. For SAP CRM 7.0, SAP Notes 1318610 and 1244479 can be useful.

*Users log on to the CRM system and then use a predefined business role to access all applications assigned to this role. Therefore, the business role is the central object for controlling the navigation bar.*

# 2    Role Concept

Due to the complexity of the role definition and profile definition in the CRM Web Client environment, we have decided to devote an entire chapter to this subject. At the beginning of this chapter, we will, once again, briefly describe the general business scenario (*Customer Interaction Cycle*) and its role concept. We will then focus on the roles and profiles used to control the CRM Web Client.

## 2.1    General Information about the Role Concept

When SAP launched version CRM 2006s, the SAP CRM application was based on a simple role concept. In its standard delivery, the user interface of the CRM Web Client is already adjusted to the role used and with version CRM 2007, SAP delivered more than 35 predefined business roles in the standard system. Sample business roles include marketing, sales, and service employees as well as IC agents. You can adjust the business roles that SAP delivers in the standard system to your individual business processes, and thus incorporate your typical business requirements into the system. We recommend that before making any adjustments, you always copy the standard business role to the customer namespace first. Often, the business roles delivered in the standard system provide a good basis for subsequent adjustment to your business requirements.

SAP CRM 2007 provides a range of business scenarios and business processes that describe end-to-end business processes involving several SAP and non-SAP components. Figure 2.1 shows a universally valid business scenario with the following four standard business roles: *Marketing Professional*, *Sales Professional*, *Service Professional*, and *IC Agent*.

General business scenario

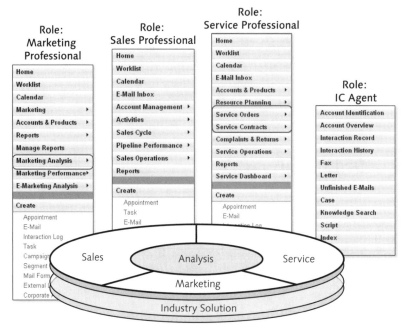

**Figure 2.1** General SAP CRM Business Scenario

Standard business
roles The navigation bar in the CRM Web Client is tailored to the specific employee tasks and roles within an enterprise. While an employee who has been assigned the business role *Marketing Professional* has a menu option entitled Marketing so that he can create campaigns or segment target groups, this menu option is missing for employees who have been assigned the business role *Sales Professional*, *Service Professional*, or *IC Agent*. The same goes for employees who have been assigned the business role *Service Professional*. The navigation bar for such employees contains additional menu options (e.g., Service Orders and Service Contracts) that are not required for employees who have been assigned other business roles. For this reason, these menu options are not displayed in their navigation bar. On a day-to-day basis, users of CRM applications specialize in one area within the value chain. Accordingly, they see only a specialized extract of the business scenario. In the standard delivery of the CRM Web Client, however, this extract has already been adjusted to their precise task within the enterprise. Before we discuss the various types of roles and profiles used to control the CRM Web Client, we will take another look at the central roles in the general business scenario from a CRM perspective.

Even though this book does not focus on mapping the different scenarios available in SAP CRM 2007, we want to briefly bring your attention to some theoretical aspects that will help your understanding of the CRM Web Client role concept. We also recommend that you read the book *mySAP CRM* [by Buck-Emden/Zencke, SAP PRESS 2004], which provides you with detailed information about the CRM Business Scenario.

> **Note**
>
> A detailed description of the functions used in the SAP CRM business scenarios and business processes is available in SAP Library under SAP CUSTOMER RELATIONSHIP MANAGEMENT • COMPONENTS AND FUNCTIONS and on the SAP Service Marketplace at *service.sap.com/okp*.

### 2.1.1  Marketing Professional

To enable enterprises to fulfill complex marketing tasks, SAP's CRM Web Client provides CRM applications with a comprehensive, open, modular, and customizable solution for the entire Marketing process.

The marketing solution works very closely with the other areas within the general business scenario (sales and service). Interaction channels are used to make existing data available to other enterprise areas for further processing. Let's take a closer look at the user interface for the *Marketing Professional* role, which is contained in the standard delivery (see Figure 2.2).

Marketing solution

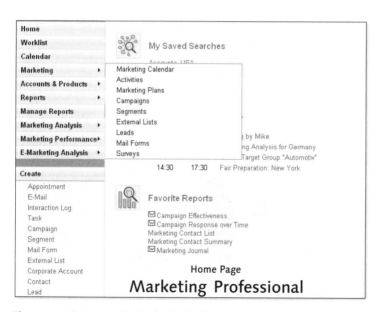

**Figure 2.2**  Business role: Marketing Professional

The navigation bar of the user interface is tailored to marketing tasks and their areas of application. Consequently, an employee in the marketing department can quickly process the operational marketing tasks that have been assigned to him.

As is the case for all other business roles, you can always customize the business role delivered in the standard system (see Section 2.5).

### 2.1.2 Sales Professional

Sales at a glance The second phase in the general business scenario is dedicated to sales (see Figure 2.3). Information acquired from marketing activities is transferred to the sales department for further processing, that is, in order to establish business relationships with new customers and to strengthen existing relationships with old customers [Emden/Zencke, *mySAP CRM*, 2004]. For these tasks, the CRM Web Client makes planning, implementation, and control activities available to sales employees.

**Figure 2.3** Business role: Sales Professional

For special sales tasks, we recommend that you use existing, specialized business roles such as the Leasing Manager or Sales Manager business role. Because the steps that comprise the daily sales process are highly complex and rarely processed in a linear fashion, the sales user interface usually requires the most adjustment.

The navigation bar of the *Sales Professional* business role has already been tailored to sales-related areas of application. The key CRM activities for sales are grouped together under the relevant menu options in the navigation bar.

### 2.1.3 Service Professional

In the general business scenario, service is key to ensuring long-term customer retention. Of all enterprise areas, customers have the most contact with the service enterprise area. For this reason, SAP has acknowledged the importance of service by introducing a wide range of functions into its integrated CRM solution. In addition to the classic *Service Professional* business role, which takes care of the entire service process (from the initial contact through to rendering services, shipping spare parts, and billing), there are other specialized service business roles.

Service at a glance

The service functions are therefore closely coupled with the other application components in the general business scenario. Existing interfaces can also be used to establish links with external systems (see Figure 2.4).

**Figure 2.4** Business role: Service Professional

Once again, the navigation bar of the user interface has already been adjusted to the requirements of the employee role within the enterprise. Here, there are no menu options that are particularly necessary for the sales or marketing roles.

### 2.1.4  IC Agent

IC Agent at a glance

In many enterprises, the IC employee (also known as an IC agent) is the direct interface to the customer. Both orders and complaints are received via this user interface. An IC agent may be employed anywhere within the general business scenario. In marketing, he can perform telemarketing tasks, while in sales, his activities relate to telesales. You should make use of the many business roles delivered in the standard system, for example, IC Agent – Insurance, IC Agent – Leasing, or IC Manager.

IC Agent: task areas

Figure 2.5 shows the user interface of an IC Agent. This user interface clearly differs from the other role-dependent user interfaces. Here, the header area has been adjusted to the needs of the IC Agent.

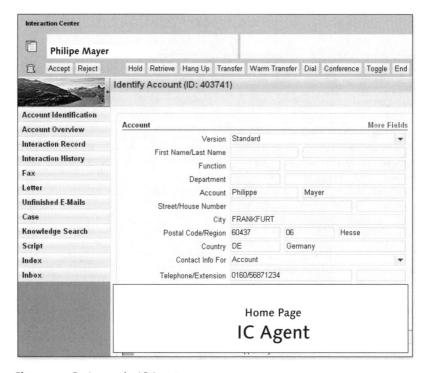

**Figure 2.5**  Business role: IC Agent

In addition to the information box for messages if a caller contacts the IC, functions for controlling the call have also been defined in the header area of the user interface. We will not continue our discussion of the IC scenario in the chapters that follow. Instead, we refer you to the book entitled *Maximizing Your SAP CRM Interaction Center* by John Burton, which is also published by SAP PRESS.

## 2.2  Technical Description of the Role Concept

To display individual user interfaces for your employees, you need a well-devised role concept. The role concept for the CRM Web Client ensures that all of the enterprise areas in the general business scenario can be mapped via a user interface. Before we actually implement the role concept in the CRM system, we will first introduce you to the specific terms used in conjunction with the CRM role concept. If you are already familiar with this terminology, you can skip the sections that follow.

Roles are collections of activities that enable a user to participate in one or more business scenarios within an organization. The navigation bar in the CRM Web Client is used to access the transactions, reports, or web-based applications contained in the roles. The navigation bars should contain only those functions generally used by a particular user in his daily work.

Role assignment also ensures the integrity of business data. Authorization profiles that limit the range of actions that can be performed by individual users in the SAP CRM system are created in accordance with the activities contained in roles. We will now take a look at the tasks of the various roles and profiles available to you when devising a role concept for the CRM Web Client.

Roles and profiles at a glance

### Definition: User Master Record

A user master record (SAP logon user) is a prerequisite for logging on to the SAP system. It is used to assign a role to a user, that is, to determine the activities intended for a particular user and the authorizations granted to that user.

### Definition: Business Partner

This generic term stands for partners in which an enterprise has a business interest. Partners also include organizations (e.g., enterprises) and persons in different roles (e.g., contact partners within an enterprise).

### Definition: Business Role

The business role is a role in the CRM system that contains business content from CRM applications (e.g., marketing, sales, and service). This content is then displayed in the CRM Web Client. The user logs on to the CRM Web Client and uses a defined business role to access the CRM applications assigned to him. Business roles are the central unit of the role concept.

### Definition: Authorization Role

The authorization role (also known as the *PFCG role*) is created using a profile generator. An authorization role is used to automatically or manually generate an authorization profile for users. This role can then be assigned to the user master record or business role by using the report CRMD_UI_ROLE_ASSIGN. You can create authorization roles as single roles or composite roles, which comprise two or more single roles.

### Definition: Authorization Profile

The authorization profile is a technical container for authorized functions (e.g., SAP transactions) and the organizational area (e.g., plant or cost center) in which the functions must be executed (limited organizational level). Therefore, the profile contains authorizations that can be identified using the name of an authorization object and the name of an authorization.

### Definition: Navigation Bar Profile

The navigation bar profile contains the logical structure for calling internal and external applications from the CRM Web Client. It describes the navigation bar of the user interface, and its structure is specifically designed for individual business roles.

### Definition: Technical Profile

The technical profile is assigned to the business role. The call for the Internet page loaded after you log off from the CRM Web Client is defined here. For downward compatibility reasons, SAP recommends that you retain all other settings. It is possible to adjust the settings for browser navigation (SAP Note 1002385). However, SAP advises against using browser navigation.

### Definition: Function Profile

The function profile activates functions for the IC agent user interface, among others. Configurations that belong to the functions are generally defined and processed in separate Customizing activities (e.g., Personalization). PARAMETERS and RUNTIME are examples of function profiles that the framework has validated for non-IC scenarios. The function profile is assigned to the business role.

### Definition: Layout Profile

The layout profile defines the navigation frame of the CRM Web Client. This navigation frame can be used to define the header area, footer area, work area, and navigation bar. The layout profile, on the other hand, is assigned to the business role.

## 2.3    Role and Profile Dependencies

The roles and profiles defined in the CRM Web Client depend on each other, and the business role is at the core of this role dependency. Business roles are used to encapsulate the content defined for a user interface. Figure 2.6 shows the dependencies between profiles, roles, and the organizational model for the business role.

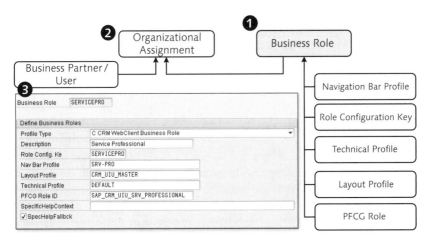

**Figure 2.6**   Business Role and Dependencies

The business role is the central object for controlling a user interface with a navigation bar, logical links, and authorizations (❶ in Figure 2.6). The following profiles or keys are assigned to the business role:

Business role

73

- **Navigation bar profile**
  Structure of the navigation bar displayed on the user interface
- **Role configuration key**
  Parameter that defines a configuration that is based on the business role
- **Technical profile**
  Profile that defines technical parameters (e.g., memory threshold, browser back support, or delta handling)
- **Layout profile**
  Customization of the navigation frame, which comprises the header, footer, and work areas
- **Function profile**
  Activation of additional functions (e.g., personalization of the user interface)
- **Authorization role**
  Gives the user predefined access rights to interface objects

Implementation
Guide: business
role

You access the business role configuration in the SAP Implementation Guide under the path CUSTOMER RELATIONSHIP MANAGEMENT • BUSINESS ROLES • DEFINE BUSINESS ROLES or in Transaction CRMC_UI_PROFILE.

In the sections that follow, we will show you the structure of the business role and the assigned profiles in detail. We will then assign this business role to the organizational model (❷ in Figure 2.6; see also Section 2.4). As a result of this assignment, each employee in the enterprise obtains his own business role and therefore his specific user interface for his daily work with the CRM Web Client. In a final step, the SAP logon user or a business partner with the role *Employee* is assigned to the organizational model (❸). The necessary Customizing settings for creating a business role are shown in the practical example discussed in Section 2.5.

### 2.3.1    Navigation Bar Profile

When starting the Customizing activities for setting up a separate user interface, you should create a new navigation bar profile or copy a navigation bar profile that already exists in the standard system. The navigation bar contains links to all work centers that belong to a role and the work centers contain links to the search pages of the business objects that belong to each work center. The navigation bar also contains direct links to the user's calendar or work list. After the navigation bar profile has been configured, it is assigned to a new or copied business role.

You start the navigation bar profile configuration in the SAP Implementation Guide under the path CUSTOMER RELATIONSHIP MANAGEMENT • UI FRAME-WORK • TECHNICAL ROLE DEFINITION • DEFINE NAVIGATION BAR PROFILE or in Transaction CRMC_UI_NBLINKS.

Implementation Guide: navigation bar profile

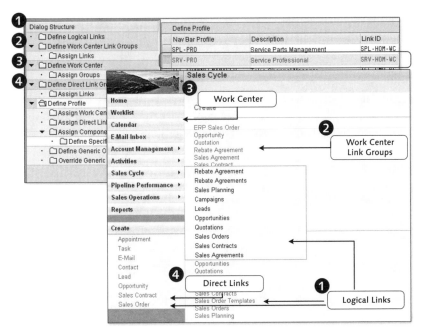

**Figure 2.7** Navigation Bar Profile

Figure 2.7 shows the navigation bar profile configuration and sample user interface for the business role *Service Employee*. All of the logical links, direct links, and work center pages for the navigation bar are defined here. Logical links are found under the direct links in the navigation bar, on the lower-level navigation, and in the info blocks for the work center pages (❶ in Figure 2.7). Logical links are also used to call the work center pages themselves. You can group logical links into link groups (❷). Such link groups are found, for example, in the info blocks for the work center pages. In addition to the logical links, you also use the navigation bar profile to define the work center page for the navigation bar. ❸ also shows that you can group logical links into groups known as *work center link groups*, which you can then assign to one or more work center pages. These result in the context menus provided in the navigation bar, for example. The direct links are created under ❹, that is, in the dialog structure of the navigation bar profile. Direct links are found in the lower part of the navigation bar. They can call both internal and external applications either directly in the work area or in an external window.

After you have defined the logical links, direct links, and work center pages, you must assign them to the navigation bar profile. In this way, you can determine the sequence in which the work center pages and direct links appear on the navigation bar. Finally, the navigation bar profile you have just created is assigned to your business role.

### 2.3.2 Technical Profile

You can use the *technical profile* to disable Internet browser navigation and frame swapping in an effort to reduce screen flickering. Here, you also reserve the corresponding memory requirement for business processes.

Implementation Guide: technical profile

You start the technical profile configuration in the SAP Implementation Guide under the path CUSTOMER RELATIONSHIP MANAGEMENT • UI FRAMEWORK • TECHNICAL ROLE DEFINITION • TECHNICAL PROFILE.

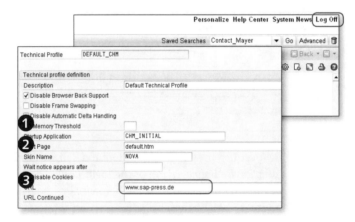

**Figure 2.8** Technical Profile

Figure 2.8 shows a standard profile for the *Channel Manager* business role. You can define the memory threshold under ❶. This value represents the server memory space requirement in megabytes (MB) and determines when a new application session is started. A check is performed to determine whether the current memory consumption is higher than the threshold specified in the technical profile of the business role. If memory consumption is higher than the threshold, the system ends the current session and starts a new session. We recommend that you define a higher threshold for business scenarios that have high memory requirements. We recommend a threshold of 70MB for standard business scenarios and 100MB for business scenarios associated with marketing or trade promotions.

For information about assigning a new default skin (❷ in Figure 2.8), see SAP Note 1137677. You can also adjust the cookie settings here. In very general terms, *cookies* are information sent by a web server to an Internet browser or information generated on the client side. Client-side cookies comprise persistent/saved data. Here, the session information is defined as a session cookie or coded as part of the URL (*mangling*). If you enable this checkbox in the technical profile, a URL parameter is set and the use of cookies is not permitted.

Default skins and settings for cookies

You can use the technical profile to specify which Internet page is called when a user logs off from the CRM Web Client (❸ in Figure 2.8). Here, you define a new URL, which is called when a user logs off from the CRM Web Client. In the standard system, the Internet page for SAP AG (*www.sap.com*) is entered by default.

Internet page when logging off

After you have configured all of the settings, you add the technical profile to your business role. In business scenarios, the technical role is primarily used with the IC.

### 2.3.3 Layout Profile

You can use the *layout profile* to design or control the structure of the entire navigation frame. Various different layouts are delivered in the standard system, even for the IC.

You start the layout profile configuration in the SAP Implementation Guide under the path CUSTOMER RELATIONSHIP MANAGEMENT • BUSINESS ROLES • DEFINE NAVIGATION FRAME.

Implementation Guide: navigation frame

❶ in Figure 2.9 shows the configuration overview of the layout profile. You use the layout profile to define the navigation frame for your user interface, which comprises the header, footer, and work areas as well as the navigation bar. The header area is a static area within the user interface. You cannot scroll here and only one header area is provided for all applications in the CRM Web Client.

This layout, which is used to structure the header area, is the standard implementation. You can customize your own header area for your layout profile. The layout components for customizing the header area are available in the SAP Implementation Guide under the path CUSTOMER RELATIONSHIP MANAGEMENT • UI FRAMEWORK • TECHNICAL ROLE DEFINITION • DEFINE LAYOUT COMPONENTS. ❷ in Figure 2.9 shows an extract from the layout configura-

Implementation Guide: layout components

tion. You can reconfigure parts of the layout here or you can create new individual parts for the navigation frame.

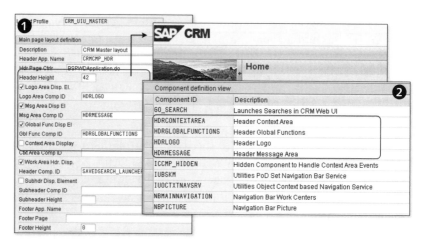

**Figure 2.9** Layout Profile

**Tip**

We recommend that you access standard layout profiles because these layout profiles, which are delivered in the standard system, will satisfy most of your requirements. Do not forget to assign your newly created layout profile to the business role.

### 2.3.4 Role Configuration Key

In addition to the navigation bar profile, the technical profile, and the layout profile, you also assign a *role configuration key* to the business role. The use of a role configuration key ensures that you do not have to change any standard SAP views. You use the UI Configuration Tool to assign a role configuration key to a copied view. Later on, you will also use the UI Configuration Tool to design the user interface for a particular business role (see Chapter 5, Section 5.1). To identify the screen configuration you have created, the role configuration key is assigned to your business role.

Implementation Guide: role configuration key

You define the role configuration key in the SAP Implementation Guide under the path CUSTOMER RELATIONSHIP MANAGEMENT • UI FRAMEWORK • UI FRAMEWORK DEFINITION • DEFINE ROLE CONFIGURATION KEY or by using the view CRMV_UI_CONFIG (Transaction code SM30).

After you have created a role configuration key (❶ in Figure 2.10), you assign this key to your business role (❷). If you now want to make changes to the user interface for this business role, you select your new role configuration key in the UI Configuration Tool (❸) and copy the configuration for the standard SAP view to the namespace for the configuration key you have created. You can now make changes to the layout, while the standard view remains unchanged. If a user in the business role you have created uses the assigned role configuration key to log on to the CRM Web Client, this key is used to determine the new layout. The standard role configuration key is <*>, which always uses the standard view. SAP Note 1248281 uses an example to describe this scenario.

**Assigning the role configuration key**

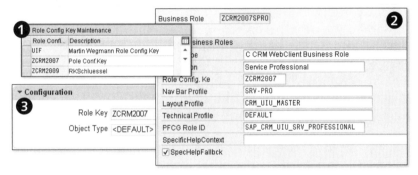

**Figure 2.10** Role Configuration Key

### 2.3.5 Authorization Role

The authorization role, also known as the *PFCG role*, is also assigned directly to the business role. It contains the authorizations required to perform the business functions that comprise the business role. Most authorizations do not have a direct impact on the CRM Web Client (aside from the authorization object UIU_COMP). You start the authorization role configuration in the SAP Implementation Guide under the path CUSTOMER RELATIONSHIP MANAGEMENT • UI FRAMEWORK • TECHNICAL ROLE DEFINITION • DEFINE AUTHORIZATION ROLE or in Transaction PFCG.

**Implementation Guide: authorization role**

In general, SAP recommends that you define the CRM Web Client functions in Customizing. If Customizing does not serve your purposes, you can use report CRMD_UI_ROLE_PREPARE and Transaction SU24 to determine the necessary authorization objects. Report CRMD_UI_ROLE_PREPARE supports you in generating and assigning authorization objects to an authorization role. After you have created the authorization role, it is assigned to the business role. The defined authorizations are active the next time the user uses

**Authorization role structure**

the modified business role to log on to the system. For additional information about determining the correct authorization objects, see Chapter 6, Section 6.3 and SAP Notes 551478 and 449832. In addition, general information about creating authorizations is available in the SAP Library at *help.sap.com* under the path SAP R/3 AND R/3 ENTERPRISE • SAP R/3 AND R/3 ENTERPRISE 4.70 • SAP NETWEAVER COMPONENTS• SAP WEB APPLICATION SERVER • SECURITY • USERS AND ROLES • FIRST INSTALLATION PROCEDURE AND UPGRADE PROCEDURE and in the documentation for the IMG activity under the path CUSTOMER RELATIONSHIP MANAGEMENT • UI FRAMEWORK • TECHNICAL ROLE DEFINITION • DEFINE AUTHORIZATION ROLE or Transaction code PFCG.

---

**Note**

If, while copying a business role, the system issues an error message indicating that one PFCG role cannot be assigned to several business roles, please refer to SAP Note 1155828.

---

## 2.4   Organizational Model and Role Assignment

Now that we have taken a detailed look at the structure of the business role, the next step involves assigning the business role to the organizational model.

Implementation Guide: organizational model

You start the organizational model in the SAP Implementation Guide under the path CUSTOMER RELATIONSHIP MANAGEMENT • BUSINESS ROLES • DEFINE ORGANIZATIONAL ASSIGNMENT or in Transaction PPOMA_CRM.

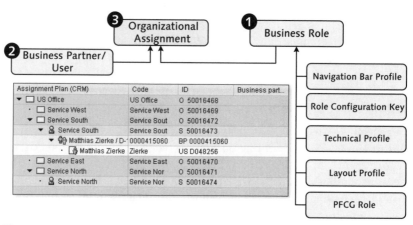

**Figure 2.11**   Organizational Model Within an Enterprise

Figure 2.11 shows the organizational structure of an enterprise in organizational units. The structure of the organizational model reflects the regional structure of the enterprise. The model is created using the elements outlined in Table 2.1.

| Icon | Definition | Short Description |
|---|---|---|
| ☐ | Organizational unit | Branch office or department |
| ⚇ | Position | Available position within a department |
| 👥 | Employee | Business partner |
| 🗿 | User | User master record |

**Table 2.1**  Icons Used in the Organizational Model

In the first step, you replicate the structure of your enterprise. Organizational units enable you to depict the structure of your enterprise in detail. For each enterprise unit, you define the address and function, which comprises sales, service, or marketing. Here, you can also define attributes for each scenario (sales, service, or marketing). Therefore, each scenario depicts a different view of the organizational structure. In addition to the defined attributes, which are valid for the relevant scenario, you must also decide whether each organizational unit is to be considered in the scenario. If so, you must define an indicator here.

*Enterprise structure*

> **Note**
>
> The Web Client UI framework will still operate successfully if you do not explicitly define an address or describe a function for each enterprise unit. However, we have mentioned both for the sake of completeness.

In the next step, you assign positions to each organizational unit. Here, you can assign several positions to one organizational unit. You define the validity period for a position and identify a manager for the organizational unit. You can also maintain a function (sales, service, or marketing) for each position. If this does not happen, the position inherits the attributes of the parent organizational unit. Note that performance problems may occur if you create too many positions (see SAP Note 389869).

*Position*

After you have assigned the positions to the organizational units, the employees are assigned to the positions. To do this, you can assign a user (user master record, Transaction SU01) or business partner with the role *Employee*

*Employees and users*

(Transaction BP) to the position. Both settings are possible and there are no disadvantages to either when logging on to the CRM Web Client. Before you assign a business partner with the role *Employee*, check the following:

1. Start Transaction BP.

2. Select a business partner that has the role *Employee*.

3. Select the IDENTIFICATION tab. Is the user master record (SAP logon user) defined?

Figure 2.12 shows the assignment of a business partner with the role *Employee*. You can use the menu bar above the organizational model to edit organizational units, and you can use the context menu to assign the business partner with the role *Employee* or to assign the user. The drag-and-drop function is also supported here.

**Business role assignment**      How are business roles assigned to employees within your enterprise? In general, it is possible to assign the business role at the organizational unit level. All employees below this organizational unit then obtain the assigned user interface.

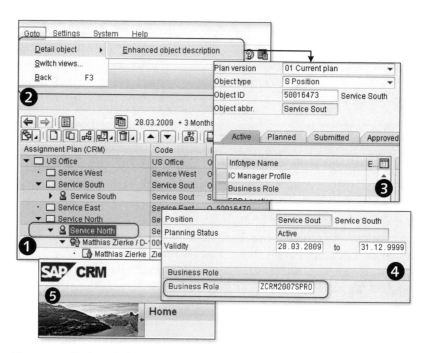

**Figure 2.12**    Business Role Assignment

Select the location in the organizational model to which you want to assign the business role. In Figure 2.12, the position is in the SERVICE NORTH (❶) organizational unit. Then, use the menu path GOTO • DETAIL OBJECT • ENHANCED OBJECT DESCRIPTION (❷) to assign the business role to the position. Select the entry BUSINESS ROLE for the position (❸) and store the business role you have created for the position within the SERVICE NORTH organizational unit. Finally, log on to the CRM Web Client and check whether the system calls your business role.

For information about assigning authorizations when creating users or business partners (report CRMD_UI_ROLE_ASSIGN), see Section 2.3.5.

Assigning<br>authorizations

You have already created the authorization profile in the PFCG role and maintained authorizations there. However, they have not been assigned to the users/business partners that require the PFCG role (based on the business roles assigned to them in the organizational model). This is done using report CRMD_UI_ROLE_ASSIGN, which also assigns PFCG role SAP_CRM_UIU_FRAMEWORK (required by the Web Client) to users. According to SAP Note 1282024, you can also run report CRMD_UI_ROLE_ASSIGN via central user administration.

> **Note**
>
> If you want to upgrade your CRM system from CRM 5.0 to CRM 2007 or CRM 7.0 and want to migrate existing authorization roles (PFCG), you can check SAP Note 1259665 for additional information.

## 2.5    Practical Example: Business Role

The practical example in this section describes the following steps:

1. Creating an authorization role
2. Creating a business role (service)
3. Using the organizational model to assign the business role
4. Logging on and testing the new business role

### 2.5.1    Creating an Authorization Role

We recommend that you create the authorization role (PFCG role) before you create a new business role.

Creating an
authorization role

1. **Call the authorization role.**

   To call an authorization role, access the path CUSTOMER RELATIONSHIP MANAGEMENT • UI FRAMEWORK • TECHNICAL ROLE DEFINITION • DEFINE AUTHORIZATION ROLE in the SAP Implementation Guide or call Transaction PFCG.

2. **Copy an authorization role.**

   In role maintenance, select authorization role SAP_CRM_UIU_SRV_ PROFESSIONAL and copy it to the customer namespace (ZCRM2007_ UIU_SRV_PROFESSIONAL). In the standard system, authorization role SAP_CRM_UIU_SRV_PROFESSIONAL is used for service business role SERVICEPRO (see Figure 2.13).

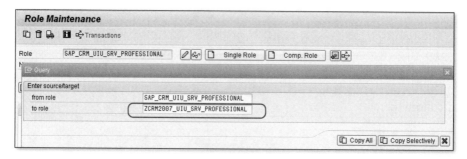

**Figure 2.13**   Copying the Authorization Role

## 2.5.2   Creating a Business Role (Service)

After you have created the authorization role, the next step is to create a new business role. In the example that follows, we chose to create a service business role. Once again, we will access the business roles already created in the standard system and customize them accordingly.

Customizing
existing business
roles

1. **Call the business role.**

   You are already familiar with the path used in the SAP Implementation Guide to call the business role: CUSTOMER RELATIONSHIP MANAGEMENT • BUSINESS ROLES • DEFINE BUSINESS ROLE. Alternatively, you can use Transaction CRMC_UI_PROFILE.

2. **Copy the business role.**

   Select the standard business role SERVICEPRO and copy it to the customer namespace (ZCRM2007SPRO), as shown in Figure 2.14 (**❶**).

You already know the definition of business role ZCRM2007SPRO, which comprises the Role Configuration Key, Navigation Bar Profile, Layout Profile, Technical Profile, and Authorization Role assignments. These entries have already been maintained for the copied standard business role SERVICEPRO.

3. **Assign the authorization role.**
   After you have copied business role ZCRM2007SPRO, authorization role ZCRM2007_UIU_SVR_PROFESSIONAL is assigned to the newly created business role (❷).

Assigning the authorization role to the business role

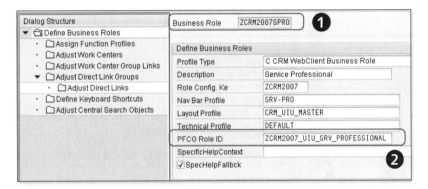

**Figure 2.14** Creating a Business Role

### 2.5.3 Using the Organizational Model to Assign the Business Role

The business role you have created (ZCRM2007SPRO) will now be assigned to one or more employees within your enterprise. You must then call report CRMD_UI_ROLE_ASSIGN to assign the PFCG role.

1. **Call the organizational model.**
   Use the now familiar path for calling the organizational model (Customer Relationship Management • Business Roles • Define Organizational Assignment), or call Transaction PPOMA_CRM.

2. **Create an organizational unit.**
   Find the organizational unit US Office. Under the service unit Service West, create the new position Service West PL (❶ in Figure 2.15).

Creating the organizational unit and position

85

3. **Create a position.**
   After you have created the SERVICE WEST PL position, you can enter an additional description. Activate the SERVICE function for the position.

4. **Assign a business partner.**
   Assign 1 to n business partners with the role *Employee* (Transaction BP) or *User* (Transaction SU01) to the SERVICE WEST PL position. To do this, right-click the position and select the ASSIGN (❷) option from the context menu.

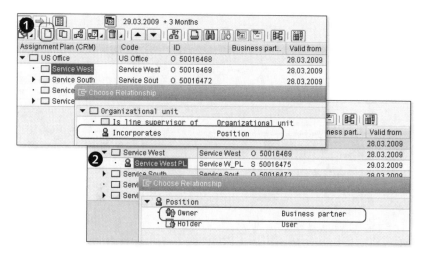

**Figure 2.15** Assigning a Position and Business Partner

Assigning the
business role

5. **Assign the business role.**
   After you have assigned the business partner or user to the organizational model, the next step is to assign the business role you created (ZCRM-2007SPRO). You can assign the business role to organizational units or to positions. In this case, select the position you created (SERVICE WEST PL) and follow the menu path GOTO • DETAIL OBJECT • ENHANCED OBJECT DESCRIPTION to assign the business role to the postion SERVICE WEST PL (❶ in Figure 2.16).

6. **Create a business role.**
   Select the business role you created (ZCRM2007SPRO, ❷) and assign it to the position you have selected (SERVICE WEST PL, ❸).

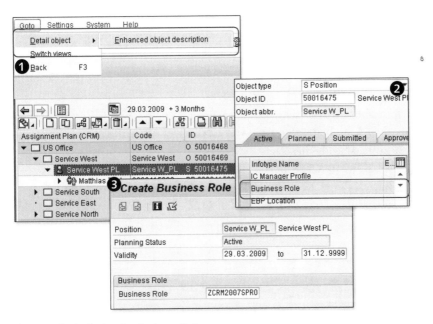

**Figure 2.16**  Assigning the Business Role

### 2.5.4  Logging On and Testing the New Business Role

After you have assigned business role ZCRM2007SPRO to the position Ser- Testing an
vice West PL, log on to the CRM Web Client (see Chapter 1, Section 1.4) application
and test the settings.

---

**Tip**

To check whether the correct business role is determined after you have
logged on to the CRM Web Client, you can move the mouse pointer over the
Personalize system link in the header of the user interface. The business role
will then be displayed in the lower status bar of the Internet browser. The
name of the business role is shown at the end of the URL.

---

## 2.6  Practical Example: Customizing the Corporate Identity

The practical example in this section describes the following steps:

1. Localizing the data on SAP NetWeaver AS

2. Replacing the company logo

3. Customizing the color and font

4. The content of important files at a glance

### 2.6.1 Localizing the Data on SAP NetWeaver Application Server

Before adjusting the user interface to include a new corporate identity design, you should familiarize yourself with NetWeaver AS, which controls the structure of the browser pages.

Creating the network path

1. **Create the network path.**

   Start Windows Explorer and select MY NETWORK PLACES (❶ in Figure 2.17). Then select ADD NETWORK PLACE to add a new network address (❷).

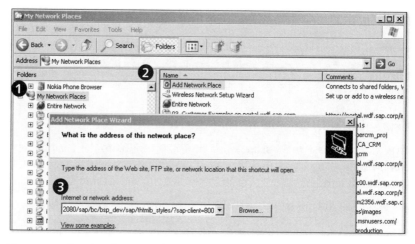

**Figure 2.17** Creating the Network Path

2. **Define the network path.**

   In the HELP window, define the path in which information about the CRM Web Client is stored (❸) and then enter a meaningful description for the network drive you have created. The standard system uses the following path:

Standard path for layout templates

*http://<server>:<port>/sap/bc/bsp_dev/sap/thtmlb_styles/?sap-client= <client>*

Important information about the server name and port is available in Transaction SMICM (or under the menu path GOTO • SERVICE).

All of the layout templates that can be selected via PERSONALIZE (system links) are available under the network drive you have just created. For a new layout, we recommend that you make a local copy of this folder and edit the copy offline. We do not recommend online editing because it can be very slow.

### 2.6.2 Replacing the Company Logo

It goes without saying that the company logo, which you can customize as follows, is an integral part of the corporate identity:

1. **Create a local copy.**
   Copy the DEFAULT folder to a local hard disk. This may take several minutes.

2. **Change the company logo.**
   There are two ways in which you can adjust the company logo. You can create a new company logo (111 × 42 pixels) and assign it a relevant file name (e.g., *logo_sap.gif*). You then copy the company logo to the directory *… /styling/lshape* for your local copy. In this case, you must adjust the style sheets in the file *thtmlb_stand.css* in accordance with the new file name for the company logo (*logo_sap.gif*).

   This brings us to the second way in which you can adjust the company logo: Replace the old company logo with a new logo that has the same file name. In this case, you do not have to adjust the program code. You then copy the modified files back to SAP NetWeaver AS.

3. **Activate the layout profile.**
   You make the layout profile known in table CRMC_THTMLB_SKIN (Transaction SM30). Define the new skin name ZSAP_PRESS, the description, and the source path of the layout profile.

   *Activating the new layout profile*

4. **Test the application.**
   Now test the application. The new entry, SAP PRESS, is now available under PERSONALIZE (system links).

Additional information about customizing the *corporate identity* for the CRM Web Client is available at *http://help.sap.com* (search word: SKIN).

### 2.6.3 Customizing the Color and Font

You can use the file *thtmlb_stand.css* to customize the colors for the navigation bar, header, and work area. This file is very well documented. Find the HTML program code that describes the part of the user interface you want to customize, and change the color accordingly.

*Redesign: color*

Redesign: font   You can also use the file *thtmlb_stand.css* to customize the font. In the standard system, the fonts Arial and Helvetica are defined for the DEFAULT user interface. You can supplement the HTML program code with your own preferred fonts. A great deal of additional information about customizing the font and color is available in the SAP Help Portal (*http://help.sap.com*).

## 2.6.4   Content of Important Files at a Glance

Table 2.2 provides an overview of key file names and their properties when personalizing the user interface.

| CSS File Name | Description |
| --- | --- |
| thtmlb_core_stand.css<br>generic.css | Launch file for all layout applications |
| thtmlb_stand.css<br>main.css | The settings for background color, browser-independent colors, and the position of the company logo are defined here. There are also files for special browser versions. |
| thtmlb_visuals_stand.css | Controls effects in the navigation bar (e.g., mouse-over movements). |
| printpreview.css | Screen display for printers |

**Table 2.2**   Overview of Important CSS Files

*The business role and navigation bar profile control the structure of the navigation bar and the way in which links to the home page, report home page, and work center page are displayed.*

# 3    Enhancing and Customizing the Navigation Bar

In this chapter, we will introduce you to the properties of the CRM Web Client navigation bar and describe which changes you can make to the navigation bar without having any programming knowledge. The navigation bar is located in the left-hand area of the user interface and, together with the header area for CRM Web Client, comprises the navigation frame.

The main menu options in the navigation bar are called work centers (❶ in Figure 3.1). Direct links, which you can use to define and immediately call CRM and ERP applications or to access pages on the Internet, are positioned in the lower part of the navigation bar (❷). The applications selected here are called in the work area or in a new window within the user interface. Direct links are grouped into groups and assigned to the navigation bar profile, among others.

Structure of the navigation bar

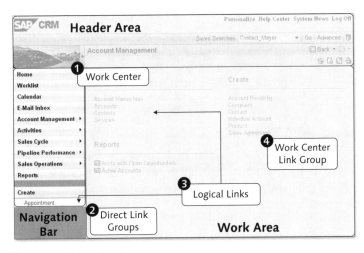

**Figure 3.1**   Navigation Bar

Logical links (❸) are the basis for all links and work center pages in the navigation bar. They are used to define the link type, the page to be called, and the link title displayed in the user interface. The page type called in the example shown in Figure 3.1 (*Work Center*) comprises three info blocks: FIND, CREATE, and REPORTS. For these info blocks, you can use Customizing for the navigation bar to group logical links into link groups for display purposes. You will find an example of this in Section 3.4.

## 3.1    Configuring the Navigation Bar

Implementation Guide: navigation bar

In the navigation bar configuration, you can completely restructure your navigation bar profile, or you can customize the standard navigation bar profiles. This configuration takes place in the SAP Implementation Guide under the path CUSTOMER RELATIONSHIP MANAGEMENT • UI FRAMEWORK • TECHNICAL ROLE DEFINITION • DEFINE NAVIGATION BAR PROFILE or in Transaction CRMC_UI_NBLINKS.

You can use the transaction for configuring the navigation bar to not only create the navigation bar profile, but also to define logical links, direct link groups, work center pages, and work center link groups. Figure 3.2 illustrates the diversity of activities you can perform using this transaction.

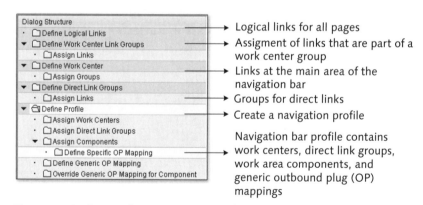

**Figure 3.2**  Configuring the Navigation Bar Profile

Logical links

We will now take a closer look at the individual options (dialog structure, Figure 3.2) in the transaction for configuring the navigation bar. We will start with logical links, differentiating between four types that you can reference after they have been created:

▶ Link

▶ Work center

► Launch transaction

► BW report

You use a link to reference additional CRM applications, such as search pages (❶ in Figure 3.3) or pages to create a new contact person. If you define a logical link of type WORK CENTER, the *work center* page type is called. ❷ in Figure 3.3 shows a Service Reports work center page.

**Types of logical links**

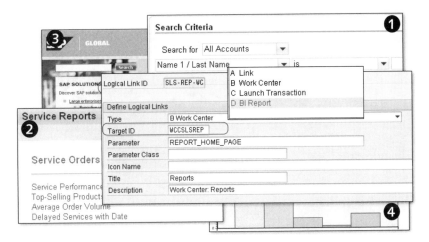

**Figure 3.3** Logical Links

You can use a logical link of type LAUNCH TRANSACTION to open Internet pages (❸), and a logical link of type BW REPORT (BI REPORT) to start evaluations (❹). To define a logical link that will subsequently be integrated into the navigation bar, you must define the task associated with the link at the start of the configuration process. In addition to the logical link type, you must also determine the target ID, which points to the inbound plug of a UI component for interaction between pages. Furthermore, you must select a parameter and parameter class that correspond to the task associated with the logical link. In this example, the logical link SLS-REP-WC will be used to call *sales reports*. To complete the definition of the logical link, you must provide a title and meaningful description. The logical link ID and the target ID are structured according to a particular template. Therefore, this section concludes with a table containing the most important abbreviations. These will help you interpret the link IDs used in the standard system. You can also use your own non-standard link ID and target ID abbreviations. The work center link groups are created below the logical links in the dialog structure of the navigation bar (see Figure 3.4).

Work center link groups

The link group ID comprises the same abbreviations that have been defined for the logical links. Existing logical links can be divided into the following three groups: FIND, CREATE, and REPORTS. Figure 3.4 (❶) shows the group ID SLS-ACC-RE. The suffix RE indicates that this group is associated with *reports*.

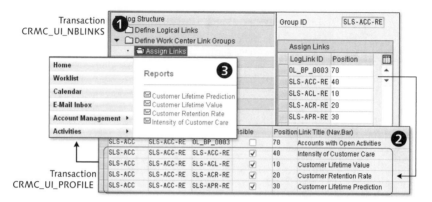

**Figure 3.4** Creating Work Center Link Groups

Defining a work center page

Before you can display the logical links or groups of logical links on a work center page, you must create a new work center page or assign your link group to an existing work center page. If you select an existing work center page, you should first copy it to the customer namespace. In the next step, you will create a work center page under DIALOG STRUCTURE • DEFINE WORK CENTER (❶). To do so, you assign a logical link of type WORK CENTER to the work center page and provide a meaningful title and description. Because the title will be used later as a menu option in the navigation bar, you should keep it as concise as possible. You can then assign your link group to the work center page.

Assigning the work center page to the navigation bar profile

Next, the work center page you have created is assigned to your navigation bar profile; however, we will skip this step for the moment. We will return to it later when we provide detailed information about the navigation bar profile (see Figure 3.6).

The last step in displaying logical links on the user interface is performed in the business role configuration, which is called via the now familiar Transaction CRMC_UI_PROFILE. Here, you select your defined business role and make sure that the navigation bar profile that you have created is stored with the defined work center page and link group. Use the menu option ADJUST WORK CENTER GROUP LINKS (❷ in Figure 3.4) to ensure that the logical links you have created for the reports are also displayed in the REPORTS info block for the work center page. Figure 3.4 (❸) shows the CRM Web Client after you have marked the logical links in the Visible column. You can also use the business role configuration to specify whether you want your logical links to be displayed on the work center page only or also in the menu within the navigation bar.

Up until now, we have somewhat neglected two dialog structure options from Customizing for navigation bars: customizing direct links on the navigation bar and customizing the navigation bar profile itself. First, let us take a look at the assignment of direct links. The configuration principle here is similar to that of the work center link groups. The DEFINE DIRECT LINK GROUPS menu option in the dialog structure (❶ in Figure 3.5) groups links into a group (SLS-CREATE in our example). You then assign the logical links to the group that you want the system to later display as direct links in the navigation bar.

*Defining direct link groups*

Next, the direct link group is assigned to a navigation bar profile. ❶ in Figure 3.5 shows the assignment of the direct group SLS-CREATE to the navigation bar profile SLS-PRO (Sales).

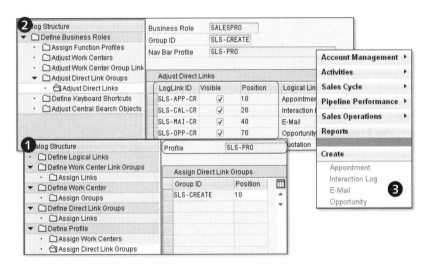

**Figure 3.5**  Assigning Direct Links

The business role configuration (Transaction CRMC_UI_PROFILE) not only ensures the sequence in which direct links appear on the navigation bar, but also which direct links are displayed (❷). If a logical link is set to inactive here, it will not be displayed in the user interface. ❸ in Figure 3.5 shows a configured application after a user has logged on to the CRM Web Client.

Creating a
navigation bar
profile

The navigation bar profile encapsulates all of the settings configured for an assigned business role. We recommend that you create your own navigation bar profile. To do so, access the existing profiles in the standard system and copy them to the customer namespace.

You must always select the home page of the corresponding business role as the link ID for the navigation bar profile and you cannot delete the home page from your navigation bar. Figure 3.6 shows the structure of the navigation bar profile, which comprises the description and ID of the logical link for the home page (SLS-HOM-WC).

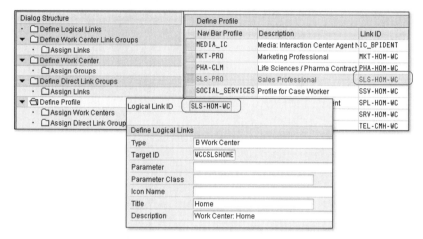

**Figure 3.6**  Navigation Bar Profile

Overview of
abbreviations

You have most likely noticed that the identification numbers defined in the standard system for logical links, groups, and work center pages follow a certain pattern. Because it is difficult to interpret this pattern at first, we have listed the main abbreviations and their descriptions in Table 3.1.

| Abbreviation | Description |
|---|---|
| ACT/ACC | Account |
| ACY | Activity |
| BP | Business Partner |
| CHM | Channel Management |
| CR | Create |
| HOM | Home |
| IC | Interaction Center |

**Table 3.1**  Abbreviations at a Glance

| Abbreviation | Description |
|---|---|
| MKT | Marketing |
| OPP | Opportunity |
| ORD | Order |
| RE | Report |
| SLS | Sales |
| SR | Search |
| SRV | Service |
| WC | Work Center |

**Table 3.1** Abbreviations at a Glance (Cont.)

Examples:

▶ **Service home page**

  ▶ Work center page ID: SRV-HOME

  ▶ Logical link ID: SRV-HOM-WC

▶ **Marketing work center page**

  ▶ Work center page ID: MKT-REPORT

  ▶ Logical link ID: MKT-REP-WC

## 3.2 Navigation from the Navigation Bar

Among other things, the way in which pages are called is controlled from the navigation bar profile. Before we take a closer look at the assignment in the CRM system, Figure 3.7 shows you how pages are called from the navigation bar.

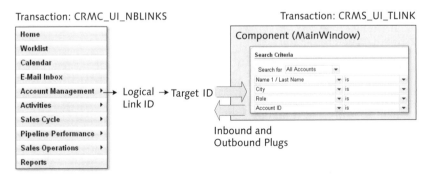

**Figure 3.7** Page History from the Navigation Bar

As you know, the navigation bar profile is managed in Transaction CRMC_UI_NBLINKS and logical links are assigned to this profile (e.g., using work center pages). When defining the logical links, you must define a target ID that specifically addresses an inbound plug for a UI component. Chapter 9 will provide technical information about UI components.

You maintain the components and the assigned inbound and outbound plugs in the SAP Implementation Guide under the path CUSTOMER RELATIONSHIP MANAGEMENT • UI FRAMEWORK • TECHNICAL ROLE DEFINITION • DEFINE WORK AREA COMPONENTS REPOSITORY or in Transaction CRMS_UI_TLINK. The table to be maintained is a cross-client table. Here, you will find the target ID defined for the logical links as a description for an inbound plug of a UI component. All available UI components and their inbound and outbound plugs are defined in the repository for *work area components*. Only the UI components that have been defined in the repository can be included in the work area. Thanks to cross-component navigation, you can navigate to a UI component without having to know the target implementation. To release your UI component for cross-component navigation, you must proceed as follows:

1. **Create an outbound plug.**
   The outbound plug facilitates navigation from your component to a target component.

2. **Create an inbound plug.**
   The inbound plug facilitates navigation from another UI component to your UI component.

As part of the outbound plug definition, you must also provide suitable data collection for the target component. For the inbound plug, you need data collection for the source component.

Figure 3.8 shows the page history in the CRM system. After you have selected a navigation bar profile (❶), the assigned work center pages (❷), for example, are used to determine the target ID of the logical link (❸).

You can use Transaction CRMS_UI_TLINK to establish a link between the target ID and the inbound plug for an object component (❹). In the CRM Web Client, you can press F2 at any time (see Chapter 5, Section 5.1.3) to check which UI component is hidden behind the user interface displayed (❺).

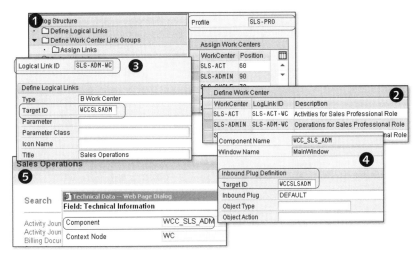

**Figure 3.8** Page History in the CRM System

## 3.3 Integrating a Transaction Launcher

The *transaction launcher* is a tool that enables you to integrate additional functions into the user interface. When supported by the transaction launcher, the CRM Web Client can display the following functions:

- Internet pages
- Business Server Pages (BSPs) from your own or other systems
- Business Object Repository (BOR) transactions
- Front office processes

Functions supported by the transaction launcher

Any of the programs or pages you call are displayed in the work area of the user interface or in a separate browser window. Data can flow to and from a separate browser window, but with some limitations. If you wish to exchange data between the CRM Web Client and the destination page, you must ensure that both applications have been integrated into the same Internet domain.

> **Note**
>
> The transaction launcher integrates only SAP applications identified as *SAP GUI for HTML*. You can check this in Transaction SE93.

### 3.3.1 Prerequisites and Limitations

The transaction launcher supports integrating the aforementioned functions. However, you should not consider it your main integration tool for customizing the user interface and should use it only for highly laborious integration tasks. Simple adjustments to the navigation bar can be made using Transaction CRMC_UI_NBLINKS.

**Required settings**

To successfully use the transaction launcher, you must configure the following settings:

1. Define the RFC connection(s).
2. Define a logical system.
3. Assign the RFC connection to the logical system.
4. Connect the logical system to the URL of the Internet Transaction Server (ITS).

**Defining an RFC connection**

When you define an RFC connection (Transaction SM59), you establish the technical interaction between the CRM system and the target system (SAP ERP or CRM) from which a program should be called. In the standard system, the RFC ID of the target system comprises the system ID and the client (<system_ID>CLNT<client>). However, this is just a recommendation; you do not have to adhere to it. When defining the RFC destination, you should select Type 3 (*ABAP Connection*) and, in addition to the logon data, provide a unique description.

**Defining a logical system**

After you have established the RFC connection, you must define the logical system, which uniquely identifies a system in the system landscape. From the SAP perspective, a logical system corresponds to a client. You define a logical system in the SAP Implementation Guide under the path CUSTOMER RELATIONSHIP MANAGEMENT • CRM MIDDLEWARE AND RELATED COMPONENTS • EXCHANGING DATA WITH EXTERNAL COMPONENTS • XIF ADAPTER SETUP • INBOUND DIRECTION • SET UP LOGICAL SYSTEMS or in Transaction BD54. You then call the client administration in the target system (Transaction SCC4) and check whether the logical system is defined there. Finally, you check whether the entries in the target system and CRM system correspond with each other. If not, you must adjust them accordingly. When assigning names, we recommend that you consider the SAP naming convention (<system_ID>CLNT<client>).

> **Note**
>
> In general, logical system names should not contain any special characters because they may cause technical problems in a multilingual environment (SAP Note 606757).

After you have successfully defined the RFC connection and the logical system, you should assign the RFC connection to the logical system. However, if you do not want to call any applications in external systems (*remote access*), you can skip this step. This assignment is made in Transaction BD97.

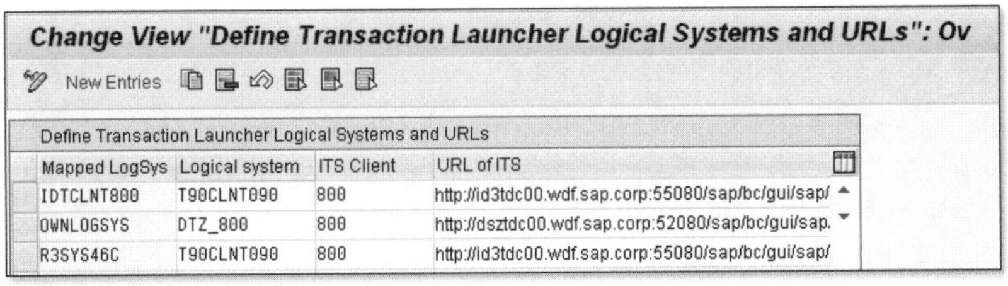

Assigning the RFC connection to the logical system

**Figure 3.9** Assigning Logical Systems

As a final step, you should check the connection between the logical system and the ITS URL. The ITS is necessary to represent graphical user interfaces as HTML pages. It supports not only the presentation of SAP's own applications in the Internet browser but also the operation of user-developed programs. You use Transaction CRMS_IC_CROSS_SYS to define your logical system and ITS URL (see Figure 3.9). Note that your definition must contain the logical system you assigned to the RFC connection. You then enter the ITS URL that calls the Web GUI service. The URL is composed as follows:

Connecting the logical system to the ITS URL

*<protocol>://<host>:<port>/<path>/!?*
*~transaction=<transaction>&~okcode=ICEXECUTE&~disconnectonclose=1*

Table 3.2 will help you gather the information you need to create the ITS URL.

| Abbreviation | Description |
| --- | --- |
| <host> | Call Transaction SMICM (remote). Obtain the host and port names under the menu path GOTO • SERVICE. |
| <port> | See <host>. |
| <path> | Call Transaction SICF (remote). Find the Web GUI service. The standard system uses the following path: *sap/bc/gui/sap/its/webgui*. |
| <transaction> | Here, you have three options: |
| | If the ITS is running on the same CRM system, use Transaction IC_LTX. |

**Table 3.2** Components of the ITS URL

| Abbreviation | Description |
|---|---|
| | If the ITS is running on an ERP system, use Transaction IC_LTXE (SAP_ABA 700 and higher). |
| | If the ITS is running on an older ERP system (R/3 system), use Transaction IC_LTXR. |

**Table 3.2** Components of the ITS URL (Cont.)

SAP Notes 990216 and 888931 provide additional information on how to correctly configure the ITS, as well as troubleshooting measures when integrating SAP GUI transactions.

---

**Note**

These preparations are necessary for BOR transactions only. They are not required to call an external Internet page. URL transactions require the specified preparations only if you want the system to automatically determine the host and port. In that case, the URL field contains only the path.

---

### 3.3.2 Creating New Transactions

Now that we have successfully completed the preparations, we will next integrate an Internet address into the navigation bar. ❶ in Figure 3.10 shows the integration goal with the transaction launcher.

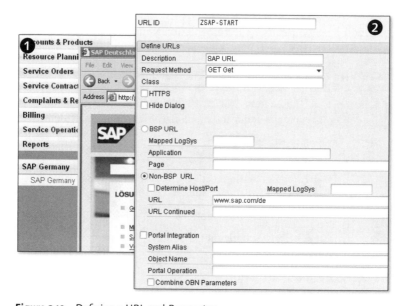

**Figure 3.10** Defining a URL and Parameter

To integrate an Internet page into the navigation bar, before you use the transaction launcher, you must first make the Internet page known. Define an Internet address of your choice (❷ in Figure 3.10) in the SAP Implementation Guide under the path CUSTOMER RELATIONSHIP MANAGEMENT • UI FRAMEWORK • TECHNICAL ROLE DEFINITION • TRANSACTION LAUNCHER • DEFINE URLS AND PARAMETERS or in Transaction SM34, where you specify the view cluster CRMV_IC_LTX_URLS.

Implementation Guide: defining a URL

Enter a URL ID and a unique description for the defined Internet address. Then, select the request method GET. The request method you select determines how additional parameters are transferred, either as a form field or as part of the Internet address. When you select HTTPS (*Hypertext Transfer Protocol Secure*) as the method for transferring data, you should select the POST method instead of GET because, in the case of HTTPS, only the body of the HTTP request is protected from prying eyes. The URL still remains visible. With GET, however, (possibly information-sensitive) parameters are clearly displayed in the URLs. The HIDE DIALOG indicator can be used for adjustments within the IC Web Client. It also makes sense for warnings that concern a loss of data outside the IC. The important factor here is the integrated Internet page. An e-mail program such as Google Mail should be protected from being inadvertently closed. A *stateless* page such as Google search, on the other hand, does not need to be protected.

Next, you should decide whether you want to call a BSP URL application or an Internet page. If you decide to call a BSP URL application, the prerequisite from Section 3.3.1 (*Connecting the logical system to the ITS URL*) must be fulfilled. Here, you define the name for the logical system and the application.

To call an Internet page, you simply enter the URL (❷ in Figure 3.10). If the URL is longer than 255 characters, insert the remaining characters in the URL CONTINUED field. Here, it is important that the destination page can be accessed via HTTP(S). Access via FTP (*File Transfer Protocol*) is not possible without development work.

The settings for portal integration are available as of CRM version CRMUIF600 SP02 (see Chapter 6, Section 6.2). If you want to execute a transaction in SAP NetWeaver Portal, you must set the Portal Integration indicator. After you have set the indicator, the system first checks whether the CRM Web Client is running in SAP NetWeaver Portal. If so, *object-based navigation* (OBN) is performed within the portal. Otherwise, the project-specific settings of the transaction launcher are simply ignored.

Portal integration: transaction launcher

After you have defined the URL and transfer parameters, start the transaction launcher wizard to link the defined URL settings with a launch transaction

Implementation Guide: transaction launcher wizard

that will subsequently be integrated into the navigation bar. You start the wizard in the SAP Implementation Guide under the path Customer Relationship Management • UI Framework • Technical Role Definition • Transaction Launcher • Configure Transaction Launcher or in Transaction CRMC_UI_ACTIONWZ. The transaction launcher wizard guides you, step by step, through the creation process. As a result of this tool, the system creates an event handler class and the relevant configuration entries.

Step 1: Select entries — Each transaction is identified by a unique launch transaction ID (❶ in Figure 3.11). If you want to change an existing transaction, you can find it using the input help F4. If you want one of the transfer parameters to be automatically filled from the *Global Data Context* (GDC), you require an entry for the *Generic Interaction Layer* (GenIL) component set (see Chapter 12, Section 12.1.2). As a result of selecting the GenIL component set, the input help for the parameter values is restricted in such a way that the system offers only those GDC entries that are suitable for the GenIL component set. Therefore, the field can usually remain blank.

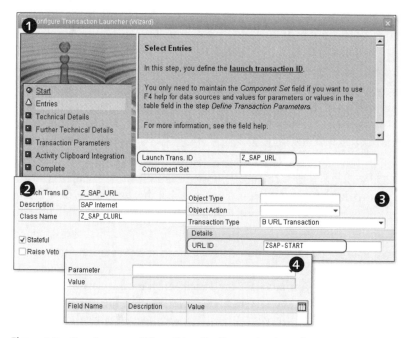

**Figure 3.11** Step Sequence When Using the Transaction Launcher

Step 2: Define technical details — You define the technical details in the second step of the transaction launcher. In addition to a description, you also specify your own class name in the customer namespace (❷). The class will later contain generated statements in relation to handling events that have been defined for the transaction. In the second step, you also specify whether the subsequent application is displayed in a separate window (STATEFUL) or in the work area of the user interface. When you use the IC scenario, you can specify here whether you want the IC agent to receive an error message and the system to close the current transaction before the contact can be ended. This message is displayed only if you have selected STATEFUL and RAISE VETO for the launch transaction.

In the third step of the transaction launcher (DEFINE FURTHER TECHNICAL DETAILS), you define the URL ID for a transaction type. The OBJECT TYPE (see Chapter 5, Section 5.2.2) and OBJECT ACTION fields are optional. However, it is important to specify the transaction type. The following transactions are offered:

**Step 3: Define further technical details**

- ▶ BOR transaction
- ▶ URL transaction
- ▶ Front office transaction

The input fields shown change in accordance with the transaction type selected. If you have selected the BOR transaction, you must define the logical system, the BOR object type, and a method name. For the BOR object type, you enter the technical name of the business object you want the system to call. You also define a BOR-object-dependent method (for example, BOR object PRODUCT BUS1178 with the `Display` method for displaying products). In Transaction SWO1, you can check whether the defined BOR object is available. Note that the BOR object has the status IMPLEMENTED.

In our example, we will select URL TRANSACTION as the TRANSACTION TYPE. For identification purposes (❸ in Figure 3.11) we must therefore specify only the URL ID. Similar to the transaction type URL TRANSACTION, front office transactions reference an ID in the target system. Because the front office transactions are available as an industry solution for ISU (*Industry Utilities*) only, we will skip this transaction type for the moment.

In the fourth step of the transaction launcher, you define the parameters and values you want the new launch transaction to use. The parameters and fields depend on the transaction you selected in step 1. BOR object methods have interface import parameters (Transaction SWO1) that you can define here. The transaction launcher cannot subsequently address parameters that are not defined here.

**Step 4: Define transaction parameters**

The transaction launcher supports only one return parameter and this parameter represents the object that is processed. You can determine whether the

**Step 5: Define an activity clipboard**

transaction results should be saved in the activity clipboard, depending on the individual parameters of the launch transaction. This is only of interest in the IC scenario. When you have completed the fifth step, close the transaction launcher. When you are finished with the wizard, the system generates program code in the background to connect the transaction. This process may take some time to complete.

### 3.3.3    Integration into the Navigation Bar Profile

Now that we have created the transaction for calling an Internet page, we can integrate it into the navigation bar profile. Use Transaction CRMC_UI_NBLINKS to open the navigation bar profile configuration.

Creating a logical link

First, a logical link that contains information about the transaction launcher is created. The logical link type must be LAUNCH TRANSACTION, the target ID is always EXECLTX, and the parameter class is usually CL_CRM_UI_LTX_NAVBAR_PARAM (see ❶ in Figure 3.12). You then define a group of direct links and assign the logical link created previously to the group (❷).

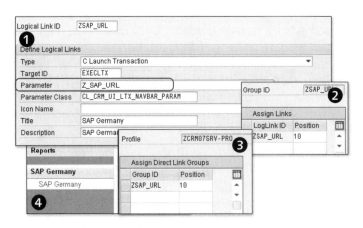

**Figure 3.12**   Integrating a Transaction

Integration into the navigation bar profile

The group of direct links you have created is now assigned to the navigation bar profile (❸). Note that the link must still be enabled using the business role transaction. ❹ in Figure 3.12 shows the CRM Web Client URL integrated into the navigation bar.

### 3.3.4    Changing an Existing Transaction

You can also use the transaction launcher to copy and subsequently change the configuration of existing transactions. After you call the transaction launcher wizard, you can adjust some (but not all) entries. If, for example, you want to adjust a BOR transaction, you can redefine the transfer parameters. You must then use the transaction launcher to regenerate the program code.

### 3.3.5 Copying and Deleting Transactions

You can copy or delete existing transactions in the SAP Implementation Guide under the path Customer Relationship Management • UI Framework • Technical Role Definition • Transaction Launcher • Copy/Delete Launch Transaction. Alternatively, you can also call view CRMV_IC_LTX_ ID in Transaction SM34. We recommend that you do not use this transaction to create a new launch transaction because it will not generate the required program code. You should use the transaction launcher wizard to create new entries for launch transaction IDs. When copying a launch transaction, note the correct version and definition entries (see Figure 3.13). The wizard increments the version number each time processing takes place.

Copying and deleting transactions

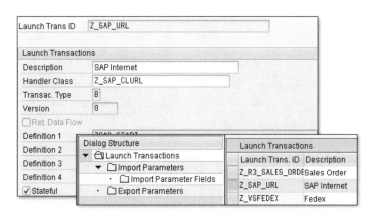

**Figure 3.13** Deleting a Launch Transaction

You can delete a launch transaction as follows:

Step sequence when deleting a launch transaction

1. Call the IMG activity (Copy/Delete Launch Transaction).

2. Identify the correct launch transaction.

3. Determine the name of the event handler class.

4. Use Transaction SE24 (BOR and FO transactions only) to delete the event handler class.

5. Delete the launch transaction.

> **Note**
>
> Before you delete a URL transaction, you should check whether the launch transaction has been integrated into the CRM Web Client only once. You can use table CRMC_IC_LTX_ID to perform this check. If this table contains only one occurrence of this entry, you can delete the URL transaction.

## 3.4    Practical Example: Navigation Bar

The practical example in this section describes the following steps:

1. Creating and assigning a role configuration key
2. Deactivating a work center page
3. Adding a work center page
4. Creating links on a work center page
5. Customizing the lower-level navigation
6. Customizing direct links

### 3.4.1    Creating and Assigning a Role Configuration Key

We recommend that you customize the user interface (view) in the customer namespace only. To do so, you have to create a role configuration key (see Chapter 2, Section 2.3.4).

1. **Define the role configuration key.**
   Call the role configuration key using the now familiar path in the SAP Implementation Guide: CUSTOMER RELATIONSHIP MANAGEMENT • UI FRAMEWORK • DEFINITION OF THE UI FRAMEWORK • DEFINE ROLE CONFIGURATION KEY.

2. **Create a role configuration key.**
   Create the role configuration key ZCRM2007 and enter a meaningful description (see Chapter 2, Section 2.3.4).

3. **Assign the role configuration key.**
   Call Transaction CRMC_UI_PROFILE for the business role definition and assign role configuration key ZCRM2007 to business role ZCRM2007SPRO.

Assigning the role configuration key to the business role

In the standard system, role configuration keys have not been defined for some business roles. In Customizing, this is indicated by the placeholder <*>.

### 3.4.2 Deactivating a Work Center Page

We will now show you how to hide the WORKLIST and CALENDAR menu options in the navigation bar. To do this, you must first identify the navigation bar profile assigned to your business role. ❶ in Figure 3.14 shows the navigation bar for business role ZCRM2007SPRO before you deactivate the WORKLIST and CALENDAR menu options.

1. **Identify the navigation bar profile.**
   Open business role ZCRM2007SPRO and identify the navigation bar profile SRV-PRO, which is defined there (❷).

2. **Call the navigation bar profile.**
   Using this information, start Customizing for the navigation bar profile in the SAP Implementation Guide under the path CUSTOMER RELATIONSHIP MANAGEMENT • UI FRAMEWORK • TECHNICAL ROLE DEFINITION • DEFINE NAVIGATION BAR PROFILE or in Transaction CRMC_UI_NBLINKS.

3. **Copy the navigation bar profile.**
   Select the navigation bar profile SRV-PRO and copy it to customer namespace ZCRM07SRV-PRO (❸ in Figure 3.14). In addition, assign a suitable description for the copied navigation bar profile.

   Copying the navigation bar profile

4. **Assign the navigation bar profile to the business role.**
   Next, assign the copied navigation bar profile ZCRM07SRV-PRO to business role ZCRM2007SPRO (❹).

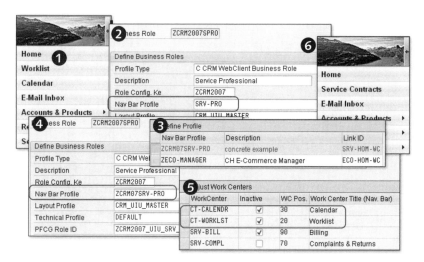

**Figure 3.14** Customizing the Navigation Bar

5. **Hide existing work center pages.**

Hiding existing
work center pages
In the business role configuration (❹), select the ADJUST WORK CENTERS menu option. You can use this menu option to display or hide work center pages (❺). In our example, you can use the INACTIVE indicator to deactivate the CALENDAR and WORKLIST menu options.

6. **Test the application.**

The CALENDAR and WORKLIST menu options are no longer available in the navigation bar (❻).

### 3.4.3 Adding a Work Center Page

In this section, we will show you how to add a new work center page to the navigation bar as a menu option:

1. **Call the navigation bar profile.**
In the SAP Implementation Guide, select the path CUSTOMER RELATIONSHIP MANAGEMENT • UI FRAMEWORK • TECHNICAL ROLE DEFINITION • DEFINE NAVIGATION BAR PROFILE or call Transaction CRMC_UI_NBLINKS.

2. **Create a new work center page.**

Creating a new
work center page
Select navigation bar profile ZCRM07SRV-PRO and copy the work center page SRV-CONTR to customer namespace ZCRM07SRV (❶ in Figure 3.15). Then replace the logical link ID with CT-EMAI-SR. Enter the title "My Work Center" and the description "My Work Center." The title will later display in the navigation bar.

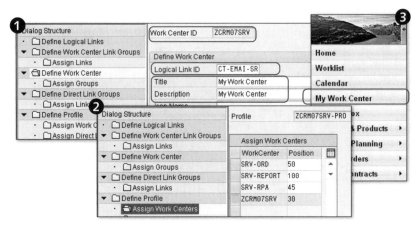

**Figure 3.15** Creating a Work Center Page

The logical link IDs are used to call the actual work center pages. If you call the menu option DEFINE LOGICAL LINKS via the dialog structure for the navigation bar configuration, you can check which work center page the logical link ID CT-EMAI-SR now opens behind the copied menu option SERVICE CONTRACTS.

1. **Assign the work center page.**
   Assign the newly created work center page ZCRM07SRV to the navigation bar profile ZCRM07SRV-PRO (❷ in Figure 3.15). Select the position of the newly created work center page on the navigation bar. In our example, we have selected Position 30. HOME and E-MAIL INBOX have lower positions.

   *Assigning the work center page*

2. **Test the application.**
   A new work center (MY WORK CENTER) is displayed in the navigation bar (❸).

## 3.5 Practical Example: Transaction Launcher

The example in this section will show you how to integrate the SAP GUI application BUSINESS PARTNER (Transaction BP) into the CRM Web Client as an HTML page. This involves the following steps:

1. Setting up a logical system
2. Using the transaction launcher to integrate the application
3. Integrating the application into the navigation bar

### 3.5.1 Setting Up a Logical System

You can use BOR object TSTC, which is delivered in the standard system, to display an SAP GUI transaction in the CRM Web Client (via ITS). However, we recommend copying BOR object TSTC to customer space ZCRM_TSTC using Transaction SE80. Then, activate the SYNCHRONOUS flag for method `Execute` (in Figure 3.16). Next, you should check whether the logical system and the ITS URL required to call an SAP GUI transaction have been set up (Transaction CRMS_IC_CROSS_SYS). Additional information is available in Section 3.3.1 and SAP Note 606757.

### 3.5.2 Using the Transaction Launcher to Integrate the Application

1. Use the relevant IMG activity or Transaction CRMC_UI_ACTIONWZ to call the transaction launcher. Define the launch transaction ID Z_CRM2007_

   *Step sequence for the transaction launcher*

BP (see Figure 3.16). To save memory, the ALL component set is no longer delivered in newer releases.

2. Next, enter a class name of your choice (for example, Z_BP_INTEGRA-TION). Then, set the STATEFUL indicator for calling the CRM application BUSINESS PARTNER in a separate window.

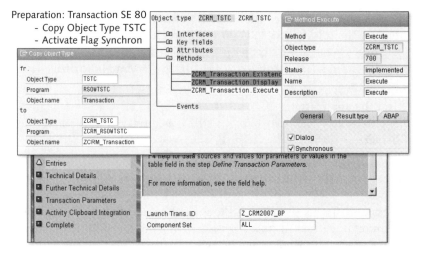

**Figure 3.16**  Step Sequence for the Transaction Launcher

3. Now, define logical system OWNLOGSYS, BOR object ZCRM_TSTC, and method name Execute. Then, select the object key as a parameter entry and define the value BP in the input field. This is the SAP GUI transaction you will call later. In our example, Transaction BP is used to display and edit business partners.

You can skip the remaining steps in the wizard. The wizard will then generate the required program code.

> **Note**
>
> Use Transaction SE93 to ensure that the SAP GUI transaction you have se-lected can be displayed as an HTML page. This is possible for the CRM ap-plication BUSINESS PARTNER.

### 3.5.3  Integrating the Application into the Navigation Bar

The now familiar path or Transaction CRMC_UI_NBLINKS is used to integrate the SAP GUI application BUSINESS PARTNER into the navigation bar.

1. **Logical link**

   First, create logical link ZSAP_BP, which will be subsequently integrated into the CRM application BUSINESS PARTNER. Here, define C LAUNCH TRANSACTION as the logical link type, EXECLTX as the target ID, Z_CRM2007_BP as the parameter, and CL_CRM_UI_LTX_NAVBAR_PARAM as the parameter class (❶ in Figure 3.17).

   *Creating the logical link*

2. **Direct link group**

   Then, define a new direct link group (ZCRM_BP) and assign logical link ZSAP_BP to this group.

3. **Profile assignment**

   Select your current navigation bar profile ZCRM07SRV-PRO and add your direct link group to the profile.

**Figure 3.17** GUI Integrated into CRM Web Client

In the business role configuration (Transaction BSP_WD_PROFILE), make sure that your newly created application for displaying business partners has been activated (❷). ❸ shows the HTML page (BUSINESS PARTNER) called by the navigation bar.

*Activation via the business role*

*As part of the L-shaped design, the header area is located in the upper section of the CRM Web Client. This area provides you with both comprehensive and general shortcuts as well as special functions.*

# 4   Enhancing and Customizing the Header Area

In addition to the navigation bar, the header area of the CRM Web Client is often the starting point for navigation within the user interface. You can use the header area to access the page history, any saved searches, and system links. You can also use the header area to obtain information about the page content you call (work area title) as well as possible adjustments to the page content (work area toolbar). The header area for marketing applications can also contain a working context (see Section 4.5).

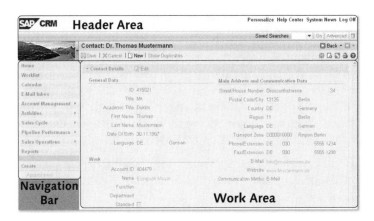

**Figure 4.1**   Header Area

The header area of the user interface is a static area within the Web Client UI framework that you cannot scroll. Furthermore, only one header area is provided per session. You can hide and display some of the areas (e.g., the saved searches and the central search), or you can change their position within the header area. You can also adjust the color and screen skins (see

*Header area: technical information*

Chapter 2, Section 2.6) as well as the size of the header area (see Section 4.2). You can customize the areas within the header in Customizing for the navigation frame, among others. You must also remember that the header area of the navigation frame comprises three areas, which are represented by the attributes UI_COMPONENT_1, UI_COMPONENT_2, and UI_COMPO-NENT_3, which, in turn, are available in the UI component CRM_WORKAR-EAHDR. In these areas, you can, for example, customize the position of the central search (see Section 4.4), saved search, or the working context (see Section 4.5).

> **Note**
>
> The UI component CRM_WORKAREAHDR is used to position header applications such as *central search*, *saved search*, and *working context*.

## 4.1 Configuring the Header Area

**Activating the central search**
To display the central search in the header area of the navigation frame, you can configure the necessary settings in the UI component CRM_WORK-AREAHDR. As a prerequisite, you must have activated the WORKAREA_HEADER component for your selected layout profile (see Section 4.3).

**Activating the saved search**
To display a saved search in the header area, you activate the SAVEDSEARCH_LAUNCHER component for your selected layout profile in the same Customizing activity (see Section 4.3).

You use the Component Workbench (see Chapter 8, Section 8.2) and the UI component CRM_WORKAREAHDR for the WORK AREA HEADER view to configure the header area for your business role. On the CONFIGURATION tab page, you select your role configuration key (❶ in Figure 4.2). Here, you can use the MORE • ATTRIBUTES button to display the attributes UI_COMPO-NENT_1, UI_COMPONENT_2 and UI_COMPONENT_3.

**Default configuration: central search**
To display the *central search* on the right-hand side of the header area, define, for example, the following value for UI_COMPONENT_3 (❷):

```
UI_COMPONENT_3:Window=CRM_ALLSEARCHES.CRM_ALLSEARCHES/LauncherW
indow;horizontalAlignment=right;
```

To ensure that the central search has sufficient space within the header area, you should define WIDTH=0PX for UI_COMPONENT_1 or UI_COMPO-NENT_2 if one of these components will not be used.

**Figure 4.2** Configuring the Header Area

To ensure that *saved searches* are displayed on the right-hand side of the header area, define the following value:

```
UI_COMPONENT_3:Window=CRM_SAVEDSEARCH.LauncherWindow;horizontal
Alignment=right;
```

Default configuration: saved search

If you want to display the *working context* on the right-hand side of the header area, define the following value:

```
UI_COMPONENT_3:Window=CMP_WCTXT.CMP_WCTXT/
MainWindow;Width=350px
```

Default configuration: working context

If you want to center the working context in the header area of the CRM Web Client, specify the aforementioned value (`UI_COMPONENT_2:Window=CMP_WCTXT.CMP_WCTXT/MainWindow;Width=350px`) in UI_COMPONENT_2.

## 4.2    Defining the Navigation Frame

The navigation frame for the header area is customized in the SAP Implementation Guide under the path CUSTOMER RELATIONSHIP MANAGEMENT • BUSINESS ROLES • DEFINE NAVIGATION FRAME. Here, you select the navigation frame specified for your business role (❶ in Figure 4.3).

Implementation Guide: navigation frame

The name of the header application, the component ID for the logo area, the message bar, and global functions for the header area are defined in the sample definition of the navigation frame. You can use the *Component Workbench* (see Chapter 8, Section 8.2) to customize the header application in greater detail (❷). In addition, you can use the layout profile to change the height of the header area (❸). This entry is useful if you want to define a larger company logo for the user interface. ❶ in Figure 4.3 also shows that, in this example, the saved search (SAVEDSEARCH_LAUNCHER) has been defined for the header area.

Structure of the header for the user interface

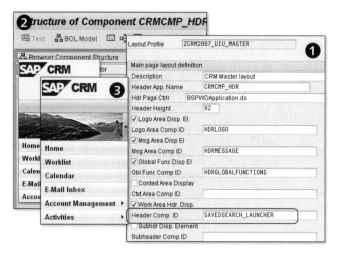

**Figure 4.3**  Navigation Frame for the Header Area

## 4.3  Defining the Layout Components

Implementation
Guide: layout
components You define the layout components in the SAP Implementation Guide under the path Customer Relationship Management • UI Framework • Technical Role Definition • Define Layout Component. Here, you also see the component IDs from the navigation frame definition (❶ in Figure 4.4). The layout component describes the component definition view (❷).

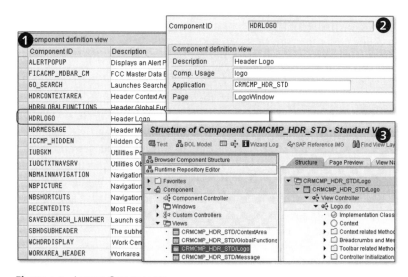

**Figure 4.4**  Layout Components

Using the information from the layout component (application name), you can use the Component Workbench (see Chapter 8, Section 8.2) to customize parts of the header area.

## 4.4 Displaying the Central Search

You can use the central search to find business objects both in the standalone CRM Web Client and in the CRM Web Client integrated into SAP NetWeaver Portal (see Chapter 6, Section 6.2). In both applications, the central search is available in the header area and is therefore displayed at all times. You can always access the header area irrespective of the business object displayed.

The visual appearance of the central search in the CRM Web Client integrated into the portal is similar to the appearance of the central search in the standalone CRM Web Client. The search menu comprises a hierarchical list of business objects and saved searches are available in the upper work area. You can also use the ADVANCED link to navigate to a search page or a saved search.

Integration

Figure 4.5 shows examples of integrating the central search and saved search into the header area of the user interface.

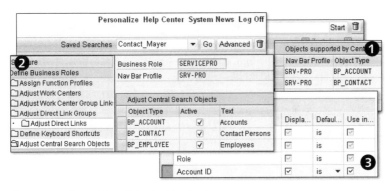

**Figure 4.5** Central Search in the Header Area

If you have entered search criteria and started the central search from the header area, the system navigates to the search page for the corresponding CRM business object and performs the search in accordance with the search criteria you have entered. The result is displayed on the search page for the business object.

You define the relevant Customizing settings for each business object to be supported by the central search in the SAP Implementation Guide under the path CUSTOMER RELATIONSHIP MANAGEMENT • UI FRAMEWORK • TECHNICAL

Implementation Guide: central search

ROLE DEFINITION • DEFINE CENTRAL SEARCH (❶ in Figure 4.5). To enable new settings to be displayed at the business role level in the central search, they are made known in Customizing for the business role (❷). However, the new search criterion has not yet been integrated into the search page. Therefore, use the UI Configuration Tool (see Section 5.1) to set the USE IN CENTRAL SEARCH (❸) indicator for the search criterion you have created.

Example: central search

To configure, for example, the search criterion for account IDs in the central search for your business role, start the UI Configuration Tool and select the UI component BP_HEAD_SEARCH and the MAINSEARCH view. Then, set the USE IN CENTRAL SEARCH indicator for the search criterion you want to display in the central search.

Additional information about the central search is available under the path SAP LIBRARY • CUSTOMER RELATIONSHIP MANAGEMENT • UI FRAMEWORK AND CONFIGURATION OF THE USER INTERFACE (UI) • SEARCH • CENTRAL SEARCH.

> **Note**
>
> You can perform the central search for business objects in the standalone CRM Web Client or in the CRM Web Client integrated into the portal. Its usage restrictions (special characters, Internet browser, etc.) are summarized in SAP Notes 1247914 and 1252827.

Implementation Guide: define parameters

Before you conclude the configuration, you should check whether the two search parameters CNTRLSEARCH_UI_TYPE and SEARCH_MAX_HITS are enabled (SAP IMPLEMENTATION GUIDE • CUSTOMER RELATIONSHIP MANAGEMENT • UI FRAMEWORK • TECHNICAL ROLE DEFINITIONS • DEFINE PARAMETER). The two search parameter values are contained in the standard delivery. The parameter CNTRLSEARCH_UI_TYPE specifies the number of fields displayed in the central search. You must also enable the SEARCH_MAX_HITS parameter. It determines the number of data records displayed in the results list (100 by default).

## 4.5   Using the Working Context

The working context is a group of attributes that are used as default values during an advanced search or when creating a new object. Working contexts are available for marketing applications only. You can use this function to select attribute values the system then uses to automatically prepopulate the user interface. The values you specify for a working context are, for example, displayed as default entries on the pages for advanced searches, the pages for creating marketing objects, and the master data pages.

First, let's take a look at a brief example: A *product manager* (PM) is responsible for a range of chocolate products and works primarily with the business partner "Chocolate Ltd." The PM creates a working context and assigns it the name "Chocolate." The working context comprises CHOCOLATE LTD. as an account, a product group for chocolate, and a planning horizon. If CHOCOLATE is the active working context, the system preassigns the account name and product group as well as the start and end dates each time the PM creates a new promotion.

Example: working context

You define the working context profile in the SAP Implementation Guide under the path CUSTOMER RELATIONSHIP MANAGEMENT • UI FRAMEWORK • TECHNICAL ROLE DEFINITION • DEFINE WORKING CONTEXT PROFILES (❶ in Figure 4.6). Here, you determine the control level (e.g., STRICT) of the function profile and assign one or more provider classes (e.g., CL_CRM_TPM_ WORKING_CONTEXT) to the working context profile under ASSIGN WORK-ING CONTEXT PROVIDERS). Next, you define language-dependent descriptions for the attributes under ADJUST WORKING CONTEXT ATTRIBUTES. You must then assign the newly created working context profile to the business role under ASSIGN FUNCTION PROFILES (❷).

Implementation Guide: working context

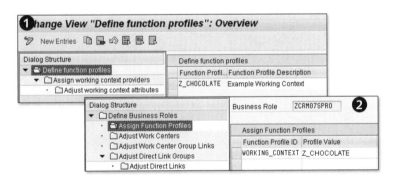

**Figure 4.6**  Working Context

The behavior of the working context depends on whether you set the STRICT indicator (Column 3 – DEFINE WORKING CONTEXT PROFILE) for strict monitoring of the working context profile.

Defining the control level

If you enable strict monitoring, you cannot override the working context. For example, you cannot search for a product that differs from the product specified in the working context. Otherwise, you can disable and override the working context. You can, for example, create *trade promotions* for an account other than the account defined in the working context.

> **Note**
>
> At present, SAP delivers only one working context profile: TPM. You can only use the TPM profile in trade promotion management (including receivables management and funds management). If you need to restrict the attributes for certain business roles, you can create additional working context profiles.

*The work area displays the information required by Web Client users. SAP CRM 2007 provides a range of new, integrated tools for customizing the work area.*

# 5 Enhancing and Customizing the Work Area

You can adapt and rearrange the work area of the CRM Web Client to a large degree without any programming knowledge.

In many cases, tasks such as showing new input fields, changing field labels, repositioning input and output fields, or enhancing business objects can be performed without any development expertise.

A range of tools is provided for this, which greatly simplifies the process of customizing the CRM Web Client work area. In this chapter, we will introduce you to the individual tools and demonstrate the options provided. In addition, the limitations of these tools are also discussed. Note that you will still need to master some development skills to complete some of the tasks involved in reorganizing and adapting the user interface; these will be discussed in the technical chapters that follow.

The work area of the CRM Web Client (see Figure 5.1) is located at the center of the user interface. In most cases, you navigate using the header area and the navigation bar, which frame the work area. Information is displayed on various page types in the work area, which are determined by each task and provided by the Web Client UI framework. The main page types used are as follows:

- ▶ Home page
- ▶ Work center
- ▶ Search page
- ▶ Overview page
- ▶ Edit page
- ▶ Reports page

**Page types**

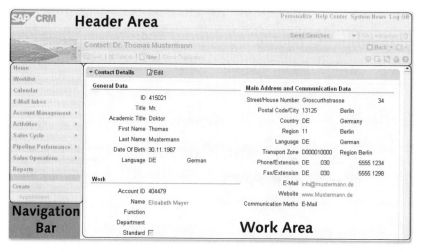

**Figure 5.1**  The Work Area

For more information about page types, see Chapter 1, Section 1.2.3, where the structure and properties of each page type are discussed in detail.

## 5.1  UI Configuration Tool

The User Interface Configuration Tool (*UI Configuration Tool*) is part of the Component Workbench (see Chapter 8, Section 8.2). The Component Workbench supports new developments and enhancements of the user interface. The UI Configuration Tool, meanwhile, is used only to design the presentation layer, that is, the layout.

Prerequisites and authorizations

Configuration of the user interface is based on the CRM_CONFIG authorization object (see SAP Note 1042187). This authorization object allows you to restrict configuration of the user interface. Authorization is based on the name of the UI component, the BSP view name, the UI object type, and the role configuration key. You can use activity "02" to create, change, or delete authorizations for configuring the user interface. Use the CRMCONFMODE authorization object (configuration mode, see Section 5.1.2) if you want to configure the user interface directly from a CRM application of the CRM Web Client.

Task area of the UI Configuration Tool

CRM application data is displayed in views, which can be grouped together in view sets (see Chapter 9, Sections 9.1 and 9.2). Views and view sets are displayed in windows and SAP provides both configurable and non-configurable views in the standard system. A view is configurable if a configuration tab is

124

assigned to it (on the CONFIGURATION tab). Most of the CRM views delivered as standard are configurable. You can configure the following settings with the UI Configuration Tool:

▸ Add, delete, and change screen elements

▸ Add and change labels

▸ Change field properties (e.g., display only)

▸ Configure additional options (e.g., load options for assignment blocks, visible search criteria, and standard search operators)

Section 5.4 provides an example of the customization of an overview page and a search page and the modification of field labels and field properties using the UI Configuration Tool.

SAP delivers at least one default configuration for each configuration view and the standard configuration should not be changed by customers. Instead, it is intended to be used as a template for customer-specific configurations. All SAP standard configurations are stored in cross-client SAP tables while configurations created or modified by customers are stored in client-specific customer tables. The configurations are determined using a configuration access sequence at runtime (see Section 5.1.1). The system begins by checking whether a customer configuration already exists, and if a customer configuration is found, it is displayed. Otherwise, the SAP configuration is used. If a customer configuration for the user interface is deleted, the SAP configuration is accessed instead.

SAP configuration and customer configuration

### 5.1.1    Configuration Access Sequence

An access sequence comprising two steps is used to determine the configuration of the user interface and the field label. In the first step in the sequence, a configuration is determined based on parameters. The parameters used for this purpose are the role configuration key, component usage, UI object type, and subobject type. If the search is not successful, the number of parameters used is gradually decreased. The parameters with which a configuration is determined are referred to as the *successful key*.

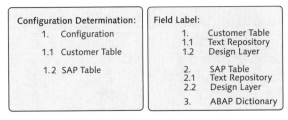

**Figure 5.2**  Access Sequence

In the second step, the successful key is used to determine the field label in the text repository. If the field label is not explicitly defined in the configuration, it can be determined from the ABAP Dictionary. The medium-length field label is always selected here. In addition to configuring the user interface with the UI Configuration Tool, you can also configure Customizing settings for the design layer in SAP CRM (see Section 5.2). The design layer allows you to link settings for the user interface with a new generic design object that spans several views.

Implementation Guide: Access sequence

It is possible to change the standard access sequence used to determine configurations. To use your own access sequence, you must implement the BSP_DLC_ACCESS_ENHANCEMENT Business Add-In (BAdI) in Customizing (SAP IMG: CUSTOMER RELATIONSHIP MANAGEMENT • UI FRAMEWORK • UI FRAMEWORK DEFINITION • BUSINESS ADD-INS (BADIS) • BADI: CONFIGURATION ACCESS DETERMINATION).

> **Note**
>
> Parameters are used to determine the user interface configuration and field label. You can implement a BAdI to change the access sequence used.

### 5.1.2    Calling the UI Configuration Tool

You can call the UI Configuration Tool in one of the following two ways:

▶ From the configuration mode in the CRM Web Client

▶ From the Component Workbench

Calling the tool in configuration mode

You can only call the UI Configuration Tool from the configuration mode if the configuration mode is already enabled. You enable the configuration mode in the system link personalization settings (see Figure 5.3).

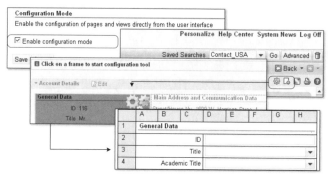

**Figure 5.3**  Calling the UI Configuration Tool from the Configuration Mode

In addition, the CRMCONFMOD authorization object must be assigned to your user. You can then select the relevant page and click the PAGE CONFIGURATION button to call the UI Configuration Tool.

The UI Configuration Tool is integrated into the Component Workbench in the SAP GUI (see Section 8.2). You can start the tool from the CONFIGURATION tab of the selected view. However, this tab is only active if a view can be configured. We will illustrate this point with a brief example: Assume that you need to identify the name of the UI component and the view for purposes of UI configuration and to call the Component Workbench. You press the F2 key to obtain this technical information (see Section 5.1.3).

**Example: Calling the UI Configuration Tool**

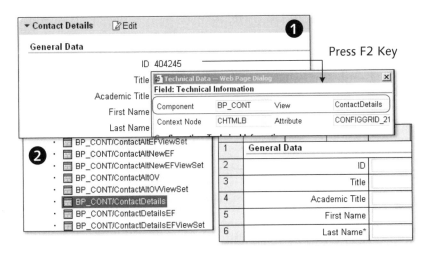

**Figure 5.4** Calling the UI Configuration Tool from the Component Workbench

❶ in Figure 5.4 shows the F2 dialog box, displaying the technical data for the selected screen area. You can then start the Component Workbench with the identified names of the UI component and view (SAP Implementation Guide: CUSTOMER RELATIONSHIP MANAGEMENT • UI FRAMEWORK • UI FRAMEWORK DEFINITION • CONFIGURE USER INTERFACE or Transaction BSP_WD_CMPWB). Specify the component name (e.g., BP_CONT) and select

**Implementation Guide: Component Workbench**

127

the correct component view (e.g., ContactDetails) (❷). Then, navigate to the UI configuration from the CONFIGURATION tab.

> **Note**
>
> To access the view configuration in your system administrator role in the CRM WebClient, assign the logical links BSP-DLC-VC and BSP-DLC_FC to the work center CT-ADMIN for your navigation bar profile.

### 5.1.3 Technical Information (F2 Key)

The F2 key in your web browser is an important tool for determining technical information in the CRM Web Client environment. The following example illustrates the functionality of this key: If you are, for example, on the Accounts overview page and want to reconfigure the page, click on an input field in the detail area. Then, press the F2 key to display a dialog box showing the technical details of the selected UI component (❶ in Figure 5.5).

In addition to the name of the UI component, the dialog box provides information about the selected view, context node, and attribute. It also indicates whether a role configuration key (see Chapter 2, Section 2.3.4) is already defined for the view. As of service pack 5, the package used is shown in the header area of the F2 dialog box (❷). Additional information about the design layer (see Section 5.2) is provided with SAP CRM 7.0.

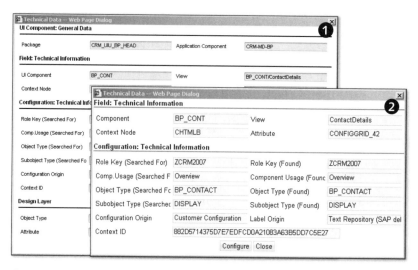

**Figure 5.5** Technical Information with the F2 Key

### 5.1.4 Structure of the UI Configuration Tool

The UI Configuration Tool is organized into rows and columns for the purpose of editing form views in table form. This structure allows you to position the arrangement of input fields and their labels in the view concisely in the table rows and columns without needing to specify an exact position in the view. Figure 5.6 shows the UI Configuration Tool and the work areas (*panels*) used to configure views. The organizational structure of the UI Configuration Tool depends on both the page type and the view type (table view or tree structure). Our discussion of the UI Configuration Tool is limited to the display and adaptation of form views.

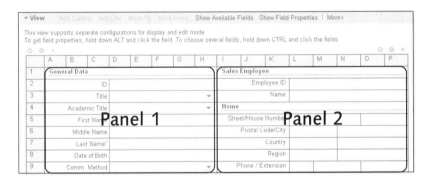

**Figure 5.6** UI Configuration Tool

Views may have different structures. The following three display options are available in the UI Configuration Tool:

> Options for splitting views

1. The view consists of a single work area with eight columns.

2. The view consists of a single work area with 16 columns.

3. The view consists of a two work areas with eight columns each.

The UI Configuration Tool offers various options for customizing views, all of which are discussed here. The buttons above the work area(s) provide the following options:

> Customizing options for views

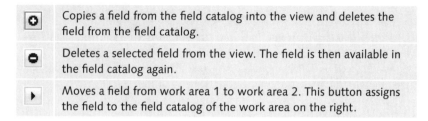

| | |
|---|---|
| ⊕ | Copies a field from the field catalog into the view and deletes the field from the field catalog. |
| ⊖ | Deletes a selected field from the view. The field is then available in the field catalog again. |
| ▸ | Moves a field from work area 1 to work area 2. This button assigns the field to the field catalog of the work area on the right. |

The toolbar of the UI Configuration Tool allows you to add a new caption (ADD CAPTION) or additional lines (ADD LINE) to the selected view. Use the MOVE UP and MOVE DOWN buttons to position new captions, input fields, or additional lines in the view. If you click SHOW AVAILABLE FIELDS, a field catalog opens that contains all available attributes for this view. If an attribute you require is not available, you need to enhance the business object. The *Easy Enhancement Workbench* (EEWB) (see Section 5.3) can be used for certain enhancements. For all other enhancements, refer to the technical chapters later in this book.

Field properties
In addition to displaying all AVAILABLE FIELDS (❶ in Figure 5.7), you can also show the FIELD PROPERTIES of a selected attribute (❷). In the field properties, you can change field labels, specify whether fields are optional or required entry fields, and display technical information about the attribute.

For historical reasons, some views exist in both display and change mode (❸). These views are used to display and maintain business partners or products. The UI Configuration Tool allows you to adapt or compare both views.

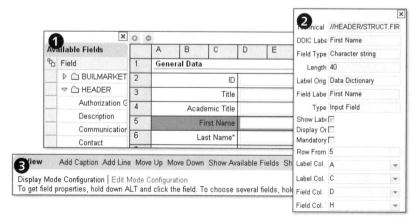

**Figure 5.7** Detail View of the UI Configuration Tool

Navigation behavior changes when you upgrade from CRM 2006s to CRM 2007. For SAP CRM 2007, navigation behavior was converted to editable overview pages (see SAP Note 1223874).

## 5.1.5 Role-Based Customizing of the User Interface

When customizing the user interface (views), we strongly recommend to ensure that changes made to views are role-based and that views used in the SAP standard system are not changed. The required view configuration is determined at runtime using the role configuration key, component usage, UI object type, and subobject type as parameters.

The role configuration key (❶ in Figure 5.8) must be assigned to a business role (❷) (see Section 2.3). Next, you assign the role configuration key to the relevant views in the UI Configuration Tool. If a user with the relevant business role then logs on to the CRM Web Client, the role configuration key is used to determine the customized views for this business role (❸). Press the F2 key to display the technical properties of the user interface.

*Example: Role configuration key*

To assign the role configuration key to a view, start the UI Configuration Tool for an SAP standard view that you want to customize.

*Role-based customizing of views*

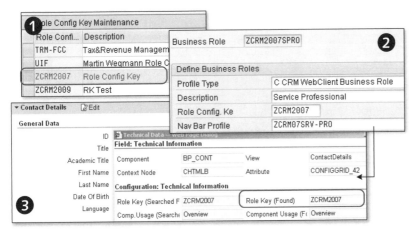

**Figure 5.8** Assigning a Role Configuration Key to a View

Switch to change mode in the UI Configuration Tool and copy the configuration of the SAP standard view (see Figure 5.9). In the dialog box that opens, define the role configuration key of the business role for which you want to adapt the view.

**Figure 5.9**  Assigning the Role Configuration Key

You can also define the COMPONENT USAGE, OBJECT TYPE, and OBJECT SUB-
TYPE parameters here. The view is accessed on the basis of these parameters
(see Section 5.1.1). You need to specify a UI object type and subobject type if
the view is used for several applications but you only want to customize the
view for one of them.

After you log on to the CRM Web Client, press the [F2] key to view all technical properties of the selected view. The dialog box that opens shows you
the view configuration found by the system based on the defined parameters
(See Figure 5.10).

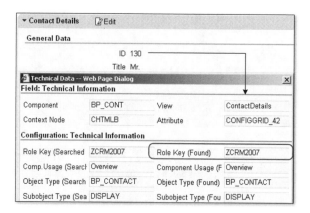

**Figure 5.10**  View with Role Configuration Key

> **Note**
>
> Check which business role is displayed after you log on to the CRM Web Cli-
> ent by positioning the mouse pointer over PERSONALIZE (system links). The
> business role is displayed at the end of the URL shown in the footer area of
> the web browser.

## 5.2 Design Layer

In the CRM Web Client, you can customize screen elements of the user interface using the UI Configuration Tool and the Component Workbench. However, changes need to be made for each view (each configuration) individually, which is not always convenient. If a screen element appears in various views, you want to be able to make the changes only once and then apply them to the relevant views. The design layer allows you to do just that.

The design layer links user interface settings with design objects, which comprise several views that share the same business content. Design objects define the field settings for the user interface and can be assigned to several views that are used in the same business context. You can use the design layer to:

**Design objects**

- Rename field labels
- Hide fields that are not required
- Assign existing input helps from the ABAP Dictionary without any customer-specific development

The design layer controls field labels in form views, table columns, and in the search criteria of the advanced search. It also controls field visibility on the UI at runtime and in the available field selection in the UI Configuration Tool. These settings are determined by design objects, which you can configure in the design layer Customizing settings.

> **Note**
>
> With the design layer, you can, for example, change field labels for several views. The changes can be explicitly overridden in the relevant views and also by the view-specific Customizing. A relevant example is provided in Section 5.5.

### 5.2.1 Structure of the Design Layer

In relation to the UI architectural concept (see Chapter 8), the design layer is logically located between the presentation layer and the business object layer (BOL) (see Figure 5.11). This means that adjustments made to the UI can be made available to all areas of the user interface.

**UI architectural concept**

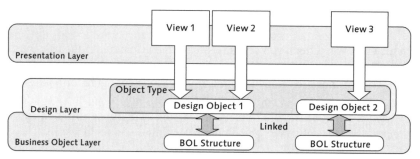

**Figure 5.11** Location of the Design Layer

Implementation
Guide: Design
object

You can define design objects and assign these to views in the design layer Customizing settings. Select CUSTOMER RELATIONSHIP MANAGEMENT • UI FRAMEWORK • UI FRAMEWORK DEFINITION • MAINTAIN DESIGN LAYERS in the IMG. You then begin by selecting or defining a UI object type (see Section 5.2.2). This UI object type does not necessarily have to be the same object type that is used by the application control units and the multilevel configuration. In other words, this UI type may be a "generic" UI object type for use with the design layer. Generic object types serve only to define reference design objects. Normal design objects should be defined in accordance with their business content for the relevant UI object types. After you define or select the UI object type, you can create a new design object or edit an existing one.

Assigning design
objects

When you define design objects, you can set one or more parameters for customizing the user interface. These parameters then have a direct influence on the assigned views. You use the Component Workbench to assign the created design objects. Here, you assign the design objects to a context node or to an individual attribute below a context node in a selected view.

This means that all adjustments you make to the user interface are available to several related views. The design object is permanently linked to the assigned structure of the BOL (see Figure 5.11). As a result, design objects can be used to adjust each attribute of the BOL structure and make these attributes transparent for all applications (views).

Several design objects can be grouped together in a UI object type. The concept of UI object types is essential to define and modify design objects completely independently of an existing BOL object. UI object types allow ABAP callback classes to be defined. These allow you to determine subobject types, for example. You can also define the name of the GenIL component and the corresponding BOL and BOR objects for UI object types. The BSP_DLC_OBJ_TYPE table contains this important information for linking UI object types, ABAP callback classes, components, and BOR and BOL objects.

## 5.2.2    UI Object Types

SAP introduced the concept of UI object types to enable the definition of business content (e.g., the design layer) independently of BOL objects. Configurations can be defined for the user interface based on UI object types. A subobject is a subordinate UI object type and can also be used as a form of differentiation.

The following example from CRM Service illustrates one way in which UI object types can be used. The UI objects COMPLAINT, IN-HOUSE REPAIR and RETURNS can be introduced for the COMPLAINT business object (BUS2000120), based, for example, on the use of various UI object types that are based on a BOL object. The user interface can then be reconfigured to suit the purposes of each usage.

**Example: Using UI objects**

If you use UI object types and subobjects, you can therefore map various UI configurations for different business processes. The UI object type and subobject type are determined by the application at runtime. The component usage is automatically assigned by the framework at runtime. You can press the F2 key to display the TECHNICAL DATA dialog box and check which UI object type is used at runtime (see Section 5.1.3).

Existing standard UI object types are displayed in Transaction BSP_DLC_SDE-SIGN (see Figure 5.12). The assigned design objects are used to show or hide standard field labels. Here, it is not possible to define new UI object types for customer-specific components in the customer namespace. The standard UI object types are valid for all clients.

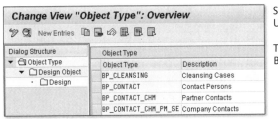

Standard UI Object Type

Transaction BSP_DLC_SDESIGN

**Figure 5.12**    UI Object Types

You can override the SAP default setting for the object types by creating a new UI object type that was created with the same name in the customer table. This may be necessary if, for example, another ABAP callback class should be assigned. These changes are client-specific and are made under CUSTOMER RELATIONSHIP MANAGEMENT • UI FRAMEWORK • UI FRAMEWORK DEFINITION • DEFINE UI OBJECT types in the IMG.

**Implementation Guide: UI object types**

You can also create new UI object types in your own namespace (Y*, Z*) in this IMG activity. This involves the optional definition of an ABAP callback class for determining subobject types. Examples of callback classes for UI object types are defined in the BSPDLCV_OBJ_TYPE maintenance view and in the BSP_DLC_OBJ_TYPE table. In addition to the callback class, you can also define other details such as a description of the object type, the GenIL component, BOL object name, and BOR object type. You can then assign design objects to the UI object types you created. Note that Customizing settings for the UI object types are client-specific.

**Determining UI object types**

For a UI object type to be determined at runtime, the DO_CONFIG_DETERMI-NATION method needs to be redefined at the level of the window controller or view controller. The SET_CONFIG_KEYS and SET_CONFIG_KEYS_4_CHIL-DREN methods are called within the DO_CONFIG_DETERMINATION method. As import parameters, the SET_CONFIG_KEYS method receives the details of the UI object type, subobject type, and a Boolean indicator that determines whether the UI object type and subobject type should also be inherited by dependent elements such as views.

### 5.2.3 Design Layer Data Model

**Linking object types and design objects**

The data model of the design layer defines the relationships between the design object, UI object type, and BOL object. Figure 5.13 shows the data model of the SAP standard tables. The only difference between these and customer-specific tables is that customer-specific tables do not use an "S" in the definition of the table names (e.g., BSP_DLC_DOBJ). The BSP_DLC_SDOBJ table defines a link between the UI object type and the design object. The name of the BOL object is also defined here. The textual descriptions for the defined languages are taken from the BSP_DLC_SDOBJ_T table. The BSP_DLC_SDESIGN table specifies which attribute of the BOL object is customized and whether this attribute should subsequently be hidden in the view or displayed as a required entry field or display field.

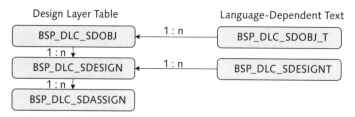

**Figure 5.13** Design Layer Data Model (SAP Standard Tables)

The view for which the changes are active is specified in the BSP_DLC_SDASSIGN table. Here, you will also find the context node to which you assigned your design object when you activated it.

### 5.2.4 General Field Customizing

The following example serves to illustrate general field customizing for the CONTACT DETAILS CRM application. Here, the business partner number is changed from ID to BUSINESS PARTNER ID (❶ and ❸ in Figure 5.14).

To create a new design object, choose CUSTOMER RELATIONSHIP MANAGEMENT • UI FRAMEWORK • UI FRAMEWORK DEFINITION • MAINTAIN DESIGN LAYER in the SAP IMG. First, select the BP_CONTACT object type (contact details). Then, define a name and a meaningful description for the new design object. Refer to the BUILCONTACTPERSON BOL object and the BP_NUMBER attribute (business partner number) (❷). Finally, define the new field label BUSINESS PARTNER ID for the design object.

Implementation Guide: Design object

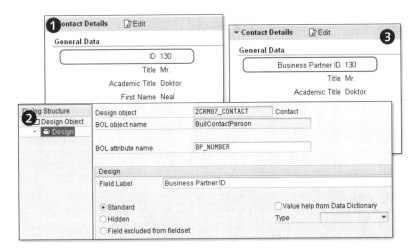

**Figure 5.14**  General Field Customizing

You can also specify whether the new field label should be hidden as a rule. This is useful, for example, in the case of the AREA CODE or TELEPHONE NUMBER input fields. If you set the VALUE HELP FROM DATA DICTIONARY indicator, input helps that already exist in the ABAP Dictionary can be accessed without any additional development effort. Generic V and P *getter methods* are implemented, which define the input help (from the ABAP Dictionary: search help, value table, and domain values) and field type (input help, checkbox, and selection list). Generic V and P getter logic is only used if this indicator is set.

> **Note**
>
> For more information about using a design object to activate an input help from the ABAP Dictionary or to define the field type, refer to SAP Note 1242566.

Assignment to context nodes

You assign the design object you created to the view of the CONTACT DETAILS CRM application in the Component Workbench (Transaction BSP_WD_CMPWB). Select a context node or an individual context attribute to which you want to assign the design object for the component (BP_CONT). Then, select the ASSIGNMENT TO DESIGN LAYER option from the context menu. The DESIGN LAYER ASSIGNMENT dialog shows which design objects are assigned to the context node. You define the assignment using the key fields (COMPONENT, VIEW, CONTEXT NODE, CONTEXT NODE ATTRIBUTE, OBJECT TYPE, and COMPONENT USAGE). Finally, choose ADD ASSIGNMENT and select the UI object type you created earlier. After you save your changes, the assignment is complete (❸ in Figure 5.14).

### 5.2.5  Modifying the Shared Memory Settings

Implementation Guide: Modifying shared memory settings for the design layer

The design layer data, in other words, the Customizing settings for design objects, can be saved in shared memory. All running applications are connected to this memory, from which they read the information they require. The total memory requirement of your CRM system is significantly reduced by connecting each application with this memory area. You can make adjustments to the shared memory settings under CUSTOMER RELATIONSHIP MANAGEMENT • UI FRAMEWORK • UI FRAMEWORK DEFINITION • EDIT SHARED MEMORY FOR DESIGN LAYER in the SAP IMG or in Transaction SHMM.

> **Note**
>
> If you want to optimize memory consumption while using the CRM Web Client, refer to SAP Notes 1276708, 1042618, and 1281896.

## 5.3  Easy Enhancement Workbench

The EEWB is a tool that allows you to enhance business objects without any development knowledge. In the EEWB, customer enhancements of a business object are defined using *wizards*. The Workbench handles all other development activities that are required. It creates database tables, UI elements, and application logic and integrates these into the SAP standard system. This way, the EEWB enables users without any ABAP expertise to enhance the SAP standard system. It makes customer developments much faster and easier to implement.

From a technical perspective, enhancing business objects with the EEWB is no different from doing so manually. In both cases, transportable ABAP objects are created and the same *customer exits, business transaction events,* or *BAdIs* are implemented. The only discernable difference is in the actual procedure for enhancing the business object. Automatic enhancement of business objects with the EEWB is implemented using generation sequences based on application-specific template objects. Because of this automation, the EEWB can only be used for business objects that have been specially prepared, most of which come from the CRM environment. Section 5.3.1 includes a selection of business objects that can be enhanced in this manner. In addition to the business objects that can be enhanced, restrictions also apply to the type of enhancement that can be performed with the EEWB. In most cases, it is only possible to add customer-specific database tables or database fields.

*Enhancement restrictions*

In general, the enhancements can extend across systems. For example, if you enhance the sales order in CRM, you can also enhance the exchange of data and the database of the connected SAP ERP system. This functionality is currently only fully supported by sales orders. On the other hand, data exchange can be enhanced for most business objects in CRM.

The system landscape must be configured to allow you to use cross-system generation. To configure the relevant configuration settings, choose CROSS-APPLICATION COMPONENTS • GENERAL APPLICATION FUNCTIONS • EASY ENHANCEMENT WORKBENCH • MAINTAIN SYSTEM LANDSCAPE in the SAP IMG or start Transaction EEWC.

*Implementation Guide: System landscape maintenance*

> **Note**
>
> For more details on this subject, refer to SAP Note 649336. The process of implementing data exchange with other systems for business partners is described in SAP Note 864222.

### 5.3.1 Differences Between the EEWB and the UI Configuration Tool

So, why do you need to use the EEWB in addition to the UI Configuration Tool to customize the user interface? The UI Configuration Tool only allows you to show or hide fields (attributes) that already exist for the business

*Differences between the EEWB and the UI Configuration Tool*

object. In terms of the CRM Web Client architectural model, you can only customize the presentation layer (see Figure 5.15) with the UI Configuration Tool.

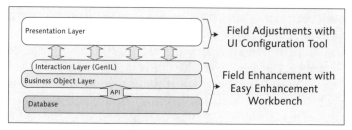

**Figure 5.15**  Field Enhancement with the EEWB

With the EEWB, on the other hand, you can implement field enhancements for business objects below the presentation layer. The EEWB can enhance structures and tables on which GenIL objects operate. Only after these enhancements are made can the UI Configuration Tool be used to show a new input or output field on the user interface. Note that the enhancement functions of the EEWB can only be used for specially prepared business objects.

Business objects that can be enhanced with the EEWB

You can use the EEWB to enhance the ACTIVITY, COMPLAINT, LEAD, OPPORTUNITY, SALES PROCESS, and SERVICE PROCESS *business transactions*, for example. The ACCOUNT PLAN, BUSINESS PARTNER, BUSINESS PARTNER RELATIONSHIPS, SALES AND SERVICE CONTRACT, COUNTER, INSTALLED BASED, PRODUCT RELATIONSHIPS, and MARKETING ELEMENTS business objects can also be enhanced with the EEWB.

### 5.3.2  Structure of the Easy Enhancement Workbench

Implementation Guide: EEWB

To make the design of the EEWB as user-friendly as possible, SAP used the familiar design of the ABAP Workbench (the screen layout and navigation options are identical). To access the EEWB, select CUSTOMER RELATIONSHIP MANAGEMENT • CRM MIDDLEWARE AND RELATED COMPONENTS • EASY ENHANCEMENT WORKBENCH in the SAP IMG or start Transaction EEWB. The object list hierarchy is adapted to the structure of a customer project.

A PROJECT is created at the highest level in the EEWB (see Figure 5.16). It comprises several enhancements and allows you to define the project documentation and a list of participants. The project is also used to define the development class (PACKAGE) of the generated objects. All of the generated objects belonging to a project are transported together. It is not possible to transport an individual enhancement of a business object.

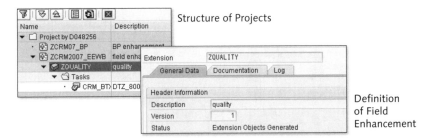

**Figure 5.16**  Project Structure in the EEWB

The ENHANCEMENTS are displayed at the next level in the EEWB. An enhancement always refers to one business object and one enhancement type. The content of the enhancement is defined using the business object-specific EEWB tool. After an enhancement has been defined and generated, the POST-PROCESSING object type often appears at the next level. This indicates manual postprocessing activities you are required to perform. An enhancement is only considered complete when it has been generated correctly and when you have completed all required post-processing activities.

*Project creation and enhancements in the EEWB*

To facilitate monitoring of the generation and to lend transparency to the technical process, all generator calls are displayed as *tasks* in the object list. After an enhancement is generated, all generated objects are visible in a task, and you can double-click to display each of these. In addition, all generation error and warning messages are described and stored in a log (see Section 5.3.4).

*Monitoring the enhancement*

### 5.3.3  Field Enhancement with the Easy Enhancement Workbench

The following steps must be completed (using the tools provided) to ensure a successful field enhancement for a business object:

1. Generate the enhancement with the EEWB.

2. Enhance the BOR object.

3. Position the enhancement on the user interface.

First, all technical steps required for the enhancement are completed automatically by the EEWB (enhancement of tables, structures, and BOL objects).

*Table or structure enhancements*

You then call the EEWB (Transaction EEWB) and create a project using the context menu (❶ in Figure 5.17). Specify a project name (e.g., ZCRM2007_EEWB), a description (field enhancement), and packages and namespaces for each system used.

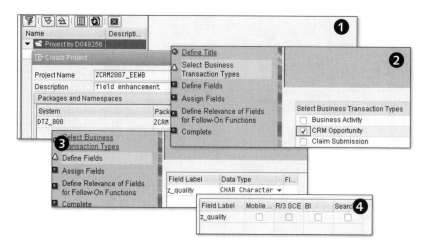

**Figure 5.17** Step Sequence in the EEWB Tool

You can then use the ENHANCEMENTS context menu to create enhancements of business objects. You also need to define a name and a description for the enhancement. In addition, the name of the business object to be enhanced (e.g., OPPORTUNITY) and an enhancement type (e.g., CUSTOMER_H) must be specified. After you have done this, position the cursor in the newly created enhancement and start the EEWB wizard from the context menu. After you have defined a title for the enhancement, you can select the business transaction types you want to enhance under SELECT BUSINESS TRANSACTION TYPES (❷ in Figure 5.17). In the next step of the wizard, you define the field in the business object that will be enhanced (❸). Here you need to define both the data type (e.g., CHAR) and the field length. You also need to specify whether the field enhancement should be performed at the header or item level. In the final step of the wizard, you define the relevance for follow-on functions (❹). Here you specify whether the field is relevant for mobile solutions, BW applications, R/3 systems, or advanced searches. The subsequent generation process may take several minutes. Both development transports and configuration transports are required for this process. If you have not yet created any transports, the system will prompt you to do so at this point. Project objects and enhancement objects are created as a result, which then need to be generated.

---

**Tip**

Note that the EEWB wizards are application-specific and may differ slightly depending on the application (see also the example provided in Section 5.6).

---

To start the generation process, position the cursor in the enhancement and select GENERATE in the context menu (❶ in Figure 5.18). If manual postprocessing of the enhancement is required, additional nodes (*postprocesses*) will appear below the enhancement in the object list. In this case, position the cursor in the first new postprocess in the object list, select EXECUTE in the context menu, and follow the instructions provided. When manual processing is finished, the entire enhancement process is complete.

**Enhancing the BOL object**

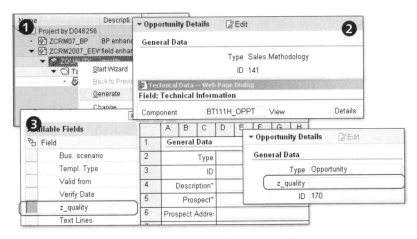

**Figure 5.18**  Positioning the Enhancement on the User Interface

You use the UI Configuration Tool to position the generated field on the user interface. To do so, select the correct UI component (❷) and start the UI Configuration Tool from the Component Workbench (Transaction BSP_WD_CMPWB). You then need to select the view to be enhanced. After you have done so, you can select the AVAILABLE FIELDS menu option to position the newly created input field (e.g., Z_QUALITY) in the view (❸).

**Positioning the enhancement on the user interface**

### 5.3.4  Troubleshooting

As you can see, an entire sequence of steps is required to get from the point of entering the relevant data to actively using the generated business objects. Various tools are called in the background during this process. This level of complexity may mean that errors are collected rather than being output immediately. In this case, the error messages are collected on the log tab of the enhancement. In this section, we will suggest solutions to some of the error messages you may encounter.

If you are unable to select the CREATE, CHANGE, or DELETE options from the context menu, this means that you do not have change authorization for the development objects. If this occurs, contact the Basis consultant responsible or the administrator to ensure that you are assigned the necessary authorizations.

Another error may occur after you exit the EEWB wizard. A message may appear, indicating that the enhancement and/or task(s) contain errors. If this happens, check the LOG tab on the detail screen of the enhancement and tasks. Then, follow the steps that are proposed in the message to correct the error. Select the CREATE OR GENERATE option from the context menu to proceed with the generation.

> **Note**
>
> For more information about the EEWB, refer to composite SAP Note 494966, which provides general information as well as instructions for correcting errors.

### 5.3.5 Notes on the Easy Enhancement Workbench

Transport of
generic
enhancements

One drawback of the EEWB is that you can only transport generated enhancements but not the definition of the enhancements (metadata). If you call the EEWB outside of the original system, no enhancements are displayed. SAP Note 1086848 describes a manual solution that can be used for a system migration.

The EEWB works in the SAP GUI. However, your enhancements can also be used in the CRM Web Client. The *Application Enhancement Tool* (AET) is delivered with CRM Version 7.0. This tool enables the direct creation of customer fields from the CRM Web Client. Chapter 17 includes a brief discussion of the benefits of using the AET. At this point, it is sufficient to note that the AET solves the problem of the missing metadata transport option in the EEWB.

As of SAP CRM 7.0, the EEWB is only required under specific circumstances (e.g., for time-dependent customer tables for business partners). However, in SAP CRM 7.0 and subsequent releases, you can still use the EEWB for enhancements in parallel with the AET. SAP does not currently plan to replace the EEWB with the AET. For this reason, a migration of EEWB enhancements into the AET is not currently supported.

## 5.4 Practical Example: Using the UI Configuration Tool

The following practical example illustrates some of the options for customizing the user interface that are available in the UI Configuration Tool:

1. Customizing the overview page

2. Customizing the search page

3. Showing input fields in a view

4. Changing field labels in a view

### 5.4.1 Customizing the Overview Page

In our example, the objective is to only display selected assignment blocks on the Contact Details overview page; in other words, to only make certain assignment blocks available for personalization. For this purpose, you need to specify which assignment blocks should be open when the overview page is called and which can be opened by the user.

Customizing assignment blocks

1. **Determine the required technical details**
   Begin by determining the technical properties of the overview page. To do this, start the CRM application Contacts from the CRM Web Client. Position your cursor in the upper area of the overview screen and press the F2 key (❶ in Figure 5.19). The dialog box that opens shows the technical properties of the selected area. Make sure that the BP_CONT UI component and the BPCONTOVERVIEW view are displayed in the pop-up window. If not, the technical properties shown do not belong to the overview page.

2. **Call the UI Configuration Tool**
   Start the Component Workbench with Transaction BSP_WD_CMPWB and specify the name of the component (BP_CONT UI) you found in the previous step. Select the BPCONTOVERVIEW view and select the CONFIGURATION tab. The UI Configuration Tool starts for the BPCONTOVERVIEW view.

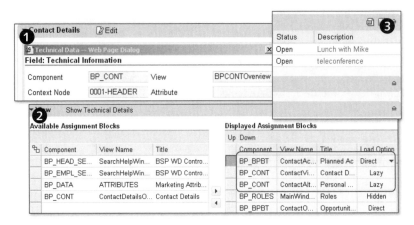

**Figure 5.19** Customizing the Assignment Blocks

3. **Copy the default configuration**

   Copy the configuration of the selected view (BPCONTOVERVIEW) and define role configuration key ZCRM2007.

4. **Select the assignment blocks**

   Select the assignment blocks you want to be displayed on the overview page. Only the assignment blocks from the DISPLAYED ASSIGNMENT BLOCKS table are displayed (❷). In this example, the assignment blocks with the titles PLANNED ACTIVITIES, CONTACT DETAILS, PERSONAL CONTACTS, and ROLES are available for the overview page.

Load options for assignment blocks

You can also specify whether the assignment blocks should be expanded when the Contact Details overview page is called (DIRECT) or whether they can be opened by users (LAZY, ❷ in Figure 5.19). Select the DIRECT option for the assignment block with the title PLANNED ACTIVITIES, the LAZY option for CONTACT DETAILS and PERSONAL CONTACTS, and the HIDDEN option for ROLES. Selecting HIDDEN means that users can choose to show or hide the assignment block themselves, using the personalization settings for the page. The only way to prevent users from accessing the personalization settings for the overview page is to delete the assignment block from the list of DISPLAYED ASSIGNMENT BLOCKS. In addition to customizing the sequence of assignment blocks, you can also modify the titles of the assignment blocks here. You then need to test the new configuration of the Contact Details overview page. ❸ in Figure 5.19 shows that the PLANNED ACTIVITIES assignment block is already open when the Contact Details overview page is started. The CONTACT DETAILS and PERSONAL CONTACTS assignment blocks are closed when the page is called.

### 5.4.2 Customizing the Search Page

The objective of this exercise is to define search operators and search fields for the CONTACT DETAILS search page. Here, we will also restrict the user's options for personalizing the search page.

1. **Determine the required technical details**
   Press the F2 key to display the technical details for the CONTACT DETAILS search page (❶ in Figure 5.20). The UI component name is BP_CONT_SEARCH and the view name is SEARCH.

2. **Start the UI Configuration Tool**
   Start Transaction BSP_WD_CMPWB to call the Component Workbench. Next, specify the UI component name you determined in Step 1 (BP_CONT_SEARCH). Then, click on the SEARCH view and start the UI Configuration Tool from the CONFIGURATION tab.

3. **Create the configuration in the customer namespace**
   Copy the configuration of the SEARCH view and define role configuration key ZCRM2007.

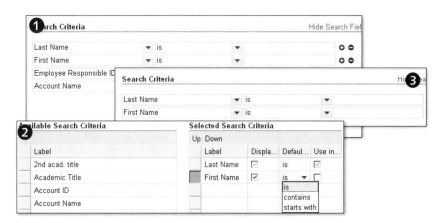

**Figure 5.20** Customizing the Search Page

Select the LAST NAME and FIRST NAME search attributes, and specify whether the search attributes should be displayed when the search page is called and which operator should be shown (❷). In our example, the IS operator is selected for both search attributes. To finish, you can choose to hide the search attribute for the central search, which is described in detail in Chapter 4, Section 4.4. Test your new configuration (❸). A practical example of the technical implementation of a search page is provided in Chapter 16, Section 16.3.

*Selecting search attributes and operators*

### 5.4.3    Showing Input Fields in a View

The following example demonstrates how to show and hide input fields using the UI Configuration Tool. For this purpose, we will access the available fields in the *field catalog* of the selected CONTACTDETAILS view. In this example, we want to hide the DATE OF BIRTH field and show the NATIONALITY field in the CONTACT DETAILS application (❶ in Figure 5.21).

1. **Determine the required technical details**
   Press the ⌨F2 key to determine the name of the component (BP_CONT UI) and of the view (CONTACTDETAILS) for the detail area of the Contact Details overview page.

2. **Call the Component Workbench**
   Start Transaction BSP_WD_CMPWB to call the Component Workbench. Specify the name of the component you found in the previous step (BP_ CONT UI) and click on the CONTACTDETAILS view. Start the UI Configuration Tool from the CONFIGURATION tab.

3. **Copy the configuration**
   Copy the configuration of the CONTACTDETAILS view and create the ZCRM2007 role configuration key.

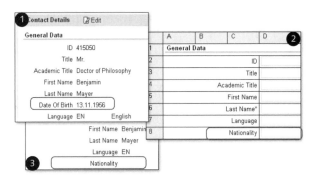

**Figure 5.21**   Showing and Hiding Fields

4. **Hide field**
   Select the DATE OF BIRTH field and select ⊖ to hide it.

5. **Show field**
   Add the NATIONALITY field to the CONTACTDETAILS view from the field catalog. You can use the UP and DOWN buttons to reposition the field in the CONTACTDETAILS view (❷, see Figure 5.21).

6. **Test your configuration**
   Save and test the new configuration (❸).

### 5.4.4 Changing Field Labels in a View

The UI Configuration Tool also allows you to change *field labels*. However, you should use the design layer (see Section 5.5) rather than the UI Configuration Tool to make changes to field labels for several fields or to a single field label for all views in the same business context.

*Customizing field labels*

In our example, we want to change label of the LAST NAME field to FAMILY NAME on the Contact Details overview page.

1. **Determine the required technical details**
   Start the CONTACT DETAILS CRM application in the CRM Web Client. In the detail area of the Contact Details overview page, select a field from the GENERAL DATA information block (❶ in Figure 5.22). If you then press the ⌈F2⌉ key to display the technical details, you will see that the name of the UI component is BP_CONT and the view name is CONTACTDETAILS.

2. **Start the UI Configuration Tool**
   Start Transaction BSP_WD_CMPWB to call the Component Workbench. Specify the BP_CONT component and start the UI Configuration Tool for the CONTACTDETAILS view on the CONFIGURATION tab.

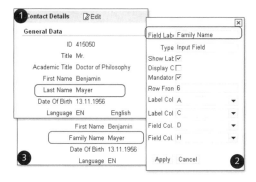

**Figure 5.22** Changing a Field Label

3. **Copy the view configuration**
   Copy the configuration of the CONTACTDETAILS standard view and enter the ZCRM2007 role configuration key. Then switch to change mode in the copied view and select the LAST NAME input field. Display the FIELD PROPERTIES from the toolbar (❷).

4. **Change field label**
   Change the label of the selected LAST NAME field to FAMILY NAME. You can now test the CRM application (❸).

## 5.5 Practical Example: Using the Design Layer

The following example demonstrates how you can use the design layer to change several views that have the same business context without having to adjust each CRM application separately with the UI Configuration Tool. This process involves the following two steps:

1. Creating a design object
2. Assigning the design object to the context node

### 5.5.1 Creating a Design Object

In this exercise, you create a design object to change the field label for the WEBSITE field to INTERNET SITE for all views. Figure 5.23 shows the "before" and "after" field labels for this scenario.

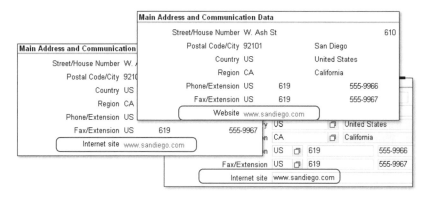

**Figure 5.23** Using the Design Layer to Change a Field Label

1. **Select the UI object type**

Editing the design layer
To create a new design object, select CUSTOMER RELATIONSHIP MANAGEMENT • UI FRAMEWORK • UI FRAMEWORK DEFINITION • MAINTAIN DESIGN LAYERS in the SAP IMG. Select BP_ADDRESS as the UI object type.

2. **Create the design object**

BOL attribute assignment
Enter ZCRM07_BPADRESSE as the name of your design object and BP WEBSITE as the description (see Figure 5.24). Then, add the BuilADDRESS BOL object. This object contains the attribute name URIURI for displaying the WEBSITE field label.

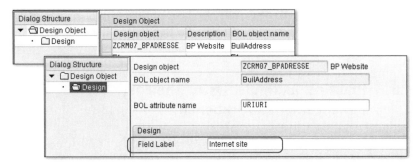

**Figure 5.24** Creating a Design Object

Next, in the dialog structure, select the URIURI BOL attribute and change the field name to INTERNET SITE.

### 5.5.2 Assigning the Design Object to the Context Node

In this step, you use the Component Workbench to make the field changes known to the application views. Use Transaction BSP_WD_CMPWB to start the Component Workbench for the BP_ADDR UI component you want to customize.

After you select the STANDARDADDRESS view, the design object you created is assigned to a context node or directly to the attribute. Figure 5.25 (**❶**) shows the assignment via the STANDARDADDRESS context node. Select the correct object type (BP_ADDRESS) for the new assignment. You can then select the ZCRM07_BPADRESSE design object you created earlier (**❷**).

Assignment to the design layer

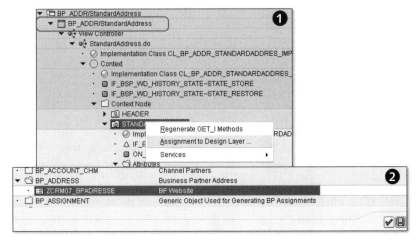

**Figure 5.25** Assignment to the Design Layer

Remember to click 🖫 to save your changes. You then need to click ✅ to confirm your entries. Finally, test the application by logging on to the CRM Web Client or using the UI Configuration Tool.

## 5.6    Practical Example: Using the Easy Enhancement Workbench

The following example demonstrates how you can use the EEWB to enhance a business object (sales contract) and then use the UI Configuration Tool to integrate the enhancement into a view. This involves the following two steps:

1. Creating a new field with the EEWB

2. Adding the field to the view with the UI Configuration Tool

### 5.6.1    Creating a New Field with the EEWB

In this example, we want to add a new field (z_customer_nr) to the sales contract business object. This field will serve to display a customer-specific number.

Creating a project

To start the EEWB, choose CUSTOMER RELATIONSHIP MANAGEMENT • CRM MIDDLEWARE AND RELATED COMPONENTS • EASY ENHANCEMENT WORK-BENCH in the SAP IMG or start Transaction EEWB.

1. **Create project**
   Create a project in the EEWB environment. Enter the name ZCRM2007-CON, a description, and package ZCRM for the project (❶ in Figure 5.26).

   A package can be created in the ABAP Workbench (Transaction SE80). All necessary source code extensions are assigned to this package using the EEWB.

2. **Create transport requests**

Creating transport requests

   After you create the ZCRM2007-CON project, the system prompts you to create Workbench and Customizing transport requests and to assign these to the project (❷).

3. **Create the extension**

Creating an extension

   Use the context menu (❸) to create the field enhancement for the SALES CONTRACT business project.

   Give your enhancement the name ZSALESCONTRACT and enter a description (❹ in Figure 5.26). Select the business object SALES_CONTRACT as the enhancement from the list of possible entries for the EEW BUS. OBJECT field. The list shows all options of business objects that can be extended using the EEWB. Select Customer_H as the EXTENSION TYPE.

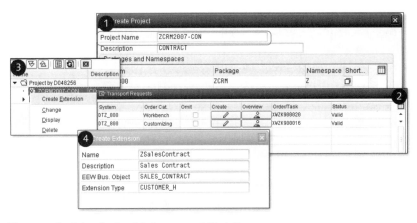

**Figure 5.26** Sales Contract Enhancement (Part 1)

4. **Start the wizard**

   Next, call the EEWB wizard. In the window that opens, enter a description and, in the next step of the wizard, specify which fields should be added to the business object (❶ in Figure 5.27). In our example, the fields defined include the Z_CUSTOMER_NR field with the NUMC data type (❷).

   **EEWB tool**

   You must specify the field type and field length when creating the field. You can then define a check table for the field enhancement.

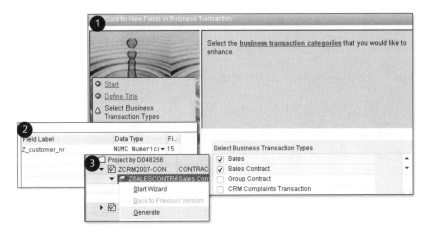

**Figure 5.27** Sales Contract Enhancement (Part 2)

5. **Field usage**

   In the next step, you specify the field usage. Here, you decide where exactly the field enhancement is to be used (e.g., SAP NetWeaver BW or mobile solutions). In our example, neither of these options is relevant.

   **Field usage**

You can then close the EEWB wizard. The subsequent process of source code generation may take several minutes.

### 5.6.2 Adding the Field to the View with the UI Configuration Tool

After you have successfully enhanced the SALES CONTRACT business object, start the Component Workbench (Transaction BSP_WD_CMPWB) for the BT121H_SLSC component. Select the DETAILS view and open the UI Configuration Tool (❶ in Figure 5.28).

1. **Copy the default configuration**

*Positioning the new field*   Copy the DETAILS standard view and define the ZCRM2007 role configuration key. Switch to change mode and select the Z_CUSTOMER_NR field you created earlier from the field catalog (❷).

Use the menu bar in the UI Configuration Tool to position the newly added Z_CUSTOMER_NR field in the view.

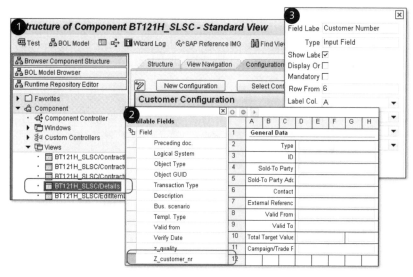

**Figure 5.28**   Sales Contract Enhancement (Part 3)

2. As a final step, change the field label to CUSTOMER NUMBER (❸) and specify whether the field is a required entry field.

*CRM 2007 offers technical capabilities for integrating SAP NetWeaver BW and CRM applications into SAP NetWeaver Portal. It also allows you to set up an authorization concept to protect confidential data.*

# 6 Application Integration and Authorization

This chapter discusses the integration of internal and external applications with the CRM Web Client. The main focus is on integration with SAP NetWeaver BW and SAP NetWeaver Portal (also referred to here as "the portal"). It is not strictly essential to integrate the CRM Web Client into the portal, as is the case with the *People Centric User Interface* (PCUI). However, this integration option allows you to copy existing portal roles. We will examine the integration of SAP NetWeaver BW reports into the CRM Web Client only from the perspective of the user interface. The steps required to successfully implement the integration in SAP NetWeaver BW or in SAP NetWeaver Portal are not covered. Issues relating to authorization in the CRM Web Client environment are addressed in the third section of this chapter. Here, we will provide a number of examples to illustrate how the authorization concept is structured in the CRM Web Client.

> **Note**
>
> As of January 2009, the name *SAP NetWeaver Business Intelligence* has been superseded by *SAP NetWeaver Business Warehouse (BW)*. This chapter therefore refers to BW reports.

The practical example at the end of the chapter involves setting up a basic authorization concept for the CRM Web Client and defining which areas should be visible to which users.

## 6.1 SAP NetWeaver Business Warehouse Integration

Prerequisites and recommendation

All BW reports based on BW 3.x and 7.x technology can be integrated into the CRM Web Client. Work center pages, overview pages, report pages, and the navigation bar of the user interface can all be integrated. Reports that are run on a regular basis can be defined as direct links. For more information about integrating BW reports, refer to SAP Note 1242033.

### 6.1.1 Basic SAP NetWeaver Business Warehouse Configuration

Implementation Guide: Defining BW reports

To integrate BW reports, you must first define them in Customizing. In the SAP Implementation Guide, choose CUSTOMER RELATIONSHIP MANAGEMENT • UI FRAMEWORK • DEFINE UI FRAMEWORKS • DISPLAY SAP NETWEAVER BI REPORTS IN CRM or start Transaction CRMC_UI_BI. To ensure that a BW report can be recognized in the CRM Web Client, the entries BI REPORT ID, LONG DESCRIPTION, BI OBJECT TYPE, and BI OBJECT KEY must be defined. The BI SYSTEM entry is optional. The BI REPORT ID identifies the report. It is therefore important to define a unique ID for each BI report. This ID is used later to call the report (logical link) in the user interface (see Figure 6.1). Next, enter a descriptive text for the report. The long text description has a maximum length of 60 characters and should describe the purpose of the report.

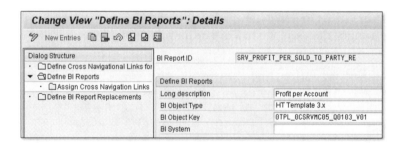

**Figure 6.1** Basic Configuration for Integrating BW Reports

Defining key BW parameters

The BI OBJECT TYPE specifies the type of the BW report. SAP currently supports only two report types. Your BW reports should therefore be based on either 3.x or 7.x BW technology. The BI OBJECT KEY is based on the BI object type of the report and identifies the object itself. The BI SYSTEM entry is optional. Here, you can specify the RFC destination of the BW system if the report should be called in a second BW system.

## 6.1.2    Links for Cross-Component Navigation

You can configure settings in Customizing that allow you to define links for navigating to other CRM components from any characteristic in a BW report. For example, if your BW report contains a list of business partners, you can configure the BUSINESS PARTNER characteristic so that you can simply click on one of the listed business partners to display the DETAILS of that partner. This triggers direct navigation to the business partner details component, which is defined as a link for cross-component navigation in your configuration (❶ in Figure 6.2). Here, the *InfoObject* is the technical name of an analysis object from which you want to navigate. You define the cross-component navigational link for an InfoObject as your next entry. Several navigational links can be defined for an InfoObject. The number defined in the SEQUENCE field is the menu option in the context menu of the BW report. The object action and the name of the object key are specified in the next two fields. The object action specifies the navigation target, whereas the object key defines the field name that corresponds to the value selected in the BW report.

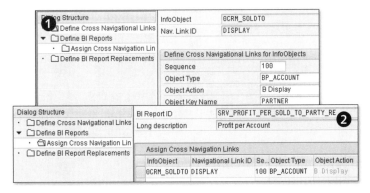

**Figure 6.2**   Cross-Component Navigation

To use a link for cross-component navigation, you must assign it to a BW report (❷ in Figure 6.2). Here, you must assign both the InfoObject and the navigational link created.

> **Note**
>
> We recommend using the following views to maintain BW reports and create links for cross-component navigation: CRMV_BI_NAVLINKS, CRMV_BI_RE-PLACE and CRMV_BI_REPORTS.

### 6.1.3 Integrating Reports into the User Interface

You need to create a logical link before the BW report created can be displayed as a direct link on the navigation bar of the user interface or as a link in the work center page.

Creating a logical link Start configuration of the navigation bar using the familiar IMG path, or start Transaction CRMC_UI_NBLINKS. Then, create a new logical link. Assign a unique logical link ID and select REPORT as the link type (see Figure 6.3). Enter the unique BW report ID as the PARAMETER. Before you give the BW report a descriptive title, you need to select the correct parameter class (CL_CRM_GEN_UI_BI_UTIL).

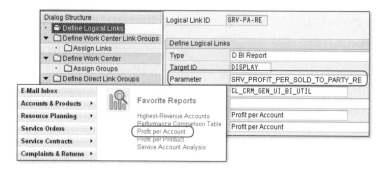

**Figure 6.3**  Logical Link for BW Integration

Finally, assign the logical link to a group of direct links or add it to a work center page.

### 6.1.4 Integration into Custom Components

If you want to display a BW report in a UI component you developed yourself, you need to create a component usage for each BW report. You can then use the BW report wherever a *reuse component* can be used. Use the *framework enhancement concept* for integration.

Creating a component usage A component usage for a BW report can be created using the Component Workbench and the Runtime Repository Editor. Here, you need to assign the usage a PARAMETER ID (that is, a unique identifier for your component) and specify "GSBIRP" as the USED COMPONENT and "MAINWINDOW" as the INTERFACE VIEW (❶ in Figure 6.4).

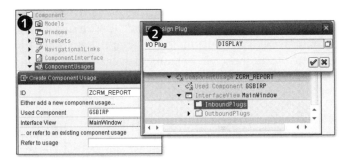

**Figure 6.4** Creating a Component Usage

Enter "DISPLAY" as the inbound plug (❷). This inbound plug is required if you want to navigate to the embedded BW report within your component. If you want to display the BW report without navigation, you must specify the REPID parameter in the WD_USAGE_INITIALIZE method. Listing 6.1 shows a segment from the program code:

```
METHOD wd_usage_initialize.
DATA: bicontext TYPE REF TO cl_bsp_wd_context_node.
CASE iv_usage->usage_name.
   WHEN 'BW-REPORT'.
   TRY.
   bicontext = iv_usage->get_context_node('BW-REPORT').
   bicontext->set_s_struct(
   attribute_path = '' component = 'REPID' value = 'BW_ID' ) .
   CATCH cx_root.
   ENDTRY.
ENDCASE.
ENDMETHOD.
```

**Listing 6.1** Displaying a BW Report Without Navigation

Note that you need to replace BW_ID with the ID name of the BW report from the configuration. For more information about cross-component navigation for BW reports, see SAP Note 1268401.

## 6.2 Integration into SAP NetWeaver Portal

The CRM Web Client can be integrated into SAP NetWeaver Portal. This allows you to start the CRM Web Client in a full-page iView (content area) in the portal. However, integration into the portal is optional rather than essential.

Integration possibilities
You can only integrate CRM Web Client business roles into SAP NetWeaver Portal. Business roles with the "CRM on-demand" and "IC Web Client" profile types, on the other hand, cannot be integrated. You therefore need to check the profile type of the business role you want to integrate. You will find this information in the master data record of the business role (Transaction CRMC_UI_PROFILE).

> **Note**
>
> For more information about integrating the Web Client into SAP NetWeaver Portal as an external BSP application, refer to SAP Notes 1175127 and 1175590.

### 6.2.1 Prerequisites and Functional Scope

Prerequisite: Business package
A number of prerequisites must be fulfilled before you can start the process of portal integration. First, check that you have installed the latest *business packages* for SAP CRM 2007, and install the latest package if required. The system requirements for portal integration in SAP CRM 2007 are as follows:

▶ SAP NetWeaver Portal 7.0 SP 12, Patch 3, and SAP Note 1103115

▶ SAP NetWeaver Portal 7.0 SP 12, Patch 4

▶ SAP NetWeaver Portal 7.0 SP 13 and SAP Note 1135723

▶ SAP NetWeaver Portal 7.0 SP 13, Patch 5

▶ SAP NetWeaver Portal 7.0 SP 14, Patch 1

You will find additional information about configuring business packages and their role in SAP Solution Manager under BASIC SETTINGS FOR SAP CRM • BUSINESS PACKAGE FOR SAP CRM • CONFIGURATION • BUSINESS PACKAGE CONFIGURATION.

Prerequisite: WorkProtect mode
*WorkProtect mode* is used to handle unsaved data during navigation in the portal. A distinction is made here between default portal settings and user-specific settings. Defined default portal settings apply to all users. However, these settings can be overwritten by any user. Default portal settings are defined under SYSTEM ADMINISTRATION • SYSTEM CONFIGURATION • SERVICE CONFIGURATION. Then select the EPCFLOADER service under BROWSE • APPLICATIONS • COM.SAP.PORTAL.EPCF.LOADER • SERVICES. SAP recommends the following configuration settings:

▶ *workprotect.mode.default = 3* (the desired system behavior can be selected each time the dialog box is displayed)

- *workprotect.mode.personalize = on*
- *workprotect.window.features = blank*

User-specific settings that are only valid for the individual user in question can also be defined. To do so, click on PERSONALIZE in the header area and select WORKPROTECT MODE in the detailed navigation of the portal. SAP recommends that you select the ACTION IN DIALOG BOX option for unsaved data to ensure that the dialog box referring to data loss is displayed.

In addition to defining WorkProtect mode, you also need to make some adjustments to the CRM portal desktop. The header area of the CRM portal desktop comprises the following CRM portal objects:

*Prerequisite: Adapting the CRM portal desktop*

- CRM desktop (*com.sap.crm.fnd.crmDesktop*)
- CRM framework page (*com.sap.crm.fnd.crmFrameworkpage*)
- CRM portal masthead (*com.sap.crm.fnd.crmMasthead*)
- CRM tools (*com.sap.crm.fnd.crmToolArea*)

The objects listed here are copies of the standard portal objects that have been enhanced with CRM-specific functions. SAP CRM comes with its own CRM portal masthead iView and CRM tools iView. For a detailed description of how to adapt these CRM portal objects, refer to the SAP Library under SAP CUSTOMER RELATIONSHIP MANAGEMENT • COMPONENTS AND FUNCTIONS • BASIC FUNCTIONS • UI FRAMEWORK AND CONFIGURATION • PORTAL INTEGRATION • ADAPTING THE CRM PORTAL DESKTOP.

Portal integration includes, for example, the following functions:

*Functional scope of portal integration*

- **Navigation highlighting**
  The portal highlights the navigation target when you navigate from within the portal navigation frame to the SAP CRM system, from the SAP CRM system to portal content, or from one CRM iView to another.

- **Session management**
  When you navigate from the portal to the SAP CRM application for the first time, a logon is started in the SAP CRM system. When a portal session is finished, all open CRM sessions are closed and a dialog box informs users that they need to save their changes to avoid a loss of data.

- **Export of role definitions to XML**
  You can use the role upload function to generate an XML file from your CRM standalone business role. This file can then be imported into SAP NetWeaver Portal to generate a portal role.

▶ **Central search**
You can use the central search function to search for CRM applications from the portal.

▶ **Mapping the portal theme to the CRM skin**
To align the look and feel of SAP NetWeaver Portal and SAP CRM, you can map a portal theme to its most similar CRM skin.

> **Note**
>
> For more information about the prerequisites for portal integration, refer to the SAP Help Portal at *http://help.sap.com* and SAP Notes 1103115 and 1135723.

### 6.2.2 Communication Between the ABAP System and the Portal

Configuring the SAP authentication assertion ticket

To enable communication between an ABAP system and SAP NetWeaver Portal, you must verify the RFC connection (Transaction SM59 – Name: CRM_EP_DEST) and configure the use of the SAP authentication assertion ticket. The authentication assertion ticket is a logon ticket with a limited validity period. It is used primarily for communication between the J2EE Engine and SAP NetWeaver Application Server (ABAP) for single use when setting up an RFC or HTTP connection. To configure the authentication assertion ticket, start the export of the ABAP system certificate from the system PSE (Transaction STRUSTSSO2). Then, load the ABAP certificate into the J2EE Engine and configure the relevant application with the ABAP system certificate. After configuration is completed, export the engine certificate and import the certificate into the relevant ABAP system. To do so, log on to the ABAP system again, start Transaction STRUSTSSO2 and click on the IMPORT CERTIFICATE icon to select the engine certificate created for import.

> **Note**
>
> If communication between the ABAP system and the portal does not work, we recommend that you also refer to SAP Note 1224422. For more information, see the Security Guide for SAP NetWeaver 7.0 (2004s) in the SAP Help Portal.

### 6.2.3 Uploading Business Roles from the CRM System

Implementation Guide: Uploading business roles

You use the role upload function if you want existing business roles (CRM Web Client business roles only) to also be used as portal roles. You must have completed all required configuration settings for a business role before it can be uploaded as a portal role. The uploaded portal role has exactly the same content as the business role. To upload business roles, select the menu path CUSTOMER RELATIONSHIP MANAGEMENT • UI FRAMEWORK • PORTAL INTEGRATION • UPLOAD BUSINESS ROLE in the SAP Implementation Guide or start Transaction GENEPXML.

Select the business role you want to upload (❶ in Figure 6.5). Next, define the parameters for the subsequent generation of portal content (❷). If the role has already been uploaded into the portal, the ROLE indicator cannot be set. This prevents you from overwriting the role element. If you select the checkbox next to TEMPLATES, iViews are generated using templates. Templates need to be generated unless they have already been uploaded and are available in the target path.

**Business role content and generation parameters**

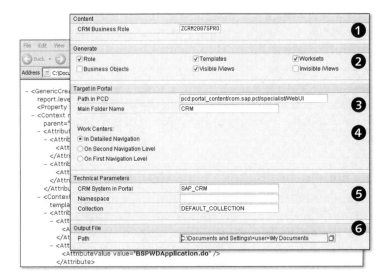

**Figure 6.5** Uploading a Business Role into the Portal

The same applies to *worksets, invisible iViews,* and *visible iViews*. Invisible and visible iViews must be available in the portal if you want to ensure access to the full functionality of links on the navigation bar.

The next step involves defining the target in the portal (❸ in Figure 6.5). This path indicates the main directory in the *portal content directory* (PCD) to which the generated portal content should be saved. It is advisable to use a directory name that helps the portal to identify the CRM system. For example, if the name of your CRM system is XYZ, you could name the main directory CRM_XYZ. Your role content is then saved in a separate directory within the CRM_XYZ main directory.

**Target in the portal**

163

Navigation in the
portal

The configuration of the work center pages allows you direct control over the navigation structure of business roles in the portal (❹). If you select IN DETAILED NAVIGATION, the generated work center pages are displayed in the portal's detailed navigation. If you enter "CRM" at the first level in the navigation bar in this case, the name of the business role is displayed on the second navigation level. If you select work center pages ON SECOND NAVIGATION LEVEL, the name of the business role is displayed on the first level of portal navigation, whereas the work center pages of the navigation bar are displayed on the second level. If you select ON FIRST NAVIGATION LEVEL, all work center pages of the navigation bar are displayed on the first level of the top portal navigation area, with logical links displayed on the second level.

Technical
parameters

Enter CRM SYSTEM IN PORTAL, NAMESPACE, and COLLECTION as technical parameters (❺ in Figure 6.5). The system alias is defined in the CRM SYSTEM IN PORTAL input field, the NAMESPACE serves to group objects (iViews and worksets), while COLLECTION is used for translation purposes. Enter DEFAULT_COLLECTION as the standard value.

Output data

The output file path indicates where the XML file is stored after the upload (❻). The name of the XML file matches the name of the business role. You can enter a path to the local host or a network path in this field. Next, execute the program. An XML file is generated, which you must then implement via the portal.

### 6.2.4 Integrating Business Roles into the Portal

To load the generated XML file into the portal, select the menu path SYSTEM ADMINISTRATION • TRANSPORT • XML CONTENT AND ACTIONS • IMPORT. After verifying that the file has been transferred successfully, select the portal menu path CONTENT ADMINISTRATION • PORTAL CONTENT to check whether the newly created portal navigation exists for the transferred business role. Then, assign the newly available portal role to your portal user and test the application in the portal.

### 6.2.5 Tips and Tricks for CRM Web Client Integration

Mapping a portal
theme to a CRM
skin

To create a consistent look and feel in both SAP NetWeaver Portal and SAP CRM, you can map a portal theme to a CRM skin. You can do this in the SAP Implementation Guide under CUSTOMER RELATIONSHIP MANAGEMENT • UI

FRAMEWORK • PORTAL INTEGRATION • ASSIGN PORTAL THEME TO CRM SKIN. If you then select the FOLLOW PORTAL THEME option under PERSONALIZE CRM • PERSONALIZE LAYOUT, the portal theme maintained in this IMG activity is displayed.

In addition to integrating the CRM skin into the portal, you can also highlight—in color—any logical links you created. Logical links that are integrated into the roles delivered in the standard system are already highlighted in color. The HIGHLIGHT indicator allows you to specify whether a logical link for cross-component navigation should be highlighted. You define highlighting in the CRM portal Customizing settings under CUSTOMER RELATIONSHIP MANAGEMENT • UI FRAMEWORK • TECHNICAL ROLE DEFINITION • DEFINE NAVIGATION BAR PROFILE. Then, select your navigation bar profile and set the HIGHLIGHT indicator for the logical link under GENERIC OP ASSIGNMENT. The OVERRIDE GENERIC OP ASSIGNMENT FOR COMPONENT option allows you to define highlighting for exceptions in individual UI components.

*Navigation in the portal*

## 6.3    Authorization Concept

The general *SAP authorization concept* provides protection against unauthorized access to transactions, programs, and services in SAP systems. Based on the authorization concept, the system administrator assigns authorizations to users, which define the actions the users can execute in the SAP system after logon and authentication. The CRM Web Client authorization concept allows you to define which areas are visible and which are hidden on the user interface. An example of how this concept works in practice is provided in Section 6.4.

### 6.3.1    Basic Principles of Authorization

The authorization concept for the CRM Web Client differs slightly from the SAP authorization concept in terms of structure. The authorization concept for the CRM Web Client is based on business roles rather than on SAP logon users that are used for logon. Business roles contain the essential business content of CRM applications that a user needs to carry out routine tasks. The business role is therefore used to control, among other things, the navigation bar and content of the user interface for displaying the various applications required by each user (see Figure 6.6).

*Authorization role dependencies*

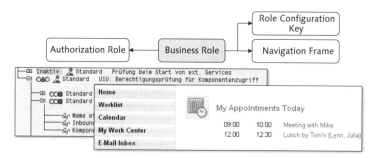

**Figure 6.6**  Authorization Concept Based on Business Role

You assign authorizations for the CRM Web Client using an authorization role, which is assigned to the business role. The authorization role (or PFCG role, see Chapter 2, Section 2.3.5) grants or denies the user permission to specific areas of the user interface.

### 6.3.2  Implementing Authorization

Identifying the relevant authorization objects

The first step towards implementing the authorization concept is to identify the relevant authorization objects. Up to ten authorization fields can be defined for an authorization object. If a user does not have authorization for an object field, access to further actions associated with that field is denied. You can identify the authorization objects that are accessed when actions are executed in the CRM Web Client in the transaction for assigning authorization objects (Transaction SU24) and in the system trace (Transaction ST01). When you call the program for maintaining the assignments of authorization objects, the type of the external service is shown. For the CRM Web Client, this is UIU_COMP (❶ in Figure 6.7). You can track the assignment of authorization objects and assignments in the USOBX_C and USOBT_C tables.

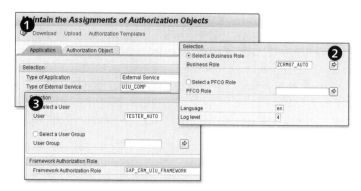

**Figure 6.7**  Steps Involved in Identifying Authorization Objects

If you do not want to have to use the system trace to determine all authorization objects for each business role, we recommend the CRMD_UI_ROLE_PREPARE program (❷). It extracts all information relating to the structure of the navigation bar and external services used into a TXT file. The external services and their checked authorization objects can also be found in the transaction for maintaining authorization object assignment (Transaction SU24). The TXT file is saved in the *SapWorkDir* directory on the local host (see SAP Note 1171286).

Business role and authorization

You use the CRMD_UI_ROLE_ASSIGN program to assign an authorization role to an SAP logon user via the business role (❸ in Figure 6.7). To execute this program, both the user and the business role must be assigned in the organizational model (see Section 2.4). When you call the program, define the SAP logon user and the SAP_CRM_UI_FRAMEWORK framework authorization role. This authorization role grants authorization to use the navigation frame (L shape) of the CRM Web Client without specifying components such as work center pages or logical links.

Assignment of SAP logon user and business role

The authorization role you created and assigned to the business role is now added to the structure of the navigation bar. When you select IMPORT FROM FILE, the TXT file is accessed and the content of the business role is also accessed. The structure of the navigation bar is then shown on the MENU tab (❶ in Figure 6.8). Next, on the AUTHORIZATIONS tab, define the access authorizations for the various areas of the user interface. To hide individual logical links or work center pages using the authorization role, search for the UIU_COMP authorization object. This object is used to control the authorization check for component accesses (❷). You now need to assign specific access rights for the components by deactivating components that are no longer required or by adding new components. Next, generate the authorization profile for the settings. For more information about selecting the correct authorization objects and about setting up authorization roles, refer to SAP Notes 551478 and 449832. If you want to migrate authorization roles from CRM 5.0 to CRM 2007, we recommend that you refer to SAP Note 1259665.

Adapting the authorization role

To assign users, it is not essential to execute the familiar CRMD_UI_ROLE_ASSIGN program again at this point. However, we recommend that you do so because the framework authorization role (SAP_CRM_UI_FRAMEWORK) is part of the user master record and is called immediately after logon to the CRM Web Client. The USER tab in the authorization role configuration indicates which SAP logon user has been assigned the authorization role. You will also find the authorization role in the master data of the SAP logon user (Transaction SU01).

Execute CRMD_UI_ROLE_ASSIGN again

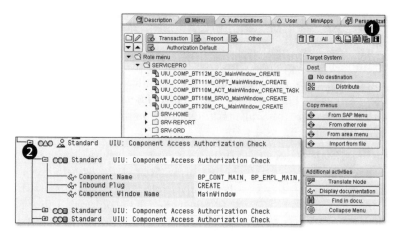

**Figure 6.8** Assigning Authorizations

> **Note**
>
> Transactions SUIM (user information system), SU53 (authorization data of the user currently logged on), and SU20 (all available authorization objects) also provide useful information relating to authorization issues. We also recommend that you refer to Composite SAP Notes 551478, 449832 and 1129682.

## 6.4 Example of Setting Up an Authorization Concept

The following example illustrates how to set up a basic authorization concept for the CRM Web Client and details the following aspects of this process:

▸ Creating a business role

▸ Creating and assigning an authorization role

▸ Authorization concept for the user interface

### 6.4.1 Creating a Business Role

In this section, we will explain how to set up an *authorization concept* for the CRM Web Client using the example of the new business role ZCRM07_ AUTO. You already know the steps involved in creating a new business role; therefore, we will keep our discussion of this part of the process brief.

Creating an authorization role

▸ **Creating the authorization role**
Before you create the business role, you must create the new authoriza-

tion role ZCRM2007_AUTO using the familiar menu path (see the earlier text) or Transaction PFCG. You need this role to create the business role in the next step.

▶ **Creating the business role**

Create the new business role ZCRM07_AUTO (Transaction CRMC_UI_ PROFILE) and assign it the ZCRM2007_AUTO authorization role you created in the previous step (❶ in Figure 6.9).

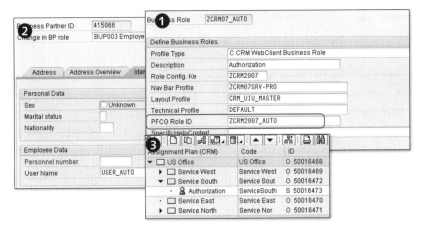

**Figure 6.9** Creating a Business Role

After the business role has been created, you must create a new business partner with the role of *Employee* (❷) and assign the new SAP logon user USER_AUTO to the business partner on the IDENTIFICATION tab (Transaction BP). We recommend that you create a new SAP logon user (Transaction SU01) for the purpose of creating and subsequently testing the application. You then assign the new logon user to the business partner you created with the role of Employee.

*Assigning an SAP logon user to a business partner*

▶ **Organizational model**

In the next step, the ZCRM07_AUTO business role you created is assigned to the organizational model (❸). To do this, start Transaction PPOMA_ CRM (see Section 2.4) and create a new AUTHORIZATION position within the SERVICE SOUTH organizational unit. Then, assign the business partner you created with the role of *Employee* to this position.

*Business role and organizational model*

If you select the menu option GOTO • DETAIL OBJECT • EXTENDED OBJECT DESCRIPTION, the ZCRM07_AUTO business role you created is assigned to the SERVICE SOUTH organizational unit. Test whether the new business role with the newly created SAP logon user is used when you call the CRM Web Client.

### 6.4.2 Creating and Assigning an Authorization Role

**Adapting the navigation bar**
You now need to use authorization characteristics to restrict access to the navigation bar. To do so, you first determine the navigation bar structure of the ZCRM_AUTO business role and then assign it to the ZCRM2007_AUTO authorization role. You can then use the authorization role to define authorization characteristics for the user.

▶ **Determining the navigation structure**

To determine the navigation structure, start program CRMD_UI_ROLE_ PREPARE in Transaction SA38 and define the ZCRM_AUTO businesses role you created earlier (❶ in Figure 6.10).

The CRMD_UI_ROLE_PREPARE program generates a TXT file and saves this file to the *SapWorkDir* directory (path: *C:\Documents and Settings \<user>\SapWorkDir*). The TXT file describes the structure of the navigation bar for the defined ZCRM_AUTO role. Next, the structure of the navigation bar must be assigned to the ZCRM2007_AUTO authorization role so that this role can be used to control access to the navigation bar.

▶ **Creating the navigation structure**

**Navigation bar and authorization role**
Start Transaction PFCG and call the ZCRM2007_AUTO authorization role you created earlier. On the Copy Menus tab, choose Import from File and import the information from the TXT file into the ZCRM2007_AUTO authorization object (❷).

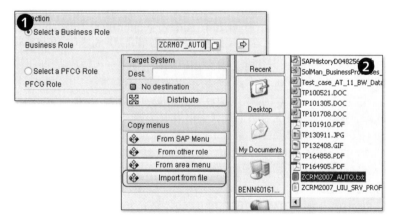

**Figure 6.10** Navigation Bar and Authorization Role

You use the CRMD_UI_ROLE_ASSIGN program (Transaction SA38) to assign the ZCRM2007_AUTO authorization role to the USER_AUTO SAP logon user. When you call the program, define the USER_AUTO SAP logon user and the SAP_CRM_UI_FRAMEWORK framework authorization role. You define the navigation frame (L shape) of the CRM Web Client without specifying authorization pages.

*Assigning the authorization role*

### 6.4.3 Preparing an Authorization Concept for the User Interface

To successfully prepare an authorization concept for a user interface, you need to consider which areas of the CRM Web Client should be visible to users and which should be hidden. You can specify to show or hide individual work center pages and logical links.

▶ **Deactivating access**

Call the transaction for defining the ZCRM2007_AUTO authorization role again (Transaction PFCG). Check all entries on the MENU tab of your PFCG role. Each entry corresponds to a work center page or a logical link. Delete the entries for which you do not want the new PFCG role to have authorization. When you do this, the entries are also deleted from the UIU_COMP authorization object of the PFCG role (❶ in Figure 6.11). Save your changes and open the AUTHORIZATIONS tab. Switch to change mode and edit your PFCG role. Search for the UIU_COMP authorization role and deactivate the authorization object with the field values COMP_NAME:*, COMP_WIN:* and COMP_PLUG:*. Finally, choose PROFILE to generate the authorization profile.

*Authorization based on authorization objects*

Alternatively, you can deactivate the entries in the UIU_COMP authorization object on the AUTHORIZATIONS tab. However, because this procedure may be rather complicated, it is more reliable to follow the steps specified previously in the role menu on the MENU tab. Your roles are then compatible for upgrades or migrations. After this step is completed, log on to the CRM Web Client with the newly created ZCRM07_AUTO business role and test the application. The navigation bar should now only show the menu items you defined in the role menu of the PFCG role.

You can use the system trace (Transaction ST01) to determine the correct content for the UIU_COMP authorization concept for the selected menu options (e.g., HOME, ACCOUNT MANAGEMENT, and ACTIVITIES) on the navigation bar for the business role you created. The system trace allows you to determine which authorization objects are called for each action executed on the user interface.

*Showing selected authorization pages*

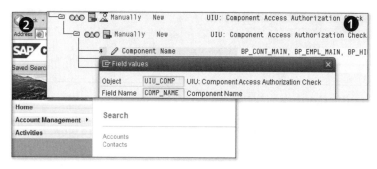

**Figure 6.11** Deactivating Areas on the User Interface

▶ **Activating access**

If, on the navigation bar, you only want to activate the three menu options specified previously, maintain the following content for the UIU_COMP authorization object for the ZCRM2007_AUTO authorization role: HOME (WCC_SLS_HOME), ACCOUNT MANAGEMENT (WCC_SLS_ACC), and ACTIVITIES (WCC_SLS_ACT). You also need to set the inbound plug to DEFAULT and the component window name to MAINWINDOW.

You use the same sequence of steps to show logical links. Show two logical links in the SEARCH logical block (inbound plug: SEARCH) for the BP_HEAD_MAIN and BP_CONT_MAIN components.

Generating the authorization role

Before you test the application (❷ in Figure 6.11), you need to generate the new settings for the ZCRM2007_AUTO authorization role.

> **Note**
>
> If the menu options or direct links are still visible after you log on to the CRM Web Client with the newly created business role, check whether additional roles or authorization profiles are assigned to the SAP logon user.

*This chapter deals with the integration of office applications. It first introduces the basic principles of web services; then you will learn how to model web services with the web service tool and use them as a data source for documents.*

# 7 Integrating Office Applications

In addition to CRM software, many users also require documents for their daily work, for example, if an employee of the marketing department wants to draw attention to new products by attaching a PDF document to an email. An integration of CRM software and software solutions by third-parties such as Microsoft or Adobe is thus indispensable. The integration of the SAP CRM solution and third-party software saves a lot of time and frees up capacity for performing additional tasks.

Real-life requirements

Generating PDF or Microsoft Word documents, as well as linking these documents with business objects from CRM applications, are key functions for many customers. In SAP CRM 2007, business objects are integrated with office applications based on *web service technology*.

Web service technology

Before you can generate documents (Microsoft Word or PDF) at runtime, you must fulfill some prerequisites. First, you have to create a web service as a data source for a document template. Here, you can model web services using the SAP CRM 2007 web service tool. Then, you have to create a document template with the *Template Designer* (*Document Template Designer*) and assign a web service to this template. You position the attributes of a web service as text placeholders in the document template. During the definition in the Template Designer, you also assign the document template to a business object. When the document template has been processed, it is stored in *content management*.

This enables you to create a document on the basis of a web service and a document template from the SAP CRM application at runtime. You can then further edit the new document (only MS Word documents) or print it via the application.

Creating a document based on a template and a web service

Service-oriented
consumers
However, the integration of third-party software is not restricted to solutions by Microsoft or Adobe—you can couple any application that follows the service-oriented pattern and that can process web services with the SAP CRM system and access business objects and their data there. Possible consumers of a web service include:

▶ Mobile applications

▶ User interfaces

▶ Widgets

▶ SAP NetWeaver Portal

▶ Composite applications

The following sections explain the steps that are necessary for the creation of web services using the web service tool. They also describe the creation of document templates with the Template Designer for a successful integration of Microsoft Word and Adobe Forms with SAP CRM 2007.

> **Note**
>
> SAP Note 1018674 summarizes the prerequisites for a successful integration of office applications. SAP Note 1114557 contains further general information regarding the use of the Mozilla browser.

## 7.1    Web Service Tool

Before we discuss the web service tool in detail in this section, we will define some critical concepts that lay the foundation for using this tool. Let us begin with the web service concept.

WSDL    A *web service* is used for the platform-independent communication in a heterogeneous system landscape between various applications via common Internet protocols such as SOAP and HTTP. A web service is described in the *web service description language* (WSDL). WSDL is a meta language used to describe the functions of a web service. WSDL documents are available in XML notation.

Service operations    A web service is a service that offers one or several service operations. A *service operation* is a specific function that provides a service. The service operation is in itself complete and is always executed when a web service is called. A web service is also called a *black box*. How a web service was implemented is not visible from the outside. The internal structure is also not relevant; the behavior and functions of the web service are much more interesting.

*Payload* generally refers to the entirety of the data that is sent to a service operation or returned from a service operation in a dedicated manner.

Payload

Up until release SAP CRM 2006s, you had to create web services manually by programming function modules first and then generating the web service interfaces using the *SAP NetWeaver Web Service Wizard*. Due to the high complexity, this implementation could take days or even weeks.

Since version 2006s, SAP provides a web service tool you can use to model web services on the basis of an object model in the Internet browser. The web service tool allows you to considerably facilitate the creation of web services because it enables you to model them from various business objects. A wizard guides you through a four-level selection process that finishes with the creation of the web service. With the web service tool SAP provides, for the first time, a simple and user-friendly tool that lets you integrate web service-consuming applications by third parties. The web services that have been created with the web service tool comply with the *world wide web consortium* (W3C) standard.

Modeling web services

A web service that has been modeled and generated with the web service tool is always stateless and can map the Read, Create, Update, and Query operations on a business object. In this context, stateless means that a web service call is always independent of its predecessors. In the Template Designer (see Section 7.2), however, you can only use web services with Read operations. The system generates a function module for each selected operation in the design mode of the web service tool.

Web service operations

The web service tool also enables you to model a web service that is based on multiple business objects (*compound service*). A compound service provides addresses of the business partners for a sales order as a *payload*, for example.

Compound service

Because web services that have been generated with the web service tool exist only locally on the ABAP server, you cannot implement a mapping to global data types; the local web service is also not included in SAP Enterprise Service Repository.

You start the web service tool via the Component Workbench (Transaction BSP_WD_CMPWB) using the WS_DESIGN_TOOL UI component.

Starting the web service tool

> **Note**
>
> For some business roles (for example, *Sales Professional*), the web service tool can be called via the navigation bar of the user interface. For simplicity, this section only discusses starting the tool via the Component Workbench.

Service object

The home page of the web service tool is a search page that enables you to search for service objects or create additional service objects. A service object is a container that contains all attributes and properties of a web service definition, based on one or several business data objects. To create a new service object, click NEW. A wizard opens that guides you through a four-level selection process that finishes with the creation of a service object.

Roadmap element

The roadmap element in the header area of the web service tool shows the four-level selection process and the current step of the wizard. You can navigate to the dialogs of the individual process steps at any time by clicking on the roadmap element. The selection process consists of the following steps:

1. Creation of a service object
2. Selection of the web service attributes
3. Editing of the web service attributes
4. Configuration of the settings and completion of the process

Step 1: creation of a service object

You maintain the basic data for the definition of the service object (first step of the wizard) in the central area of the home page. First, you assign a name to the service object. (Keep in mind that you have to specify a customer namespace.) In addition to defining a name, you specify the business object and the root object (see Section 12.1.3) that should form the data basis of the service object. Here, you also define which service operations (read, create, or modify) can be performed for this business object. Select a component set if you want to create a compound service based on multiple business objects.

> **Note**
>
> A plain web service is generally based on the root object of a GenIL component and its dependent objects in the object model. Consequently, a relationship to other objects in different GenIL components may not always be possible. If you define a component set, you can use the objects from the GenIL components contained therein to define a service object.

In the bottom part of the page of the first step for the creation of a web service, you can add search objects of the service object definition, but only the search objects of the selected business object.

Step 2: selection of attributes

In the second step, you select the required and descriptive attributes for the new service object that should be created. The attribute selection of the service object displays in the left screen section in a tree structure that hierarchically maps the object model of the selected business object. It also displays the possible operations you can perform for the objects that are linked to the root object in the object model. From the tree structure, select the required operation attributes for the service object. To do so, select the row with the attribute structures in the table. Clicking on the CONFIRM SELECTION button transfers the selection to the right screen section.

In the third step of the wizard (EDIT ATTRIBUTES), you include all selected operation attributes in a table. In the overview of the operation attributes, you can define the reference name of the attributes or use the default value. The reference name of the attribute is used in the WSDL file as the name for the attribute in the XML structure. In the SERVICE DEFAULT VALUE column, you can define a default value for the attribute. If you set the EXCLUDED option for an attribute, this attribute is read but cannot be modified.

Step 3: editing of attributes

The fourth step of the wizard summarizes the settings of the service object. When the service object is created, it first has a status of DRAFT. If you click the SAVE button, the system provides you with a new button, CHECK, so that you can check the consistency of the service object definition. The ACTIVATE, PRODUCTIVE, and NOT PRODUCTIVE buttons influence the status of service objects.

Step 4: settings

During its lifecycle, a status object can adopt four different statuses:

Status of a service object

- Draft
- Active
- Productive
- Not productive

The *initial* status of a web service upon creation is DRAFT. In this status, you can modify, copy, and delete the service definition at any time. To be able to use the web service, you must set the status to ACTIVE. If you want to modify a service object, you should reset the status of the service object to DRAFT. In the ACTIVE status, you can test the web service and call the web service description file (WSDL file). To be able to transport a web service, you must set its status to PRODUCTIVE. Be careful; you can no longer change the definition of the service object after the status is set to PRODUCTIVE. If you want to delete a web service that is set to PRODUCTIVE, you must deactivate the web service by assigning the NOT PRODUCTIVE status to it. Only then can you select it. Keep in mind that the selected status is not adopted until you click on the SAVE button.

After having completed the wizard for the creation of the web service, you should test the service. For this purpose, the status must be set to ACTIVE. You can test web services using the web service home page to which you can navigate via the TEST PAGE button in the last step of the wizard. It is a *Java server page* (JSP page), and you need a configured SAP J2EE server to execute

Testing the service object

it. Furthermore, to use this function, the address of the J2EE server must be defined in the system.

> **Note**
>
> Up until SAP NetWeaver 7.0 support pack 13, you can define the address of the J2EE server in Transaction WSADMIN under Settings • Administration. From SAP NetWeaver 7.0 support pack 14 on, you must use Transaction SOA-MANAGER for this purpose. Alternatively, you can test the web service from one of these two transactions.

Generating objects

The web service tool generates numerous *Data Dictionary* (DDIC) objects such as structures, function groups, and function modules in the /CRMOST/ namespace in the background.

The CRMOST_GENSTATUS_MONITOR report lets you search for service objects and view a graphical overview of all generated DDIC objects for the service object in a tree structure. In this view, you can navigate forward by clicking on the DDIC objects as well as export and import service object definitions.

## 7.2    Template Designer

No document template in the standard version

The Template Designer is a web-based tool that enables you to create document templates you can provide with business data via the web service technology from a CRM system at runtime. From SAP CRM 2007 on, PDF and Microsoft Word documents are supported. You must create your own document templates because SAP does not deliver document templates and web services with the standard version.

In general, you have to distinguish between two phases when creating and using document templates—design time and runtime.

Design time and runtime of the application

During the *design time*, you create the document template. To help you, you can use the Template Designer. At *runtime*, you create new documents on the basis of the created template in the CRM application and assign them to a business object. The newly created documents are stored in *content management*.

Starting the Template Designer

We will first take a look at the creation of a document template during the design time using the Template Designer. Before starting the Template Designer, you have to fulfill certain prerequisites. Section 7.6.3 provides more information on this. You can also start the Template Designer via the Component Workbench (Transaction BSP_WD_CMPWB). To do so, select the

CRM_OI_TEMPLDSG UI component and click on the Test button. The system then starts the Internet browser and takes you to the home page of the Template Designer.

The home page of the Template Designer provides various options for searching for existing document templates. When you enter search criteria, keep in mind that the search differentiates between upper and lower case spelling. The bottom area displays the result list of the search as a table. The header area of the table contains buttons that enable you to copy, delete, or modify existing document templates. To perform one of these actions, you should first select a document from the result list.

*Template Designer: search page*

As with creating web services (see Section 7.1), you can create a document template using the New button of the search page. The system then takes you to an editing page where you can define a new document template.

*Template Designer: new creation of document templates*

In the File Type selection list, you define in which format the document template should be created. You can select either Microsoft Word or Adobe XML Form File (PDF). In the Name field, you define the technical name of the document template; enter a unique name and a meaningful description.

The Object Type field serves to assign a document template to a business object. If you assign a document template to a business object in the Template Designer, you can use it at the runtime of a CRM application. The Attachment assignment block on the overview page of a business page is used to generate and assign the corresponding document from the defined template with the information of the business object. Therefore, the specification for Object Type in the Template Designer is binding.

*Template Designer: assignment to the business object*

You do not have to assign a web service to the document template. However, if you want to define a web service, use the input help for the search. If the system does not offer the required web service for selection, check whether the status of the web service is set to Productive and whether it contains a read operation. Always remember that you can only assign a web service to a document template when the web service has been created using the web service tool.

*Template Designer: assignment of a web service*

When you have assigned a web service to a document template, you can use the WEB SERVICES TOOL button in the toolbar to navigate to the web service. The WSDL button enables you to call the WSDL definition of the web service.

Making a selection in the LANGUAGE field links a language key to a document template so that the document template depends on the logon language.

> **Tip**
>
> If you want to use a document template in multiple languages, you must copy the template on the home page of the Template Designer. Then, save the copy with the new language key.

**Starting the Template Designer**

If you click on the START DESIGNER button, the system saves your specifications for the definition of the document template. Depending on the selection of the document format (file type), the system starts the respective Template Designer for Microsoft Word or Adobe Forms. The following sections discuss the creation and modification of document templates for Microsoft Word and Adobe Forms.

## 7.3 Document Templates in Microsoft Word

**Creating and storing a document template**

If you have used MICROSOFT WORD as the data type during the definition of the document template, the system calls the Template Designer for Microsoft Word.

Figure 7.1 shows a document template in the Template Designer for Microsoft Word with an assigned XML schema (❶). The XML schema is generated from the WSDL definition via *extensible stylesheet language* (XSL) or XSL Transformation (XSLT). Here, the system stores a document template that has been created with Microsoft Word in content management of the SAP CRM system after it has been saved in Microsoft Word as an XML form.

❷ in Figure 7.1 shows all available attributes the service object provides for the document template. The attributes and their relationships are displayed in a hierarchical tree structure. If you deselect the LIST ONLY CHILD ELEMENTS OF CURRENT SELECTION option, the system outputs the available attributes one below the other.

**Modifying a document template**

You can edit the document template in Microsoft Word as usual. To design the template, you can use the Microsoft Word functions in the function list. Now, position the available attributes from the service object (see Section 7.1) in your document (❸). The system inserts the attribute as a purple XML tag in the document. XML tags are not output when they have child elements. Only XML tags that are mapped as the last node in a hierarchical tree structure have associated text. This text is then output in the print output.

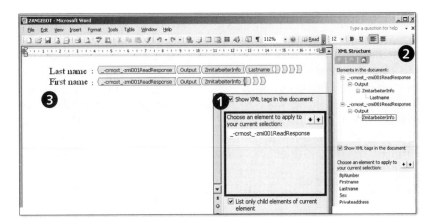

**Figure 7.1** Template Designer (Microsoft Word)

You can also use multiline attributes, which are used to display tables, for example. Multiline attributes are always mapped in a table. To do so, insert the nested XML tags in the document until you reach the ITEM nesting level. Here, insert a table with the required number of columns and two rows in the document. The first row contains the heading of the table columns. In the second row, an attribute from the ITEM XML node is added for each cell of the row. **Multiline attributes**

You can map complex structures such as a 1:n or m:n relationship of business objects by implementing a respectively deep nesting for the tables. **Complex structures**

## 7.4 Document Templates in Adobe LiveCycle Designer

If you select the Adobe XML format for the definition of the document template, the system provides options different from those for creating a template using Microsoft Word. For example, you can download a schema definition from the content management system if you have defined a name for the web service. Furthermore, you can download an already created Adobe form template or store a newly created template in the SAP CRM system. To map the properties of business objects, you can use only templates that are stored in the SAP CRM system.

**Starting Adobe LiveCycle Designer**

If you click on the START DESIGNER button, the system opens *Adobe LiveCycle Designer* in a new window. You can then create a new document. Next, you define the data connection to a web service using a schema definition (XSD file). The data connection is required to connect the service object attributes and text controls in Adobe LiveCycle Designer. Download the schema definition from the CRM system and store it locally. In the menu bar of Adobe Live-Cycle Designer, select the FILE • NEW DATA CONNECTION entry (❶ in Figure 7.2), and call the data description from the locally stored XML schema. The attributes of the services object are now available in the template (❷).

**Embedding the web service attributes**

After you have successfully established a data connection, you can drag the attributes of the web service (XML schema) to the drawing area (center) using drag-and-drop (❷). Here, you are additionally provided with an Adobe Live-Cycle Designer library, including controls. However, you have to connect these controls to the attributes of the web service manually.

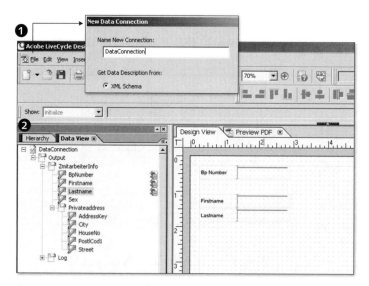

**Figure 7.2**  Document Template with Data Connection

**Publishing the template**

After you have completed the modification of the document, save it as an *Adobe XML Data Package* (XDP) file, which is a special Adobe document format. You can then make the created template available in the SAP CRM system by uploading the newly created template to the CRM system. You can now use the template in any SAP CRM application. The next section describes how you use document templates in the CRM application.

> **Tip**
>
> You do not have to create each document from scratch. Adobe LiveCycle Designer enables you to import existing PDF or Microsoft Word files. The quality of the templates, however, can vary after the import.

## 7.5  Documents in the CRM Application

So far, we have described how you create Microsoft Word and PDF document templates. Next, you will learn how these document templates become concrete documents with information of business objects. As you already know, you specify an object type when defining a document template. Only if a document template exists for this business object can you populate a document template with data at the runtime of the CRM application. Begin by starting a CRM application and selecting a business object. The overview page of the standard version contains the ATTACHMENTS assignment block. You can select the template that has been created for this business object in the function list of the assignment block using the WITH TEMPLATE button (see Figure 7.3).

**Access via assignment blocks**

**Figure 7.3**  Assignment Block "Templates" — Buttons

If the button displays as inactive, a document template has not yet been assigned to the business object. If you click the button, another dialog opens where you can select a document template (see Figure 7.4).

**Figure 7.4**  Dialog for Selecting a Document Template

Select a document template. After you have made your selection, the CRM application reads the stored document template from content management. It then calls the assigned web service and links the payload to the document template. For Adobe XML formats, the read process is implemented via *Adobe Document Services* (ADS).

## 7.6 Advanced Topics

Document templates and service objects are not automatically linked to the transport system; you have to manually assign them to a transport request. Sections 7.6.1 and 7.6.2 discuss the manual transport of document templates and service objects. Section 7.6.3 discusses the prerequisites for using the Template Designer. The chapter closes with notes on Adobe Document Services.

### 7.6.1 Transport of Document Templates

Implementation Guide: transporting document templates

When document templates are created, they are not automatically assigned to a transport request. This has to be done manually as soon as a transport to target systems is required. You assign document templates in the SAP Implementation Guide to a transport request of the Customizing type via the menu path CUSTOMER RELATIONSHIP MANAGEMENT • BASIC FUNCTIONS • CONTENT MANAGEMENT • TRANSPORT DOCUMENT TEMPLATE. You can also assign them via the CRM_KW_TEMPLATE_TRANSPORT program (Transaction SE38) (❶ in Figure 7.5). After you have called the IMG activity, the system prompts you to enter an object type. The object type should correspond to the object type in the dialog for generating a document template in the Template Designer (see Section 7.2).

**Figure 7.5** Home Page: Transport of a Document Template

Assigning document templates to the transport

Clicking on the EXECUTE button takes you to the next dialog where you select the document templates from a list that should be transported and assign them to a transport request using the TRANSPORT DOCUMENT TEMPLATES button (❷).

> **Note**
>
> If you want to transport a document template that is assigned to a web service, you must ensure that the corresponding web service is also transported to the respective target system and released.

## 7.6.2    Transport of Service Objects

For service objects, an automatic transport mechanism is also not available. To transport a service object within a system landscape from the development system to the consolidation system and production system, you need a transport request of type "workbench". Keep in mind that you can only transport service objects that are set to PRODUCTIVE.

You can assign service objects to an existing transport request in the SAP Implementation Guide via the menu path CUSTOMER RELATIONSHIP MANAGEMENT • UI FRAMEWORK • DEFINE UI FRAMEWORKS • WEB SERVICES • WEB SERVICE TOOL: TRANSPORT SERVICE OBJECTS. Alternatively, you can use the CRMOST_TRANSPORT report (Transaction SE38). You can bundle any number of service objects that should be transported in a transport request using the application. If you want to delete a service object definition in the target system, you can select and delete the corresponding object type in the SERVICE OBJECT DELETION TO BE TRANSPORTED field.

*Implementation Guide: transporting service objects*

Remember that a transport to a target system does not transport technical DDIC objects such as function modules or structures to the target system, only the service object's runtime settings that are configured in the web service tool are transported. After the transport to the target system has been completed, you perform an *after import function*, which generates the technical DDIC objects in the target system.

> **Note**
>
> If you transport data to the target system, the system does not create a runtime configuration. You have to do this manually using Transaction WSCONFIG (since NetWeaver 7.0 support package 14, this is Transaction SOAMANAGER). In this case, the security settings that have been configured in the web service tool apply. However, they do not apply in development systems. Here, you always use the BASIC AUTHENTICATION option to release the runtime configuration of a service after activation.

## 7.6.3    Prerequisites for Using the Template Designer

To use the Template Designer, the CRM_OI service must be activated in the SAP CRM system. You can use Transaction SICF in the SAP GUI to check whether a service is active.

*Prerequisite: service*

Furthermore, the Internet browser must be ActiveX-enabled, that is, it should be able to execute ActiveX controls. In addition, ActiveX must be activated in

*Prerequisite: browser*

the browser settings. You must also ensure that the following security settings have been configured in the Internet browser for LOCAL INTERNET:

▶ Agent scripting

▶ Execute ActiveX controls and plug-ins

▶ Initialize and execute ActiveX controls that are not secure

Prerequisite: MS Word

Both during the design time in the Template Designer and when using Microsoft Word templates at runtime (via the WITH TEMPLATE button in the Attachments assignment block), ActiveX needs to be activated in the browser. In addition, at least Microsoft Word Version 2003 Professional needs to be installed on your computer because the Microsoft XPath technology is used for the Microsoft Word integration.

Prerequisite: Adobe

The Template Designer for PDF document templates does not necessarily require ActiveX: If ActiveX is activated in the browser, Adobe LiveCycle Designer is started after you click the START DESIGNER button. If ActiveX is not activated, you can start Adobe LiveCycle Designer manually. To use PDF document templates, it is not relevant whether ActiveX is activated at runtime. In general, note that you need Adobe LiveCycle Designer if you want to create document templates based on the PDF format. You can download and install it separately, from the SAP Service Marketplace. To display the PDF document, Adobe Acrobat Reader must be installed on the client that is supposed to display the document.

Prerequisite: Adobe Document Services

To be able to generate PDF documents from document templates, an SAP NetWeaver Application Server with Adobe Document Services must be installed and configured in the system landscape. You can test the connection to Adobe Document Services using the FP_PDF_TEST_00 program (Transaction SE38). If the connection to Adobe Document Services has been established successfully, the system displays the current version number.

Table 7.1 lists additional useful SAP notes for the integration of office applications:

| SAP Note | Short Text |
| --- | --- |
| 1018674 | Prerequisites for the CRM Office Integration |
| 955221 | ADS Installation |
| 834573 | SAP Interactive Forms by Adobe: Acrobat/Reader |

**Table 7.1**  SAP Notes on the Integration of Office Applications

*This chapter introduces the Web Client UI framework in detail. It describes the terms and relations that are necessary for adapting and developing components and includes examples and listings that will help you become familiar with the programming of components for the user interface.*

# 8 Web Client UI Framework

The Web Client UI framework is based on the IC Web Client UI framework. In SAP CRM 2005, the *Interaction Center* was the only business application that was based on the Web Client UI framework; as of CRM 2006s, all CRM applications are based on it. As a result, significant extensions of the framework have become necessary.

With the Web Client UI framework available as of CRM 2006s, SAP provides an option of component-based application development according to the *model view controller* (MVC) *architecture pattern*. An essential aspect of the MVC architecture pattern is the separation of the units, data retention, layout, and program control into different components of an application. The Web Client UI framework is based on the latest technologies such as *asynchronous JavaScript and XML* (AJAX) and enables functions such as drag-and-drop in the Internet browser using integrated JavaScript libraries. The basic principle of the Web Client UI framework rests on the classification into components and on reuse, that is, a web application can be structured into various components that are called by applications and can be reused by other components. Thus, the idea behind the component-based application development is to orchestrate an application from a set of components.

Component-based application development

## 8.1 Basic Principles

The greatest part of an application runs on *SAP NetWeaver Application Server* (SAP NetWeaver AS); users only use an Internet browser that displays predefined screen content and forwards user actions to the server. The Internet browser only knows the screen to be displayed; business logic or context are completely unknown to it. The actions triggered by users influence the flow logic considerably, along with the screen content to be displayed. The application server receives the actions sent by users and returns a transformation result to the Internet browser in the form of new screen content. This process is referred to as *roundtrip*.

> **Note**
>
> Up to and including SAP CRM 2007, the framework is an SAP_ABA add-on called CRMUIF, that is, CRM UI framework. As of CRM Release 7.0, the framework is a separate software component called *Web Client User Interface Framework* (WEBCUIF).

Web Client architecture model  Figure 8.1 shows the Web Client architecture model. You can see the software layers of the CRM Web Client that build on one another. Each software layer usually communicates with the subordinate or superordinate layer.

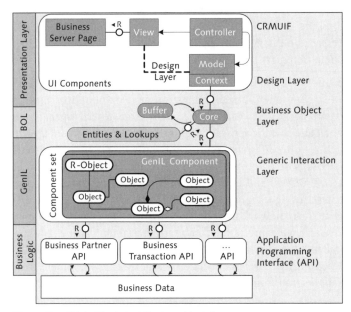

**Figure 8.1**  Web Client Architecture Model

We will now discuss the different layers of the Web Client architecture model, from top to bottom:

▶ **Presentation Layer (Web Client UI framework)**
Layer 1, which presents the CRM application in the Internet browser (from which requests resulting from user interactions are sent) and processes and

presents responses of the application server. A Web Client-based application consists of multiple components that interact with one another via interfaces. Each component follows the established MVC approach, that is, the layout (view) is strictly separated from the program control (controller) and the data retention (model).

▶ **Design Layer**
The Design Layer is located between the View and BOL layers. Its goal is to control UI-specific settings with a business process orientation.

▶ **Business Object Layer (BOL)**
Layer 2, which includes the BOL, which provides a uniform interface for access to object models. An instance of an object is referred to as a BOL entity. Chapter 13 covers the BOL in detail.

BOL entities

▶ **Generic Interaction Layer (GenIL)**
Layer 3, which includes the GenIL, which provides object models based on component sets. Objects of an object model are provided with data from the respective APIs of the busine HTML /ss data objects, depending on the context. Chapter 12 describes the architecture of the GenIL in detail.

Object models based on component sets

▶ **Business Logic (APIs)**
Layer 4, which presents the software layer with interfaces (*APIs*) for access to business data and provides data from the database or from other systems to the GenIL.

## 8.1.1 BSP Programming Models

SAP NetWeaver AS provides business server page (BSP) technology for a page-based programming model to implement web applications. The definition of the layout of a BSP page can only contain static source code; the layout receives the dynamic using information—determined at runtime—that is integrated with the layout. This means that at the runtime of a BSP page, the layout consists of a static part and a dynamic part, for example, data of a database table. The static part of a BSP page can be defined in *hypertext markup language* (HTML) or *extensible markup language* (XML). The dynamic part is implemented using server-side scripting. You can use ABAP or JavaScript as scripting languages.

Page-based programming model

You can use *page fragments* for the modularization of a BSP page. They include the layout of a BSP page and can be embedded in BSP pages at runtime using the include technique.

Page fragments

**Screen elements**    To optimize performance, BSP pages are compiled in normal ABAP classes at runtime the first time they are accessed. You can use ActiveX controls, Java applets, or style sheets in a BSP page as required. The application developer is responsible for arranging the screen elements. A BSP page can contain multiple screen elements: A distinction is made between screen elements for displaying data and screen elements that send an event to the server due to a user action, for example, buttons or links. Table 8.1 shows a selection of common screen elements of CRM applications.

| Screen Element | Meaning |
| --- | --- |
| | Input field with value help (F4 help) |
| | Disabled input field |
| Date of Birth | Field label, standard field |
| Last Name* | Field label, mandatory field |
| Activities, Opport. and Orders | Link |
| Save | Buttons (toolbar) |
| Synchronize | Button |
| | One-Click Action (OCA) |
| | Checkbox |
| 03.11.2008 | Date selection |
| Mr. / Dr. / Mr. / Ms. | Dropdown list/picklist |

**Table 8.1**  Screen Elements of SAP CRM 2007 Applications (Excerpt)

**BSP Extensions**    To not overload a BSP page with HTML and script coding and consequently make it unreadable and unmaintainable, SAP introduced the concept of BSP extensions. BSP extensions contain a set of BSP elements that provide more powerful functions than regular HTML tags and offer the benefit of a holistic look and feel in all BSP applications.

**Note**

*Tag library* is another common term for BSP extensions. Consequently, elements of a BSP extension are simply referred to as tags. The terms tag library and tag will be used throughout the rest of this book. Characteristics of tags are referred to as *attributes*.

The concept of BSP extensions drastically reduces the complexity of a BSP page, the pages have a clear arrangement, and thanks to the reusability of tags, you do not need to program each function multiple times. Tags are written in XML notation.

Actions that are triggered by the user in the user interface are processed in the event handler of the page. An event handler corresponds to a method in the ABAP OO environment.

However, the page-based programming model also had drawbacks. The processing of user input (request) and the formatting and updating of the screen display (response) had to be programmed again for each additional BSP page. It was quickly determined that you could swiftly obtain good results using the page-based programming model but that the close integration of the layout and program control resulted in disadvantages. This gave rise to poorly maintainable applications that could only be modularized and reused with a great deal of effort.

Something new had to be found, and the *model view controller architecture* pattern found its way into BSP technology, giving birth to the term *BSP-MVC*. This architecture pattern was developed in *Smalltalk* by XEROX in the 1980s for user interfaces. It describes an architecture pattern that is meant to ensure the maintainability and extensibility of the three units *model*, *view*, and *controller*, and achieve a separation of layout and program control.

But what does "model view controller" mean in detail, and what are the tasks of the three units? This can be best illustrated as shown in Figure 8.2.

The *controller* assumes the control of the model and view units, processes the user actions implemented by the user—such as keyboard inputs and mouse clicks—from the *hypertext transfer protocol* (HTTP) request. In BSP-MVC, the controller is represented as a BSP controller to which you assign an implementation class derived from the `CL_BSP_CONTROLLER2` class.

The *model* unit manages the data of the application. In BSP-MVC, the model is mapped by a class that inherits from the `CL_BSP_MODEL` class.

*Reusability of tags*

*Model View Controller (BSP-MVC)*

*HTTP request*

191

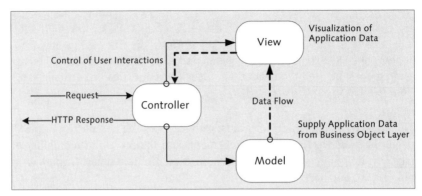

**Figure 8.2** Model View Controller Design Pattern

HTTP response    The *view* unit represents the presentation layer that requests data from the model via the controller and is responsible for the output of this data in an HTTP response. Usually, the view unit does not contain any program logic. Figure 8.3 illustrates this in a flowchart.

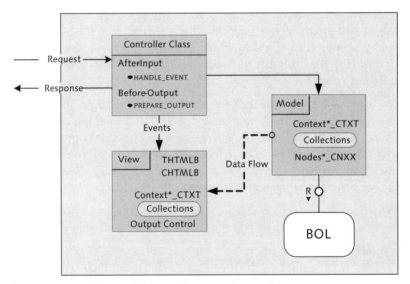

**Figure 8.3** Model View Controller Component Presentation

Table 8.2 summarizes the responsibilities of the three units model, view, and controller.

| Unit | Responsible for |
|------|-----------------|
| Model | Manipulation of data |
| | Data retention |
| | Data formatting |
| View | Data display |
| Control-ler | Event control |
| | Data distribution |
| | Navigation |

**Table 8.2** Responsibilities of Model, View, and Controller

Conclusion: The controller-based approach provides for separation between data retention, layout, and program control in BSP applications. The goal of the MVC approach is to create a better structuring of the applications to be maintained.

### 8.1.2 Web Client UI Framework

The Web Client UI framework is implemented with an object orientation, is based on BSP-MVC technology, and extends this technology with new facets. As you already know, the Web Client UI framework works on a component-basis, that is, it is not the application that plays the leading part but the components. A component consists of a multitude of objects such as views, windows, and controllers.

Web Client UI framework

---

**Caution: Possible Confusion of Terminology**

The last section discussed the MVC architecture pattern. This section also describes views; however, a view in this context is a part of a visual interface and should be considered a technical object. In the Web Client UI framework, each view is based on the MVC architecture pattern.

---

Views are a part of the visual interface of a UI component. Each view is assigned to a BSP page of the *BSP-View* type; conversely, this means that a change to a BSP page immediately impacts the output of a view. Views must be assigned to a window so that they can be displayed. If multiple views should be displayed at the same time, you must organize them in view sets and assign them to a window. Chapter 9 discusses the visual parts of a component.

Views and windows

With views, the Web Client UI framework consistently implements the MVC design pattern:

- **Model**
  The view context corresponds to the model unit and is responsible for data retention.

- **View**
  The view layout is controlled by an assigned BSP page.

- **Controller**
  The view controller connects the context and layout, responds to user interactions, and assumes program control.

Controller types

In total, there are five different types of controllers in the Web Client UI framework:

- View controller
- Window controller
- Component controller
- Custom controller
- Interface controller (virtual)

Each controller type fulfills its specific tasks. For example, one of the tasks of a view controller is to control the event handling within a view. The component controller and custom controller are used to exchange data beyond the view boundaries (see Chapter 9, Section 9.4). The interface controller manages the interface of the UI component to the outside. Each controller has an implementation class, the *controller class*. On the basis of object-oriented programming a controller class includes attributes and methods.

Context and context nodes

The context is another model variant SAP introduced with the Web Client UI framework. The context consists of context nodes which in turn can have attributes that are similar to an internal table. Context nodes can be linked with BOL entities from an object model offered by the GenIL (see Chapter 13) and screen elements of a view using data binding. Consequently, a context acts as a kind of intermediate layer between a model and a view. Another advantage of context nodes is that they have the ability to format data for the user interface. From a technical point of view, context nodes are classes that are derived from the CL_BSP_WD_CONTEXT_NODE class, which in turn inherits from the CL_BSP_MODEL class. Context nodes are always assigned to a context. Chapter 9, Section 9.4 describes the context and context node elements, as well as the connection to a data model.

The interaction of many different components calls for a sophisticated concept to control the navigation within an application. Within CRM applications, you must differentiate between the variants *easy navigation with navigational links* and *cross-component navigation*.

Easy navigation and dynamic navigation

A navigation is considered easy if the navigation is between views of a component or between views of different components within a component use. To describe an easy navigation, you need *inbound* and *outbound plugs*. A *plug* is a connection point via which a view or window can be accessed or exited. A description of an easy navigation is called a *navigational link*. An outbound plug is linked with an inbound plug in a navigational link. In addition, the navigational link receives a unique name. Thus, a navigational link describes a *navigation path* from the start to the target and can be understood as a directed relationship.

Inbound and outbound plugs

The control of cross-component navigation is based on customizing the CRM application (see Chapter 3, Section 3.2). It is used when navigation is required from one work area component to another that have no direct usage dependency. Chapter 9, Section 9.5 discusses the topic of navigation in detail.

### 8.1.3 Tag Libraries

To display screen elements in the user interface, the Web Client UI framework uses *tags* from different *tag libraries*. CRM 2005 used tags of the HTMLB tag library. As of CRM 2006s, using these tags has been replaced by using tag libraries THTMLB and CHTMLB. The TAJAX tag library is only used for grouping tags from THTMLB and CHTMLB to define areas in the layout that must be *rendered* again, if required (see note box), without having to recreate the displayed page. The goal of this delta handling is both better performance and "smoother" display without having to completely refresh the website after each user interaction.

Delta handling

> **Note**
>
> *Render* refers to the process of displaying a graphical content or the mechanism for calculating or creating an image.

The THTMLB library tags are independent of the Web Client UI framework and can therefore also be used in other BSP applications. They support functions for data management, event handling, and positioning of screen elements in the layout. Furthermore, the THTMLB library contains tags for displaying screen elements, for example, input fields (THTMLB:inputField) or

THTMLB library

dropdown list boxes (THTMLB:dropdownListBox). The appearance of these screen elements can be changed without modifications (see Section 2.6).

> **Note**
>
> To obtain an overview of all screen elements offered by the THTMLB tag library, call the CRM_THTMLB_COMP UI component in the Component Workbench using Transaction BSP_WD_CMPWB. Click on the TEST button to start the component in the Internet browser. The system displays a list of all standard screen elements. Click on one of the links to view the screen element in action.

CHTMLB library    Contrary to the THTMLB library, CHTMLB library tags cannot run without the Web Client UI framework because they require context nodes for the data binding or the existence of other framework parts. CHTMLB tags are also *composite tags* that do not generate a separate output in the form of HTML, but position the THTMLB tags and delegate the output in HTML to the embedded THTMLB tags. For example, the CHTMLB:config tag represents a form and internally delegates to the tags of the THTMLB tag library to display screen elements. Table 8.3 lists the most important CHTMLB tags.

| Tag | Function | Note |
| --- | --- | --- |
| CHTMLB:config | Form or edit mode | |
| CHTMLB:configTree | Presentation of a configurable tree structure | |
| CHTMLB:configCellerator | Presentation of a configurable table | |
| CHTMLB:configTable | Presentation of a configurable table | Obsolete—use the CHTMLB:configCellerator tag instead |
| CHTMLB: overviewFormConfig | Form or edit mode | Obsolete—use the CHTMLB:config tag instead |
| CHTMLB: overviewTableConfig | Table display | Obsolete—use the CHTMLB:configCellerator tag instead |

**Table 8.3**   Tags of the CHTMLB Tag Library

> **Note**
>
> Approximately 95% of the table views in CRM applications work with the CHTMLB:configTable tag. As much as possible, the CHTMLB:configTable tag is first delegated to the THTMLB:tableview tag and then to the CHTMLB:configCellerator tag. For custom implementations, you should use the more modern tag CHTMLB:configCellerator because the CHTMLB:config Cellerator tag provides improved performance and a better interface as compared to the CHTMLB:configTable tag.

The CHTMLB tag library (C stands for *configurable*) was introduced to be able to configure views without programming effort. You can influence the display of the tags either using the UI Configuration Tool in the Component Workbench at design time or using the UI Configuration Tool in the Internet browser at runtime (see Chapter 5, Section 5.1) without requiring an adaptation via programming.

For example, you can map a table that is based on the context node and its attributes using the CHTMLB:configCellerator tag. You determine the mapping of table columns using the UI Configuration Tool; the column set of the UI Configuration Tool depends on the quantity of defined context node attributes, among other things. Using the CHTMLB library is aimed at creating a configurable layout instead of "hard-coded" BSP pages.

CHTMLB:config Cellerator

To determine the layout of a CHTMLB tag, it requires a structure description in XML notation. The XML structure is read from the storage system for configurations at runtime and bound to the XML attribute of a CHTMLB tag.

Usage of a tag library

The example in Listing 8.1 shows the source code of a BSP page that specifies an XML structure of the view controller at runtime and binds the XML attribute of the CHTMLB:config tag:

```
<%@page language="abap" %>
<%@extension name="chtmlb" prefix="chtmlb" %>
<%@extension name="thtmlb" prefix="thtmlb" %>
<chtmlb:config xml = "<%=
controller->configuration_descr->get_config_data( )
%>"
                mode = "RUNTIME" />
```

**Listing 8.1** Activating the Configuration Tool

### 8.1.4 Web Client Component

As already discussed, the basic principles of the Web Client UI framework are reusability and componentization. The CRM application is structured into different components to create modules that can be reused at other points of the CRM application. The principle of component-based development was introduced in CRM 2006s and adopted by *Web Dynpro*, another SAP technology for creating web applications.

**Properties of a Web Client component**

Before continuing, we will first identify certain properties of a Web Client component:

- It represents a self-contained, reusable unit.
- It does not know the users.
- It encapsulates reusable elements such as windows, controller, context, context nodes, and their attributes.
- It is assigned to a BSP application.
- It exposes a visual interface to the outside (optional).
- It is extendable without requiring a modification.
- It is created and processed with the Component Workbench.
- It is subject to the transport system.

**Structure of a UI component**

Figure 8.4 illustrates the structure of a UI component. As a technical container, the UI component encapsulates reusable elements such as windows, views, and controllers and controls the restricted access to these elements via an interface (component interface).

A UI component that uses another UI component could access the context of an interface controller of the embedded UI component to impact the UI component from the outside. A direct contact with the component controller of the UI component to be embedded is not possible from the outside.

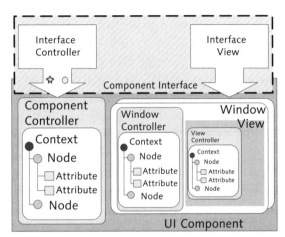

**Figure 8.4** Structure of a UI Component

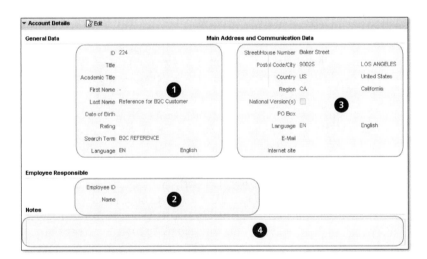

**Figure 8.5** Components in the CRM Web Client

Up until now, the UI component has been looked at in rather abstract and theoretical terms. Perhaps you are asking yourself the following question: "What does a UI component look like at runtime?" Figure 8.5 shows an excerpt of a CRM application, including the dialog for processing account

UI component at runtime

199

details. This dialog includes multiple UI components (❶ to ❹) that have a usage dependency, and each form a visible part of the CRM application via their *interface views* (see Chapter 9, Section 9.6.1).

The number of UI components displayed in the Internet browser cannot be determined immediately by looking at the Web Client user interface because it is possible that the system is currently displaying only the elements of a single UI component.

Division of a UI component

When you create your own UI components, you face the question into how many UI components you should divide the application. This strongly depends on the complexity, the design, and possibly the content of the respective application and must be decided for each case individually. However, there are some rules of thumb that are generally valid:

▸ For performance reasons, you should use as many UI components as necessary, but as few as possible.

▸ A UI component should form a logical unit.

▸ A UI component should contain a manageable number of views.

Although there is no difference from a technical point of view, in SAP CRM, you must differentiate three types of components according to their function (see Table 8.4).

| Type | Function/Example |
| --- | --- |
| Generic components | UI components that start with the GS name prefix (*generic services*) offer generic services such as text management, and so on. |
| Technical components | Technical UI components such as the web service tool (see Chapter 7, Section 7.1) are used for the modeling of a web service. |
| Business object components | All other UI components that do not correspond to the two previously mentioned types but can be allocated to a concrete business object, for example, the BP_ADDR component for managing business partner address information. These UI components constitute the majority of available UI components. |

**Table 8.4** Component Types According to Their Function

Multiple instances of a UI component can be available at the same time in the main memory of the SAP NetWeaver AS server. An instance of a UI component is always assigned to a user session.

## 8.2    Component Workbench

To create or process a UI component, you need a development environment. The *Component Workbench* is the development environment for UI components of the Web Client UI framework. You can call it in the SAP GUI by starting Transaction BSP_WD_CMPWB. The Component Workbench is independent and not integrated with the ABAP Workbench. It is the only tool to process UI components that are based on the Web Client UI framework. Wizards within the workbench support the application developer in the processing of UI components and generate or modify technical objects such as implementation classes.

*Code generation development environment*

In the initial screen of the Component Workbench, you are provided with the functions DISPLAY, CREATE, and TEST. Furthermore, you can activate the ENHANCEMENT SET field to implement customer-specific enhancements. Chapter 11, Section 11.1 discusses using enhancement sets in great detail.

*Initial screen of the Component Workbench*

When you open a component for processing, the system takes you to the component structure overview (see Figure 8.6).

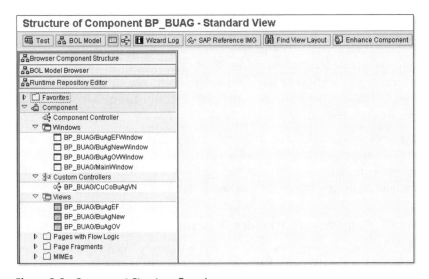

**Figure 8.6**  Component Structure Overview

The component structure overview is divided into three areas. The toolbar in the top area of the screen provides several functions that are summarized in Table 8.5:

*Component structure overview*

| Pictogram | Function Description |
|---|---|
|  | You can test an existing component using the Test button. |
|  | With this button, you can display the model of a component set without having to switch to the GenIL Model Browser. |
|  | Full-screen mode (on/off) |
|  | The where-used list enables you to find the UI components that embed the selected UI component. |
|  | This function shows the results of the UI component wizards that were used last. |
|  | You use this button to navigate to the IC Web Client in the SAP Implementation Guide. |
|  | You can search the view layout for a view controller implementation class using this function. |
|  | This function lets you enhance a component using the enhancement set technology. |

**Table 8.5**  Pictograms of the Component Workbench

Component structure browser
The left area of the screen provides different browsers for selection. The component structure browser is displayed by default. In the right area of the screen, on the STRUCTURE tab, the system displays the details of the respectively selected object from the component structure browser. From now on, this area will be referred to as the *detailed overview*.

Runtime repository editor
The browsers that are most frequently used in the Component Workbench are the *component structure browser* and the *runtime repository editor*. They are presented later on. After a model connection has been established in the runtime repository editor, the BOL model browser is also available.

### 8.2.1    Component Structure Browser

In the component structure browser, you can process objects such as views, windows, or custom controllers or add them to a UI component.

Parts of a UI component
Figure 8.7 shows the structure of a UI component in the component structure browser. The presentation of the parts of a UI component such as window, view, and controller is hierarchical. By clicking on an element in the tree structure of the component structure browser, on the right side of the screen, the system displays the corresponding details in another tree structure (see Section 8.2.2).

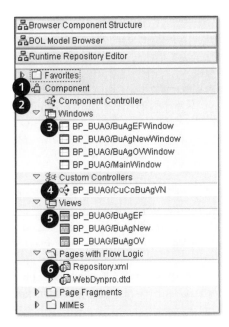

**Figure 8.7**  Structure of a Component

The COMPONENT (❶) serves as the root node for the nodes WINDOWS, CUS-
TOM CONTROLLERS, VIEWS, PAGES WITH FLOW LOGIC, PAGE FRAGMENTS, and
MIMEs.

The essential parts of a component are as follows:

▶ **Component controller**
Each UI component has a component controller (❷) in whose context you
can store cross-view data in the context node. The context nodes defined
in the component controller can be "published" in the component interface and thus provided to other UI components.

▶ **Window**
A window (❸) is a special type of view but has no *BSP page* assigned to
it. It manages views or view sets (see Chapter 9, Section 9.2) and is used
for the visual output of UI components. A window has its own controller and a context and can be published as an interface view for reuse of a
component.

▶ **Custom Controller**
Like the component controller, a custom controller (❹) is available for
all other controller types within a UI component for additional data storage. In contrast to the component controller, however, multiple custom

controllers can exist within a UI component and must be created using a wizard before they can be used. Custom controllers are loaded only when required.

▶ **Views**

Within the Web Client UI framework, from a technical point of view, a view (❺) is a BSP page. This BSP page uses the CHTMLB and THTMLB tag libraries. Therefore, a view is a "drawing area" and forms an element of an application's user interface. You can assign a view to a window only once.

▶ **Repository.xml**

The *Repository.xml* file (❻) is assigned to each UI component. This file contains specifications (in XML notation) for the functioning of the UI component regarding component usage, the component interface, inbound and outbound plugs, and the object model (component set) used. A manual change of this XML structure is possible but not recommended because the entire UI component becomes useless in the event of an error. You use the runtime repository editor to process and display the *Repository.xml* file. Section 8.2.4 presents this editor.

## 8.2.2 Detailed Overview

Details When you select an object from the nodes VIEWS, WINDOWS, COMPONENT CONTROLLER, or CUSTOM CONTROLLERS in the component structure browser, the system displays a detailed overview with details on the selected object, in a tree structure on the right side of the Component Workbench. Figure 8.8 shows the detailed overview for a view. The display of a window or a controller looks similar. The nodes of the detailed overview represent the implementation classes (❶), context node (❷), context-related methods (❸), event handler (❹), plugs (❺ and ❻), and other objects, such as *BSPs* (❼, only for views), or *controllers*. For nodes of the IMPLEMENTATION CLASS, METHODS, EVENT HANDLER, and PLUGS type, you can jump to the *class builder* (Transaction SE24) using the forward navigation.

Context menu Depending on the node type, you can call actions from a context menu to redefine the methods or start wizards you can use to create event handlers, plugs, or context nodes.

The node with the .DO description represents the view controller. By clicking on the .DO node, you open a dialog that shows the technical properties of the view controller. In this dialog, you can view and process the assignment of the view to the controller class, troubleshooting, caching, and lifecycle. The last level of the detailed view (❼) shows the VIEW LAYOUT node. If you double-click the subnode with the .HTM description, you open the BSP page of the view and its source text.

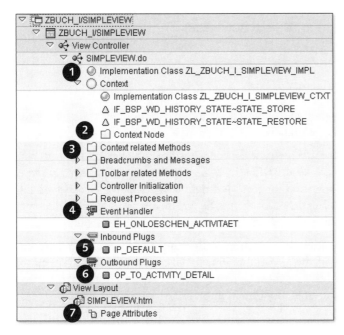

**Figure 8.8** Detailed Overview of a View

### 8.2.3 View Navigation

The VIEW NAVIGATION tab visualizes the runtime repository information and presents the use of the view in the UI component. A prerequisite is that the view is directly or indirectly assigned to a window.

### 8.2.4 Runtime Repository Editor

As already discussed, the runtime repository editor is a tool for visualizing and processing the *repository.xml* file. This means that if you make changes in the runtime repository editor, your changes impact the content of the *repository.xml* file after you have clicked on the SAVE button in the runtime repository editor. Changes to the runtime repository can be implemented by selecting a node in the hierarchical tree structure and selecting actions in the context menu. Furthermore, you can make changes to view assignments using drag-and-drop.

Tasks    Tasks you can carry out using the runtime repository editor are as follows:

- ► Connecting the UI components to a component set (model connection)
- ► Assigning views and view sets to windows
- ► Assigning views to view sets (view areas)
- ► Creating navigational links
- ► Defining the component interface
- ► Embedding components (creating a usage dependency)

Figure 8.9 shows the hierarchical structure of the runtime repository editor in the Component Workbench.

New entries in    To add new entries in the runtime repository editor, click on the EDIT but-
the runtime    ton in the toolbar (❶) to switch to change mode. Select the main node of
repository editor    the object type you want to create and right-click to open the corresponding
context menu. Select the ADD action. The system opens a dialog in which you complete your entries; confirm them by clicking on the SAVE button.

Check for    The general rule applies that entries in the runtime repository are based on
inconsistencies    existing objects of the UI component, for example, views, plugs, context nodes, or view sets. This means that you cannot create additional objects of this type in the runtime repository editor.

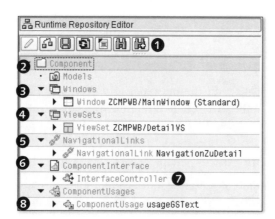

**Figure 8.9**    Runtime Repository Editor

Deleting these objects may lead to inconsistencies in the runtime repository. You can check the runtime repositories for inconsistencies using the CHECK button.

The connection of an object model to the UI component is carried out in the runtime repository editor. You can only assign a GenIL component set to the MODELS node (❷). When you have assigned a GenIL component set, the BOL model browser (see Section 8.2.5) is available in the Component Workbench. In Chapter 12, separate sections are dedicated to the topics of object model and GenIL component set.

Connecting an object model

You define inbound and outbound plugs for the window in the WINDOWS node (❸). Moreover, the assignment of a view or view set to a window is carried out at this point. You can assign multiple views to a window, and the first view in the list is the standard view. You can change the position of the views in the list using drag-and-drop. Below the WINDOWS node in the hierarchy, you can find the VIEWSETS node (❹). Here, you can assign views to a view set. Note that you must first create views and view sets in the component structure browser. Chapter 9 discusses views, view sets, and windows in detail.

Assignment to windows

In the NAVIGATIONALLINKS node (❺), you define the easy navigation from a source view to one or more target views. A prerequisite for the complete description of a navigation is that you have defined inbound and outbound plugs. A *navigational link* contains a unique name and the specification of an outbound plug (source) and at least one inbound plug (target). The name of the navigational link is required to execute a navigation. Chapter 9, Section 9.5.1 discusses the topic of *easy navigation* in detail.

Easy navigation with navigational links

The COMPONENTINTERFACE node (❻) describes the characteristic of a UI component regarding its use by other UI components. In the INTERFACECONTROLLER (❼), for example, you add context nodes of the component controller to the component interface (see Chapter 9, Section 9.6) and they are then visible from the "outside" for other UI components.

Component interface

In the COMPONENTUSAGES node (❽), you manage component usages. A component usage represents the relation to a UI component to be embedded. The goal is to reuse this UI component in the embedded UI component. Chapter 9, Section 9.6.4 discusses component usages in detail.

Definition of component usages

## 8.2.5 BOL Model Browser

If you assigned a component set to the UI component in the runtime repository, the *BOL model browser* is available as an additional browser within the Component Workbench. Like the GenIL model browser, it hierarchically displays the object model of the used component set.

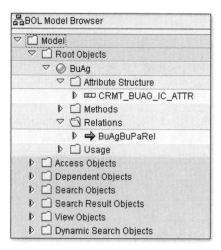

**Figure 8.10** BOL Model Browser

The system only displays objects contained in the component set. The display is categorized according to object type. You can navigate to the data dictionary by double-clicking an attribute structure. The RELATIONS node points to other objects in the object model using relations, while the USAGE node shows how the object is referenced by other objects (see Chapter 12, Section 12.1.4). Existing methods of the object are listed in the METHODS node, if applicable.

Overview of the object model | The BOL model browser lets you quickly gain an overview of the object model without having to switch to Transaction GENIL_MODEL_BROWSER (see Chapter 12, Section 12.2.1).

*An application generally consists of an array of UI components. Defined interfaces are required to ensure that UI components can cooperate with each other. In this chapter, we will introduce you to the architecture and parts of a UI component.*

# 9    UI Component Architecture

In the previous chapters, we have explained basic concepts and principles of the Web Client UI framework. We have described its component-based approach and the tools for creating your own UI components. It therefore now makes sense to discuss the architecture and parts of a UI component.

The architecture of a UI component differentiates between an internal view and an external view. In the internal relationship of a UI component, the view, window, controller, and context node units are assigned to the UI component. Initially, these units can only make contact with each other. For a component to be able to provide *services*, and thereby functions in the form of views, context data, and events to other users, these elements must first be added to the component interface (see Figure 9.1).

Visibility of a UI component internally and externally

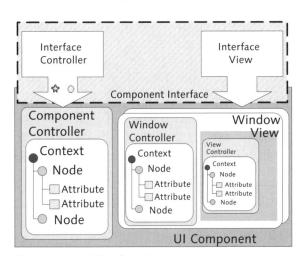

**Figure 9.1**    Visibility of a UI Component

This view is also reflected in the order of topics presented in this chapter. In the following sections in this chapter, we will describe the structure of a UI component and explain in detail individual elements such as views, windows, and controllers. We then apply a data model to the context and integration and learn mechanisms for defining *simple* and *cross-component navigation*.

In Section 9.6 at the end of this chapter, we will discuss the declaration of the component interface and explain how to create a usage dependency to other UI components.

## 9.1 View

**View as a visual unit**

Before we discuss different implementations of views, we first want to explain what a view in the Web Client UI framework actually means in the traditional sense. Previously, we discussed that views form a part of the visual interface of a UI component and that views are each assigned to a BSP page. Users of web applications are accustomed to these web applications using the entire screen to display contents. This is no different for the Web Client UI framework; however, it follows a special approach because it assembles the screen content from smaller units. These units are called *views*. They are organized in *view sets* to display several views on the screen at the same time. You can use view sets to combine and nest views within each other in different ways. We will discuss view sets in detail in Section 9.2.

**Creating a view**

A view can only exist within a UI component. You therefore need a UI component to create a view. You use the Component Workbench for this purpose. To start the wizard that supports you when creating a view, select the VIEWS level within the component structure browser and select the CREATE option from the context menu. Figure 9.2 shows the hierarchical structure of a view in the detailed overview within the Component Workbench.

The topmost elements of a view are the view controller (❶) and its implementation class (❷). CONTEXT (❸) and CONTEXT NODES (❹) are lower-level elements of the view controller. The following levels contain the most common methods (❺) of the implementation class of the view controller that are processed by the framework at runtime:

▶ Context-Related Methods

▶ Breadcrumbs and Messages

▶ Toolbar-Related Methods

▶ Controller Initialization

▶ Request Processing

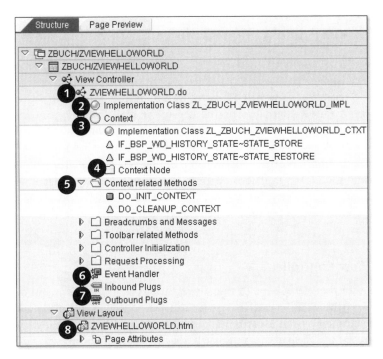

**Figure 9.2** Parts of a View

These methods control the program flow of the view and can be redefined to influence the flow logic.

Other elements of the view controller are the event handler (❻ in Figure 9.2) for processing user events, and plugs (❼) for controlling navigation. The layout of a view is produced by the assigned BSP page (❽).

> **Note**
>
> Not every view is assigned to a BSP page all at once. For example, an OVER-
> VIEW PAGE view (see Section 10.5) does not have its own BSP page. This is
> because the layout of an overview page can, in principle, only be processed
> with the UI Configuration Tool. After you create an overview page, the UI
> Configuration Tool is immediately available in the Component Workbench.

**Assignment to a window**

You cannot execute a view without windows; therefore, you must always assign it to a window. You perform this step in the runtime repository editor (see Section 9.3). If you neglect to assign a view to a window, the view will not be displayed at runtime and different functions will not be available in the runtime repository editor at the design phase—the view subsequently cannot be taken into consideration in a definition of a navigational link. Alternatively, you can also assign a view to a view set (see Section 9.2). However, you must then, in turn, assign the view set to the window to display the view.

### 9.1.1 View Controller

**View controller tasks**

Every view in the Web Client UI framework has exactly one view controller. The view controller is responsible for processing the entries made and actions performed by the user and managing the data relating to the view in the view context. The view controller is assigned an implementation class that contains the methods for controlling the behavior of a view in relation to navigation, event handling, and data binding. If the user clicks a button for a view, the controller contains the logic to process this mouse click and start a navigation. The view controller is instantiated and initialized when the view is displayed. The instance of the view controller is deactivated when the view is no longer displayed. The data in the context is discarded when you deactivate the view controller.

### 9.1.2 View Context

**View context**

The view context manages the data relating to the view. At design time, the context presents, along with its context nodes, the attributes required by the component for the program flow. At runtime, the context with its context nodes and attributes is provided with values from screen elements (e.g., due to user entries) or with values from BOL entities of an object model. It is therefore used as a linking layer between presentation and data retention. An implementation class is assigned to the context, and the name of the implementation class generally ends with the _CTXT suffix. The implementation class of the view context can be addressed as an attribute of the implementation class for the view controller.

Before we continue, we first want to identify certain general properties of a context node:

- It identifies a table of the same types of objects with several attributes.
- It can refer to other context nodes.
- It can be part of a context node hierarchy (see Section 9.4.6).

Context nodes are assigned to the context, and there can be any number of context nodes in the context. Context nodes can either exist independently of each other or form a hierarchy. We differentiate between two types of context nodes: *value nodes* and *model nodes*. You can select the type of context node when you create it using the wizard.

A model node refers to a GenIL object of an object model (see Chapter 12, Section 12.1.1) and represents the link between a screen element and object model. The reference to the GenIL object in the object model is created by the `BaseEntityName` attribute in the implementation class of the context node. The attributes of a GenIL object from the object model can be transferred completely or partially into the model node in the wizard. A value node, in contrast, does not have any reference to an object model and can have any number of attributes with any number of data types. You can have a combination of model nodes and value nodes.

You create context nodes using a wizard. The wizard generates an implementation class for each context node. When context nodes are generated with the wizard, their implementation classes are assigned a unique name that contains a two-digit sequential number and ends with the CN suffix.

Attributes are the smallest parts of a context node and are used to link screen elements to the context. This means that entries in a view are automatically transported to the linked attributes by extracting the data from the HTTP request and transporting it into the view context. By contrast, the data from the attributes is read for compiling the HTTP response. A data type is assigned to attributes, which can have their own getter and setter methods (see the following paragraphs). By linking attributes to screen elements with the view controller, you decouple the layout and program control.

Linked screen elements on a view can only process *string* data type information. On the database, however, you must be able to store contents in different data formats. You therefore need to convert the string data type to DDIC data types (*ABAP Dictionary*). This occurs for every roundtrip through the processing of a getter method by the framework for which the DDIC data type of an attribute is converted to the string data type and displayed on the screen. In contrast, when you enter data, the content of a screen element of the string data type is converted into a DDIC data type of the relevant attribute and updated in the context by processing a setter method.

Binding context attributes with STRUCT

Model nodes with the `BaseEntityName` reference to a GenIL object are beneficial for the Web Client UI framework in that the attributes of a model node can be accessed generically. The Web Client UI framework uses the STRUCT virtual structure for this purpose, the components of which correspond to the attributes of the BOL entity. For example, access to the STRUCT.BP_GUID component corresponds to access to the `BP_GUID` attribute of the `BuilHeader` GenIL object. The Web Client UI framework uses the `GET_S_STRUCT` and `SET_S_STRUCT` methods to access attributes generically.

Generic getter and setter method calls

You can replace generic getter and setter method calls with non-generic method implementations. You create non-generic getter and setter methods using either a wizard (see Figure 9.3) in the Component Workbench or by manually copying the template methods in the context node implementation class. You can identify the template methods by their method name—they all end with the _XYZ suffix.

> **Note**
>
> We recommend that you use the wizard because this procedure is quicker, more user-friendly, and, above all, less prone to errors. However, sometimes the wizard is not available and you therefore have to create the methods manually.

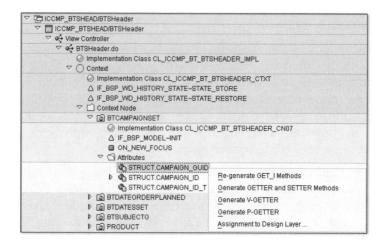

**Figure 9.3** Getter and Setter Methods

By changing the values that the getter methods return to the framework, you can influence the appearance, function, and input readiness of screen elements (linked to context attributes) of configurable views at runtime. The Web Client UI framework processes four types of getter methods:

Appearance and function of screen elements

### P Getter (Property)

A P getter method defines other properties of a screen element. A screen element that is linked to an attribute changes its appearance or adopts the set properties of the attribute. You set properties of screen elements by setting the RV_VALUE return parameter of the P getter method. The possible properties of a screen element are defined as constants in the IF_BSP_WD_MODEL_SETTER_GETTER interface. Table 9.1 gives you an overview of possible properties.

| Property | Description |
| --- | --- |
| FP_DETAIL_LINK | Displays a link next to an input field |
| FP_SERVER_EVENT | Sets the event name for a roundtrip |
| FP_ONCLICK | Sets the name for the onClick event |
| FP_TOOLTIP | Sets a tooltip text |
| FP_GROUP | Sets a radio button group |
| FP_FIELDTYPE | Sets the field type (see Table 9.2) |
| FP_RADIO_COLS | Sets the columns for radio buttons |
| FP_TEXTAREA_ROWS | Sets the rows for text area elements |
| FP_TEXTAREA_COLS | Sets the columns for text area elements |
| FP_SORTABLE | Sets the sortable/not sortable property |
| FP_DISABLE_FILTER | Sets the filter for a column |

**Table 9.1** Properties of Attributes

If attributes of a context node do not have a P getter implementation, the Web Client UI framework uses a heuristic method to determine the field type of the column when displaying a table. The heuristic approach for determining the field type is especially time-consuming for tables. In technical jargon, this is also known as "intensive." To avoid this, create a P getter method for every additional attribute and return the field type. Also implement SAP Note 1179315, which will cause the result of the heuristic approach to be buffered for attributes without a P getter implementation when the first row is rendered. The buffered result can then be accessed when the second row

Determining the field type

onward is rendered, without the heuristic method having to be used again. This benefits performance.

You can therefore use the FIELD TYPE property to manipulate the type of screen element at runtime. The instances of the FIELD TYPE property outlined in Table 9.2 are possible.

| Property | Displayed As |
| --- | --- |
| FIELD_TYPE_INPUT | Input field |
| FIELD_TYPE_PICKLIST | Picklist (dropdown box) |
| FIELD_TYPE_CHECKBOX | Checkbox |
| FIELD_TYPE_LINK | Hyperlink (external) |
| FIELD_TYPE_EVENT_LINK | Hyperlink (server event) |
| FIELD_TYPE_RADIO | Radio button |
| FIELD_TYPE_TEXT | Text field |
| FIELD_TYPE_IMAGE | Image |
| FIELD_TYPE_TEXTAREA | Multiline textbox |
| FIELD_TYPE_PASSWORD | Password field |
| FIELD_TYPE_TIMEPICKER | Time picker field |
| FIELD_TYPE_OCA | One-click action (OCA) |

**Table 9.2**  Instances of the FIELD TYPE Property

The constants are contained in the IF_BSP_DLC_VIEW_DESCRIPTOR interface.

### V Getter (Value Help)

Value help/ dropdown box

You need to implement a V getter method when you want to provide value help (F4 help) or a dropdown box for an input field that is linked to an attribute of a context node. We will show you how to implement a dropdown box in Chapter 16, Section 16.4.6.

### M Getter (Metadata)

Metadata of a screen element

The M getter method provides metadata such as the data type from the ABAP Dictionary or field lengths for an attribute.

### I Getter (Input Readiness)

You use an I getter method to control whether a screen element linked to a context attribute is ready for input at runtime. Input fields that are not ready for input are displayed grayed out in the layout. You can use the Boolean RV_DISABLED returning parameter of an I getter method to activate (FALSE value) or deactivate (TRUE value) input readiness.

**Input readiness**

> **Note**
>
> We will explain the procedure for creating context nodes and attributes in Section 9.4.3.

If the context node of the attribute is a model node, the default implementation of the I getter method uses the IS_PROPERTY_READONLY method to check whether the attribute of the BOL entity can only be read, not changed. In this case, you are not allowed to edit the input field on the user interface and the I getter method returns the TRUE value with the RV_DISABLED returning parameter.

**IS_PROPERTY_ READONLY**

## 9.1.3 Event Handler

Event handlers are required to be able to react to user actions on the user interface. For example, if a user clicks a button on the user interface, this triggers an event that can be processed accordingly by an event handler method. Event handlers are implemented as methods of the view controller. Within the view controller, the DO_HANDLE_EVENT method in the view controller distributes the events to the generated event handler methods of the view.

To create an event handler, you must select the EVENT HANDLER level in the view controller of the Component Workbench and start the CREATE option from the context menu (see Figure 9.4).

**Creating an event handler**

**Figure 9.4** Creating an Event Handler in the View Controller

In the dialog that appears, you need to define the name of the event (server event) and confirm it with ✔.

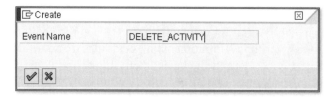

**Figure 9.5** Defining the Event Name for an Event Handler

> **Note**
>
> When the event handler method is being created, it receives the name of the event that is entered in the wizard, including the EH_ON prefix. The event name is case sensitive.

By creating an event handler with the wizard, a call for the event handler method is automatically added to the DO_HANDLE_EVENT method implementation in the implementation class for the view controller. Pay attention to case sensitive spelling when entering the event name in the wizard. Chapter 16, Section 16.3.3 contains a practical example for creating an event handler.

### 9.1.4 Plugs

Inbound and outbound plugs

A *plug* is a transfer point of a view and fulfills an inbound or outbound function. We differentiate between *inbound plugs* and *outbound plugs*. Plugs are required to describe *navigation* within an application. Navigation means the different ways a user can move in an application.

Inbound plugs identify possible navigation into a view, and outbound plugs are required for navigating from the view. A *navigational link* connects an outbound plug to an inbound plug, and plugs are generally located in different views.

Creating plugs

You create inbound and outbound plugs in the detailed overview of the Component Workbench. To create an inbound plug, use the wizard (which you can start from the context menu) at the INBOUND PLUGS level (see Figure 9.6). You create outbound plugs in the same manner.

**Figure 9.6** Creating an Inbound Plug

After you create a plug, the method implementation of the plug is available in the controller. The name of the method is composed of the IP_ prefix for inbound plugs (or OP_ for outbound plugs) and the name of the plug. From the detailed overview, you can navigate forward into the method implementation.

Plug method

If the two views do not have a common data context by way of context node binding (see Section 9.4.4), you can exchange data between views using the DATA_COLLECTION parameter of the NAVIGATE method of the view manager. The DATA_COLLECTION parameter is an IF_BOL_BO_COL interface type, which means that a collection can be transported from the source view into the target view. The IV_COLLECTION parameter is the only parameter contained in the method implementation of the receiving inbound plug.

Exchange of data between views

> **Note**
>
> Because many different scenarios occur in relation to navigating within CRM applications, we have dedicated a separate part of this chapter, Section 9.5, to the complex topic of navigation. Furthermore, Chapter 16, Section 16.5.1 contains a practical example for creating plugs.

Like a view, a window can also have inbound and outbound plugs and therefore becomes part of a navigation. To exit a window through its outbound plug and thereby start the navigation, you must call the CALL_OUTBOUND_PLUG method of the window controller with the name of an outbound plug. You create plugs in the detailed overview for windows. Window plugs play an important role in the navigation of work area components (see Section 9.5.2).

Window plugs

After you create a plug in the detailed overview of a window, the plug method implementation is initially empty and should be implemented fully using the following statement:

```
me->fire_outbound_plug(
  iv_outbound_plug   = 'PLUG_NAME'
  iv_data_collection = iv_data_collection ).
```

You can provide inbound plugs for a window with a follow-up navigation so that they can be delegated further to an inbound plug of a view. To do so, select the ADD PLUG WITH FOLLOW-UP NAVIGATION option from the context menu on the INBOUND PLUGS level of a window in the runtime repository editor. A dialog appears, as shown in Figure 9.7. You then enter the name of the inbound plug and the name of the navigational link to be created and select the view and corresponding inbound plug.

Delegating inbound plugs

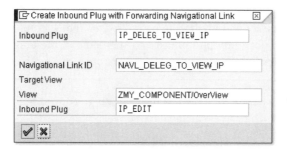

**Figure 9.7** Defining a Follow-Up Navigation

The newly defined navigational link then appears in the runtime repository editor under the specification of the FOLLOW_UP virtual outbound plug. The new window inbound plug you have created appears in the runtime repository under the specification of the follow-up navigational link.

> **Note**
>
> You can also program the delegation of inbound plugs in the plug method implementation. However, the advantage of declaring a delegation of inbound plugs in the runtime repository is that it offers a better overview.

### 9.1.5 View Layout (BSP Page)

View layout as a BSP page

As already discussed, the view output is produced by statements in the BSP page. This can be done either directly with HTML and JavaScript or with tags (see Chapter 8, Section 8.1.3). You can use scripting statements to influence the output dynamically.

> **Note**
>
> Although technically feasible, you should avoid dynamic outputs with scripting statements as much as possible and only use them in absolutely exceptional cases. Instead, use the tags from the CHTMLB and THTMLB tag libraries.

You should use tags from the THTMLB and CHTMLB tag libraries for BSP pages in UI components because these tags can guarantee that the layout is output without any errors. Within the BSP, you can position screen elements such as input fields, picklists, or buttons and, if necessary, link them to the context.

Page attributes

A BSP page has access to the view controller and view context; context nodes are available as page attributes in the BSP page. Page attributes are the data interface of a BSP page.

> **Note**
>
> CHTMLB tags are the preferred tags to use compared to all other alternatives. It is only with configurable views (see Chapter 10) that the user obtains the required flexibility for configuring and personalizing the user interface.

You start the editor for editing a BSP page by double-clicking the VIEWNAME. HTM node in the detailed overview of the Component Workbench. The *tag browser*, which you can activate through the ENVIRONMENT • WEB TOOLS • TAG BROWSER path in the menu bar, is useful for editing BSP pages. All tags and their attributes available in the system are displayed in a hierarchical tree structure in the tag browser and you can add them to the source code of the BSP page using drag-and-drop (see Figure 9.8).

**Tag browser**

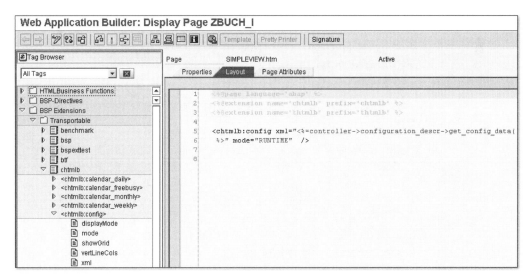

**Figure 9.8** Activated Tag Browser in a BSP Page Editor

If you use ABAP language constructs within the BSP page, you must include the following BSP directive as the first line in the BSP page:

```
<%@page language="abap" %>
```

BSP directives or statements, which the server must interpret at runtime, are identified by the scripting tag in the layout. This means they are enclosed between <% and %>. Other important directives are the INLINE CODE and OUTPUT OF VARIABLE VALUES directives. You use the INLINE CODE directive to identify ABAP or JavaScript source text in the layout of a BSP page.

**BSP directives**

The following is an example:

```
<%
  data l_str type string.
       l_str = 'Hello World!'.
%>
```

You use the OUTPUT OF VARIABLE VALUES directive to output the value of a basic variable at the time the page is processed.

The following is an example: `<%= ls_builheader-bp_number %>`

When you use a tag in the BSP page, the use must be displayed by including the tag library, as shown in the following example:

```
<%@extension name="chtmlb" prefix="chtmlb" %>
```

You can link tag properties to context nodes to provide a tag with values from the context or to transport values from a tag into the context. The syntax for binding attributes is //<CONTEXTNODE>/<ATTRIBUTE>, and //<CONTEXT-NODE>/TABLE for binding a context node to tag properties for displaying a table.

> **Note**
>
> In the //<CONTEXTNODE>/TABLE syntax, note that only the name of the context node is variable. The context node must be of the CL_BSP_WD_CONTEXT_NODE_TV type.

BSP page parameters

A BSP page provides you with various parameters you can use to access the view controller, page context, environmental data of the BSP page, or contents of the request/response cycle. Within the BSP page, you can access public attributes and methods of the view controllers by using the CONTROLLER parameter as a reference to the view controller. You can obtain an overview of all addressable references by clicking the SIGNATURE button in the toolbar. The toolbar provides even more functions such as source code formatting, syntax checks, and activations. Changes to a BSP page only become active after you activate the BSP page explicitly.

In addition to the option to create "hard coded" BSP pages, the Web Client UI framework lets you configure a view using the *UI Configuration Tool*.

The UI Configuration Tool is based on the context; in other words, on context nodes and their attributes. The attributes available in the context form the field selection and column selection of a configuration tool. Unlike "hard coded" BSP pages, the UI Configuration Tool therefore determines the number of visible screen elements and the area where the screen elements are positioned.

The UI Configuration Tool is based on dynamic layout processors that are implemented in CHTMLB tags or in controllers of overview pages. A layout processor is responsible for displaying and positioning screen elements correctly on the user interface. This implies that you must use CHTMLB tags within the BSP page to activate the configuration tool. We already discussed using CHTMLB tags and activating the UI Configuration Tool in Chapter 8, Section 8.1.3.

**Layout processors**

> **Note**
>
> Due to the simple layout design and the personalization option available to users, the preference should be to use configurable views and only create "hard coded" BSP pages in exceptional cases.

## 9.2    View Set

In the previous sections, we mentioned that a single view can completely fill a window area. However, you can also display several views on the screen simultaneously. To do so, you must organize views in a *view set*. A view set is an available area that can be divided into several areas (*view areas*) in grid form. You can place views in each view and these views can then be displayed next to or underneath each other on the screen. Figure 9.9 shows common view set grids. More complex grids can only be achieved by nesting view sets. A view set can also consist of only one view area.

**Dividing view sets into view areas**

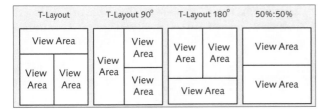

**Figure 9.9**    Common View Set Grids

To be able to display view sets, they, like views, must be assigned to a window in the runtime repository. You also assign views to view areas in the runtime repository. From a technical point of view, a view set is a special view type. It contains a controller and context; however, the context generally does not have any context nodes. Like a view, a view set can also have event handlers and plugs.

**Assigning view sets to windows**

223

Creating view sets and defining the grid size
You create view sets in the *component structure browser* of the Component Workbench. You create them with the support of a wizard tool. You can call the wizard from the context menu at the VIEWS level in the component structure browser by starting the CREATE VIEW SET option. The wizard then performs a four-step process that ends with it creating a view set. In the first wizard step, you get a brief description about how the wizard works. In the second step, you define the view set by naming it and specifying the grid size in lines and columns. Figure 9.10 shows the definition of a view set that is divided into two view areas.

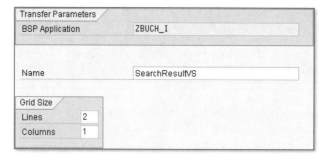

**Figure 9.10** Defining a View Set

Naming view areas
After you define the grid size, in the third step you must name the view areas uniquely and define their positions in the grid. You can also define other properties such as the column and line spans of a view area (see Figure 9.11). The column span defines the number of columns you want to be used to link the current cell, and the line span defines the number of lines.

In the fourth and last step, the view set is displayed schematically as a grid. You end the process by clicking the COMPLETE button, which causes the view set to be generated. An entry is automatically made in the runtime repository.

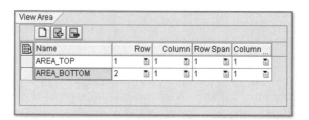

**Figure 9.11** Defining View Areas

Changes to view sets are not supported by the wizard; instead, you must implement them manually. It is therefore worthwhile to take a look at the BSP page of the view set. The code generator creates a BSP page for the view set with the statements shown in Figure 9.12.

```
<%@page language="abap" %>
<%@extension name="thtmlb" prefix="thtmlb" %>
<%@extension name="bsp" prefix="bsp" %>
<thtmlb:grid xmlns:thtmlb="CRMThinHTMLBLibrary" cellSpacing="1"
             columnSize="1" height="100%" rowSize="2" width="100%">
  <thtmlb:gridCell colSpan="1" columnIndex="1" rowIndex="1" rowSpan="1">
<bsp:call comp_id = "<%= controller->GET_VIEWAREA_CONTENT_ID( 'AREA_OBEN' ) %>"
          url      = "<%= controller->GET_VIEWAREA_CONTENT_URL( 'AREA_OBEN' ) %>" />
</thtmlb:gridCell>
<thtmlb:gridCell colSpan="1" columnIndex="1" rowIndex="2" rowSpan="1">
<bsp:call comp_id = "<%= controller->GET_VIEWAREA_CONTENT_ID( 'AREA_UNTEN' ) %>"
          url      = "<%= controller->GET_VIEWAREA_CONTENT_URL( 'AREA_UNTEN' ) %>" />
  </thtmlb:gridCell>
</thtmlb:grid>
```

**Figure 9.12** Technical Mapping of a View Set (BSP)

We can clearly recognize the use of the `THTMLB:grid` and `THTMLB:gridCell` tags for arranging the view areas and the specifications for the grid size of the view set in XML notation requested by the wizard. The content of a view area is determined and displayed at runtime by the `CALL` tag of the BSP tag library.

You assign views to view areas in the runtime repository editor by selecting the ADD VIEW option from the context menu (see Figure 9.13). Note that to do so, you must be working in change mode.

**Figure 9.13** Assigning a View to a View Area

In the dialog that subsequently appears for assigning the view, choose the name of the view and confirm it with the ⌈Enter⌋ key to assign the selected view to the view area. You must do this in the same way for all view areas. You can also assign several views to a view area, however, only one view (by default, the uppermost view) will be displayed within a view area. You can change the sequence of views using drag-and-drop. One alternative to display several views simultaneously in a view set is to nest view sets.

> **Note**
>
> You can only assign a view to a view area once. If you try to perform an assignment multiple times in the runtime repository editor, the system will issue an error message when you try to save the assignment.

Interface views (see Section 9.6.1) of other UI components are handled like normal views and can therefore also be assigned to a view area in a view set. Chapter 16, Section 16.3.5 contains a practical example for creating a view set.

## 9.3 Window

So far, we have discussed the individual visual parts of a UI component, views, and view sets. You have learned that a view is a section of a screen display and that views can be organized in view sets to display several views at the same time. However, a view cannot be executed alone. To be able to display it, you must always assign it to another visual unit, the *window*. A window represents a layer on a UI component and is used for arranging and navigating views or view sets. It forms the visual interface of a UI component and therefore, ultimately, the application's visual interface. Like a view, it has a controller that is also known as a *window controller*. You implement both visual units in the same manner, but with one exception: Unlike a view, a window does not have a layout. Whereas a view only displays a subarea of the screen, a window represents the entire work area (see Chapter 1, Section 1.2.3). If you navigate from one window to another, the work area display also changes.

Interface view | Another important function of a window is that you can add it to the component interface as an interface view and, with the assigned views, it becomes part of the reusable, visual interface of a UI component. The component interface is illustrated in Section 9.6.

Each UI component can consist of several windows and each window can in turn have several views. A window can only display one view at runtime. If you want several views to be displayed, you must group them in a view set and assign them to the window.

Adding windows | When creating a UI component, the Component Workbench also automatically generates a window. If the name has not been changed, the name of the generated window is MainWindow. You can add windows to a UI component by selecting the Windows level in the component structure browser and starting the Create option from the context menu to start the wizard for creating windows. From the dialog that appears, you are led through an eight-step creation process where, in addition to naming the window, you can also add model nodes or value nodes to the context of the window controller. The procedure for creating context nodes is the same for all controller variants; therefore, we have summarized it in Section 9.4.3. After you generate a window, an entry is automatically made in the runtime repository.

You assign views and view sets to a window in the runtime repository editor by starting the ADD VIEW option from the context menu.

*Assigning views and view sets to a window*

> **Note**
>
> As you can see in Figure 9.14, the FLAG AS DEFAULT option is also available in the context menu. This is because several windows can exist next to each other within a UI component and the framework must be able to identify which of these windows should be displayed by default when you call the UI component.

**Figure 9.14**  Adding a View to a Window Definition

In the next dialog, you choose a view and assign it to the window by confirming this with the ⌷Enter⌷ key. You must save the changes you make in the runtime repository editor by clicking the SAVE ( ⊟ ) button. You can assign several views to a window. By default, the topmost view is also displayed in the first position in the window. You can change the order of views using drag-and-drop. To ensure that the other views are displayed at runtime, they must be part of a navigation. Chapter 16, Section 16.3.6 contains a practical example where we explain how to assign a view set to a window.

## 9.4    Controller and Context

Up until now, we have only briefly looked at the controller and context by explaining the view controller and view context in Sections 9.1.1 and 9.1.2. However, this does not in any way mean we have exhausted the potential of the controller and context. We still have to explain other concepts such as

*Context node binding and model integration*

context node binding and model integration (integrating the context into a data model) to get a full picture of a UI component's options. Because these concepts apply for all controller variants, we have decided to summarize them in this section. Where there are small differences, we will explicitly highlight them.

### 9.4.1 Component Controller

Central data store    The component controller is used as a central data store of a UI component instance and can be addressed by all objects within the UI component. Like all view controllers, the component controller has a context and, if necessary, model nodes or value nodes with attributes. There is exactly one component controller for every UI component. Context nodes of a component controller can be published in the component interface (see Section 9.6.2) and therefore made accessible in read and write mode for other UI components. When a UI component is embedded in another UI component, if necessary, the component controller transfers the data binding to the context of the embedded UI component (see Section 9.6.4). The component controller is created during the component instantiation and removed from the store again when the Web Client UI framework discards the instance of the UI component.

BSPWD
Component.do    The component controller is assigned the name BSPWDCOMPONENT.DO by default. To access an instance of a component controller, use the COMP_CON-TROLLER reference which, as an attribute, is a part of every controller implementation class.

### 9.4.2 Custom Controller

A custom controller is suitable for encapsulating different controller tasks and can be optionally assigned to a UI component by the application developer. Like the component controller, the custom controller is available as an additional central data store within a UI component. There can be several custom controllers within a UI component. Context nodes for a view can be linked to context nodes for a custom controller. This process is known as *context node binding*. We discuss the topic of context node binding in detail in Section 9.4.4. A custom controller is instantiated when the controller is accessed the first time. The instance of the custom controller can be discarded, if required. However, at the latest it will be removed from the store when the instance of the UI component is discarded.

Through the provision of the GET_CUSTOM_CONTROLLER method, each controller implementation class allows access to an instance of a custom controller.

Every custom controller will be globally available if you put the GLOBAL. prefix in front of the custom controller name when calling the GET_CUS-TOM_CONTROLLER method.

In addition to custom controllers in UI components, there are also global custom controllers that are instantiated when you start the application. You can define these controllers in the SAP Implementation Guide by following the IMG path CUSTOMER RELATIONSHIP MANAGEMENT • UI FRAMEWORK • UI FRAMEWORK Definition • MAINTAIN RUNTIME FRAMEWORK PROFILE.

*Global custom controller*

### 9.4.3 Context Nodes and Attributes

We have not yet explained how you can add context nodes and attributes to a context; we will do so now. Creating context nodes is supported by a wizard in the Component Workbench. You can create context nodes using the wizard for creating views or windows in the component structure browser or using a wizard by selecting the context in the controller in the detailed overview. We will explain the latter option in detail because we believe that this is the one used more often.

*Creating context nodes using the wizard*

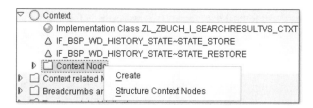

**Figure 9.15** Creating a Context Node in the Controller

You can start the wizard from the context menu of the CONTEXT NODE in the detailed overview in the context of a controller by selecting the CRE-ATE option. The wizard consists of a maximum of seven steps and must be worked through from start to finish. After you start the wizard, the first step provides you with brief information about the way it works. In the second step, you define the context node by selecting the context node type, including model nodes, value nodes, and nodes for storing dropdown box values. If you want to define a model node, you must also select an object from an object model (see Figure 9.16). Note that when naming the context node, you are not allowed to use any special characters such as underscores, for example.

*Starting the wizard*

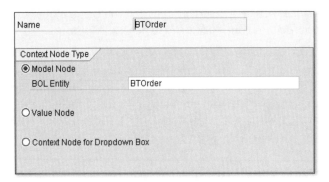

**Figure 9.16**  Wizard for Creating a Context Node

**Adding attributes**

In step three of the wizard, you can add attributes of a BOL entity to a model node. This gives you the advantage of being able to define the names of the attributes individually. If you do not add any attributes, the attributes of the BOL entity can nevertheless be addressed through the STRUCT virtual structure of the context node (see Section 9.1.2).

> **Note**
>
> The "Context Node for Dropdown Box" option (see Figure 9.16) is an obsolete construct. Implement the V getter method of a context node attribute instead (see Section 9.1.2).

**Model attributes**

Figure 9.17 shows an example of the BUILHEADER BOL entity that was selected as the BOL entity of the model node. The two attributes LASTNAME and FIRSTNAME were selected as model attributes. The LASTNAME attribute was changed to SURNAME in the wizard. After the wizard generates the context node, all attributes of the BOL entity with the exception of the SURNAME (❶) attribute are available via the STRUCT virtual structure. The SURNAME attribute does not contain a STRUCT. prefix, but does have its own getter and setter methods. However, these methods continue to reference the LASTNAME attribute of the BUILHEADER BOL entity.

Because of the selection of the FIRSTNAME (❸) model attribute, separate getter and setter methods were generated for this attribute.

The attribute can continue to be addressed with the STRUCT.FIRSTNAME name because the original name was not changed. All other attributes of the BOL entity (❷) can be addressed with the STRUCT. prefix but do not contain any separate getter and setter methods. However, you can generate them at any time in the Component Workbench (see Section 9.1.2).

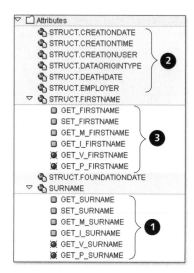

**Figure 9.17** STRUCT Virtual Structure and Getter and Setter Methods

If you previously selected a model node as your context node, attributes from other objects related to the selected object can also be included in the attribute selection. The name of the BOL attribute then consists of the subobjects in the object model and attribute name itself (see Figure 9.18).

| Model Attribute | Model Node | BOL Attribute |
|---|---|---|
| GUID | BTOrder | BTOrderHeader/GUID |
| OBJECT_ID | BTOrder | BTOrderHeader/OBJECT_ID |
| PROCESS_TYPE | BTOrder | BTOrderHeader/PROCESS_TYPE |
| POSTING_DATE | BTOrder | BTOrderHeader/POSTING_DATE |
| DESCRIPTION | BTOrder | BTOrderHeader/DESCRIPTION |

**Figure 9.18** Attribute Selection of a Model Node

In the fourth wizard step, you can add attributes to the value node. The attributes defined in this step are assigned a basic data type from the ABAP Dictionary (see Figure 9.19). The entries in this step are optional.

Adding value nodes

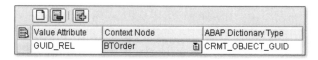

| Value Attribute | Context Node | ABAP Dictionary Type |
|---|---|---|
| GUID_REL | BTOrder | CRMT_OBJECT_GUID |

**Figure 9.19** Adding Value Attributes

Links to custom controller

The fifth step lets you define context node binding (see Section 9.4.4) to a custom controller. If you want to link the context node with a context node of the custom controller, you use input help to enter the name of the BSP application, the custom controller, and the context node of the custom controller. This step is necessary when you want to manage data across views in the context of the UI component. The entries in this step are optional.

Context node dependencies

In the sixth step, you can define dependencies to other higher-level context nodes (see Figure 9.20). This can be useful if an application should be informed that the user has selected another line in a table and BOL entities must therefore be updated in dependent context nodes (see Section 9.4.6).

**Figure 9.20**  Dependencies to Higher-Level Context Nodes

If you enable the ALWAYSCREATEINSTANCE option, additional statements are integrated when code is generated for the ON_NEW_FOCUS method of the implementation class of the dependent context node. This integration serves to create a BOL entity of the dependent context node automatically when the focus of the higher-level context node changes.

In the last wizard step, you are provided with an overview of the attributes you have created. You use the COMPLETE button to close the process for creating a context node.

> **Note**
>
> The procedure for creating context nodes with the wizard in the detailed overview also applies for all other controller variants such as the custom controller, window controller, and component controller.

The Web Client UI framework provides an abundance of ABAP classes for mapping context node types, which we have summarized in Table 9.3. The framework uses some of these ABAP classes when generating the implementation class. In areas where a wizard does not provide any support, you must manually access these ABAP classes. Let us take a look at the following example: A tree view (see Section 10.3) is based on context nodes of the CL_BSP_ WD_CONTEXT_NODE_TREE type. In the Web Client UI framework, you cannot create this type of context node with the wizard. You must therefore manually change the superclass of the implementation class of the context node from `CL_BSP_WD_CONTEXT_NODE` to `CL_BSP_WD_CONTEXT_NODE_TREE`.

| Context Node Type | Technical Mapping by ABAP Class |
|---|---|
| Model node | CL_BSP_WD_CONTEXT_NODE |
| Value node | CL_BSP_WD_CONTEXT_NODE |
| Table | CL_BSP_WD_CONTEXT_NODE_TV |
| Deep table | CL_BSP_WD_CONTEXT_NODE_DTV |
| Dropdown box | CL_BSP_WD_CONTEXT_NODE_DDLB |
| Tree structure | CL_BSP_WD_CONTEXT_NODE_TREE |
| Advanced search pages | CL_BSP_WD_CONTEXT_NODE_ASP |

**Table 9.3** Types of Context Nodes with Superclass

### Adding Context Attributes using a Wizard

When you first define a context node, you can add other model attributes to it. Select the ATTRIBUTES level of the corresponding context node in the detailed overview and choose the CREATE option from the context menu. A wizard guides you through a four-step creation process. In the second wizard step, you confirm the type of attribute. Only the MODEL ATTRIBUTE type is currently supported (see Figure 9.21).

Adding attributes

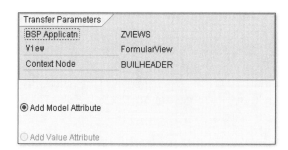

**Figure 9.21** Attribute Type Selection

In the third step, you define the name of the attribute and the origin of a BOL entity. The attribute does not have to belong to the defined BOL entity directly. You can also select an attribute of a BOL entity that can be accessed using relations (see Figure 9.22).

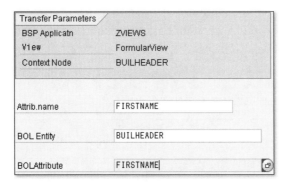

**Figure 9.22** Defining the Attribute Name

In the fourth and last step, you see a summary. To add the attribute to the context node, click the COMPLETE button.

### 9.4.4 Context Note Binding

Lifetime of a view

As already mentioned, the lifetime of a view is limited by its visibility and use. When you display a view, the view controller undertakes the instance creation of the context nodes. When the view is no longer visible, it is deactivated and the context is removed from the store again together with the context nodes. If you need to keep the values of a view context, you can bind context nodes of the view context to context nodes of custom controllers or component controllers.

Provided a context node binding was defined between two controllers, when a context node is changed, the data is automatically updated and "transported" into the bound context node.

> **Note**
>
> For the sake of completeness, we should mention that a "real" transport of data does not take place with context node binding because the framework internally works with type references and the context data is therefore only available once in the store.

If the view context is removed from the store, the data remains in the context of the other controller. Figure 9.23 schematically illustrates the context node binding (❶) between the view controller (❷) and the custom controller (❸).

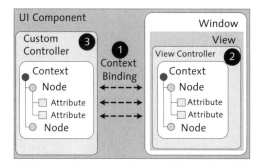

**Figure 9.23** Context Node Binding between Controllers

Context node binding between view controllers and custom controllers is not absolutely necessary but it is an option we recommend using. Because components generally do not consist of only one view, custom controllers are a useful structuring tool in a UI component. Direct context node binding between view controllers and component controllers is also possible but is not supported by a wizard.

**Custom controller as a structuring tool**

The prerequisite for successful context node binding is that the context nodes to be bound have the same attributes. You bind the context nodes of the view controller to the custom controller either using the wizard when you create a new view, window, or context node or manually by retrospectively inserting the code from Listing 9.1 into the CREATE method of the implementation class of the context:

```
owner->do_context_node_binding(
     iv_controller_type = cl_bsp_wd_controller=>co_type_
custom
     iv_name = '{NAME_CUSTOM_CONTROLLER}'
     iv_target_node_name = '{NAME_OF_TARGET_CONTEXT_NODE}'
     iv_node_2_bind = {NAME_OF_SOURCE_CONTEXT_NODE} ).
```

**Listing 9.1** Context Node Binding on Custom Controller

The name of the CREATE method is composed of the CREATE_ prefix and the name of the context node.

In addition to the context node binding of the view controller to the custom controller, you can also carry out context node binding from the view controller to the component controller. In this case, you use the cl_bsp_wd_controller=>co_type_component constant (see Listing 9.1).

An important aspect for context node binding is that the relationship between the controllers is always *directional*. This means that the view controller

**Directional relationship**

235

"knows" the custom controller or component controller and, conversely, custom controllers and component controllers do not have any direct relationship to the view controller.

Display in the Workbench In the Component Workbench, you can identify whether a context node is bound (see Figure 9.24). The node display shows a small black arrow (❶). Another lower-level node shows the binding to the controller (❷).

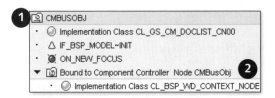

**Figure 9.24**  Displaying Context Node Binding in the Workbench

We will use a practical example in Chapter 16, Section 16.4.4 to explain context node binding to a component controller in detail.

### 9.4.5  Model Integration

So far, we have discussed that screen elements are bound to attributes of context nodes in a view context and how you can create context nodes and attributes. We also detailed concepts for context node binding. However, we have not yet answered one question: How does data arrive in the context for it to be output on the user interface? If you recall the Web Client architecture model from Chapter 8, Section 8.1, you will notice that the BOL is arranged under the presentation layer. You would then assume the following correctly: To provide model nodes with data, you can use elements from the BOL.

Collection wrapper A *collection wrapper* that refers to a BOL collection is assigned to each context node. With BOL entities, the BOL collection contains the actual data. The collection wrapper type is CL_BSP_WD_COLLECTION_WRAPPER and it implements the IF_BOL_BO_COL interface for accessing a collection.

> **Note**
>
> A *wrapper* is an implementation based on the adapter design pattern. The collection wrapper practically "wraps" the collection and provides indirect access to the entities of the collection through the *collection interface*.

To fill a context node with values, you must therefore transfer a collection with BOL entities to the corresponding collection wrapper. The implementation class of a context node has the SET_COLLECTION method, which expects a collection of the IF_BOL_BO_COL reference type as an import parameter and can be called to fill the context node with data.

Filling context nodes with values

A controller implementation class has an attribute called TYPED_CONTEXT that points to the context instance as the type reference and can be used for accessing context nodes.

**TYPED_CONTEXT**

You can use the following program statement to transfer a collection with BUILHEADER BOL entities to a context node called BUILHEADER:

```
...
DATA lr_collection TYPE REF TO cl_crm_bol_bo_col.
me->typed_context->builheader->set_collection( lr_collection ).
```

You also use the collection wrapper to determine the current BOL entity from the BUILHEADER context node, as shown in the following example:

Current BOL entity from context nodes

```
DATA lr_entity TYPE REF TO if_bol_bo_property_access.
lr_entity =
me->typed_context->builheader->collection_wrapper->get_
current( ).
```

Listing 9.2 illustrates how you can fill a context node based on the BUIL-HEADER BOL entity type with the result of a contact search.

```
DATA lv_dyn_query TYPE REF TO cl_crm_bol_dquery_service.
lv_dyn_query =
  cl_crm_bol_dquery_service=>get_instance(
'BuilHeaderAdvancedSearch' ).
  lv_dyn_query->set_property( iv_attr_name = 'MAX_HITS'
                              iv_value    = '100' ).
lv_dyn_query->add_selection_param(
   iv_attr_name = 'COUNTRY'
   iv_sign      = 'I'
   iv_option    = 'EQ'
   iv_low       = 'DE'
   iv_high      = '' ).
DATA lv_result TYPE REF TO if_bol_entity_col.
lv_result = lv_dyn_query->get_query_result( ).
typed_context->builheader->set_collection(
 lv_result ).
```

**Listing 9.2** Filling a Context Node with Search Results

> **Note**
>
> The framework instantiates the BOL core (see Chapter 13, Section 13.3) when the application is started. The GenIL component sets are loaded through the UI component.

The BuilHeader context node is provided with the first one hundred BOL entities found from the BuilHeaderAdvancedSearch search.

### 9.4.6 Dependent Model Nodes

In the following section, we will discuss in detail how dependent model nodes work. Dependent model nodes are used for displaying a 1:n object relation. When you create model nodes in the wizard, you can define hierarchies of model nodes (see Figure 9.25).

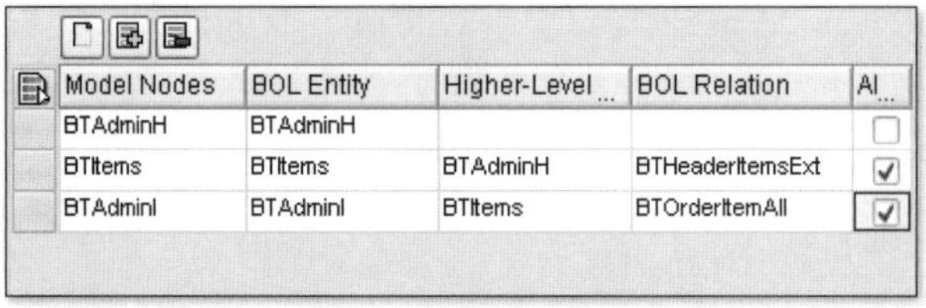

| Model Nodes | BOL Entity | Higher-Level... | BOL Relation | Al... |
|---|---|---|---|---|
| BTAdminH | BTAdminH | | | ☐ |
| BTItems | BTItems | BTAdminH | BTHeaderItemsExt | ☑ |
| BTAdminI | BTAdminI | BTItems | BTOrderItemAll | ☑ |

**Figure 9.25** Defining a Model Node Hierarchy

**ON_NEW_FOCUS supply function**

During the generation of model nodes, the ON_NEW_FOCUS supply function of a dependent model node is implemented with statements to determine the BOL entities of the dependent model node (based on the current BOL entity of the higher-level model node) as a collection at runtime and to assign them to the collection wrapper of the dependent model node.

The ON_NEW_FOCUS supply function is a type of event handler for the NEW_FOCUS collection wrapper event. If the focus of the collection of the leading context node changes (see Section 13.2), its collection wrapper sends the NEW_FOCUS event. The data of the dependent context node is therefore automatically adjusted through the event handler. You can also use this construct for updating the context structure automatically. To do so, trigger the NEW_FOCUS event explicitly by calling the PUBLISH_CURRENT method on the collection wrapper of the leading context node.

Figure 9.26 shows the hierarchical display of dependent context nodes in the detailed overview. To see this display in the Component Workbench, select the Context Node node in the detailed overview and choose the Structure Context Node option from the context menu.

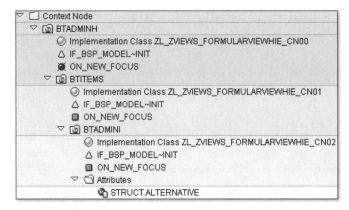

**Figure 9.26** Model Node Hierarchy in the Detailed Overview

## 9.5 Navigation

*Navigation* refers to the different ways a user can move in a CRM application. For the user, the result of navigation is a change in the screen display that can occur either by partially or fully changing views or windows. A view is always the starting point for navigation.

As you know, SAP CRM applications consist of different UI components that due to direct usage dependency interact among themselves or indirectly with one another based on the Customizing settings. We therefore need to separate two important aspects when describing navigation. Navigation can be described in the runtime repository using *plugs* (see Section 9.1.4) and *navigational links*. This procedure applies for view-to-view or window-to-window navigation, even if visual elements such as views and windows that are involved in the navigation are contained in different UI components. The prerequisite for this cross-component navigation with navigational links is that there is a usage dependency between the UI components. This *tight* coupling of UI components is based on definitions in the runtime repository.

**Aspects of navigation**

The second procedure is more flexible, that is, it concerns navigation between *loosely* coupled UI components that are not "known" among each other and therefore must provide interfaces for navigation based on settings in the SAP Implementation Guide (not on specifications in the runtime repository). As an example of this type of scenario, we can use a generic UI component that, due to its generic character, cannot know all targets of a navigation. Independent, loosely coupled UI components are also known as work area components.

**Loose and tight coupling of UI components**

> **Note**
>
> For the sake of completeness, we should mention that the specifications for navigating from independent, loosely coupled UI components are stored in the Customizing of the navigation bar and in the *repository for* work area components.

### 9.5.1 Navigating with Navigational Links

In this section, we will first look more closely at navigating with navigational links. To understand this, we recommend that you read Section 9.1.4, which explains how you create plugs and how they work in the Component Workbench.

Navigation path and navigational links

The navigation path for navigating from a source view to target views is uniquely defined by navigational links in the runtime repository editor because a plug does not formally "know" anything about a navigation. To add a navigational link in the runtime repository, you choose the ADD NAVIGATIONAL LINK option from the context menu on the NAVIGATIONAL LINKS level of the runtime repository editor (see Figure 9.27).

**Figure 9.27**   Adding a Navigational Link in the Runtime Repository

A navigational link is assigned a unique name when it is created. You should use a "descriptive" name that reflects the direction of the navigation. You can also specify the source view with its outbound plug and the target view with its inbound plug (see Figure 9.28).

DEFAULT plug

The inbound plug does not necessarily have to exist. If you do not specify an inbound plug when defining a navigational link, the DEFAULT inbound plug is used by default.

> **Note**
>
> You can add targets to an existing navigational link in the runtime repository editor.

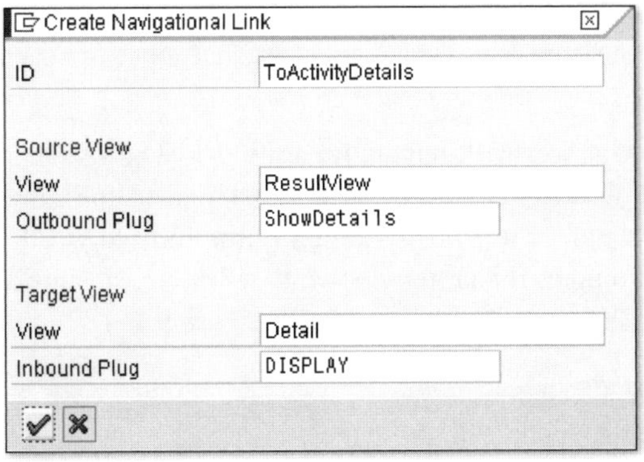

**Figure 9.28** Defining a Navigational Link

You can start the navigation from the view after you define a navigational link with the following `navigate` method call of the view manager:

```
view_manager->navigate(
source_rep_view  = rep_view
outbound_plug    = '{NAME_NAVIGATIONALLINK}' ).
```

**Listing 9.3** Starting a Navigation

<table>
<tr><td>Note</td></tr>
<tr><td>The parameter OUTBOUND_PLUG needs the name of the navigational link, not the name of the outbound plug, which you might incorrectly assume based on its name.</td></tr>
</table>

An empty method implementation is generated with every definition of an outbound plug. This empty implementation should be implemented completely by calling the `view_manager->navigate` method. Instead of then calling the `view_manager->navigate` method directly, you only need to call a method whose name derives from the `OP_` prefix and name of the outbound plug. The benefit of this procedure is that if the name of a navigational link should change, the `view_manager->navigate` call only has to be changed in one place.

*Implementing the outbound plug method*

The name of the navigational link is used in the method call for starting the navigation to ensure that the Web Client UI framework identifies to which target view it should navigate. Chapter 16, Section 16.5.2 contains a practical example for defining navigational links.

We will now look in more detail at different scenarios for simple navigation with navigational links to illustrate the special features that exist for each scenario.

**View-to-view navigation scenario**

The simplest scenario for navigation with navigational links is when navigation needs to be defined between two views that are assigned to the same window. For this scenario, you only need to create an outbound plug in the source view and an inbound plug in the target view and define a corresponding navigational link. This is illustrated schematically in Figure 9.29.

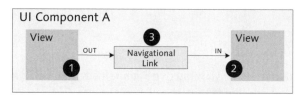

**Figure 9.29** View-to-View Navigation Scenario

The outbound plug (❶) is connected to the inbound plug (❷) through a navigational link (❸).

**Technical implementation of a view-to-view navigation**

What could a technical implementation of this type of scenario look like in practice? If we assume that navigation within a UI component should be started from a source view to a target view by clicking a button, a chain of events occurs during the execution, as illustrated schematically in Figure 9.30.

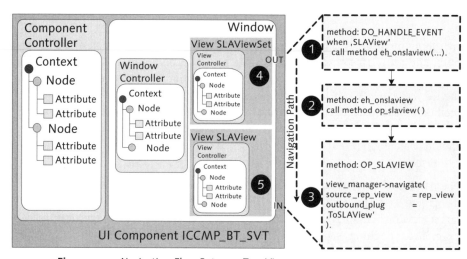

**Figure 9.30** Navigation Flow Between Two Views

> **Note**
>
> You can easily reproduce an implementation for this type of scenario in the standard SAP system using the ICCMP_BT_SVT UI component. The ToSLA-View navigational link is used in this UI component to navigate from the *SLAViewSet* view to the *SLAView* view. The navigation is called in the EH_ON-SLAVIEW event handler of the *SLAViewSet* view.

Screen elements such as buttons generate an event when you click them that is processed by the event handler of the controller. This event is first processed by the DO_HANDLE_EVENT (❶) method in the view controller and delegated to another event handler method, for example, EH_ONSLAVIEW (❷). This method then calls the method implementation (❸) of the outbound plug (❹) to start the navigation.

When the VIEW_MANAGER->NAVIGATE() method is called, the navigation starts asynchronously. The automatically generated method implementation of the inbound plug (❺) is called and the target view is displayed.

This scenario shows a navigation from a view in UI component A to an interface view of an embedded UI component B. The interface view of UI component B is handled like a regular view in component usage.

View-to-component navigation scenario

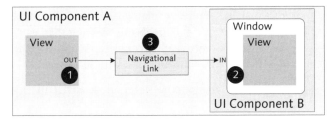

**Figure 9.31** View-to-Component Navigation Scenario

The scenario in Figure 9.32 illustrates a more complex option, with three UI components involved. When the outbound plug of the view (❶) for UI component B is called, the call is forwarded to the outbound plug of the window (❷) in UI component B. The outbound plug of the window is connected to an inbound plug of a window (❸) in UI component C through a navigational link (❹) in UI component A. The name of the navigational link (❹) in UI component A must match the name of the outbound plug of the window from UI component B. The outbound plug of the window from component B must be declared in the runtime repository of component B.

Component-to-component navigation scenario

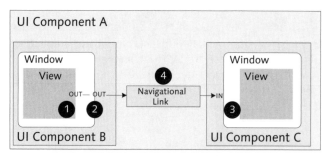

**Figure 9.32** Component-to-Component Navigation Scenario

The outbound plug of the view (❶) is forwarded to the outbound plug of the window (❷) by determining the window controller and CALL_OUTBOUND_PLUG method call, as shown in Listing 9.4:

```
data: lr_window type ref to cl_bsp_wd_window.
lr_window = me->view_manager->get_window_controller( ).
lr_window->call_outbound_plug( '{NAME_WINDOW_OUTB_PLUG}' ).
```

**Listing 9.4** Determining the Window Controller and Outbound Plug Call

### 9.5.2 Cross-Component Navigation

Cross-component navigation means navigation between components that have not defined an indirect usage dependency among each other. The control of cross-component navigation is based on mechanisms other than navigational links. However, the technical process of cross-component navigation does not differ from the process of navigating with navigational links.

Static and dynamic navigation

We differentiate between two variations for cross-component navigation:

▸ Static navigation

▸ Dynamic navigation

**Static Navigation**

Static navigation is based on settings in the repository for work area components in the SAP Implementation Guide and the generic outbound plug mapping in the Customizing of the navigation bar. The repository for work area components contains all available UI components of CRM applications including their inbound and outbound plugs, which are part of the component interface (see Section 9.6). You can open the repository for work area components through the IMG path CUSTOMER RELATIONSHIP MANAGEMENT • UI FRAMEWORK • TECHNICAL ROLE DEFINITION • DEFINE WORK AREA COM-

PONENT REPOSITORY. Each plug in the repository can be assigned to a combination of UI object types (see Chapter 5, Section 5.2.2) and UI object actions. You can choose between the DISPLAY, SEARCH, EDIT, CREATE, EXECUTE, and DELETE object actions (see Figure 9.33).

**Figure 9.33** Defining the Outbound Plug, Object Type, and Object Action

You can generically map an outbound plug to the navigation target in the DEFINE GENERIC OP MAPPING node after following the IMG path CUSTOMER RELATIONSHIP MANAGEMENT • UI FRAMEWORK • TECHNICAL ROLE DEFINITION • DEFINE NAVIGATION BAR PROFILE. The target ID of the target component from the repository for work area components is entered in the TARGET ID field.

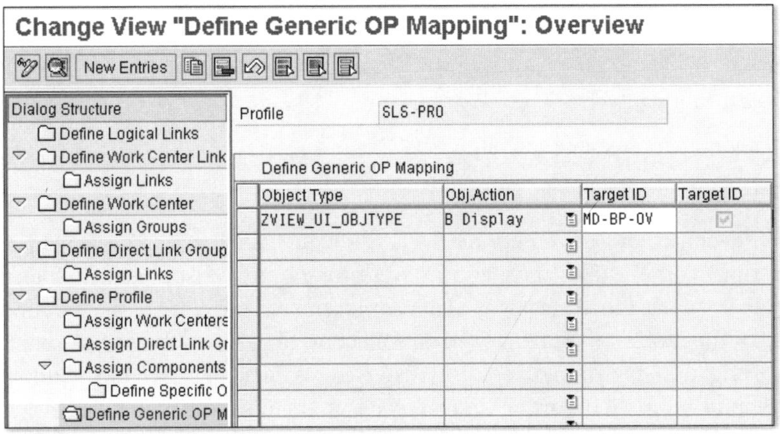

*Generically mapping an outbound plug*

**Figure 9.34** Defining Generic OP Mapping

The combination of outbound plug, UI object type, and object action describes the required navigation target more abstractly. It is used by CRM applications when a UI component currently being used in the work area of the application is exited through its outbound plugs. The result of this procedure is that all outbound plugs that use the same combination of UI object type and object action ultimately share the same navigation target. This mechanism guarantees consistent navigation across components.

### Dynamic Navigation

**Navigation descriptor object**

Dynamic navigation occurs using a *navigation descriptor object* and is very useful for generic UI components that cannot know their navigation target due to their generic character. The navigation descriptor object contains information to uniquely determine a navigation target. This could be the UI object type or a business object (as a BOL entity or BOR object) that should be processed. The object action describes what you have to do (display, edit, search, etc.) and is always part of the navigation descriptor object.

A navigation descriptor object enables you to navigate dynamically from an outbound plug to different targets. The information a navigation descriptor object contains is converted into a combination of UI object type and object action that in turn can be used to determine the navigation target. Table 9.4 lists the elements a navigation descriptor object can provide.

| Element |
|---|
| UI object type |
| Object action |
| Object (optional) |
| UI component name (optional) |

**Table 9.4**  Elements of a Descriptor Object

The developer of a UI component is responsible for creating a navigation descriptor object. This navigation descriptor object can be used to check whether a navigation target is available, or it can be transferred to the inbound plug of the target component via data collection to perform the navigation. If the navigation descriptor object is transferred via data collection to a window outbound plug, the information conveyed by the descriptor object is evaluated to determine the navigation target. If the contained information allows and requires a new instance of a BOL entity to be generated, this instance is transferred to the data collection and the navigation descriptor object is removed from the data collection. In this case, the navigation would run exactly as if a direct navigation had taken place with outbound and inbound plugs and navigational links.

To create a navigation descriptor object at runtime, you call one of the methods of the `CL_CRM_UI_DESCRIPTOR_OBJ_SRV` class:

► CREATE_BOR_BASED

► CREATE_ENTITY_BASED

► CREATE_UI_OBJECT_BASED

► CREATE_ADVANCED_SEARCH_BASED

Creating a navigation descriptor object at runtime

Listing 9.5 shows how a navigation descriptor object is created to be transferred to a `DEFAULT` outbound plug of the window controller for starting a navigation:

```
DATA lr_descrip_obj TYPE REF TO if_bol_bo_property_access.
DATA lr_nav_srv TYPE REF TO if_crm_ui_navigation_service.
DATA lr_window_controller TYPE REF TO cl_bsp_wd_window.
DATA lr_data_collection TYPE REF TO if_bol_bo_col.
call method
cl_crm_ui_descriptor_obj_srv=>create_entity_based
  EXPORTING
  ir_entity        = lr_entity
iv_ui_object_type   = space                            iv_ui_
object_action = if_crm_ui_descriptor_object=>gc_action_display
  iv_component         = '{MY_COMPONENT_NAME}'
  RECEIVING
    rr_result          = lr_descrip_obj.
lr_nav_srv = cl_crm_ui_navigation_service=>get_instance(
  me ).
IF lr_nav_srv->is_dynamic_nav_supported( ir_descriptor_
object = lr_descrip_obj ) EQ abap_true.
  CREATE OBJECT lr_data_collection TYPE cl_crm_bol_bo_col.
  lr_data_collection->add( iv_entity = lr_descrip_obj ).
  lr_window_controller =
  me->view_manager- >get_window_controller( ).
  lr_window_controller->call_outbound_plug(
    iv_outbound_plug = 'DEFAULT'
    iv_data_collection = lr_data_collection ).
ENDIF.
```

**Listing 9.5** Navigation with the Navigation Descriptor Object

The LR_ENTITY variable is a type reference of the CL_CRM_BOL_ENTITY class and represents a BOL entity of an unknown object, to whose UI component the navigation should take the user for viewing.

## 9.6 Component Interface

In Chapter 8, Section 8.1.4, we established that a UI component represents an independent, reusable unit and exposes an interface externally. A UI component is similar to a *blackbox implementation*; the user of a UI component is not interested in how the UI component is structured internally or how it works. Only the *elements* a UI component exposes are of interest. The elements that can publish a UI component are context nodes, interface views (windows), and events (see Figure 9.35). As a user of a UI component, only one other UI component is considered. To use the UI component, the user must create a usage dependency to the component and thereby almost literally embed the UI component (see Section 9.6.4).

**Publishing context nodes**  Publishing context nodes allows users to access UI component data in read and write mode. Publishing a window as an interface view enables the embedding UI component to use visual parts of an embedded UI component. Finally, UI component events enable other UI components to be informed about a status change.

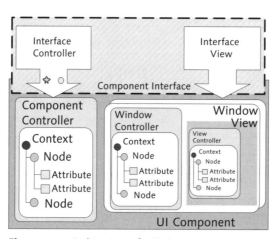

**Figure 9.35**  Architecture of a UI Component

**Interface controller**  These elements are provided declaratively by the *interface controller*, which was implemented as a virtual concept and facilitates technical access to a UI component using a usage object. Like the component controller, the interface controller is only available once for each UI component and can only be displayed externally as a single controller type of a UI component. A usage object is only instantiated at runtime if the UI component is embedded and used in another UI component.

You define the public interface of a component in the runtime repository editor by assigning existing elements of a UI component to the interface controller.

## 9.6.1 Interface View

You can declare each window of a UI component as an interface view by selecting the COMPONENTINTERFACE node in the runtime repository editor and starting the ADD INTERFACE VIEW option in the context menu (see Figure 9.36).

*Declaring a window as an interface view*

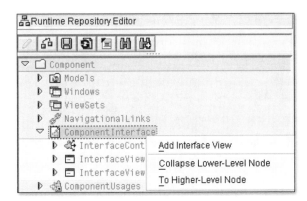

**Figure 9.36** Adding an Interface View

When you call the value help in the dialog that appears, you get a list of possible UI component windows that you can assign to the interface controller. Choose a window and complete the creation process. After you create the interface view, you will find another entry in the COMPONENTINTERFACE node in the runtime repository that contains two subnodes, INBOUNDPLUGS and OUTBOUNDPLUGS. Complete the interface view by creating the declaration of existing plugs through the context menu. Section 16.6.2 contains a practical example for declaring an interface view.

## 9.6.2 Context

Context nodes that are defined in the component controller and should be published must be explicitly assigned to the interface controller—these con-

*Publishing context nodes*

249

text nodes can be model nodes as well as value nodes. You assign a context node to the interface controller in the runtime repository editor by selecting the CONTEXT node and starting the ADD CONTEXT NODE option in the context menu. In the dialog that appears, choose the context node from the selection list and confirm your selection by pressing the ⌷Enter⌷ key (see Figure 9.37)

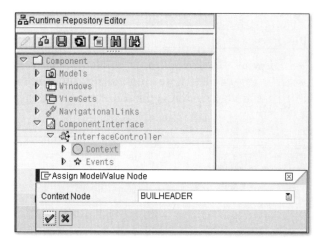

**Figure 9.37**  Adding a Context Node to the Interface Controller

In Section 9.6.4, we will explain how you can access context nodes of an embedded UI component.

### 9.6.3  Events

Component events

To conclude, we will introduce you to events for UI components. UI components can send events to inform other UI components about a status change. Alternatively, they can subscribe events to other UI components to respond to status changes for these UI components. You define events in the interface controller at the COMPONENT INTERFACE level in the runtime repository editor (see Figure 9.38).

Sending a component event

To send defined events in the component interface, you must call the RAISE_ COMPONENT_EVENT method of the component controller of the sending UI component using the name of the defined event. We describe registering for an event at the end of Section 9.6.4.

250

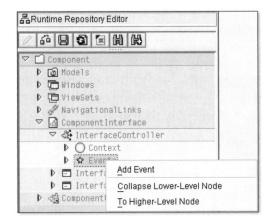

**Figure 9.38**  Events in the Interface Controller

## 9.6.4  UI Component Usage

After having discussed the interface of a UI component, we will now cover the usage of UI components. The advantage of reusing a UI component is clear—a UI component that maps a function such as a *customer search*, for example, has to be developed only once and can then be used within an application as often as desired. As a prerequisite, this UI component must have a component interface.

To use a UI component, you must first define component usage. You do this in the Component Workbench in the runtime repository editor by starting the ADD COMPONENT USAGE option from the context menu in the COMPONENTUSAGE node (see Figure 9.39).

Defining component usage

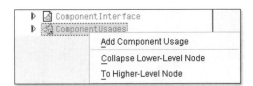

**Figure 9.39**  Adding Component Usage

In the dialog that appears, you assign an ID that uniquely identifies the usage and select the UI component with its interface view. After you define the component usage, you can add other interface views into the runtime repository.

Referring to
existing
component usage Another option is to refer to an already existing component usage during the creation process (see Figure 9.40). When you use a referenced component usage, no new component instance is loaded; instead, the component usage of the referenced instance is reused. In Figure 9.40, we also show the definition of the component usage of the GS_JOBMONITOR UI component. This is a standard SAP UI component that enables you to display and create jobs, similar to the way you can accomplish this in the SAP GUI in Transaction SM37.

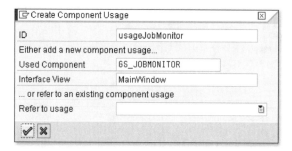

**Figure 9.40**  Defining Component Usage

After you have successfully created the USAGEJOBMONITOR component usage, it is displayed in the COMPONENTUSAGES node in the runtime repository with details of the ID, COMPONENT NAME, and INTERFACE VIEW. You can navigate forward to embedded UI components from the runtime repository (see Figure 9.41).

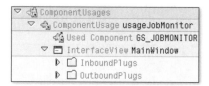

**Figure 9.41**  Component Usage in the Runtime Repository

Although we have now defined component usage, we have not yet used any element of an embedded UI component. As you know, you can use interface views, events, and public context nodes of a UI component.

### Using an Interface View

Creating an
interface view You can assign view sets or windows to an interface view as you would do for a normal view. You will know by the view name whether the view is a normal

UI component view or an interface view. Interface views have the ID of the component usage definition in the name as a prefix (see Figure 9.42).

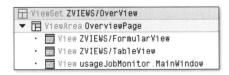

**Figure 9.42** Assigned Interface View of an Overview Page

As is also the case for normal views, an interface view may only be assigned to a window or view set once. However, you can assign an interface view several times if it is based on referenced component usage in the runtime repository.

*Assigning an interface view in the runtime repository*

## Data Exchange via Context Node Binding

You can exchange data between UI components using context nodes of the interface controller of the embedded UI component and context nodes of the component controller or custom controller of the embedding UI component. To do so, you need to set up context node binding between both context nodes. For this purpose, you implement the WD_USAGE_INITIALIZE method in the component controller of the embedding UI component. Listing 9.6 shows an example of a context node binding of two context nodes called JOBS.

*Data exchange via context node binding*

```
CASE iv_usage->usage_name.
WHEN 'usageJobMonitor'.
  iv_usage->bind_context_node
    exporting
      iv_controller_type  =
      cl_bsp_wd_controller=>co_type_component
      iv_target_node_name = 'JOBS'
      iv_node_2_bind      = 'JOBS'.
ENDCASE.
```

**Listing 9.6** Interface Controller to Component Controller Context Node Binding

The name of the component usage is analyzed in the CASE statement in Listing 9.6.

The prerequisite for context node binding is that the controller of the embedding UI component has the same type of context nodes as the interface controller of the embedded UI component.

GET_CONTEXT_
NODE method

Alternatively, the usage object (IV_USAGE parameter) provided by the WD_ USAGE_INITIALIZE method enables you to access public context nodes of an embedded UI component using the GET_CONTEXT_NODE method. You always get a usage object reference by calling the GET_COMPONENT_USAGE method of the component controller.

## Registering for a Component Event

Registering for a
component event

You must apply somewhat more effort for a UI component that wants to register for an event of another UI component. First, you must add an event handler interface called IF_BSP_WD_EVENT_HANDLER to the class implementation of the component controller. Then, you must call the SUBSCRIBE_EVENT method of the access interface for component usages in the WD_USAGE_INITIALIZE method. An implementation could look like the one shown in Listing 9.7.

```
CASE iv_usage->usage_name.
  WHEN '{USAGE_ID}'.
    iv_usage->subscribe_event(
    iv_event_name =  '{EVENT_OF_SENDING_COMPONENT}'
        iv_handler    = me ).
ENDCASE.
```

**Listing 9.7** Calling the "SUBSCRIBE_EVENT" Method

SUBSCRIBE_
EVENT
HANDLE_EVENT

When you call the SUBSCRIBE_EVENT method, you first define which event should be subscribed. At the same time, you also specify the event handler that should process the event accordingly (in our example in Listing 9.7, the (me) event handler is the implementation class of the component controller). The IF_BSP_WD_EVENT_HANDLER event handler interface makes an additional HANDLE_EVENT method available to the component controller where you can catch and handle the event accordingly.

## Delegating Outbound Plugs of Embedded UI Components

You can delegate an outbound plug of an embedded UI component to an outbound plug of an embedding UI component to enable navigation from the embedded UI component. To do so, you select an outbound plug of an interface view in the runtime repository editor of the "parent component" and select the DELEGATE TO WINDOW OUTBOUND PLUG option from the context menu. In the dialog, you select the window outbound plug of the embedding UI component to which you want to delegate and confirm this by pressing the ⟨Enter⟩ key. You can only delegate to outbound plugs of windows that use the interface view.

*Configurable views and pages are the central pillars of the Web Client UI framework; they ensure that the Web Client becomes a user-friendly user interface. This chapter describes the characteristics of the different view types and pages and their creation.*

# 10 Creating Configurable Views and Pages

After having discussed the visual elements of a UI component in detail, this chapter covers the different view variants of the Web Client UI framework. Views are divided into two categories. The first contains all view variants that are directly used to map business data. This includes form views, views to map tables (table views), and views to map tree structures (tree view). Sections 10.1 to 10.3 focus on these view variants.

*View variants*

The second category comprises all page types that are responsible for the arrangement of the first category's views, have the character of a main page, and do not use business data directly. This includes search pages, overview pages, and work center pages. Sections 10.4, 10.5 and 10.6 discuss these page types.

## 10.1 Form View

Form views are used primarily to enter data in the Internet browser. Figure 10.1 shows an excerpt of the CONTACTDETAILS form view of the BP_CONT UI COMPONENT. As you can see, the form view consists of a heading (❶), field labels (❷), and input fields (❸). Some input fields are additionally provided with an input help (❻) or displayed as a dropdown box (❹). At runtime, required entry fields are indicated by a red asterisk to the right of the field label (❺).

*Data entry in the Internet browser*

The field selection for a form view depends on the attributes of the context nodes in the view context of the form view. You can arrange the fields using the UI Configuration Tool. At design time, you can define input fields as required entry fields or display fields in the UI Configuration Tool.

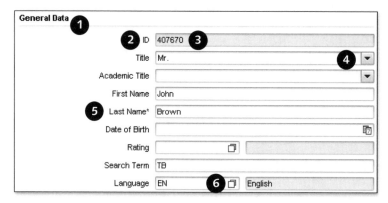

**Figure 10.1** Form View "ContactDetail" (Excerpt)

You can create form views in the component structure browser of the Component Workbench by selecting the VIEWS level and triggering the CREATE action from the context menu (❶ in Figure 10.2).

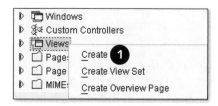

**Figure 10.2** Creating a View in the Component Structure Browser

Selecting CREATE from the context menu opens a wizard for creating a view in a new window. The wizard guides you through a nine-level entry process for the definition of the view. During this process, you specify the name of the view, define model nodes or value nodes for the view context, and enter the view type. You have to define the context node because context nodes are the field selection for the UI Configuration Tool. You can add context nodes at any time.

For a configurable form view, select the EMPTY VIEW view type and complete the wizard to have the system generate the view.

**Note**

The FORM VIEW generates a static form view with buttons only.

256

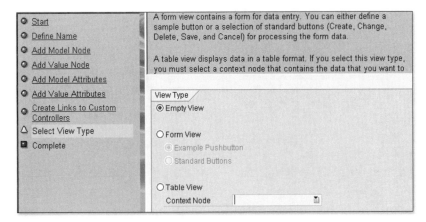

**Figure 10.3** Wizard for Creating a View

In the detailed overview of the view, you edit the content of the BSP page and replace the default coding of the BSP page with Listing 10.1 to activate the UI Configuration Tool for the form view.

*Modifying the BSP page*

```
<%@page language="abap" %>
<%@extension name="chtmlb" prefix="chtmlb" %>
<chtmlb:config xml  = "<%=
controller->configuration_descr->get_config_data( )
%>"
mode = "RUNTIME" />
```

**Listing 10.1** Activating the UI Configuration Tool for the Form View

> **Note**
>
> The `chtmlb:config` tag provides additional attributes. For space reasons, only the mandatory attributes are discussed here.

After having successfully activated the BSP page, navigate to the UI Configuration Tool and create a new default configuration using the NEW CONFIGURATION button.

When the configuration has been generated, you edit the layout of the view by moving the fields from the field list (❶ in Figure 10.4) to the panels (❷) and setting field properties (❸) such as the field position or text for field labels.

*Layout processing*

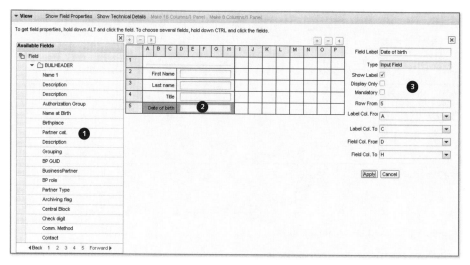

**Figure 10.4**  UI Configuration Tool for the Form View

Save the layout definition in the configuration using the SAVE button.

## 10.2    Table View

The main purpose of table views is the presentation of a wealth of information as a table. For example, table views are often used in CRM applications to display search results or as views for assignment blocks in overview pages. Figure 10.5 shows the MAINSEARCHRESULT table view from the user perspective. It displays the business partners search result of the BP_HEAD_SEARCH UI component.

| ID | Name | Phone | Street | City | Region | Country |
|---|---|---|---|---|---|---|
| 408658 | Brian Brown | | | | | |
| 404810 | Helen Brown | +44 (7808) 575-190 | | Feltham | | Great Britain |
| 407991 | IRVING BROWN | | ERIC CHANDLER H... | NEW BRUNSWICK | New Jersey | United States |
| 406411 | James Brown | | 8744 Twin Oaks A... | DALLAS | Texas | United States |
| 407143 | Jane Brown | | 607 S FIGUEROA ST | LOS ANGELES | | United States |
| 405338 | Jennifer Brown | +44 (7808) 575-718 | | Harlow | | Great Britain |
| 413385 | John Brown | | | | | |
| 135 | John Brown | | | | | |
| 407670 | John Brown | | | PHOENIX | Arizona | United States |

**Figure 10.5**  Table View "MainSearchResult"

**Structure of a table view**

The structure of a table view is organized in columns (❶) and rows (❷). Depending on the setting of the table tag, you can select individual or multiple table rows. If the presentation result exceeds a configurable size, it is divided into pages. The navigation bar (❸) then enables you to navigate to the other pages. You can also provide actions (❹) for a table view. Actions are buttons that, when clicked, send a result that can be caught and processed with event handlers.

You define a table view the same way as a form view (see Section 10.1). In the second to last step of the wizard, select TABLE VIEW instead of EMPTY VIEW (see Figure 10.3). In the dropdown box, select a context node whose attributes are the columns of the table.

Definition of a table view

In the detailed overview of the view, switch to change mode and replace the default coding of the BSP page with the statements from Listing 10.2 to activate the UI Configuration Tool for the table view. This is necessary because the presentation of a table is technically implemented via the CHTMLB:configCellerator tag.

```abap
<%@page language="abap" %>
<%@extension name="chtmlb" prefix="chtmlb" %>
<chtmlb:configCellerator
    id          = "Table"
    table       = "//<CONTEXT NODE>/Table"
    width       = "100 %" />
```

**Listing 10.2** Activating the UI Configuration Tool for the Table View

To link the table to the context, you must link the table attribute of the configCellerator tag with the name of the context node. In the BSP page of the view, replace the <CONTEXT NODE> placeholder with the name of the corresponding context node or page attribute.

Linking the table to the context

In the detailed overview of the generated view, the context node for the table has specific characteristics. The implementation class of the context node can be derived from the _BSP_WD_CONTEXT_NODE_TV class. Additionally, the GET_TABLE_LINE_SAMPLE method is generated. This method provides the columns that should be displayed as a result (see Figure 10.6). The column list is still based on the attributes of the context node that is linked to the CHTMLB:configCellerator tag.

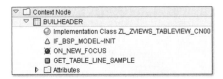

**Figure 10.6** Table Context Node Using BUILHEADER as an Example

Configuring the table view

After the BSP page has been successfully activated, you must create a new default configuration in the UI Configuration Tool and configure the table view by moving fields from the AVAILABLE FIELDS area to the DISPLAYED FIELDS area.

You have now created and configured a table view. Chapter 9, Section 9.4.5 describes how you can populate a table or context of a table with data. Chapter 16, Section 16.3.4 provides a practical example of creating a table view.

### 10.2.1 Buttons

At the beginning of this section, you learned that you can also provide buttons (actions) for a table view in the header area of the table. This is possible because the CHTMLB:configCellerator composite tag provides the ACTIONS attribute for linking a description table of THTMLB buttons. The description table corresponds to the CRMT_THTMLB_BUTTON_T type.

Inserting the "Save" button

For example, to insert the Save button (including an icon) in the header area of a table, add the following entry to the statements in the BSP page:

```
actions= "<%= controller >gt_buttons %>".
```

Add a new public attribute of type CRMT_THTMLB_BUTTON_T to the view controller. In the DO_PREPARE_OUTPUT method of the view controller, insert a new element in the gt_buttons attribute. The statements in Listing 10.3 illustrate this process.

```
DATA ls_button TYPE crmt_thtmlb_button.
clear gt_buttons.
ls_button-type      = cl_thtmlb_util=>gc_icon_save.
ls_button-enabled = abap_true.
ls_button-on_click = '{CLICK_EVENT}'.
append ls_button to gt_buttons.
```

**Listing 10.3**  Adding a Button

**Figure 10.7**  "Save" Button in the Header Area of a Table

Figure 10.7 shows the SAVE button (❶), including the floppy disk icon, in the header area of a table. To be able to respond to the event that has been triggered via the button, you must also generate an event handler for the

{CLICK_EVENT} event in the view controller (for more information, see Chapter 9, Section 9.1.3).

### 10.2.2   One-Click Actions (OCAs)

In addition to the integration of buttons in the header area of a table, you can integrate what are called *one-click actions* (OCAs) in a separate ACTIONS column (❶ in Figure 10.8). OCAs execute an action for an object that is mapped in a table on the overview page.

**Figure 10.8**   OCA in a Table Row

There is no wizard that supports creating OCAs in tables. Therefore, you have to perform the steps to create OCAs manually, as follows:

Creating OCAs in tables

- Extending the GET_TABLE_LINE_SAMPLE method
- Creating the GET_THTMLB_OCA and GET_P_THTMLB_OCA getter methods
- Activating the new column ACTIONS in the Configuration Tool
- Redefining the GET_OCA_T_TABLE method
- Creating the event handler for the OCA

The first step in implementing an OCA is to add the CRM_THTMLB_ONE_CLICK_ ACTION type to the type declaration in the GET_TABLE_LINE_SAMPLE method of the table context node's implementation class—as shown in Listing 10.4 with the structure of the BuilHeader GenIL object as an example:

Extending the type declaration

```
method get_table_line_sample.

  types: begin of line,
    thtmlb_oca type crm_thtmlb_one_click_action.
  include type crmst_header_object_buil.
  types:
        end of line.
  create data rv_sample type line.
endmethod.
```

**Listing 10.4**   Extending the Type Declaration for OCA

Next, you create the GET_THTMLB_OCA method in the implementation class of the table context node by copying an existing getter method and renaming

it accordingly or by creating the method manually. In both cases, the GET_
THTMLB_OCA method requires the signature that is shown in Figure 10.9.

The method is required to display the ACTIONS column in the table but does
not contain any statements.

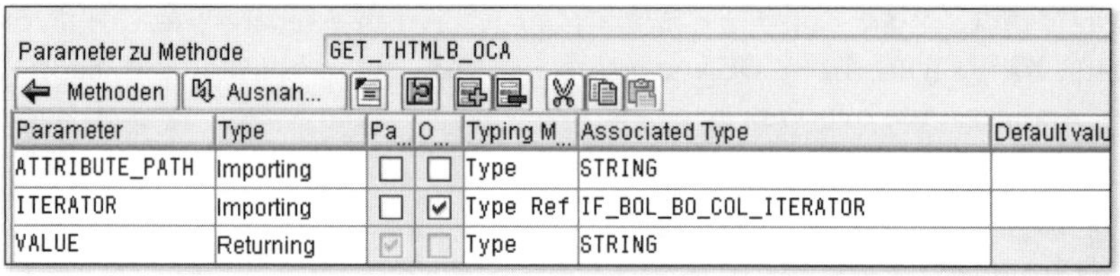

| Parameter zu Methode | | GET_THTMLB_OCA | | | | | |
|---|---|---|---|---|---|---|---|
| ← Methoden | Ⓐ Ausnah... | | | | | | |
| Parameter | Type | Pa | O | Typing M | Associated Type | | Default valu |
| ATTRIBUTE_PATH | Importing | ☐ | ☐ | Type | STRING | | |
| ITERATOR | Importing | ☐ | ☑ | Type Ref | IF_BOL_BO_COL_ITERATOR | | |
| VALUE | Returning | ☑ | ☐ | Type | STRING | | |

**Figure 10.9**  Signature of Method GET_THTMLB_OCA

Now, create the GET_P_THTMLB_OCA method in the implementation class of
the table context node by copying the _GET_P_XYZ template method. Insert
the statements in the method as shown in Listing 10.5.

```
method get_p_thtmlb_oca.
  case iv_property.
    when if_bsp_wd_model_setter_getter=>fp_fieldtype.
      rv_value = cl_bsp_dlc_view_descriptor=>field_type_oca.
    when if_bsp_wd_model_setter_getter=>fp_onclick.
      rv_value = 'OCA_CLICK'.
  endcase.
endmethod.
```

**Listing 10.5**  Statements for Method GET_P_THTMLB_OCA

The GET_P_THTMLB_OCA method confirms the field type and the event handler
for the Web Client UI framework.

Then, navigate to the Configuration Tool and move the [THTMLB_OCA] column from the AVAILABLE FIELDS column list to the DISPLAYED FIELDS area.
Save your settings.

In the implementation class of the table context node, redefine the GET_
OCA_T_TABLE method, which is part of the generic table view context. To
display an OCA for deleting an object, insert the statements from Listing 10.6
into the GET_OCA_T_TABLE method.

```
method get_oca_t_table.
data:
ls_one_click_action type crmt_thtmlb_one_click_action.
clear ls_one_click_action.
ls_one_click_action-id = 'DELETE'.
```

```
ls_one_click_action-icon = 'delete.gif'.
ls_one_click_action-text = 'Delete'.
ls_one_click_action-active = 'X'.
append ls_one_click_action to rt_actions.
endmethod.
```

**Listing 10.6**   Statements for Method GET_OCA_T_TABLE

When you reach this point, the OCA is displayed in the table's ACTIONS column. However, what is still missing is the event handler to catch the OCA_ CLICK event and trigger a function. To proceed, create a new event handler in the Component Workbench. In the wizard, enter "oca_click" in the EVENT NAME field. When the event handler has been generated, you can evaluate the row index and name of the OCA in the EH_ONOCA_CLICK method. Listing 10.7 illustrates a sample implementation.

```
method eh_onoca_click.
  data:
      lv_event type string,
      lv_index type string,
      lv_row_index type i.
  split htmlb_event_ex->event_defined at '.' into
lv_event lv_index.
  lv_row_index = lv_index.
endmethod.
```

**Listing 10.7**   Row Index of the OCA and Event Name

## 10.3   Tree View

A tree view serves to map information as hierarchical nodes (see Figure 10.10) and it inherits its appearance from the table view. It is structured in columns (❶) and nodes, which are displayed as rows (❷ and ❸).

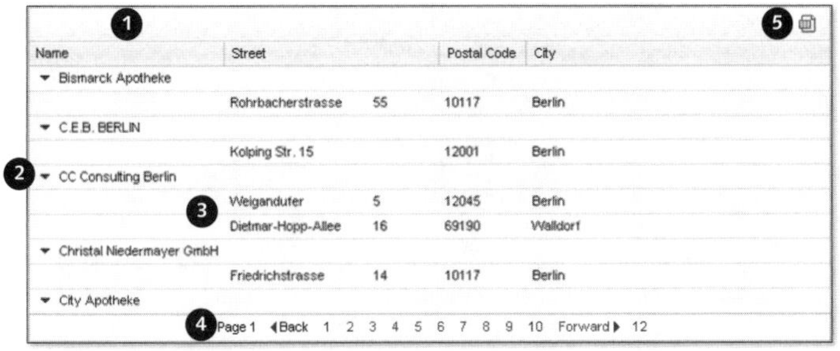

**Figure 10.10**   Tree View

If the presentation result exceeds the configurable size, it is divided into pages and the navigation bar (❹) lets you navigate to the other pages. You can also use additional functions such as exporting mapped data to Microsoft Excel (❺).

Manual creation required

Strictly speaking, a tree view is not a specific view type. Instead, only the CHTMLB:configTree tag is used in the BSP page of the tree view. There is no wizard that supports creating a tree view. Consequently, multiple manual steps are necessary to create the view. A tree view should be based on a table view; therefore, you must first generate (see Section 10.2) and adapt a table view.

One proxy class for each nesting level

At design time, you have to manually implement a proxy class for each tree view nesting level. At runtime, every tree view node corresponds to an instance of a proxy class.

> **Note**
>
> If you do not know the nesting depth, you can use recursive implementation technology. As a result, you do not have to implement a proxy class for each nesting depth. The GSMCTREE UI component can be used as a sample implementation for this.

Figure 10.11 shows the context of the tree structure from Figure 10.10 in the detailed overview of the Component Workbench.

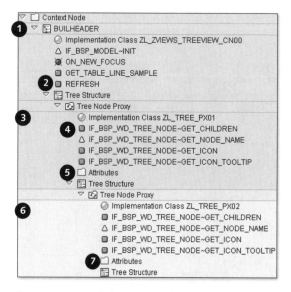

**Figure 10.11** Detailed Overview of a Tree Structure

The implementation class of the context node (❶) inherits from the CL_BSP_WD_CONTEXT_NODE_TREE class instead of the CL_BSP_WD_CONTEXT_NODE_TV class. As a result, two additional methods, GET_TABLE_LINE_SAMPLE and REFRESH, are provided as a result of the inheritance, which have to be redefined and implemented.

The GET_TABLE_LINE_SAMPLE method provides a structure as the result. The components of the structure represent the configurable columns of the tree structure presentation.

Method GET_TABLE_LINE_SAMPLE

The REFRESH method generates the instances of a proxy class (see the ZL_TREE_PX01 proxy class in Listing 10.8) as nodes of the first nesting depth using the CL_BSP_WD_TREE_NODE_FACTORY factory class. Listing 10.8 illustrates a sample implementation of the REFRESH method.

Method REFRESH

```
...
try.
    lr_iterator = me->collection_wrapper->get_iterator( ).
    lr_entity ?= lr_iterator->get_first( ).
    while lr_entity is bound.
        lr_root = me->node_factory->get_proxy(
                iv_bo        = lr_entity
                iv_proxy_type = 'ZL_TREE_PX01' ).
        lr_root->node_key = add_root_node( lr_root ).
        lr_root->expand_node( ).
      lr_entity ?= lr_iterator->get_next( ).
    endwhile.
  catch cx_sy_move_cast_error cx_sy_ref_is_initial.
endtry.
...
```

**Listing 10.8** Creating a Tree Node Using the Factory Method

A proxy class (❸ and ❻) inherits from the abstract class, CL_BSP_WD_TREE_ NODE_PROXY. It is therefore necessary to redefine and implement the GET_ CHILDREN method (❹).

**Method GET_ CHILDREN**

The GET_CHILDREN method of a proxy class creates the nodes of the subordinate nesting level in the tree structure at runtime by providing an internal table of tree node references as a result. Listing 10.9 illustrates a sample implementation of the GET_CHILDREN method.

```
...
try.
  lr_entity ?= me->bo.
  lr_coll ?= lr_entity->get_related_entities( iv_relation_
name = 'BuilAddressRel' ).
  lr_entity ?= lr_coll->get_first( ).
   while lr_entity is bound.
     lr_child = me->node_factory->get_proxy(
         iv_bo          = lr_entity
         iv_proxy_type   = 'ZL_TREE_PX02'
         iv_parent_proxy = me ).
       append lr_child to rt_children.
       lr_child->expand_node( ).
       lr_entity ?= lr_coll->get_next( ).
   endwhile.
  catch cx_sy_move_cast_error cx_sy_ref_is_initial.
endtry.
...
```

**Listing 10.9** Sample Implementation of Method GET_CHILDREN

**Creating attributes manually**

The context node delegates the call of the getter and setter methods to the proxy classes (❸ and ❼) at runtime. A proxy class must thus implement the components from the GET_TABLE_LINE_SAMPLE method as attributes. In this case, you cannot use the wizard to create the attribute. Instead, you have to create it manually by copying the _GET_XYZ and _SET_XYZ template methods of the proxy class and creating them with a new name in the proxy class. The name of the getter method must correspond to the GET_{ATTRIBUTE NAME} pattern.

You enable the development of the tree structure by calling the BUILD_TABLE method of the context node (❶) in the DO_PREPARE_OUTPUT method of the view controller (see Listing 10.10).

```
if typed_context->builheader->node_tab is initial.
  typed_context->builheader->refresh( ).
```

```
endif.
typed_context->builheader->build_table( ).
```

**Listing 10.10** Sample Implementation of Method DO_PREPARE_OUTPUT

The BSP page has to use the `CHTMLB:configTree` composite tag to display the configurable tree structure. A minimum requirement is that the mandatory attributes of the tag—`id`, `nodeTable`, and `table`—are supplied (see Listing 10.11).

```
<%@page language="abap" %>
<%@extension name="chtmlb" prefix="chtmlb" %>
<chtmlb:configTree id = "ConfigTree"
  nodeTable          = "<%= <CONTEXT NODE>->node_tab %>"
  table              = "//<CONTEXT NODE>/Table"
/>
```

**Listing 10.11** Activating the UI Configuration Tool for the Tree View

You have to replace `<CONTEXT NODE>` with the respective name of the context node (❶ in Figure 10.11).

> **Note**
>
> To display an icon at the beginning of a row, you must implement the IF_BSP_WD_TREE_NODE~GET_ICON method by assigning a URL that refers to an icon to the RV_VALUE parameter. An implementation might look as follows:

```
rv_icon = cl_thtmlb_util=>get_icon_url( 'folder.gif' ).
```

After all manual programming work has been completed, you can generate a default configuration in the UI Configuration Tool and arrange the columns (see Figure 10.12).

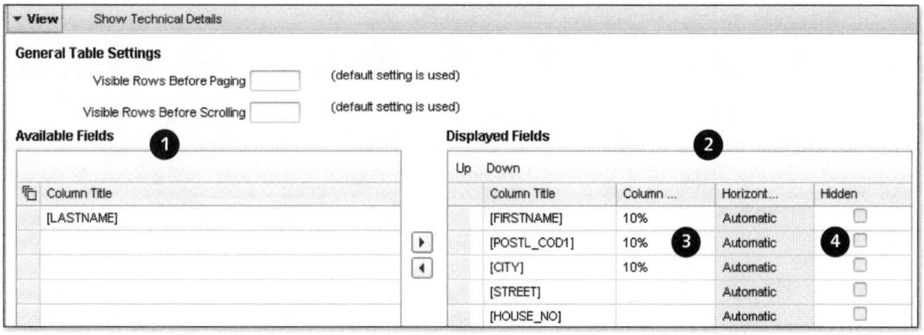

**Figure 10.12** UI Configuration Tool for the Tree View

In the UI Configuration Tool, you move the fields from the Available Fields area (❶) to the Displayed Fields area (❷) to map the fields as columns in the tree structure. You can also set additional properties such as Column Width (❸) and visibility (Hidden, ❹).

## 10.4  Search Pages

Searching for business objects

The most frequently used entry point in an application is a search for business objects. The search pages (*advanced search views*) of the Web Client UI framework provide an easy way to perform a dynamic search based on variable search criteria (❶ in Figure 10.13) and to map the result list as a table (❷).

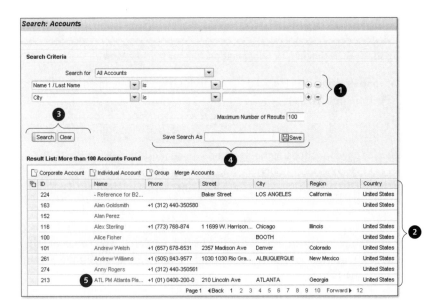

**Figure 10.13**  Page Structure of an Advanced Search

Using a search page

You can start or clear the search via the Search or Clear buttons (❸). Next to these buttons, you can save the search criteria as a saved search (❹). By clicking on a link (❺) in the result list, you can, for example, navigate to the overview page of a business object. For more information on search pages, refer to Chapter 1, Section 1.2.3.

There is no wizard that supports creating a search page. To implement a search page, you have to perform various steps. Chapter 16, Section 16.3 provides a comprehensive practical example of creating a search page.

Technically, the search for business objects is based on a dynamic search object that is contained in a component set. If you specify a component set, the GenIL model browser (see Chapter 12, Section 12.2.1) lists all existing search objects.

> **Tip**
>
> The SAP standard version provides the BSPWD_ADVSEARCH UI component, which you can use as a template for your own implementation of search pages. Figure 10.13 illustrates this UI component at runtime.

The presentation of a search page is based on tags of the CHTMLB and THT-MLB library. These are hierarchically built on each other and called sequentially (see Table 10.1). The tags can be called in different views as long as you adhere to the call sequence. The `searchFrame` tag is the root tag of this hierarchy. Search pages must be enclosed by the `CHTMLB:PageType` tag.

*Search page tags*

A search page usually consists of a view set (see Chapter 9, Section 9.2) that contains two views (search criteria and result list) in a 50%:50% presentation.

*Structure of a search page*

However, the SAP standard version also contains other implementation variants. Thus, the structure of an existing search page may differ from the variant described here.

| Tag Hierarchy of a Search Page |
| --- |
| `CHTMLB:PageType` |
| `THTMLB:searchFrame` |
| `THTMLB:searchCriteriaFrame` |
| `THTMLB:searchArea` |
| `THTMLB:searchTagArea` |
| `THTMLB:advancedSearch` |
| `THTMLB:searchButtonsArea` |
| `THTMLB:button` **(search)** |
| `THTMLB:button` **(clear)** |
| `THTMLB:searchSavingArea` |
| `THTMLB:searchResultFrame` |

**Table 10.1** Hierarchical Structure of Search Tags

Processing in the
UI Configuration
Tool

After you have activated the BSP page and created a configuration, you define the search criteria in the UI Configuration Tool (see Figure 10.14).

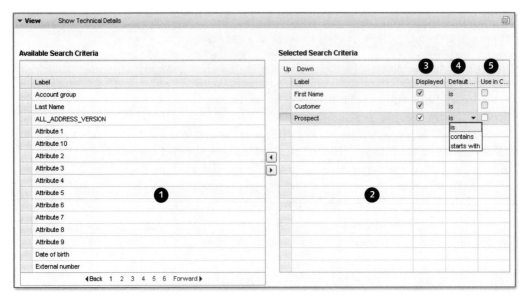

**Figure 10.14** UI Configuration Tool for Search Pages

For this purpose, assign the search criteria from the AVAILABLE SEARCH CRITERIA (❶) list to the SELECTED SEARCH CRITERIA (❷) area. In addition, define whether the search criterion should be displayed (❸) and specify the visible default operator (❹). In the USE IN CENTRAL SEARCH column (❺), you release the search criterion for a usage in the central search. Chapter 4, Section 4.4 provides more information on the activation of the central search in the CRM Web Client.

Implementing a
search page

We will now take a look at a possible variant for creating a search page. To do so, you will need to pay attention to specific aspects for the view that maps the search criteria. A wizard is used to create two model nodes in the context. The first represents the search with search criteria and is based on the dynamic search object. After the wizard has created the model node, you have to manually replace the CL_BSP_WD_CONTEXT_NODE superclass of the implementation class of the model node with the CL_BSP_WD_CONTEXT_NODE_ASP class. This defines the model node that represents the dynamic search object in the context. Among other things, the CL_BSP_WD_CONTEXT_NODE_ASP class also provides a method that lets you determine the attribute structure of the search object. This method is required by the THTMLB:advancedSearch tag for execution.

The second model node contains the result list. It is based on the result object type of the dynamic search object and is linked to a model node in the component controller using a context node binding (see Chapter 9, Section 9.4.4).

Another specific aspect is that you have to change the inheritance of the controller class in such a way that the superclass (!) of the view controller inherits from the CL_BSP_WD_ADVSEARCH_CONTROLLER class instead of the CL_BSP_WD_VIEW_CONTROLLER class. The CL_BSP_WD_ADVSEARCH_CONTROLLER class contains methods to provide definitions and search fields of the advanced search for the THTMLB:advancedSearch tag.

For the SEARCH and CLEAR buttons, you need one event handler for each button (see Section 9.1.3). Its name must correspond to the value in the onClick attribute of the THTMLB:button tag. You can implement the advanced search call in the event handler for the SEARCH button. Listing 10.12 provides the corresponding sample implementation. The SEARCH model node is used to start the advanced search. The result list is stored in the RESULT model node.

**Buttons "Search" and "Clear"**

```
data l_qs type ref to cl_crm_bol_dquery_service,
l_qs ?= me->typed_context->search->collection_wrapper->get_
current( ).
data l_result type ref to if_bol_entity_col.
l_result = l_qs->get_query_result( ).
me->typed_context->result->collection_wrapper->set_
collection( l_result ).
```

**Listing 10.12** Executing an Advanced Search

To clear the search criteria in the user interface, you can copy the implementation from Listing 10.13 to the event handler for the CLEAR button.

```
data: qs type ref to cl_crm_bol_dquery_service,
qs = me->get_current_dquery( ).
if qs is bound.
  data lr_adjustments type ref to crmt_regex_conversion_tab.
  lr_adjustments = me->get_adjustments( ).
  qs->clear_selection_param_values( lr_adjustments ).
endif.
```

**Listing 10.13** Clearing the Search Criteria

The view that maps the search result usually consists of a table view (see Section 10.2). Because of a context node binding to the model node in the component controller that contains the search result, the system can map the result list in the table.

**View with result list**

> **Tip**
>
> Before you begin implementing a search page, you must ensure that the component set that is assigned to the UI component contains the dynamic search object.

## 10.5 Overview Pages

An *overview page* contains detailed business data object information and is divided into a header area and what are called *assignment blocks*. Assignment blocks usually map information relating to the business data object (e.g., item details) in tables. The overview page is frequently the first point of contact when you navigate from a dialog to a business data object. The information in an assignment block can be displayed in different ways (see Figure 10.15):

▶ As a form view (❶)
▶ As a table view (❷, ❸, ❹)
▶ As a tree view

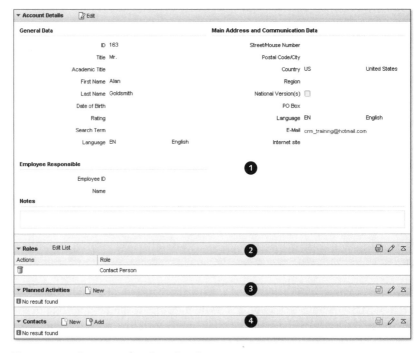

**Figure 10.15** Structure of an Overview Page

Assignment blocks on an overview page have a heading and a specific toolbar that may contain buttons for processing the data.

From a technical point of view, an overview page is a view set that contains only one view area. You can only change the layout of an overview page with the UI Configuration Tool, which does not need to be explicitly activated through tags. The CONFIGURATION tab is available when the wizard for generating the overview page has been closed.

You create an overview page in the component structure browser in the context menu of the VIEWS level by starting the CREATE OVERVIEW PAGE action.

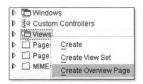

**Figure 10.16** Creating an Overview Page

Then, navigate to the runtime repository editor and create the view set (if it is not yet available). It should have the same name as the overview page. Be sure to keep case sensitivity in mind here. Next, add a view area to the view set. The name of the view area needs to be OVERVIEWPAGE. Be sure to keep case sensitivity in mind here as well. After having created the view area, add all views of the OVERVIEWPAGE view area that may be suitable as assignment blocks of the overview page.

When you have assigned the overview page of the view type to a window, navigate from the runtime repository editor to the UI Configuration Tool of the overview page and generate a new default configuration. The system then prompts you to select the configuration type. Select the OVERVIEW PAGE configuration type, as shown in Figure 10.17.

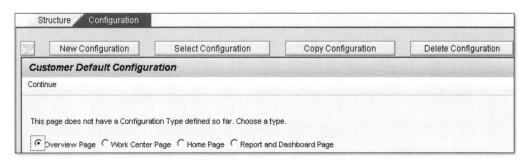

**Figure 10.17** Defining the Configuration Type of the Overview Page

The NEXT button brings you to the administration area of the assignment blocks. Assign (❷) the required views from the AVAILABLE ASSIGNMENT BLOCKS area (❶) to the DISPLAYED ASSIGNMENT BLOCKS area (❸) (see Figure 10.18).

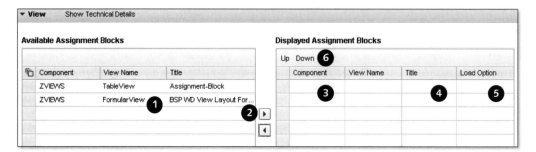

**Figure 10.18** Configuring the Assignment Blocks

Defining the load option
In the TITLE column (❹), you can define a heading for the assignment block. In the LOAD OPTION column (❺), you can choose between three different options:

▸ Lazy Load (the assignment block is displayed if necessary)

▸ Direct (the assignment block is always directly displayed)

▸ Hidden (the assignment block is not displayed)

The UP and DOWN buttons (❻) let you specify the vertical sequence in which the assignment blocks are arranged. The practical example in Chapter 16, Section 16.4 illustrates the implementation of an overview page.

## 10.6 Work Center Pages

Two-column grid
Similar to overview pages, work center pages consist of various views, arranged in a two-column grid, with any number of rows (see Figure 10.19). From the point of view of the user, work center pages usually consist of groups of links that are organized in information blocks (❶, ❷, and ❸).

Mapping an information block as a view
Technically, each information block is mapped by a view; thus, Figure 10.19 shows three views in total that are organized in one work center page. The mapping is not restricted to links; you can also integrate views with any layout into a work center page.

You create a work center page the same way as an overview page (see Section 10.5). You can also only change the layout of an overview page with the UI Configuration Tool, which does not need to be explicitly activated through tags. The CONFIGURATION tab is available in the Component Workbench when the wizard for generating the work center page has been closed.

**Figure 10.19**  Work Center Page "Account Management"

You create a work center page in the component structure browser in the context menu of the VIEWS level by starting the CREATE OVERVIEW PAGE action. This may be surprising but illustrates that a work center page is a subtype of an overview page.

Subtype of an overview page

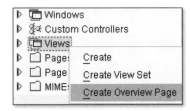

**Figure 10.20**  Creating an Overview Page

Then, navigate to the runtime repository editor and create the view set (if it is not yet available). It should have the same name as the work center page. Be sure to keep case sensitivity in mind here. Next, add a view area to the view set. The name of the view area needs to be OVERVIEWPAGE. Be sure to keep case sensitivity in mind here as well. After having created the view area, add all views of the OVERVIEWPAGE view area that may be suitable as information blocks of the work center page.

Generating a view set for the work center page

When you have assigned the view to a window, navigate from the runtime repository editor to the UI Configuration Tool of the work center page and generate a new default configuration. The system then prompts you to select the configuration type.

Creating a configuration

Select the WORK CENTER PAGE configuration type (see Figure 10.21). The NEXT button takes you to the configuration of the left and right visible columns of the work center page.

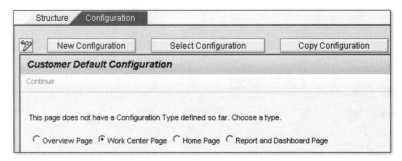

**Figure 10.21** Defining the "Work Center Page" Configuration Type

Positioning the assignment blocks

In the UI Configuration Tool for work center pages (see Figure 10.22), you select a view from the available assignment blocks (**❶**) and position it to the LEFT VISIBLE COLUMN (**❹**) or RIGHT VISIBLE COLUMN (**❺**) using the corresponding button (**❷** or **❸**). This way, you define a view as an information block. The buttons (**❻**) let you move the views from the left column to the right column and vice versa.

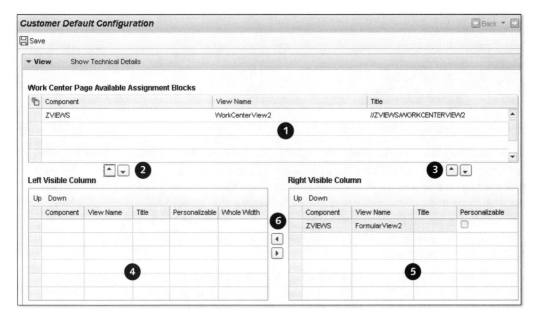

**Figure 10.22** Configuring the Columns as Information Blocks

276

**Figure 10.23** Configuring a Column

You can influence the appearance of views that are arranged in a column (❶ in Figure 10.23) using various options. For example, you can define a heading for each view (❷). The PERSONALIZABLE option (❸) defines whether a view can be personalized in the work center page at runtime. If you activate the WHOLE WIDTH option (❹), the system displays the view at the end of the work center page. The view is displayed across the entire width of the screen. In this case, you can no longer move the view using drag-and-drop.

Influencing the appearance

*This chapter introduces the enhancement concept of the Web Client UI framework. It provides options for the modification-free adaptation of UI components of a standard SAP delivery.*

# 11 UI Component Enhancement Concept

The SAP concept for the modification-free enhancement of standard UI components is feasible because the Web Client UI framework was implemented with integrated object orientation. In fact, all standard SAP classes remain unaffected by changes because the original controller class instances are not replaced by custom-developed class instances until runtime.

*Modification-free adaptation*

The motivation for enhancements of UI components derives from concrete, real-life tasks. Table 11.1 summarizes a few examples of typical tasks, to illustrate when you need to use the enhancement concept.

*Motivation for enhancements*

| Task | Object |
|---|---|
| Add context nodes or attributes | Controller and context |
| Customize event handling | View |
| Add plugs (navigation) | View and window |
| Add views, windows, and view sets | Views, windows, view sets, and runtime repository |
| Add buttons | View |
| Implement customer-specific value helps (F4 helps) | Controller and context |

**Table 11.1**  Typical Tasks for Enhancements

| Note |
|---|
| Take a look at SAP Note 1248485 on the enhancement of tree views and SAP Note 1257172 on the transport of enhancements within a system landscape. |

Enhancement
using the
Component
Workbench

You enhance UI components using the Component Workbench, which provides wizards for this specific purpose. The wizards derive standard SAP classes in customer-specific subclasses, taking the customer namespace into account. In addition to making changes to objects, you can also add objects. Furthermore, you can enhance the runtime repository.

These enhancements are assigned to a grouping element, the *enhancement set*. Thus, an enhancement is like a container of enhanced UI components that must be used for enhancing a UI component in the Component Workbench.

## 11.1    Enhancement Set

Definition in the
BSPWDVC_CMP_
EXT view cluster

As mentioned previously, an enhancement set as a grouping element is responsible for the management of controller replacements. To create an enhancement set, you need to open the BSPWDVC_CMP_EXT view cluster using the view cluster maintenance (Transaction SM34) and add a new entry in change mode. To define an enhancement set, you must first enter a name in the ENHANCEMENT SET column (e.g., "ZBOOK") and a definition in the DESCRIPTION column (e.g., "Enhancement Set Book Project").

COMPONENT_
LOADING BAdI

You can create multiple enhancement sets but only one enhancement set is used by the Web Client UI framework at runtime. At runtime, the COMPONENT_LOADING BAdI determines the active enhancement set within the default enhancement implementation from the BSPWD_EHSET_ASGN table. Within this table, you can assign the active enhancement set to a system client.

Determining the
enhancement set
dynamically

If you want to use an enhancement set dynamically at runtime, you must create and activate a custom enhancement implementation for the IF_BSP_WD_CMP_LOADING_BADI~GET_ACTIVE_ENHANCEMENT_SET method in the COMPONENT_LOADING BAdI.

> **Note**
>
> You must use the BSPWDV_EHSET_ASG maintenance view—which you can open using Transaction SM30—to maintain the BSPWD_EHSET_ASGN table.

## 11.2    Enhancing UI Components

Authorizations

After you have defined an enhancement set, you can enhance the standard SAP UI components. To implement enhancements, you additionally require the following authorizations:

▶ Authorization to maintain cross-client Customizing

▶ Authorization to create BSP applications

▶ Authorization to create ICF services

▶ Authorization to create ABAP objects

You enhance UI components using the Component Workbench (Transaction BSP_WD_CMPWB). For this purpose, start the Component Workbench via the SAP GUI, select the UI component to be enhanced in the COMPONENTS field, and switch to the detail view of the UI component. Click on the ENHANCE COMPONENT button in the detail view within the Component Workbench.

The system then displays a dialog in which you can specify an existing enhancement set. Enter the previously defined enhancement set and click ✔ to confirm.

Assigning the enhancement set to the UI component

Another dialog opens in which you define the BSP application for storing the enhanced objects. The Component Workbench automatically stores all enhanced objects in this BSP application. Press ⌈Enter⌋ to confirm.

> **Note**
>
> You should consider the name of the original UI component when specifying the name of the application. This simplifies identification if you have implemented multiple enhancements.

Another dialog opens in which you enter the runtime repository storage. Because enhancements of a UI component impact the runtime repository, you must save changes to the runtime repository in a separate storage system. This storage system is assigned to the previously created BSP application and is a copy of the *Repository.xml file*. Copy the REPOSITORY.XML name when you specify the name of the storage, and press ⌈Enter⌋ to confirm.

Storage definition

After a short generation phase, the UI component to be enhanced is displayed slightly altered in the component structure browser of the Component Workbench (see Figure 11.1). The objects of the UI component—component controller, windows, custom controllers, views, and the *Repository.xml* file—are not displayed in black but in gray in the component structure browser. The context menu now shoes the added ENHANCE entry. The runtime repository can now also be enhanced.

Display in the component structure browser

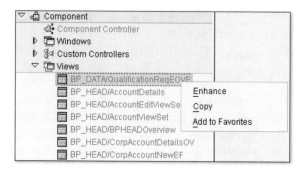

**Figure 11.1**  Enhanced UI Component in the Component Workbench

Objects that can be enhanced

Objects of a non-enhanced UI component are usually displayed in black in the component structure browser. Gray objects can be enhanced, but have not been enhanced yet. When you have enhanced an object, for example, a view, it is displayed in black again in the component structure browser.

Starting the enhancement wizard

You can enhance an existing object by selecting it in the component structure browser and then starting the enhancement wizard using the ENHANCE activity in the context menu.

> **Note**
>
> The heading in the Component Workbench also indicates whether a UI component can be enhanced. If an enhancement set is available, the system displays its name at the end of the heading.

Effects of enhancements

Figure 11.2 illustrates the technical effects of enhancements and how they influence the display within the Component Workbench. An enhanced view is displayed in black (❶). In the detailed overview on the right side of the screen, you can see that the original implementation class CL_BP_HEAD_COR-PDETAILSEF_IMPL (❸) of the view controller was replaced by the derived class ZL_BP_HEAD_CORPDETAILSEF_IMPL in the customer namespace (❷). The same applies to the implementation class of the UI context. The implementation class of a context node, however, is only derived from a subclass in the customer namespace when context attributes were added using the wizard.

> **Note**
>
> In the standard implementation of BAdI BSP_WD_APPL_WB, if an enhancement has been made, the first character of the original name of the implementation class is replaced by a Z. You can "overwrite" this name assignment procedure using a custom implementation of BAdI BSP_WD_APPL_WB.

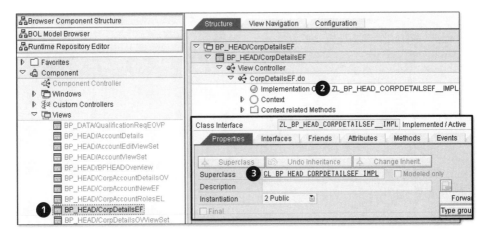

**Figure 11.2** Enhanced View in the Component Structure Browser

After you have enhanced a controller using the wizard, the ZTYPED_CONTEXT attribute is available in the controller. This attribute points to the derived implementation class of the context as a reference. If you add a new context node, you address the new context node via the ZTYPED_CONTEXT reference in your program statements.

**Enhancing a controller**

Implementation classes of context nodes are not implicitly enhanced via the Component Workbench. This is done explicitly when another attribute is added to the context node using the wizard. See also SAP Note 1247543.

**Enhancing a context node**

As mentioned previously, enhanced objects are saved in a BSP application. The display of the structure of the BSP application is performed in the repository browser in Transaction SE80; it is grouped by controller, views, and pages with flow logic (see Figure 11.3).

**Displaying a BSP application in the repository browser**

After you have enhanced a UI component, you can find the definitions of the controller replacements within the dialog structure of the CONTROLLER SUBSTITUTES level in the BSPWDVC_CMP_EXT view cluster.

> **Note**
>
> If you want to remove enhancements, select the enhanced object in the component structure browser in the Component Workbench and select the DELETE ENHANCEMENT activity from the context menu to start the wizard. Select the object types you want to delete and confirm with the [Enter] key. Refer to SAP Note 1122248 for further information on this topic.

**Removing enhancements**

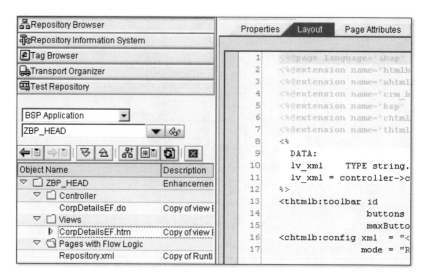

**Figure 11.3** BSP Application with Enhancement Objects in the Repository

## 11.3 Enhancement Set in the Component Workbench

The Component Workbench is the development environment for UI components (see Figure 11.4). To edit an enhanced UI component, in the initial screen, you must specify the enhancement set in the ENHANCEMENT SET field (❷) in addition to the UI component (if required). If an active enhancement set can be specified, it is preset in the ENHANCEMENT SET field.

**Figure 11.4** Calling the UI Component with an Enhancement Set

If the ENHANCEMENT SET field should not be visible, click on the button next to COMPONENT (❶) to display the field. If you do not enter a value, the system opens the standard UI component without the enhancement set. If an active enhancement set can be specified, it is preset in the ENHANCEMENT SET field.

*The generic interaction layer (GenIL) provides business data objects such as business partners or business operations in abstract object models. This chapter presents the architecture and different object types of the GenIL.*

# 12 Generic Interaction Layer – GenIL

In a model view controller architecture, the *model* unit is responsible for data retention and independent of the *layout* and *program control* units. Since CRM version 20006s/1, the SAP CRM solution is completely based on the Web Client UI framework, the BOL and the GenIL. The BOL together with the GenIL is an essential part of the Web Client architecture because it is responsible for the data management of the user interface components.

The BOL is a standardized interface for access to an object model that consists of a defined quantity of GenIL components and their objects. It separates the business logic from the user interface and program control of the CRM Web Client.

Object model

## 12.1 Benefits of the Generic Interaction Layer

Because all CRM business data objects such as BUSINESS PARTNER, PRODUCTS, and BUSINESS TRANSACTIONS are offered as GenIL objects in an object model, an application developer does not need to know and use all specific *application programming interfaces* (APIs) of the business data objects because these objects also use these APIs. Therefore, he can concentrate on the application of an object model and think that he is working with an object database. Without the object model, an application developer must ensure the persistence of the application data himself; with an object model, however, he only needs to identify the required business data object and provide the attributes of the business data object with values at runtime. He can leave the call of the APIs to the responsible GenIL components.

Another benefit is that an object model of the GenIL can be enhanced by enhancing existing GenIL objects with additional attributes using the Easy Enhancement Workbench (EEWB) (see Chapter 5, Section 5.3) or adding new GenIL objects to an object model (see Section 12.3). You can also model an entirely new object model if you desire. As of SAP CRM 2007 support package 2, you can enhance the GenIL with additional GenIL objects on the basis of web services. Section 12.3.3 provides further information on this topic.

### 12.1.1    GenIL Object Model

The model comprises a set of GenIL components that are organized in component sets. A GenIL component in turn comprises a set of GenIL objects and their interrelationships. All GenIL objects together form the already mentioned object model (see Figure 12.1).

Object model

To clarify the object model concept, the following sections discuss the *business partner* (BP) GenIL component and introduce the business partner model provided therein in extracts. The business partner model of the BP component comprises more than two hundred objects and relationships in the standard version of CRM 2007.

Object model of the BP component

Figure 12.1 shows excerpts of an object model. It consists of a search object (❶), a root object (❷; see Section 12.1.3), and three additional objects that depend on the root object (❸) and that are linked with one another via named relations (see Section 12.1.4). The BUILHEADERSEARCH search object provides a list of root objects of the BUILHEADER type for successful searches. The BUILHEADER root object represents the header structure of an object of the BUSINESS PARTNER type. The BUILADDRESS object is an object that depends on the BUILHEADER object. The BUILADDRESS object is connected with two additional dependent objects, BUILADDRESSVERSION and BUILADDRESSFAX.

> **Note**
>
> If you leave out search objects, you can assume the following rule: The root object is always the point of entry of an object model and the other objects in the model depend on the root object. Multiple root objects can exist in a GenIL component (see Section 12.1.2).

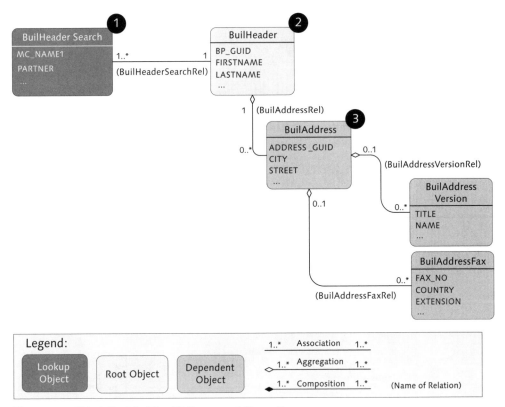

**Figure 12.1** Object Model of the BP Component (Excerpt)

## 12.1.2 GenIL Components and Component Sets

You now know the structure of an object model. The following sections discuss the parts of an object model in more detail: the GenIL component and GenIL objects.

A GenIL component provides a hierarchical object model to the GenIL. It acts as an intermediate layer between the CRM business logic and the *consumer*, the CRM Web Client in most cases. Ultimately, a GenIL component is an ABAP class. The ABAP class contains no business logic but calls the APIs that contain the business logic. Thus, it assumes the mapping between the data model it provides and the underlying APIs by accessing the database tables.

**GenIL component**

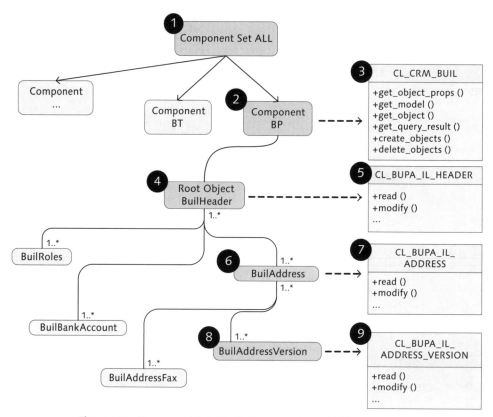

**Figure 12.2** Component Set, GenIL Components, and Objects

**Component set**  Figure 12.2 shows the component set ALL (❶), which—in addition to a few other components—contains the BP component (❷) for business partners. The IF_GENIL_APPL_MODEL~GET_OBJECT method of the CL_CRM_BUIL implementation class (❸) provides the object data of the GenIL objects for the BP component, such as root objects (❹) and dependent objects. As shown in Figure 12.2, the BUILADDRESS GenIL object (❻) is represented by the CL_BUPA_IL_ADDRESS ABAP class (❼) that contains methods for reading and modifying address data. The object classes do not access the database directly but use the API of the respective business data objects for data access instead. Each GenIL component assumes control of these object classes individually; that is, there is no standardized procedure for the implementation of a GenIL component.

> **Note**
>
> Some GenIL objects communicate with other SAP systems via RFC so that the access of APIs is not limited to the database.

By assigning a GenIL component to a component set you define the functional scope of the application. To define a GenIL component and assign a GenIL component to a component set, follow the IMG menu path CUSTOMER RELATIONSHIP MANAGEMENT • CRM CROSS-APPLICATION COMPONENTS • GENERIC INTERACTION LAYER/OBJECT LAYER • BASIC SETTINGS or use Transaction SM34 and the CRMVC_GIL_APPDEF view cluster.

**Assignment to the component set**

| Dialog Structure | Component Definition | | | |
| --- | --- | --- | --- | --- |
| ⬡ Component Definition | Comp. Na | Description | Implementation Class | Object Table |
| ▽ ☐ Component Set Definitio | BP | Business Partner | CL_CRM_BUIL | CRMC_ALLOBJ_BUIL |
| ☐ Component Assignm | BPCND | | CL_CRM_CONTRACT_BPCONDIL_COMP | CRMC_BPCOND_OBJ |
| | BPEXCN | | CL_CRM_BP_EXCEPTION_COMP | |
| | BPEXCP | | | |
| | BPORUL | | CL_CRM_FMBPO_RULE_IL | |
| | BP_AFF | | CL_CRM_BP_AFF_COMP | |

**Figure 12.3** Component Definition (Excerpt)

The SAP standard provides several components and component sets. In the dialog for the maintenance of the component definition, you must specify a unique name for a component, including an implementation class. You can optionally specify the object table and model table.

**Component definition**

If a table name is available in the columns OBJECT TABLE and MODEL TABLE for a component definition, you can generically take the model metadata such as the root objects or dependent objects (including the object relationships and specifications on the cardinality of the GenIL component) from this table data. If no entry exists, the implementation class of the GenIL component provides the dependent objects and object relationships in the methods GET_MODEL and GET_OBJECT_PROPS.

> **Note**
>
> Not every component sticks to this procedure; the specification in the OBJECT TABLE and MODEL TABLE columns can be used for information only because some components handle this logic with an individually defined implementation of the GET_MODEL and GET_OBJECT_PROPS methods of the IF_GE-NIL_APPL_MODEL interface.

In the dialog structure (left part of the screen), you can maintain the component sets and assign a component to a component set. Figure 12.4 shows the assignment of the ACP, BP, and BPORUL components to the BP_APPL component set.

**Assignment of a component to the component set**

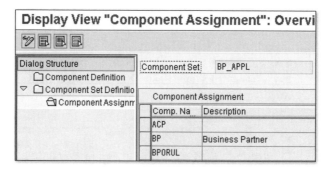

**Figure 12.4** Assignment of Components to Component Sets

Table 12.1 lists important GenIL components and their implementation classes.

| Component | Description | Implementation Class |
|---|---|---|
| BP | Business partner | CL_CRM_BUIL |
| BT | Business transaction | CL_CRM_BTIL |
| IBASE | Installation | CL_CRM_IBASE_IL |
| PROD | Products | CL_CRM_PRODIL |
| MKT* | Marketing | CL_CRM_MKT* |
| SAMPLE | Sample implementation for custom GenIL components | CL_CRM_GENIL_SAMPLE_COMP, CL_CRM_GENIL_SAMPLE_COMP_NEW |
| SO2 | Components for simple objects | CL_CRM_GENIL_SO_COMP2 |

**Table 12.1** Important GenIL Components

### 12.1.3 GenIL Objects

Characteristics of a GenIL object

The following discusses the smallest unit of an object model, the GenIL object. It is characterized by the following features:

- It corresponds to a unique object type.
- It has a flat *data dictionary* (DDIC) structure with attributes that form the object attributes of the GenIL object.
- It includes at least one key field for access control.
- It is technically represented by an ABAP class.

Business data object

At runtime, a business data object is an instance of a GenIL object. A GenIL object must correspond to one of the following types:

▶ **Root object**
Object types

A *root object* can be addressed via its unique key and can be locked and edited independently. Each root object is also an access object but not vice versa.

▶ **Search object**

A *search object* is a defined object search and provides root objects or access objects as the result set.

▶ **Dynamic search object**

A *dynamic search object* delivers more features than a simple search object. For example, it supports the use of search operators that are similar to the selection criteria (select options) in the ABAP terminology.

▶ **Dependent object**

A *dependent object* directly or indirectly depends on a root object and can only be addressed or modified via this root object.

▶ **Search result object**

A *search result object* contains different business data objects. To be able to assign business data objects to the object model, the search result object is associated with the root object of the same component.

▶ **Access object**

An *access object* can be directly addressed via its unique key but it can only be edited or locked in connection with its dependent root object. Exploding the access path from object to object within a model based on a root object can be relatively complex due to the hierarchical tree structure. Therefore, you can use access objects in the reading process. Access objects can be addressed directly as a "shortcut," so to speak.

A GenIL object usually has a separate ABAP handler class, including methods for selecting and persisting the object data. Additionally, a GenIL object can be enhanced with individual business logic in the form of object methods. The DDIC structure that contains the attributes of the object should not include any deep structures.
ABAP handler class

> **Note**
>
> Sometimes the term *BOL object* is used instead of *GenIL object* but if you are working at a higher abstraction level, the term GenIL object is more appropriate. However, although there are two terms, the meaning is ultimately the same.

### 12.1.4 Relationships Between GenIL Objects

Characteristics of an object relationship

In the object model, GenIL objects have a relationship to other GenIL objects. Such a relationship is characterized by the following features:

▸ It has a unique relationship type.

▸ It maps a "parent-child relationship," including the specification of a cardinality.

▸ In contrast to objects, it has no attributes.

Relationship types

A relationship type can correspond to one of the following variants:

▸ **Aggregation**
An aggregation describes a relationship between a child object and its root object. Only access objects and dependent objects can be part of an aggregation.

▸ **Composition**
A composition is a type of aggregation, with the only exception that a root object can never exist without its child object.

▸ **Association**
An association describes a simple relationship between two objects.

In addition, the relationship type depends on the object types that should be related. For example, the relationship between a root object and its dependent object can only be of the AGGREGATION or COMPOSITION type, whereas a relationship between two root objects can only be of the ASSOCIATION type.

Cardinality

The cardinality describes the complexity of a relationship between two sets of objects and specifies with how many other BOL entities a BOL entity of an object can or must have a concrete relationship. A *BOL entity* refers to a concrete instance of an object.

Table 12.2 lists possible values of cardinalities:

| Cardinality | Description |
| --- | --- |
| 0:1 | Each BOL entity of the first entity set is related with not more than one BOL entity of the second entity set. |
| 1:1 | Each BOL entity of the first entity set is related with exactly one BOL entity of the second entity set or vice versa. |
| 0:n | Each BOL entity of the first entity set can be related with any number of BOL entities of the second entity set. BOL entities of the second entity set can be related with a maximum of one BOL entity of the first object set. |

**Table 12.2** Cardinality Values Between BOL Entities

| Cardinality | Description |
|---|---|
| 1:n | Each BOL entity of the first entity set can be related with any number of BOL entities of the second entity set. Conversely, each BOL entity of the second entity set is related with at least one BOL entity of the first entity set. |

**Table 12.2**  Cardinality Values Between BOL Entities (Cont.)

## 12.2  Tools for Displaying Object Models

SAP provides the GenIL BOL browser and GenIL model browser analysis tools to support you in the visual analysis of the structure of an object model. The GenIL BOL browser is used to display the data of an object model that is determined using the BOL (see Chapter 13). The GenIL model browser is used to display object models with their objects and named relationships (relations). Both tools are available in the SAP GUI.

*Visualization of the object model*

| Note |
|---|
| It is recommended that you familiarize yourself with these two tools. When you implement model enhancements, these tools are very helpful for testing your own GenIL implementations. |

### 12.2.1  GenIL Model Browser

The GenIL model browser is a tool for visualizing object structures and relationships to other objects in the object model. It is started by calling Transaction GENIL_MODEL_BROWSER in the SAP GUI. After you have entered a component set in the initial screen of the GenIL model browser, and selected EXECUTE ( F8 ), the system takes you to the hierarchical presentation of the object model in the GenIL model browser (see Figure 12.5).

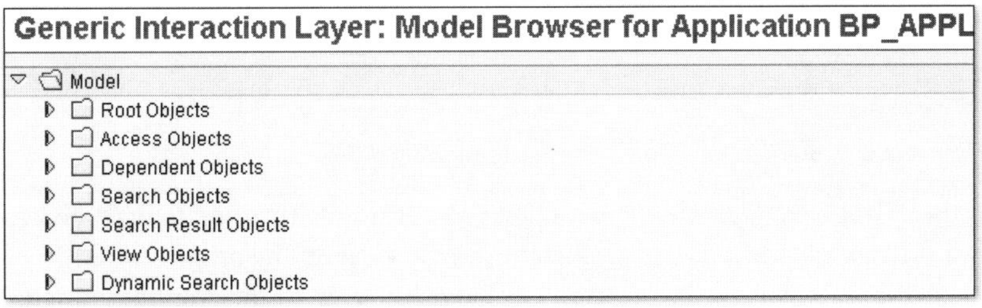

*Visualization of object structures*

**Figure 12.5**  Structure Display of the GenIL Model Browser

When you start the GenIL model browser, the display of the object model is initially hierarchically subdivided into object types in a tree structure. The following hierarchy levels are provided in the form of additional model nodes in the MODEL node:

- ▶ Root objects
- ▶ Access objects
- ▶ Dependent objects
- ▶ Search objects
- ▶ Search result objects
- ▶ View objects
- ▶ Dynamic search objects

Object network    Provided that the object model contains objects of the corresponding type, the system can display these objects by expanding the respective hierarchy level as object nodes. The GenIL model browser displays an object model in a tree structure. It actually forms an object network because a model can have recursive elements, something a tree structure can only insufficiently indicate.

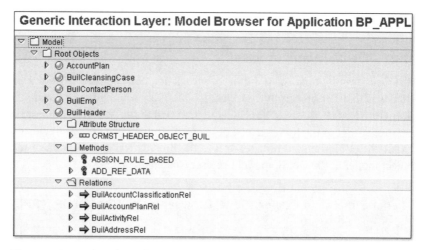

**Figure 12.6**   "BuilHeader" Object in the GenIL Model Browser (Excerpt)

If the system displays a black arrow on the left side of the hierarchy level, you can further expand this hierarchy level by clicking on the arrow. A multitude of pictograms is used in the GenIL model browser to differentiate objects, relationships, attributes, and methods. Table 12.3 lists all used pictograms of the GenIL model browser.

| Pictogram | Description |
|---|---|
| ⊘ | Object in the object model (applies to all object types) |
| ☐ | Model nodes or containers for an attribute structure |
| ▥ | Attribute structure |
| ✎ | Attribute in an attribute structure |
| ▦ | Data element of an attribute |
| ⇨ | Relationship in the object model |
| ⚷ | Object method |

**Table 12.3**  Pictograms of the GenIL Model Browser

Figure 12.6 shows an excerpt of the BUILHEADER root object that is expanded in the ROOT OBJECTS node in the GenIL Model Browser. You can view the CRMST_HEADER_OBJECT_BUIL attribute structure of the BUILHEADER object whose attributes and data elements can also be displayed in the GenIL model browser. Attributes of an attribute structure are attributes of the objects at the same time. You can also navigate forward to the dictionary maintenance by double-clicking the attribute structure.

Objects

In the METHODS hierarchy level, you can find specifications on the method implementations for some objects. A method implementation contains specific business logic that you can call using BOL programming (see Chapter 13, Section 13.11) or using the GenIL BOL browser (see Section 12.2.2).

Methods

Relationships to other objects are displayed in the RELATIONS hierarchy level. If you click on the black arrow on the left side of the relationship name, the system displays the related object—including its attributes and methods—and additional object relationships, if applicable.

Relations

The USAGE node, which contains the two subnodes ASSOCIATED BY and AGGREGATED BY (see Section 12.1.4) provides further information on the usage of the selected object in the object model. Entries in the nodes refer to objects that use the selected object and ultimately indicate the inversion of the relationship.

Object usage

**Figure 12.7** Usage of an Object in the Object Model

In contrast to the GenIL BOL browser, the GenIL model browser is only a tool for displaying the object model. You cannot change data using the GenIL model browser.

### 12.2.2 GenIL BOL Browser

The Web Client UI framework provides the GenIL BOL browser (Transaction GENIL_BOL_BROWSER) tool for implementing operations such as search, select, and change data of business data objects. In day-to-day life, the GenIL BOL browser turns out to be an essential analysis tool, for example, to test custom GenIL implementations. Because you can scan the object model and display the data of objects on the screen, you can quickly obtain an overview of the object model.

Structure of the GenIL BOL browser When you start the GenIL BOL browser, the system first prompts you to enter a *component set*. By activating the IN DISPLAY MODE option, you can ensure that the data can be displayed but not changed. If you select EXECUTE ([F8]), the system takes you to the GenIL BOL browser.

In principle, the GenIL BOL browser is subdivided into five screen areas (see Figure 12.8):

▸ A toolbar for searching, creating, and saving changes to BOL entities (❶)
▸ A display of messages from the business logic. The message browser must be displayed explicitly (❷).
▸ A view of the search objects and enhanced search objects in the model browser (❸)
▸ A presentation of the search result list in the list browser (❹)
▸ A presentation of the object details in the object browser (❺)

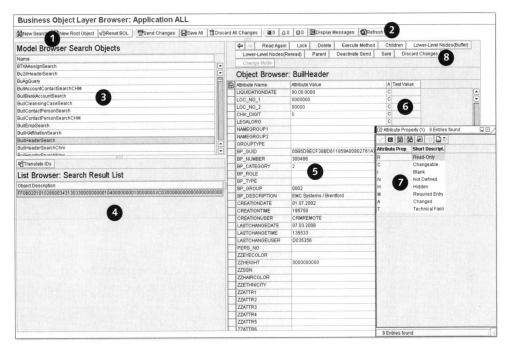

**Figure 12.8** Structure of the GenIL BOL Browser

The presentation of the screen areas varies depending on whether you are in search mode (NEW SEARCH button on the toolbar) or in creation mode (NEW ROOT OBJECT button on the toolbar). To activate the message browser, you must click on the DISPLAY MESSAGES button (❷) on the toolbar.

The essential functions of the GenIL BOL browser comprise the implementation of object searches, the creation of objects, and the implementation of changes to existing objects. If you are in search mode, the system displays the search objects of the component set you selected initially in the model browser. Note that the list of search objects first indicates all simple search objects in alphanumeric order. At the end of the list, you can then find all dynamic search objects in alphanumeric order (this was changed in release 7.0). The list browser (❹) shows the search result list if the search in the object browser (❺) (with possible restrictions of the search area) was successful. Provided that the GenIL BOL browser can determine the key type information of the search result objects, you can transform the unique IDs of the search result objects in the list browser (❹) into the respective key of the object in plain text by clicking on the TRANSLATE IDs button. When you select an object in the list browser, the display of the object browser changes, which then maps the attributes of the object in the object browser.

Functions of the GenIL BOL browser

297

Attribute
properties

Furthermore, the system outputs the attribute properties of each attribute (❻). The meaning of an attribute property is displayed in the value help that can be displayed (❼).

Because of the navigation in the list browser, you are provided with several buttons in the object browser (❽). They enable you to make changes to the objects or to go from one object to the next after you have selected an object relationship in the model browser using the object model.

Test the object
method

If the selected object has its own method implementations, you can select and execute a method in the model browser using the EXECUTE METHOD button. Using the CHILDREN button, you can have the system display the relationships to subordinate objects hierarchically in the model browser. By selecting a relationship in the model browser, the corresponding object and its attributes is displayed as an object node in the object browser and can be edited there.

New objects

If you want to create new objects, you must click on the NEW ROOT OBJECT button on the toolbar (❶). The attributes for defining an object are shown in the parameter browser below the model browser. These parameters must be supplied with values. After you have clicked the CREATE OBJECT button, the system creates the object in the API. If an error occurs during the creation of an object, you can view it in the message browser. To create BOL entities of dependent objects of the root objects, navigate to any dependent object by selecting a relationship and clicking on the INSERT ENTITY button in the list browser.

## 12.3 Enhancing Object Models

What is an enhancement of an object model? It is the enhancement of an existing object or addition of a new object to an existing object model.

In real life, you often face the problem of mapping a customer-specific field in a database table in a user interface. The user interface of the CRM Web Client, however, does not operate at the database level directly. It functions at the object model level with the BOL that is provided by the GenIL. The GenIL objects process APIs to access the database. A problem that was relatively easy to solve in traditional Dynpro programming has become somewhat more difficult due to the complexity of the Web Client UI framework.

Easy Enhancement
Workbench

SAP's EEWB (see Chapter 5, Section 5.3) is a tool used to enhance a multitude of objects and their database tables and structures. However, the EEWB cannot be used randomly for all object enhancements; it can only be used for objects (and their APIs) whose underlying DDIC structures are intended for an enhancement using the EEWB. This is why we will describe the alternatives in the following sections.

Figure 12.9 shows the schematic structure of the GenIL. To enhance a GenIL object of an object model, you must consider the following levels of an object implementation (see the black boxes in the figure):

*Handler class, API, database level*

▶ The DDIC structures of the object (e.g., object attributes)

▶ The handler class of the object

▶ The API that is processed by the object implementation

▶ The underlying database table or the RFC call

> **Note**
>
> It can sometimes be sufficient to only enhance the DDIC structures and database tables involved with additional fields so that the adaptation of the handler class can be skipped. However, this only applies to structures that can be enhanced. To find the structures involved is usually not an easy task.

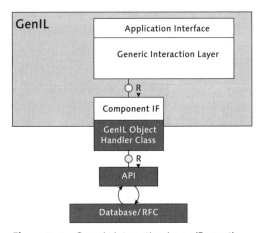

**Figure 12.9** Generic Interaction Layer (Excerpt)

To insert another object in an object model, it is necessary to create a new object implementation. This is then used to create the following elements:

*New object in the object model*

▶ DDIC structures (object attributes)

▶ A handler class

▶ A definition of the new object (object type, structure name, etc.)

▶ If required, a definition of the relationships to other objects (in Customizing)

▶ Often, you must adapt the handler classes of "adjacent" objects in the object model that should be related to the new object.

There are no threads or definite rules for the enhancement of an object model in the SAP standard because each GenIL component proceeds individually for the instantiation of its objects. In the worst case, it is not possible to enhance a component at all (or only through modification).

Sections 12.3.1 and 12.3.2 discuss options for enhancing a business partner model and business transaction model that are often required in a customer project.

**Simple GenIL objects**
Section 12.3.3 will show that simple options exist to define a new GenIL object of the ROOT OBJECT type; this section also describes the creation of simple GenIL objects on the basis of a customer-specific table. Section 12.3.4 will discuss how you can enhance an object model on the basis of a web service.

### 12.3.1 Enhancing the Business Partner Model

Some objects of the object model for business partners — for example, static search objects — cannot be enhanced using the EEWB. For such cases, SAP provides an alternative enhancement option.

An implementation class (handler class) and a structure that maps the object attributes exist for each object in the standard business partner model. You can find these specifications and information on the object relationships in the views that are listed in Table 12.4. You can open the views for view maintenance using Transaction SM30.

| View Name | Presentation of the |
| --- | --- |
| CRMV_OBJ_BUIL | Business partner objects |
| CRMV_MODEL_BUIL | Business partner object relationships |

**Table 12.4** Business Partner Object Model

You can find the option to enhance the standard business partner model by following the IMG menu path CUSTOMER RELATIONSHIP MANAGEMENT • CRM CROSS-APPLICATION COMPONENTS • GENERIC INTERACTION LAYER/OBJECT LAYER • COMPONENT-SPECIFIC SETTINGS • ENHANCE OBJECT MODEL FOR BUSINESS PARTNER (alternatively you can also start Transaction CRMC_BUIL in the SAP GUI). In this IMG activity, you maintain the metadata of the object model for business partners. You can define additional objects and relationships and replace existing standard objects. You can use the IMG activity to perform the following:

- Implement a custom search
- Filter search results to customer-specific criteria
- Supplement the business partner model with new dependent objects
- Implement new methods with business partner logic for a business partner object

You should handle the maintenance of data with care because changes can affect all applications that are based on GenIL for business partners.

The dialog structure of the IMG activity is divided into the following levels:

- Implementation class definition
- Object definition
- Model definition
- Method definition

At the IMPLEMENTATION CLASS DEFINITION level (see Figure 12.10), you must enter the name of the new object and its implementation class.

*Implementation class*

The implementation class must be derived from the CL_BUIL_ABSTR class.

At the OBJECT DEFINITION level, you maintain the specifications on the object type and the structure name. In the ROOT OBJECT NAME field, you enter the name of the root object of the enhancement (see Section 12.1.3).

*Object definition*

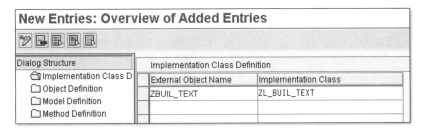

**Figure 12.10** Implementation Class Definition

At the MODEL DEFINITION level, you define a new relationship between an existing object and your new object.

*Model definition*

You define your own object methods with business logic under METHOD DEFINITION. Here, you must enter the new method name and the object for which you want to execute the method. The method must exist in the implementation class.

*Method definition*

You will recall that object implementations can be overwritten in the standard. Keeping this in mind, let us take a look at a simple example for enhancing a search object. Assume that you need to enhance the BUILEMPSEARCH search object with search criterion DATE OF BIRTH. If you enter this search criterion, the goal is to have the system output only those employees whose birthday is on a specific date. Granted, this example is not very challenging, but it is only supposed to demonstrate how you can implement a functioning enhancement. The following list of steps describes the typical procedure for enhancing the BUILEMPSEARCH SEARCH OBJECT:

**Adapting the object search**

1. First, create the new `ZCRMST_EMP_SEARCH_BUIL` structure as a copy of `CRMST_EMP_SEARCH_BUIL` and enhance it with the `BIRTHDT` attribute of the `BU_BIRTHDT` type.

2. Create the new `ZL_BUPA_IL_EMP_SEARCH` class and derive it from the `CL_BUPA_IL_EMP_SEARCH` class.

3. Redefine the `GET_RESULT_TABLE` method and insert the statements from Listing 12.1.

4. Start Transaction CRMC_BUIL and overwrite the implementation for the BUILEMPSEARCH search object.

5. Test the BUILEMPSEARCH search object in the GenIL BOL browser.

**Copy of the object attribute structure**

Create a copy of the `CRMST_EMP_SEARCH_BUIL` structure using the ABAP Dictionary Maintenance (Transaction SE11), and add the new fields. The new structure should have the name `ZCRMST_EMP_SEARCH_BUIL`. Enhance the structure with the `BIRTHDT` attribute of the `BU_BIRTHDT` type. Activate the structure.

**Creating and deriving the class**

Use the *Class Builder* (Transaction SE24) to create a new class with the `ZL_BUPA_IL_EMP_SEARCH` name. In the properties of the class, you define the `CL_BUPA_IL_EMP_SEARCH` class as the superclass. This way you ensure a derivation of the `CL_BUPA_IL_EMP_SEARCH` class.

**Redefining the GET_RESULT_ TABLE method**

Redefine the `GET_RESULT_TABLE` method of the `ZL_BUPA_IL_EMP_SEARCH` class and insert the statements from Listing 12.1. Subsequently, activate the `ZL_BUPA_IL_EMP_SEARCH` class.

```
call method super->get_result_table
  exporting
    is_parameters           = is_parameters
    it_selection_parameters = it_selection_parameters
  importing
    et_bupa_search_result   = et_bupa_search_result
    ev_max_hits             = ev_max_hits .
```

```
data ls_bupa_search_result type bus020_search_result.
data lv_tabix type i.
data l_but000 type but000.
data ls_searchpara type zcrmst_emp_search_buil.
move-corresponding is_parameters to ls_searchpara.
if not ls_searchpara-birthdt is initial.
  loop at et_bupa_search_result into ls_bupa_search_result.
    lv_tabix = sy-tabix.
    select single * from but000 into l_but000
     where partner_guid = ls_bupa_search_result-partner_
guid  and birthdt = ls_searchpara-birthdt.
    if sy-subrc ne 0.
      delete et_bupa_search_result index lv_tabix.
    endif.
  endloop.
endif.
```

**Listing 12.1** Enhancing a Search Object

Now start Transaction CRMC_BUIL. Insert a new row in the dialog structure at the IMPLEMENTATION CLASS DEFINITION level. In the OBJECT NAME field, enter the name BuilEmpSearch. Enter ZL_BUPA_IL_EMP_SEARCH in the IMPLEMENTATION CLASS field. Then switch to the OBJECT DEFINITION level in the dialog structure and insert a new row. In the OBJECT NAME field, enter the name BuilEmpSearch. Select the SEARCH OBJECT object type. Enter ZCRMST_EMP_SEARCH_BUIL in the ATTRIBUTE STRUCTURE. In the ROOT OBJECT field, enter the name of the root object, "BuilEmp". Save your settings.

*Object definition in Transaction CMRC_BUIL*

Finally, you must test the enhancement for the BUILEMPSEARCH search object in the GenIL BOL browser. Start the GenIL BOL browser. Enter BP_APPL in the COMPONENT SET field and press the [F8] key to go to the BOL browser. Select the BUILEMPSEARCH search object and start the search taking into account the BIRTHDT search criterion.

*Testing the enhancement*

## 12.3.2  Enhancing the Business Transaction Model

Section 12.3.1 described how you can enhance the business partner model. The procedure for enhancing the business transaction model is the same; the only difference is that the metadata of the object model for business transactions is saved in different tables. For the sake of simplicity, the following sections only describe the differences and specific features of the business transaction model enhancement.

To be able to implement enhancements of the object model for business trans-actions that you cannot carry out using the EEWB, it is useful to know the object model for business transactions. As already mentioned, in the object model for business transactions, a handler class and a structure that maps the object attributes exist for each object. To implement object enhancements, you must therefore adapt the structure and the handler class, if required. You can determine the assignment of an object to a handler class in the Custom-izing of the object model for business transactions.

> **Note**
>
> As of SAP CRM 2007 support package 3, you can view the Customizing for the object model for business transactions via CUSTOMER RELATIONSHIP MAN-AGEMENT • CRM CROSS-APPLICATION COMPONENTS • GENERIC INTERACTION LAYER/OBJECT LAYER • COMPONENT-SPECIFIC SETTINGS • BUSINESS TRANSACTIONS in the SAP Implementation Guide (Transaction SPRO) and enhance it with new entries.

Metadata of the object model

The ENHANCE MODEL FOR BUSINESS TRANSACTIONS WITH FURTHER NODES IMG activity summarizes the metadata of the object model in one table. The general rule applies that you should not change or delete any entries of the table in this view because this could impact other applications that are based on the GenIL for business transactions. However, you can add entries to the Customizing to enhance the object model.

In the maintenance view of the IMG activity, you can view specifications such as object name, description, object type, structure name, and handler class. Note that the HANDLER CLASS column of the table frequently has no entry for an implementation class of an object. This is because the GenIL uses a generic procedure to determine the class name during the generation of an object instance for business transactions.

> **Note**
>
> The generic procedure to determine the implementation class of a business transaction object is as follows: For example, if the name of a business trans-action object is BTQUERY1O, then the first two letters of the object name are omitted and QUERY1O remains. Then, the implementation of the searched object is CL_CRM_ + Query1O + _RUN_BTIL. Therefore, the CL_CRM_ prefix and the _RUN_BTIL suffix are used for the generic name determination of the object implementation class. As a result, the name of the implementation class is `CL_CRM_QUERY1O_RUN_BTIL`.

An entry in the DEFINE CUSTOMER-SPECIFIC HANDLER CLASSES FOR BUSINESS TRANSACTION MODEL NODES IMG activity (CRMV_OBJ_BTIL_C maintenance view) enables you to "overwrite" this procedure. This means that the system does not load the original implementation class at runtime but rather the class that you have defined in the STRUCTURE NAME column. Methods of the CL_CRM_OBJ_FACTORY_BTIL class consider the customer-specific handler classes in Customizing when loading the GenIL object classes.

Handler class

When you define the name of an ABAP class in the STRUCTURE NAME column, you must keep in mind that the technical name of this ABAP class must end with a suffix and that you must define the name of the ABAP class without a suffix in the maintenance view. The suffix consists of the literal constant _RUN_BTIL. The length of a class name in ABAP is 30 characters. If the class name has more than 21 characters, this affects the suffix, which is then truncated by the corresponding number of characters.

Consider the naming convention!

> **Example**
>
> If you specify a handler class with ZCL_BTADMINH_ADVANCED_QUERY in the maintenance view, the technical name of the class must be ZCL_BTADMINH_ADVANCED_QUERY_RU.

Keep this in mind when you specify a name during the creation of a new class using the Class Builder (Transaction SE24). When you enter the name of the class in the STRUCTURE NAME column, the system does not check whether the class is actually available in the system.

To enhance the object model for business transactions with additional relationships, you use the CRMV_ORLALL_BTIL maintenance view.

Relationships

You can manage object methods of business transactions that each contain a specific functionality for mapping business logic using the CRMV_METHOD_BTIL maintenance view.

Object methods

Table 12.5 summarizes all maintenance views for enhancements to the business transaction model.

| View Name | Function |
| --- | --- |
| CRMV_OBJ_BTIL_C | Maintenance of object data |
| CRMV_ORLALL_BTIL | Maintenance of object relationships |
| CRMV_METHOD_BTIL | Maintenance of object methods |

**Table 12.5**  Maintenance Views for the Business Transaction Model

### 12.3.3 Simple GenIL Objects

Simple GenIL objects let you enhance an object model with your own objects; these are always root objects.

In the SAP Implementation Guide (Transaction SPRO), you can find the maintenance dialog for the definition of simple objects under CUSTOMER RELATIONSHIP MANAGEMENT • CRM CROSS-APPLICATION COMPONENTS • GENERIC INTERACTION LAYER/OBJECT LAYER • COMPONENT-SPECIFIC SETTINGS • DEFINE SIMPLE OBJECTS. Alternatively, you can open the CRMVC_ GIL_SO_DEF view cluster using Transaction SM34.

| Object Name | Implementation Class | Attribute Structure | Structure of Mandatory Fields During |
|---|---|---|---|
| AUI WorkItem | CL_CRM_IC_AUI_WI | CRMST_AUI_WI | |
| AUIWFWIAttachments | CL_CRM_IC_AUI_WF_WI | CRMT_BSP_WFM_ATTACHMENTLIST | |
| AUIWFWIDetail | CL_CRM_IC_AUI_WF_WI | CRMT_BSP_WFM_DETAILLIST | |
| AUIWFWIObjects | CL_CRM_IC_AUI_WF_WI | CRMT_BSP_WFM_TAB_DETAIL_WIO | |
| AUIWFWorkItem | CL_CRM_IC_AUI_WF_WI | CRMT_BSP_WD_WF_DETAIL | |
| Assignment | CL_CRM_ASSIGNMENT_SO | CRMST_ASSIGNMENT_SO | <NONE> |
| BIReport | CL_CRM_BI_REPORT_GENIL | CRMT_BI_REPORT_NODE | |
| ChatTranscript | CL_CHAT_GENIL | ICT_CHAT_TRANS | |
| DefectDocument | CL_CRM_TELCO_SIMPLE | IST_DATA | |
| EventHistory | CL_CRM_EVENTHIST | COMT_EH_DISPLAY_GENIL | COMT_EVHIST_IMP |
| FindSurvey | CL_CRM_SURVEY_SIMPLE_BO | CRMT_SURVEY_UI | |
| ICBORWrapper | CL_CRM_IC_BOR_WRAPPER | CRMT_IC_BOR_WRAPPER | CRMT_IC_BOR_WRAPPER |
| ICFaxLetter | CL_CRM_IC_BOR_WRAPPER | CRMT_IC_BOR_WRAPPER | CRMT_IC_BOR_WRAPPER |
| MktInteractionObject | CL_CRM_MKT_IO_SO_HANDLER | CRMT_SO_IO_ATTR | |
| My Worklist | CL_TODO_BO | CRMT_MY_WORKLIST | |
| SAPOffice | CL_CRM_IC_SAPOFFICE | CRMST_IC_SO_SAPOFFICE | |
| SearchReDoResults | CL_CRM_IC_ALINK_QUERIES | TOARS_S | TOARS_S |
| SearchReDoUrls | CL_CRM_IC_ALINK_QUERIES | TOADURL_S | TOADURL_S |
| ServiceTimeRep | CL_CRM_IC_SRVTTIMEREP_SIMPLE | CRMD_TIMEREP | |
| Shortcut | CL_CRM_SHORTCUT_GENIL | CRMT_SHORTCUT | CRMT_SHORTCUT_CREATE |

**Figure 12.11** Defining Simple GenIL Objects

**Maintaining the object definition** In the dialog for maintaining the object definition (see Figure 12.11), you must specify the name of your object and enter the name of the ABAP implementation class. At this point, you must also enter the name of the structure that describes the attributes of a simple GenIL object. As another option, in the STRUCTURE OF MANDATORY FIELDS DURING CREATION column, you can maintain a structure with attributes whose attributes must be filled when you generate the BOL entity.

In the dialog structure (left area of the window), you can define search objects, relationships to other root objects, and object methods for the GenIL object. To define a search object for a GenIL object, enter the name of your search object in the SEARCH OBJECT NAME input field under SEARCH OBJECT DEFINITIONS and the structure with the search criteria attributes in the PARAMETER STRUCTURE NAME input field.

In the dialog structure for RELATION DEFINITIONS, you maintain the relationship of a simple GenIL object to other root objects by entering the name of the relation, the name of the target object including the component name of the target object, as well as the cardinality. Note that you can only define associations to root objects and access objects at this point. Such assigned objects do not depend on transactions.

Moreover, you can enhance your GenIL objects with additional business logic by entering the names of the additional methods in the METHOD DEFINITIONS dialog structure. Here, you must implement the EXECUTE_METHOD method of the IF_GENIL_SO_HANDLER interface by evaluating the IV_METH-ODE_NAME parameter accordingly and calling the methods that are necessary to fulfill the function.

Enhancement with business logic

An implementation class of a simple GenIL object must implement either the IF_GENIL_SO_HANDLER interface or the abstract class CL_CRM_GENIL_ABSTR_SO_HANDLER, provided that the access key of the GenIL object is of the GUID type (RAW16). For all other key variants, the implementation class must implement the IF_GENIL_SO_HANDLER2 interface or the CL_CRM_GENIL_ABSTR_SO_HANDLER2 basis class.

The interfaces IF_GENIL_SO_HANDLER or IF_GENIL_SO_HANDLER2 contain certain method definitions, the most important of which are listed in Table 12.6:

| Method | Function |
|---|---|
| CREATE | Creates a set of object instances according to the parameters. |
| GET_LIST | Returns a list of object instances that meet the search parameters. |
| GET_DETAIL | Returns attributes and relations of object instances. |
| MODIFY | Modifies attributes and relations of object instances in the buffer. |
| LOCK | Locks object instances. |
| DELETE | Deletes object instances. |
| SAVE | Saves object instances of object entities. |
| EXECUTE_METHOD | Executes an object instance method. |

**Table 12.6** Methods of the IF_GENIL_SO_HANDLER2 Interface

You do not have to implement all methods of the interfaces. For a GenIL object that only selects data, it is sufficient if the GET_LIST and GET_DETAIL methods are defined accordingly in the implementation class.

> **Note**
>
> Simple GenIL objects are assigned to the SO2 component set automatically.

**Generic solution approach** You probably realized that you must carry out one or more steps to implement a simple object. For recurring tasks, such as the provision of information from a user-defined database table, a generic functionality would, however, be desirable. This generic functionality is provided in the form of the CL_CRM_GENIL_GEN_TABLE_OBJ class. Using this class, you can omit a large part of programming because in Customizing, you only need to define the name of the database table that contains the data of the business data object. Moreover, you have to specify a lock object. You can structure the table as desired—the only prerequisite is that the user-defined database table contains a key field with the GUID name and the GUID data type. The reason for this limitation is that the CL_CRM_GENIL_GEN_TABLE_OBJ class implements the IF_GENIL_SO_HANDLER interface.

The following section describes how you can generically create a simple GenIL object:

1. Create a database table with the GUID key field and the corresponding attributes.

2. Create a lock object (if a lock object already exists, this step can be skipped).

3. Go to Customizing for simple objects in the SAP Implementation Guide.

4. Make an entry in the CRMC_TBLOBJ_MAP table.

5. Finally, test the object in the GenIL BOL browser.

In the first step, you create a database table with the corresponding attributes that maps the new business data object. In the second step, you create a lock object for the data record locks because the changes to the business data object should be implemented. In the third step, you define the simple GenIL object in the Customer Relationship Management • CRM Cross-Application Components • Generic Interaction Layer/Object Layer • Component-Specific Settings • Define Simple Objects IMG activity. Step four is required to link the object to the database table and to the lock object. For this purpose, you need to add an entry of the simple object to the CRMC_TBLOBJ_MAP database table (stating the corresponding lock object).

Finally, in step five, you test the new object using the GenIL BOL browser. Section 12.4 comprehensively describes a practical example for creating a simple GenIL object.

### 12.3.4  Web Service Consumption Tool (WSCT)

As of release SAP CRM 2007 support package 2, you can generate root objects and search objects that are based on a web service using the *Web Service Consumption Tool* (WSCT). For this purpose, the WSCT uses standard SAP NetWeaver technology and is based on consumer proxy definitions. Only the synchronous and stateless call of a web service is supported (see Section 7.1).

*Web Service Consumption Tool*

> **Note**
>
> A consumer proxy definition is generated using a valid WSDL file as the input file. The proxy enables the application developer to concentrate on the business functions, while technical aspects, such as the processing of a SOAP message, are automatically taken from the proxy implementation.

Thus, the WSCT requires a functioning, configured web service, including the existing consumer proxy definitions. For the sake of simplicity, this section does not describe the implementation and configuration of proxies in detail. Instead, you will learn how you can use the WSCT to generate Gen IL objects based on a web service.

To start the WSCT (see Figure 12.12), follow the IMG path CUSTOMER RELATIONSHIP MANAGEMENT • UI FRAMEWORK • UI FRAMEWORK DEFINITION • WEB SERVICES • WEB SERVICE CONSUMPTION TOOL: CREATE BOL OBJECTS.

*Starting the WSCT*

> **Tip**
>
> You can also start the WSCT in the SAP GUI using Transaction CRM_GENIL_WSC.

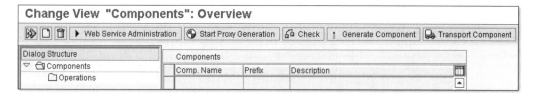

**Figure 12.12**  Initial Screen of the Web Service Consumption Tool

**Read and query operations**

The dialog of the WSCT is subdivided into a toolbar and a hierarchical dialog structure for managing the (GenIL) components and operations. An operation corresponds to a service operation and the system only supports read and query operations.

Table 12.7 lists the toolbar pictograms and describes their function.

| Pictogram | Function |
|-----------|----------|
| ▷▷ | Changes the name of a component |
| ▯ | Creates a new component definition or an operation |
| 🗑 | Deletes the component definition or the operation |
| ▶ Web Service Administration | Navigates to the web service administration |
| 🌐 Start Proxy Generation | Starts the proxy class generation based on a web service |
| 🔒 Check | Checks the definition for consistency (the check is also carried out at the attribute level) |
| Generate Component | Generates the component as a GenIL component and component set |
| Transport Component | Transports the component definition to the target systems |
| Attribute Tree | Displays the attributes of the input-output structures of a client proxy method |

**Table 12.7**  Pictograms of the Web Service Consumption Tool

To generate a new component, click on the CREATE COMPONENT button and enter a name and a description for the new component in the details dialog. Additionally, define a prefix. It is used for the name assignment during the generation of the DDIC structures and for the GenIL object names (see Figure 12.13).

**Creating an operation**

After you have saved the entry for the component, you can generate an operation based on a proxy method (see Figure 12.14).

---

**Note**

If no proxy is available, you can start the wizard for generating consumer proxy definitions based on a web service by clicking on START PROXY GENERATION.

---

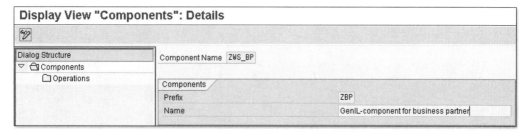

**Figure 12.13**  Creating a Component in the WSCT

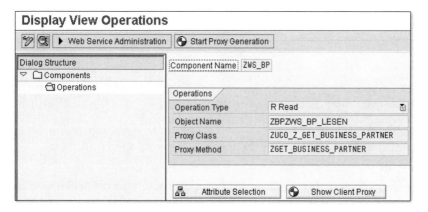

**Figure 12.14**  Defining an Operation in the WSCT

In the OPERATIONS area, you assign service operations to the component. In the OPERATION TYPE selection list, choose operation type READ or QUERY. With this selection, you also determine whether the object is a root object or a search object.

*Assignment of service operations*

Only one read operation and therefore one root object per component is permitted and it must always exist in the component.

Enter the name of the proxy class that implements the web service call in the PROXY CLASS field and specify the name of the corresponding proxy method in the PROXY METHOD field.

If you click the ATTRIBUTE SELECTION button, the system takes you to the dialog window for defining the component attributes. This dialog displays all attributes of a proxy method in a tree structure on the left side of the screen (see Figure 12.15). The tree structure is subdivided into two main nodes, INPUT (❶) and OUTPUT (❷).

*Defining the component attributes*

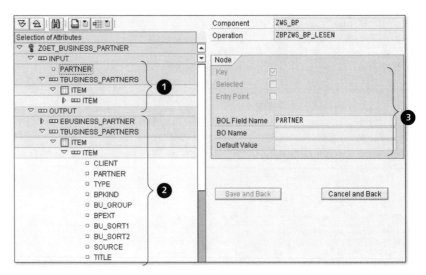

**Figure 12.15** Attribute Selection in the WSCT

Properties of
attributes

On the right hand side, you define the properties of the selected nodes or attributes (❸). You can define the following properties of an attribute:

▶ **Key**
Here you determine whether the selected attribute is a key field. The specification of the key is necessary, for example, to define the key structure of a root object.

▶ **Selected**
If you set this property, the attribute is used as an attribute for the root object or search object.

▶ **Entry Point**
With this property, you determine as of which point the root object or search object begins. This property can only be used for nodes or attributes in the output structure.

Additionally, you can specify individual names for attributes or objects; the name of an attribute must be unique. Furthermore, you can assign default values at the attribute level. This is useful for search criteria of a query operation.

Special aspects for
the assignment of
properties

When assigning properties, you must take certain aspects into account. In principle, you must differentiate between a read operation and a query operation, as follows:

▶ **Read operation**
At least one key field must exist in the input structure and the output structure. In addition, you must select a key field for each table selected in the output branch. The key fields are used to create the key structure of the dependent GenIL object in a 1:n relationship. Within the output structure, you must select a node as the entry point.

▶ **Query operation**
You must select at least one input attribute of a query operation and the output structure of a query operation must contain at least one key field. Key fields of a query operation must correspond to the key fields of the input structure of the read operation. You must determine exactly one output structure as the entry point for the query operation. This is the structure as of which the query operation begins. A table must be super-ordinate to this structure.

After you have created the operations with attributes and set the properties, you can check the consistency of the definition using the CHECK button. If the system does not display any error messages, you can generate the component using the GENERATE COMPONENT button. In addition to the component, the system also generates a component set and assigns it to the component. The name of the component set derives from the name of the component and the _WSC suffix is added.

Generating components

When you have completed the generation of the component, you can test it in the GenIL model browser and the GenIL BOL browser.

Testing the component

## 12.4 Practical Example: Creating a Simple GenIL Object

The goal of this practical example is to create a simple GenIL object on the basis of a new database table. Section 12.3.3 described the procedure for generically creating a simple GenIL object. This is used as the basis for the activity. You must perform the following steps:

1. Defining and activating a database table

2. Creating a lock object

3. Configuring a simple object in Customizing

4. Connecting with lock object and database table

5. Testing the new object using the GenIL BOL Browser

### Defining and Activating a Database Table

Before you create a simple GenIL object, you first create a user-defined database table whose structure you can view in Table 12.8. The structure of the database is intentionally kept simple in this example and it is limited to five rows. Ensure that the table contains a `GUID` key field with the `GUID` data type. The name of the table is ZCATALOG.

ZCATALOG table

| Field Name | Key Field | Init | Data Element |
|---|---|---|---|
| CLIENT | X | X | MANDT |
| GUID | X | X | GUID |
| ORDEROBJ | | | CRMT_OBJECT_GUID |
| CATALOGTYPE | | | COMT_CATALOG |
| SHORT TEXT | | | CHAR200 |

**Table 12.8**  Structure of the ZCATALOG Table

You can create a table in the SAP GUI using the ABAP Dictionary Maintenance (Transaction SE11). Additionally, maintain the technical settings (Technical Settings button) and activate the table.

### Creating a Lock Object

Lock object

Step two requires you to create a lock object because simultaneous changes to the data records should be avoided. This is also done in the ABAP Dictionary Maintenance (Transaction SE11). Enter a name for the lock object and ensure that it starts with the EZ prefix. If you work in your own customer namespace, you can also prefix the customer namespace instead of the EZ prefix. The lock object should be the only reference that refers to the ZCATALOG primary table. Ensure that the key fields `CLIENT` and `GUID` are available on the Lock Parameter tab. Activate the lock object.

### Configuring a Simple Object in Customizing

The third step involves the configuration of the simple object in Customizing. Open Transaction SPRO in the SAP GUI and select the maintenance of the simple objects in the Customer Relationship Management • CRM Cross-Application Components • Generic Interaction Layer/Object Layer • Component-Specific Settings • Define Simple Objects IMG activity. Create a new object with the name, ZCATALOG and enter the name of the CL_CRM_GENIL_GEN_TABLE_OBJ class in the Implementation Class field, and the name of the previously created ZCATALOG table as the attribute structure (as you know, a database table that is defined in the SAP system is a structure by definition). Enter the name GUID as the key name in the KEY STRUCTURE field.

To complete the maintenance of the object definition, go to the search object definition in the dialog structure (left part of the screen). There, enter the ZCATALOGQRY name in the SEARCH OBJECT NAME field and the ZCATALOG name in the PARAMETER STRUCTURE NAME field. Save these settings and exit the transaction for maintaining simple objects.

*Search object definition*

### Connecting with the Lock Object and Database Table

After you have completed this process, you must connect the lock object with the previously created object definition. Therefore, open the CRMV_TBLOBJ_MAP maintenance view using the Table View Maintenance (Transaction SM30) for mapping the simple table objects and insert a new row. Enter the name ZCATALOG in the EXTERNAL OBJECT NAME and TABLE NAME fields. The name of the lock object you defined in step two must be in the LOCK OBJECT field. Save your entries and exit the maintenance transaction.

*Mapping of the lock object and object definition*

### Testing the New Object using the GenIL BOL Browser

At this point, we have almost finished with the example. You now only need to test the new object. To do so, open the GenIL BOL browser using Transaction GENIL_BOL_BROWSER, select the SO2 component set, and continue with EXECUTE ( F8 ). You should find the ZCATALOGQRY object search in the model browser. Test the search based on some search criteria. It is also possible to create new entries. Click on the NEW ROOT OBJECT button, then select the ZCATALOG object and maintain the object attributes. Save your entries in the GenIL BOL browser and in the data browser (Transaction SE16), check whether your entries are included in the ZCATALOG table.

*Testing in the GenIL BOL browser*

*The BOL is the bulwark of the UI.*
— Uwe Reimitz, SAP AG

# 13 Business Object Layer — BOL

The BOL is a model-based software layer that provides all CRM business data objects to various consumers via a standardized interface. The BOL is therefore the layer that is connected to both the user interface and the object model.

To motivate you to read this quite technical chapter, let's first explain the necessity of the BOL. If you want to create your own UI components using windows and views and mapping data from an object model to a user interface, the BOL is indispensable. Model nodes (see Chapter 9, Section 9.1.2) refer to a GenIL object of an object model. To populate these model nodes with data, you should use the functions of the BOL.

At runtime, the BOL manages business data objects in the form of BOL entities and stores information about what changes have been made to the BOL entities. The BOL does not know to which GenIL component a business data object belongs. This is known by the GenIL because it distributes the requests (*lock*, *change*, *save*, etc.) across the relevant GenIL components.

Many consumers use the BOL to access the object model, however, the main consumer is the CRM user interface (Web Client). Other consumers also exist such as the GenIL BOL browser (see Figure 13.1).

Main consumer

Using the BOL within your ABAP programs and UI component has significant benefits:

▶ The development of UI components is facilitated by the close coupling of the BOL to the presentation layer of the Web Client UI framework.

▶ BOL-internal buffer mechanisms (caches) increase system performance (see Section 13.12).

▶ The transactional control through the BOL facilitates development and reduces development times.

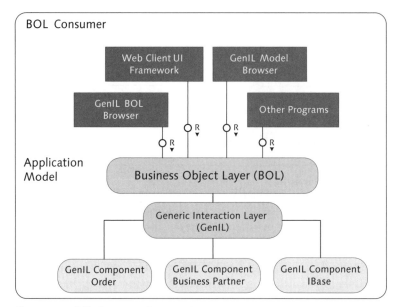

**Figure 13.1** BOL Consumer Presentation

**BOL API**  The BOL API was implemented entirely with object orientation and the usage of the different provided services, interfaces, and classes is standardized. The BOL provides standardized services for searching, generating, changing, and deleting business data objects such as PRODUCT or BUSINESS PARTNER in a transactional context.

**Buffer**  As already mentioned, the BOL has a specific buffer to temporarily store BOL entities for performance reasons. If a search service returns BOL entities, or if you navigate from one BOL entity to another in the object model, the system stores these BOL entities in the buffer (see Section 13.12).

## 13.1  BOL Entities

**Entity manager**  The system stores data of business data objects generically in attributes of BOL entities at runtime. Technically, a BOL entity is a runtime instance of the `CL_CRM_BOL_ENTITY` class and cannot stand alone, that is, it is managed within an entity manager. This procedure ensures the uniqueness of a BOL entity. Every instance of a BOL entity includes a reference to its entity manager, which contains control indicators and information on relationships to other BOL entities. This, and additional information is stored in the `ENTITY_TAB` attribute of the entity manager (`CL_CRM_BOL_ENTITY_MANAGER` class).

Table 13.1 lists certain useful attributes of the `CL_CRM_BOL_ENTITY` class. To know that they exist may be useful in real life.

| Attribute | Description |
|---|---|
| PARENT_ENTITY | Pointer to the higher-level BOL entity (parent object) |
| MY_MANAGER_ENTRY | Pointer to the entity manager |
| CONTAINER_PROXY | Pointer to the buffer |

**Table 13.1** Useful Attributes of the CL_CRM_BOL_ENTITY Class

To access the attributes of a BOL entity, you use the `IF_BOL_BO_PROPERTY_ACCESS` interface. BOL entities are often managed in collections (see Section 13.2).

## 13.2  Working with Collections

A collection is a generic list of BOL entities and is used in a similar way as an internal table with object references. The Web Client UI framework often uses collections because collections are transferred to *collection wrappers* of a context node to populate a context node with data. For more information, refer to Chapter 9, Section 9.4.5. Figure 13.2 illustrates the structure of a collection.

You have to distinguish between two variants of collections: *entity collections* and *BO collections*. Both variants are containers for BOL entities. A BOL collection, however, can additionally manage instances of search services (represented by the `CL_CRM_BOL_QUERY_SERVICE` service).

Entity collection and BO collection

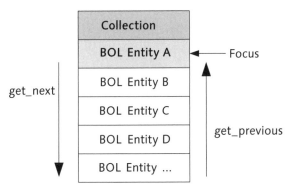

**Figure 13.2**  Schematic Diagram of a Collection

319

You can add BOL entities to a collection or delete them. To manage BOL entities within a collection, the collection provides the ADD, REMOVE, and CLEAR methods. All BOL entities are stored only as references in the collection.

### 13.2.1 Access Using Iterators

Focus change To access BOL entities that are contained in a collection, you use iterators. You can use iterators to navigate in a collection, that is, an iterator enables you to address BOL entities of a collection. A *focus object* is assigned to every collection. Initially, this focus object points to the first entry of a collection. If you use a global iterator to navigate from one BOL entity to the next, the focus also changes (see Figure 13.3).

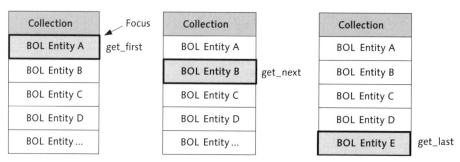

**Figure 13.3** Collection and Focus Object

Global iterator If the focus changes, the FOCUS_CHANGED event of the collection is sent. Listing 13.1 illustrates the use of a global iterator for a collection with the GET_NEXT method to navigate to the next BOL entity of the collection.

```
DATA:
lv_collection   TYPE REF TO if_bol_bo_col,
lv_property_access TYPE REF TO if_bol_bo_property_access.
lv_property_access = lv_collection->get_next( ).
```

**Listing 13.1** Using a Global Iterator

Local iterator The usage of a global iterator for a collection, including moving the related focus object, is not always required or desired. In such cases, you can use a local iterator. However, you have to explicitly request an iterator object from the collection. Listing 13.2 illustrates the use of a local iterator.

```
DATA lv_iterator TYPE REF TO if_bol_bo_col_iterator.
lv_iterator = lv_collection->get_iterator( ).
DATA lv_prop_access TYPE REF TO if_bol_bo_property_access.
lv_prop_access = lv_iterator->get_first( ).
WHILE lv_prop_access is bound.
```

```
  lv_prop_access = lv_iterator->get_next( ).
ENDWHILE.
```

**Listing 13.2** Using a Local Iterator

In addition to the GET_NEXT method to navigate from one BOL entity to the next, a collection provides additional methods for navigation within a collection, as summarized in Table 13.2.

| Method | Description |
|---|---|
| GET_NEXT | Provides, based on the current position, the next element within a collection. |
| GET_PREVIOUS | Provides, based on the current position, the previous element within a collection. |
| GET_LAST | Provides the last element of a collection. |
| GET_FIRST | Provides the first element of a collection. |
| GET_CURRENT | Provides the element on which the focus is at the moment. |

**Table 13.2** Methods for the Navigation within a Collection

## 13.2.2 Filtering Collections

Local iterators are used for navigation within a collection but also to filter a collection. Because you can use an unlimited number of iterators, you can also use any number of filters for a collection. However, keep in mind that the content of a collection can never be influenced by a filter.

Listing 13.3 illustrates the creation of a filter that should filter a collection of personal data by the *date of birth* attribute.

```
DATA:
lv_persons  TYPE REF TO cl_crm_bol_bo_col,
lv_filter   TYPE REF TO if_bol_bo_col_iterator.
lv_filter = lv_persons->if_bol_bo_col~get_iterator( ).
lv_filter->filter_by_property( iv_attr_name = 'BIRTHDATE'
                               iv_value     = '20070226' ).
```

**Listing 13.3** Filtering a Collection

When you have set the filter criterion, the iterator now uses the entries of the collection that correspond to the filter criterion. The comparison operation is implemented with the CP (*covers pattern*) comparison operator. Setting a filter criterion affects the methods of the iterator, particularly the SIZE and

**Filter criterion**

GET_BY_INDEX methods. You can further refine a filter process by calling the FILTER_BY_PROPERTY method. To remove all defined filters of a collection, call the DELETE_FILTER iterator method with the optional parameter IV_ALL and the Boolean value true (ABAP_TRUE) because a call without this parameter only removes the last set filter.

**Buffered mode versus interactive mode**

When you filter collections, you have to distinguish between two modes: buffered mode and interactive mode. The *buffered mode* is the default mode. Here, the iterator uses a copy of the collection. This procedure is beneficial for runtime but has a major disadvantage: the filter result will become invalid when you change the original collection or the BOL entities contained therein. You should consequently use this mode for read-only scenarios only. In contrast to this, an iterator in the *interactive mode* uses the original collection. The filter result is always correct because the filter process is implemented on the basis of the original collection. However, the execution of operations for the collection is somewhat slower in interactive mode.

### 13.2.3 Sorting Collections

**Sorting**

The sort method enables you to sort collections; you can define the sort sequence via parameters (see Listing 13.4).

```
DATA:
lv_address TYPE REF TO cl_crm_bol_entity_col.
lv_address->sort( iv_attr_name = 'STREET'
                  iv_sort_order = IF_BOL_BO_COL=>SORT_
DESCENDING ).
```

**Listing 13.4** Sorting a Collection

**Conversion exits**

Note that the sorting algorithm is sorted alphanumerically and the internal representation of the respective data type is used for sorting. Conversion exits are not considered here.

**Auto-cleanup mode**

If it is necessary that the system automatically removes deleted BOL entities from a collection, you must activate the auto-cleanup mode of the collection by calling the IF_BOL_BO_COL~ACTIVATE_AUTOCLEANUP method.

> **Note**
>
> Using the auto-cleanup mode means that you have to explicitly delete a collection that is no longer required, using the IF_BOL_BO_COL~CLEAR method. Otherwise, the garbage collector does not remove the collection from memory because the event handler table of your BOL entities still refers to the collection.

## 13.3   BOL Core

To be able to use the BOL to access an object model, you first have to determine an instance of the BOL core. At runtime, only one instance of the
BOL core exists for each session. The BOL core is technically mapped by
the CL_CRM_BOL_CORE class. Among other things, this class contains methods for access to the object model and for loading component sets. Listing
13.5 illustrates the determination of an instance of the BOL core using the
GET_INSTANCE method of the CL_CRM_BOL_CORE class.

Starting the
BOL core

```
DATA lv_bol_core TYPE REF TO cl_crm_bol_core.
lv_bol_core = cl_crm_bol_core->get_instance( ).
call method lv_bol_core->start_up
  exporting
    iv_appl_name          = 'ONEORDER'
    iv_display_mode_support = abap_false.
```

**Listing 13.5**   Starting the BOL Core

Calling the START_UP method starts the BOL with the defined component
set (in our example, the ONEORDER component set), which maps the data
model of the business transactions in the SAP standard version.

The CL_CRM_BOL_CORE=>GET_INSTANCE factory method provides a singleton
instance of the BOL core as the result. The BOL is started by calling the
START_UP method with the transferred component set. Set the ABAP_TRUE
value for the IV_DISPLAY_MODE_SUPPORT parameter if you want to ensure
that only locked objects can be changed. This corresponds to the implementation of a pessimistic locking procedure. In this case, all changes to objects
are ignored until the SWITCH_TO_CHANGE_MODE or LOCK method is called. The
system uses the ABAP_FALSE value for the IV_DISPLAY_MODE_SUPPORT parameter by default. This corresponds to an optimistic locking procedure.

Display mode

You can reload additional components or component sets via the LOAD_COM-
PONENT or LOAD_COMPONENT_SET method.

Reloading a
component (set)

## 13.4   Searching for BOL Entities

Searching for business data is one of the most frequently performed user
activities when using a dialog application. This leads to the question of how
you can determine business data as BOL entities. In this context, remember
the previously mentioned search services, of which two variants exist: static
searches and dynamic searches. Search criteria in static searches are always

linked with AND, whereas dynamic searches allow for additional options for formulating search queries.

**Static searches**  Let us first take a look at static searches, which provide a selected list of BOL entities. Listing 13.6 uses the static search BTQuery10 to determine a list of all business transactions of the BUSINESS ACTIVITY type (BUS2000126) by using a search service.

```
DATA lv_qs TYPE REF TO cl_crm_bol_query_service.
lv_qs = cl_crm_bol_query_service=>get_
instance(    'BTQuery10' ).
lv_qs->set_property(
iv_attr_name = 'OBJECT_TYPE'
iv_value = 'BUS2000126' ).
DATA lv_result TYPE REF TO if_bol_entity_col.
lv_result = lv_qs->get_query_result( ).
```

**Listing 13.6**  Executing a Simple Object Search

If the GET_QUERY_RESULT method is called, the LV_RESULT variable contains the search result as a collection (see Section 13.2) if the search was successful.

**Dynamic searches**  Since SAP CRM 2006s/1, the BOL also supports dynamic searches via the CL_CRM_BOL_DQUERY_SERVICE class. These have the benefit that you can formulate search criteria in ABAP in a similar way as for select options. This lets you use additional search patterns such as "greater than" or "less than" in addition to the check for equality (equal operator). Therefore, you can use OR links (*disjunctions*) within the same search criterion, whereas between search criteria, an AND link (*conjunction*) is always used.

```
DATA lv_dyn_query TYPE REF TO cl_crm_bol_dquery_service.
lv_dyn_query =
cl_crm_bol_dquery_service=>get_
instance( 'BuilEmpAdvancedSearch' ).
lv_dyn_query->set_property( iv_attr_name = 'MAX_HITS'
                            iv_value     = '100' ).
lv_dyn_query->add_selection_param( iv_attr_name = 'COUNTRY'
                                   iv_sign      = 'I'
                                   iv_option    = 'EQ'
                                   iv_low       = 'DE'
                                   iv_high      = '' ).
DATA lv_result TYPE REF TO if_bol_entity_col.
lv_result = lv_dyn_query->get_query_result( ).
```

**Listing 13.7**  Executing a Dynamic Search

If the GET_QUERY_RESULT method is called, the lv_result variable contains the search result as a collection (see Section 13.2) if the search was successful.

Due to the dynamic character of the search, the search parameters are also stored in a collection. The GET_SELECTION_PARAMS method provides this collection, which you can perform and modify using iterators.

In addition to performing dynamic searches, you can also store the search with its search criteria as a saved search (see Chapter 1, Section 1.2.3). The following statement stores the search as a search template under the name MYSEARCH:

*Generating a template for a saved search*

```
lv_dyn_query->save_query_as_template( iv_query_
id = 'MySearch' iv_overwrite = abap_true ).
```

The following statement illustrates how you can load the MYSEARCH search template using the LOAD_QUERY_TEMPLATE method:

```
lv_dyn_query->load_query_template( iv_query_id = 'MySearch' ).
```

For the user, a search template is only stored locally. This means that no transport to any other systems takes place.

## 13.5    Traversing via the Object Model

To navigate from one object to a related object within an object model using a directional relationship, you always have to traverse, that is, move, from a root object or an access object through the object model. To navigate from an object to a lower-level object in the object model, you can use the GET_RELATED_ENTITY and GET_RELATED_ENTITIES methods of a BOL entity (CL_CRM_BOL_ENTITY). The GET_RELATED_ENTITY method provides a single instance of a BOL entity and is used to determine a BOL entity from a relationship of the 1:1 cardinality. The GET_RELATED_ENTITIES method provides a collection of BOL entities as a result and is used to determine a BOL entity from a relationship of the 1:n cardinality.

Listing 13.8 illustrates how you can read the UIFCustomer BOL entity using a modeled relationship, BookCustomerRel.

*Determining BOL entities*

```
DATA lv_customers TYPE REF TO if_bol_entity_col.
lv_customers = lv_entity->get_related_entities(    iv_relation_
name = 'BookCustomerRel' ).
DATA lv_customer TYPE REF TO cl_crm_bol_entity.
lv_customer = lv_customers->get_first( ).
```

**Listing 13.8**  Accessing Related BOL Entities in the Object Model

To navigate to a higher level in the object model, you can use the GET_PAR-
ENT method. You can call it until you reach the root object in the object
hierarchy.

## 13.6 Locking BOL Entities

Before you change a BOL entity, you should lock it. This can be done by calling the LOCK instance method of the BOL entity (see Listing 13.9). You can
only lock BOL entities of root objects. The system automatically delegates
every lock request that addresses a BOL entity to the corresponding instance
of the root object.

```
DATA lv_success TYPE abap_bool.
lv_success = lv_entity->lock( ).
```

**Listing 13.9**  Setting a Lock

The return parameter of the LOCK method enables you to check whether the
lock was actually set for the BOL entity. If the lock has been successfully created, the system generates an instance of a transaction context for the locked
BOL entity. This instance is then stored in the transaction manager. To release
a BOL entity, you must go through the entire transaction cycle up to a commit, rollback, or revert (see Section 13.9).

## 13.7 Accessing BOL Entities

As already mentioned, a BOL entity is technically mapped by the CL_CRM_
BOL_ENTITY class. The class implements the IF_BOL_BO_PROPERTY_ACCESS
interface, which contains method definitions for the generic access to attributes of the BOL entity (see Table 13.3).

| Method Name | Function |
|---|---|
| GET_PROPERTY | Returns a reference to an attribute. |
| GET_PROPERTIES | Returns a structure with all attributes of the BOL entity. |
| SET_PROPERTIES | Sets all attributes of a BOL entity on the basis of a structure. |
| GET_PROPERTY_AS_VALUE | Returns an attribute. |

**Table 13.3**  Methods of the IF_BOL_BO_PROPERTY_ACCESS Interface

| Method Name | Function |
|---|---|
| GET_PROPERTY_AS_STRING | Returns an attribute as a string. |
| SET_PROPERTY | Sets an individual attribute. |
| SET_PROPERTY_AS_STRING | Sets an attribute through a string conversion. |
| IS_PROPERTY_READONLY | Checks whether an attribute is write-protected (*read-only*). |

**Table 13.3**  Methods of the IF_BOL_BO_PROPERTY_ACCESS Interface (Cont.)

To read the properties of a BOL entity, you use getter methods of the IF_BO_ BOL_PROPERTY_ACCESS interface. Listing 13.10 illustrates how you can read the value of the PUBLISHER attribute of a BOL entity.

**Properties of BOL entities**

```
DATA lv_publisher TYPE string.
lv_entity->get_property_as_value(
   exporting iv_attr_name = 'PUBLISHER'
   importing ev_result = lv_publisher ).
```

**Listing 13.10**   Listing 13.10 Reading the Properties of Entities

To change attributes of a BOL entity, you use setter methods of the IF_BO_ BOL_PROPERTY_ACCESS interface. For example, to assign the PUBLISHER attribute of a BOL entity to the GALILEO PRESS value at runtime, you can use the SET_PROPERTY method (see Listing 13.11):

```
lv_entity->set_property(
exporting iv_attr_name = 'PUBLISHER'
   iv_value = 'GALILEO PRESS' ).
```

**Listing 13.11**   Changing the Properties of an Entity

In addition to reading and changing individual attributes of a BOL entity, you can read or set all attributes of a BOL entity as a structure using the GET_PROPERTIES and SET_PROPERTIES methods.

> **Note**
>
> The IF_BO_BOL_PROPERTY_ACCESS interface is not only implemented by the CL_CRM_BOL_ENTITY class but also by classes of simple and dynamic search services, as well as by parameters of dynamic search services.

## 13.8   Generating BOL Entities

Entity factory

In general, when generating BOL entities, you have to distinguish between the generation of root objects and the generation of dependent objects. Root objects are created using the *entity factory*, whereas dependent objects are generated by calling the CREATE_RELATED_ENTITY method of their parent objects. Creating a root object entity directly implies the call of the underlying APIs. For dependent objects, you have to implement this by explicitly calling the MODIFY method of the BOL core because changes to dependent objects are collected and not forwarded until the MODIFY method is called, as a whole, to the underlying APIs. Sending new BOL entities to the APIs does not necessarily lead to persistence; they are not stored in the database until the transaction has been successfully completed. The IS_PERSISTENT method of a BOL entity enables you to check whether a BOL entity is stored in the database. Listing 13.12 illustrates the generation of a BOL entity—*business partner*, including *role*—as an example.

Entity "business partner"

```
DATA lv_bol_core TYPE REF TO cl_crm_bol_core.
lv_bol_core = cl_crm_bol_core=>get_instance( ).
lv_bol_core->start_up( 'BP_APPL' ).
DATA ls_params TYPE crmt_name_value_pair.
ls_params-name = 'BP_CATEGORY'.
ls_params-value = '1'.
DATA lt_params TYPE crmt_name_value_pair_tab.
APPEND ls_params TO lt_params.
DATA lv_buil_factory TYPE REF TO cl_crm_bol_entity_factory.
lv_buil_factory = lv_bol_core->get_entity_
factory( 'BuilHeader' ).
DATA l_bp_entity TYPE REF TO cl_crm_bol_entity.
l_bp_entity = lv_buil_factory->create( lt_params ).
l_bp_entity->set_property( iv_attr_name = 'FIRSTNAME'
                           iv_value = 'Valentin' ).
l_bp_entity->set_property( iv_attr_name = 'LASTNAME'
                           iv_value = 'Mustermann' ).
l_bp_entity->set_property( iv_attr_name = 'COUNTRYORIGIN'
                           iv_value = 'DE' ).
DATA l_role_ent TYPE REF TO cl_crm_bol_entity.
l_role_ent  = l_bp_entity->create_related_entity(
'BuilRolesRel' ).
l_role_ent->set_property( iv_attr_name  = 'PARTNERROLE'
                          iv_value = 'BUP003' ).
```

```
l_role_ent->set_property( iv_attr_
name   =   'PARTNERROLECATEGORY'
                         iv_value = 'BUP003' ).
lv_bol_core->modify( ).
DATA l_tx TYPE REF TO if_bol_transaction_context.
l_tx = l_bp_entity->get_transaction( ).
check l_tx->check_save_needed( ) eq abap_true.
check l_tx->check_save_possible( ) eq abap_true.
l_tx->save( ).
l_tx->commit( ).
```

**Listing 13.12**  Generating BOL Entity "Business Partner" in Role "Employee"

## 13.9    Transaction Context

Changes to BOL entities are not directly implemented in the database but instead are collected in a buffer in the BOL. To update the changes to the database, you need a transaction context. This ensures that changes to BOL entities are carried out as a whole (consistent) in the database and not only parts of them. In general, the system forwards only the changed attributes of a BOL entity to the API of the respective business data objects. A distinction is made between the following three variants of transaction contexts:

*Updating changes*

▶ **Global transaction context**
The global transaction context manages all modified root object entities and can be directly addressed via the BOL core instance.

▶ **Individual transaction context**
The individual transaction context is only assigned to a root object entity and is generated either via the GET_TRANSACTION method when requested, or, at the latest, when a BOL entity is locked using the LOCK method. The individual transaction context is addressed via a BOL entity.

▶ **Specific transaction context**
The specific transaction context can be used for cases between variant 1 and variant 2. To use the specific transaction context, you must generate an instance of the CL_CRM_BOL_CUSTOM_TX_CTXT class and add a transaction context.

The methods of a transaction context always use their own dataset. The creation process and lifetime of the various transaction contexts varies, but the transaction cycle remains the same (see Figure 13.4).

*Transaction cycle*

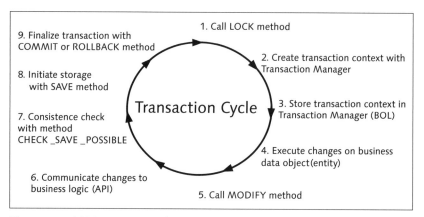

**Figure 13.4** BOL Transaction Cycle

When the LOCK BOL method is successfully called, the system automatically generates a transaction context and stores it in the transaction manager. After changes have been made to BOL entities, you must explicitly call the MODIFY method of the BOL core. Calling the MODIFY method of the BOL core is delegated to the MODIFY method of the relevant GenIL component which, in turn, calls the API for changing the data. The explicit call of the SAVE method of the transaction context is forwarded to the GenIL. The system reads the transaction context and calls the SAVE method of the relevant GenIL components. If the data is saved successfully, you must complete the transaction by calling the COMMIT method. If the data is not saved successfully, you must call the ROLLBACK method. After completion of the transaction, the system deletes the transaction context. Listing 13.13 illustrates the use of the transaction context. Note that for space reasons, the listing is not complete.

```
DATA l_core TYPE REF TO cl_crm_bol_core.
DATA l_ent TYPE REF TO CL_CRM_BOL_ENTITY.
l_core = cl_crm_bol_core=>get_instance( ).
l_core->start_up( 'ONEORDER' ).
...
check l_ent->lock( ) = abap_true.
l_ent->set_property( iv_attr_name = 'STREET'
                     iv_value = ' Dietmar-Hopp-Allee 16' ).
l_core->modify( ).
DATA l_tx TYPE REF TO if_bol_transaction_context.
l_tx = l_ent->get_transaction( ).
check l_tx->check_save_needed( ) eq abap_true.
check l_tx->check_save_possible( ) eq abap_true.
if l_tx->save( ) = abap_true.
  l_tx->commit( ).
```

```
else.
  l_tx->rollback( ).
endif.
```

**Listing 13.13**  Using the Transaction Context

Calling the COMMIT method usually removes all locks. If you want to save the context "in between," you can keep the locks if you set the IV_KEEP_LOCKS parameter to ABAP_TRUE when calling the COMMIT method.

IV_KEEP_LOCKS

## 13.10  Messages from the APIs

You can also use BOL methods to evaluate the messages that occur during processing and are generated by the respective APIs of the business data objects. Here, you also have to differentiate between messages that are object-related and messages that are not object-related. Messages are collected in message containers and can be extracted from there.

### 13.10.1  Object-Related Messages

Every BOL entity of the Assignment Object type (see Chapter 12, Section 12.1.3) includes a reference to a message container that collects the occurring messages of the business data object. Listing 13.14 illustrates how you can extract object-related messages from a message container.

```
DATA lv_mc TYPE REF TO if_genil_message_container.
DATA lv_entity TYPE REF TO cl_crm_bol_entity.
lv_mc = lv_entity->get_message_container( ).
If lv_mc->get_number_of_messages(
  if_genil_message_container=>mt_all ) > 0.
DATA lit_messages TYPE crmt_genil_message_tab.
lv_mc->get_messages( exporting iv_message_type =
  if_genil_message_container=>mt_all
importing et_messages = lit_messages ).
endif.
```

Extracting object-related messages

**Listing 13.14**  Extracting Object-Related Messages

### 13.10.2  Global Message Container

To extract messages that are not object-related from the global GenIL message container, you need a reference to the message container of the BOL core. You can retrieve this using the following statements, for example:

Extracting
messages that are
not object-related

```
DATA lr_core TYPE REF TO cl_crm_bol_core.
lr_core = cl_crm_bol_core=>get_instance( ).
...
DATA lr_global_messages TYPE REF TO cl_crm_genil_global_mess_
cont.
lr_global_messages = lr_core->get_global_message_cont( ).
```

**Listing 13.15**  Reference to the Global GenIL Message Container

The messages are extracted from the global GenIL message container in the
same way as from the object-related message container (see Listing 13.14).

## 13.11  Object Methods in the BOL

Some business data objects provide specific methods with business logic.
The BTOrderHeader object, for example, provides objects methods such as
createFollowUp, which enables you to create follow-up documents. The signature of an object method contains the import parameter IT_PARAM of the
crmt_name_value_pair_tab type, which can process values in the form of
a table. As a result, the object method returns a collection of entities. To call
an object method that is modeled in such a way, you must first populate
the import parameter of the crmt_name_value_pair_tab type. Then, the
EXECUTE method of the BOL entity is called. As an example, Listing 13.16
illustrates the generic call of the createFollowup object method via a call of
the EXECUTE method of a BOL entity.

Calling an
object method

```
DATA:  ls_param TYPE crmt_name_value_pair,
       lt_param TYPE crmt_name_value_pair_tab,
       lv_result TYPE REF TO if_bol_entity_col,
lv_order_header TYPE REF TO cl_crm_bol_entity.
ls_param-name = 'PROCESS_TYPE'.
ls_param-value = 'TSRV'.
APPEND ls_param TO lt_param.
TRY.
  lv_result = lv_order_header->execute(
          iv_method_name = 'create_FollowUp'
      it_param  = lt_param ).
CATCH CX_CRM_BOL_METH_EXEC_FAILED.
ENDTRY.
```

**Listing 13.16**  Calling an Object Method

Before an object method is processed, all pending changes in the data container are forwarded to the relevant APIs by implicitly calling the MODIFY method. Because object methods can change BOL entities, every change results in the creation of a lock and a transaction context.

> **Note**
>
> SAP CRM 2007 introduced the EXECUTE2 method, which returns any DDIC type as the return result instead of a collection.

## 13.12  BOL Buffer

The BOL has its "own" buffer to manage BOL entities. Every entity that has been determined by searching or traversing through an object model is stored in the BOL buffer. This also applies to BOL entities that represent a dependent object that is generated or deleted.

The buffers of the GenIL components are bilaterally synchronized with the BOL buffer for each roundtrip in a CRM application. This is implemented by calling the MODIFY method of the CL_CRM_BOL_CORE class. However, in some special cases, you have to explicitly synchronize the buffers. For explicit synchronization, use the REREAD method of the CL_CRM_BOL_ENTITY class (see Section 13.1). This method directly calls the APIs and should thus be used with caution for performance reasons.

*Synchronizing the buffers*

*The previous chapters discussed the different software layers of the Web Client UI framework. This chapter covers their generic application services.*

# 14 Generic Application Services

Generic application services have a cross-component character; that is, they are used across all components. They provide users that deploy services with standardized functions and interfaces, for example, for outputting messages or controlling the page history. This chapter discusses topics such as message output, breadcrumbs, view group context, dialog boxes, and buttons.

## 14.1 Message Output

For general notes on the presentation of the message bar in SAP CRM 2007, refer to Chapter 1, Section 1.2.2. In addition, you should be familiar with the creation of messages and message classes. We distinguish between four message types in SAP CRM 2007:

- Critical information messages
- Error messages
- Warning messages
- Information (and success) messages

If the system cannot display the entire text of a message, and if a long text is defined for the message, the system displays the DETAILS link to the left of the message text in the message bar (see ❶ in Figure 14.1). Clicking on the DETAILS link opens a dialog that outputs the long text of the message.

Displaying messages in the message bar

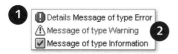

**Figure 14.1** Sample Messages

Navigable messages

You can also have the message bar display (❷) what are called *navigable messages*. In this case, the system displays the message text as a link in the message bar.

Properties of messages

Messages have a message source, message type, and message level (hierarchy level), all of which affect the sorting and filtering of messages and thus their presentation in the message bar. Table 14.1 lists the message output sequence.

| Criterion | Sequence |
|---|---|
| Message type | Critical information message, error, warning, information, and success |
| Message source | BSP framework, UI framework, object-related message, and global BOL message |
| Message level | Numeric |

**Table 14.1** Output Sequence of Messages

Message level

The Web Client UI framework distinguishes between different message levels, as you can see in Table 14.2. A message level assigns a message to a user group. Message levels are defined in a domain for the BSP_WD_MESSAGE_LEVEL data element.

| Level | User Group |
|---|---|
| 0 | Non (demo mode) |
| 1 | Customer |
| 3 | Office-based employee |
| 6 | Experienced user |
| 8 | Administrator |
| 9 | Only collect in trace mode |

**Table 14.2** Message Level

If no level is explicitly specified when a message is generated, the default level is "1."

### 14.1.1 Outputting a Message in the Message Bar

Message service

To output a message in the message bar of the user interface, the system uses the central *message service*, which manages messages from different sources as a message container. The following sources are possible for messages (see Figure 14.2):

- The BSP framework
- The Web Client UI framework
- GenIL (with and without object reference)

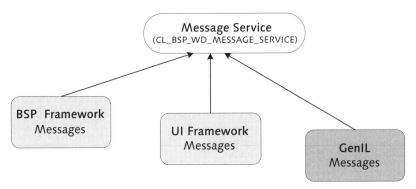

**Figure 14.2** Sources for Messages

The BSP framework is the technical basis for the Web Client UI framework. Therefore, the messages from the BSP framework always refer to fields in the user interface. Every implementation class of a context node has an ERRORS attribute as a reference to the CL_BSP_MESSAGES class. The methods of the CL_BSP_MESSAGES class enable you to create new messages and store them in or remove them from the message container.

**Messages from the BSP framework**

> **Note**
>
> If you call the ADD_MESSAGE method, for example, to add a message, you can define the severity of the error using the SEVERITY parameter. If the SEVERITY parameter contains the values "1" or "2," the system outputs an error message and you can no longer navigate from the page.

The BSP framework thus automatically generates messages when values are written from the screen elements in the context and a type conversion fails because, for example, the date was entered in the date field in the wrong format. In the next roundtrip, all messages from the BSP framework are automatically removed from the message container.

For other messages with a reference to the Web Client UI framework, you can determine an instance of the *global message service* using the following statement:

**Messages from the UI framework**

```
DATA lr_msg_service TYPE REF TO cl_bsp_wd_message_service.
lr_msg_service ?= me->view_manager->get_message_service( ).
```

Because the global message service is implemented according to the singleton design pattern, you can also determine a valid instance at any time using the following statement:

```
lr_msg_service =
cl_bsp_wd_message_service=>get_instance( ).
```

Table 14.3 provides an overview of the relevant methods of the CL_BSP_WD_MESSAGE_SERVICE class.

| Method | Description |
|---|---|
| ADD_MESSAGE | Adds a message to the message container |
| ADD_BAPI_MESSAGES | Adds BAPIRET2 messages to the message container |
| COLLECT_MESSAGES | Collects messages from different sources |
| GET_NUMBER_OF_MESSAGES | Returns the number of messages |

**Table 14.3** Methods of the CL_BSP_WD_MESSAGE_SERVICE Class (Excerpt)

Outputting a message using the global message service

To output a message, you can use the ADD_MESSAGE method of the global message service, for example. This is illustrated in the example below, which outputs an information message of the CRM_IC_APPL_UI_AUTO message class (Transaction SE91):

```
lr_msg_service->add_message(
        iv_msg_type   = 'I'
        iv_msg_id     = 'CRM_IC_APPL_UI_AUTO'
        iv_msg_number = '000' ).
```

A message that is generated this way is output only once and is no longer displayed in the next roundtrip. You can prevent this by transferring a reference to an instance of the IF_BSP_WD_MESSAGE_HANDLER interface with the IV_VERIFICATION parameter of the ADD_MESSAGE method when it is called. For roundtrips, the system processes the VERIFY_MESSAGE callback method of the IF_BSP_WD_MESSAGE_HANDLER interface for each message that contains a reference to the IF_BSP_WD_MESSAGE_HANDLER interface. If the VERIFY_MESSAGE method provides true as the Boolean result, the system keeps the message in the message bar after the roundtrip.

Outputting navigable messages

The global message service enables you to register callback methods so that you can output navigable messages, that is, you can initiate a navigation to, for example, another view, by clicking on the message in the message bar. The callback methods are of the IF_BSP_WD_MESSAGE_HANDLER~HANDLE_MESSAGE type. A registration of the message service for a message looks as follows:

```
DATA lr_service TYPE REF TO cl_bsp_wd_message_service.
lr_service = me->view_manager->get_message_service( ).
TRY.
 lr_service->subscribe_message(
         iv_message_class  = 'CRM_IC_APPL_UI_BDC'
         iv_message_number = '114'
         iv_subscriber     = me
     iv_activation         = abap_true ).
  CATCH cx_bsp_wd_dupl_mess_subscr.
ENDTRY.
```

**Listing 14.1**  Registering a Callback Method

> **Note**
>
> The ME self reference in our example points to a view controller that imple-
> ments the IF_BSP_WD_MESSAGE_HANDLER interface, including the HANDLE_
> MESSAGE method.

### 14.1.2  Message Filter

Not every message is of use for every user. A technical message, for example, is often too complex for common users Therefore, a mechanism is available that lets you filter the message output. There are two message filter variants in the Web Client UI framework:

▶ A filter that is based on a user-specific setting of the BSPWD_USER_LEVEL parameter

▶ A program-controlled filter whose default implementation outputs messages from all message sources (see the earlier text)—except for object-related messages

### Message Filter Using the BSPWD_USER_LEVEL Parameter

If the BSPWD_USER_LEVEL parameter is not set, it contains default value 3. Users can set the parameter in Transaction SU3 on the PARAMETERS tab, for example.

### Program-Controlled Message Filter

To output object-related messages of a BOL entity, you have to implement the `IF_BSP_WD_HISTORY_STATE_DESCR~GET_MAIN_ENTITY` method in the controller of a view that is mapped in the work area. To display the object-related messages, this method returns a reference to a BOL entity of the `CL_CRM_BOL_ENTITY` type to the Web Client UI framework. Because this method is also required for the breadcrumb implementation (see Section 14.3), it may have already been implemented in the controller class.

If you need more control over the message filtering, you can implement the `IF_BSP_WD_STATE_CONTEXT~GET_MESSAGE_FILTER` method. This method must always return a filter object of the `CL_BSP_WD_MESSAGE_FILTER` type. The filter object lets you activate and deactivate message sources and add BOL entities whose messages should be displayed.

> **Note**
>
> A sample implementation of the use of a filter object can be found in the `IF_BSP_WD_HISTORY_STATE_DESCR~GET_MAIN_ENTITY` method in the `CL_IUICBCO_CUCOBICO_IMPL` class in the SAP standard version.

If you do not use either of the two methods mentioned here, the system does not output object-related messages.

## 14.2    View Group Context

**Edit mode and display mode**

In applications, you must be able to distinguish between *edit mode* and *display mode*, particularly if it comes to the data maintenance in a dialog. This is because the same data record must not be processed by different users at the same time; otherwise, data may be deleted or distorted and, as a result, inconsistent. Consequently, appropriate mechanisms must be available to ensure that data that is entered in the dialog is always stored consistently.

**Application scenario**

From the point of view of users, they do not edit data records but business objects. Technically, in the Web Client UI framework, an instance of a business object corresponds to an instance of a GenIL object, that is, a BOL entity (see Chapter 13, Section 13.1). A typical application scenario is as follows: Before you can change to edit mode to edit a business object, you must technically check whether the BOL entity can be locked. For example, if the BOL entity is already being edited by another user, it cannot be locked, and the system outputs a corresponding error message. In contrast, if the lock operation is successful, the system changes to edit mode so that the user can enter his data on the user interface. After the data input, the user stores or discards the data. In both cases, you must change to *display mode* to release the data record (BOL entity) so that it can be edited by other users, if required. By changing to display mode, the fields are no longer ready for input.

The *view group context* is a mechanism that controls the input readiness of assignment blocks on an editable overview page. It forms a hierarchy from window to view set and from view set to view and is implemented at the controller level. If a controller does not define a specific view group context in this hierarchy, the controller automatically belongs to the view group context of its parent object, as illustrated in Figure 14.3.

Controlling the input readiness for assignment blocks

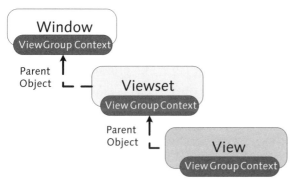

**Figure 14.3** Hierarchy of the View Group Context

Before you can use the view group context, you must instantiate it in the SET_VIEW_GROUP_CONTEXT method of a controller (see Listing 14.2):

Instantiating the view group context

```
if iv_first_time = abap_true.
  if not me->view_group_context is bound.
    if iv_parent_context is initial.
      create object me->view_group_context type cl_bsp_wd_view_
group_context.
    else.
      me->view_group_context = iv_parent_context.
    endif.
  endif.
endif.
```

**Listing 14.2** Assigning a View Group Context

We will now take a closer look at a concrete application example for the view group context using a form view. For form views that are based on the CHTMLB:CONFIG tag, you can set edit mode using the DISPLAYMODE attribute at runtime, as the following excerpt of a business server page illustrates:

Application example using a form view

```
...
<chtmlb:config
  ...
  displayMode = "<%= controller->view_group_context->is_view_
in_display_mode( controller ). %>" />
```

The DISPLAYMODE attribute of the CHTMLB:CONFIG tag is of a Boolean type and can thus only adopt the TRUE or FALSE value. In our example, the system transports the Boolean value of the IS_VIEW_IN_DISPLAY_MODE method of the view group context to the DISPLAYMODE attribute during a roundtrip at runtime. If you change to edit mode, the system processes the *I-getter method* (*input-readiness*, see Chapter 9, Section 9.1.2) of each visible field on the user interface. Depending on the return values of the I-getter method, the fields are ready for input or mapped as display fields.

Class CL_BSP_
WD_VIEW_
GROUP_CONTEXT

Technically, the view group context corresponds to an object instance of the CL_BSP_WD_VIEW_GROUP_CONTEXT class. Table 14.4 provides an excerpt of common methods of this class:

| Method | Function |
|---|---|
| IS_VIEW_IN_DISPLAY_MODE | Checks whether the view is in display mode. |
| SET_VIEW_EDITABLE | Sets edit mode for the transferred view instance. |
| SET_ALL_EDITABLE | Sets edit mode for all dependent views in the view group context. |
| RESET | Returns to display mode, and initializes the view group context. |
| SET_ASSOCIATED_TX_CONTEXT | Assigns a transaction context to the view group context. |

**Table 14.4**  Methods of the CL_BSP_WD_VIEW_GROUP_CONTEXT Class (Excerpt)

Changing to
edit mode

To set the edit mode for the current view, you can implement the following statement in the event handler implementation of an EDIT button, for example:

```
me->view_group_context->set_view_editable( me ).
```

Changing to
display mode

To change to display mode, use the reset method, as shown in the following statement:

```
me->view_group_context->reset( ).
```

Optionally, you can also couple the view group context with a transaction context (see Chapter 13, Section 13.9) using the `SET_ASSOCIATED_TX_CON-TEXT` method. If the transaction context is released, the system automatically processes the `RESET` method (see Table 14.4) and resets the view group context.

## 14.3  Breadcrumbs

If the user navigates from one work area to the next, the framework displays the heading of the last visited work area in the page history (see Figure 14.4). Such a heading is called a *breadcrumb*.

**Figure 14.4**  Breadcrumbs in the Page History

You can either navigate within the page history by selecting a displayed breadcrumb or by using the BACK and FORWARD buttons.

You can technically add breadcrumbs to the page history using what are called *sync points*. In short, a sync point is a point in the program code where the `history_trigger` event for creating a breadcrumb in the page history is generated. The `history_trigger` event is generated by the `RAISE EVENT history_trigger.` statement. An entry to the page history should only be implemented when you navigate to a completely different work area and not when you navigate from one view to the next within a work area. Therefore, sync points can be at the following points:

**Sync points**

- Within the destructor of a controller class of a window, an overview page, or a view set
- Directly before the call of a navigation that includes a change to another work area component

You implement a sync point in the destructor of a controller by redefining the `WD_DESTROY` method and calling the `history_trigger.` event. Listing 9.1 illustrates a sample implementation.

```
METHOD wd_destroy.
  raise event history_trigger.
```

```
call method super->wd_destroy.
ENDMETHOD.
```

**Listing 14.3**  Calling a Breadcrumb in the Destructor

---

**Note**

Keep in mind that the destructor of the superclass must be called.

---

The window and view controller inherit the IF_BSP_WD_STATE_CONTEXT and IF_BSP_WD_HISTORY_STATE_DESCR interfaces, including methods to handle breadcrumbs. The framework treats method implementations of these interfaces as callback methods. In the Component Workbench, these callback methods are visible in the CONTEXT (❶) and BREADCRUMBS AND MESSAGES (❷) nodes (see Figure 14.5).

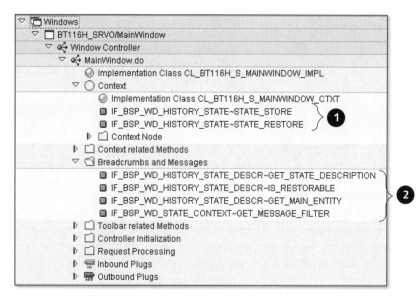

**Figure 14.5**  Callback Methods for Breadcrumbs

---

**Example in the SAP Standard Version**

For an example of how you manage breadcrumbs, refer to the BT116H_SRVO UI component in the SAP standard version. In the window controller of the UI component, all breadcrumb methods are implemented.

---

If you return to the work area, the framework must be able to restore the processed leading entity of the work area. For this purpose, you must store the leading entity in the state container before you go to the next work area. This is implemented in the IF_BSP_WD_HISTORY_STATE~STATE_STORE method by calling the ADD_ITEM method of the state container:

```
state_container->add_item
( im_name  = {name of entity}
  im_value = {entity object reference}.
```

To restore the entity, the framework processes the IF_BSP_WD_HISTORY_STATE~STATE_RESTORE method. To read the entity from the state container, use the GET_ITEM method of the state container:

```
state_container->get_item(
  exporting im_name  = {name of entity}
  importing ex_value = {entity object reference}
    exceptions others = 0 ).
```

Then, you have to bind the determined entity to the collection wrapper of a context node.

To control the creation of the breadcrumb, the framework processes the IF_BSP_WD_HISTORY_STATE_DESCR~IS_RESTORABLE callback method. In this method, you can, for example, check whether the entity is persistent and prevent the system from creating a breadcrumb if the entity is not persistent.

You can modify the work area title (see Section 1.2.2) or the text of a breadcrumb with an implementation of the IF_BSP_WD_HISTORY_STATE_DESCR~GET_STATE_DESCRIPTION method by defining a text from the online text repository (OTR) for the DESCRIPTION return parameter (see Section 14.7.2).

You can optionally implement the IF_BSP_WD_HISTORY_STATE_DESCR~GET_MAIN_ENTITY callback method to display the leading entity of the work area for the framework. The framework processes this method if the system identifies duplicates of breadcrumbs and compares the leading entities to avoid that duplicate entries are displayed in the page history.

## 14.4  Dialog Box

Dialog boxes are small, overlapping windows of the Internet browser that have their own specific content. They offer specific services to users, for example, customer searches. Dialog boxes therefore add functionality to the user interface by obtaining entries and confirmations from the user, or simply by mapping information. The best-known examples of this type in the Web Client UI framework are search help dialog boxes, dialog boxes for decision-making, or the technical data dialog box ($\boxed{\text{F2}}$ key).

For different use cases, the Web Client UI framework provides different approaches to display dialog boxes. Section 14.4.1 illustrates how you can call a dialog box for an interaction with the user (input confirmation). Section 14.4.2 describes how you can map a dialog box that embeds a view of a UI component.

### 14.4.1 Dialog Box for Queries

Figure 14.6 shows a dialog box that queries the YES or NO options, including a query text. The title bar of the dialog box also displays a heading. A dialog box for queries requires an interaction with the user, for example, selecting an option by clicking a button or directly closing the dialog box by clicking in the right top corner on the button that closes the dialog box.

**Figure 14.6**  Dialog Box with Query

Elements of a query dialog box

This means a total of three elements are required to display a dialog box for queries:

▶ Title

▶ Query text

▶ Combination of buttons

We will now take a look at how you can implement the statements for calling a dialog box for queries. A dialog box is always started from a view. Consequently, you must first define a new attribute with the following properties in the implementation class of the view controller:

▶ Name:                  M_POPUP_CONFIRM

▶ Type:                   INSTANCE ATTRIBUTE

▶ Visibility:             PUBLIC

▶ Type assignment:        TYPE REF TO

▶ Reference type:         IF_BSP_WD_POPUP

This attribute is used as a reference to the dialog box instance. The reference is first initial; to generate an instance and assign it to the M_POPUP_CONFIRM attribute, you have to call the following statement:

```
call method
comp_controller->window_manager->create_popup_2_confirm
  exporting
    iv_title           = 'This is a window title'
    iv_text            = 'Do you want to confirm your input?'
    iv_btncombination = if_bsp_wd_window_manager=>co_btncomb_
yesno
  receiving
    rv_result          = m_popup_confirm.
```

You can implement this statement in the event handler method of a button, for example. The CREATE_POPUP_2_CONFIRM method receives parameters for outputting a heading (IV_TITLE), a query text (IV_TEXT), and combinations of buttons (iv_btncombination). A set of predefined button combinations is available; these are listed in Table 14.5. The set consists of individual constants, which are defined in the if_bsp_wd_window_manager interface.

| Constant | Maps |
| --- | --- |
| CO_BTNCOMB_OK | OK button |
| CO_BTNCOMB_CLOSE | CLOSE button |
| CO_BTNCOMB_OKCANCEL | OK and CANCEL buttons |
| CO_BTNCOMB_YESNO | YES and No buttons |
| CO_BTNCOMB_YESNOCANCEL | YES, No, and CANCEL buttons |
| CO_BTNCOMB_NONE | Does not map any buttons, only text |
| CO_BTNCOMB_CUSTOM | Individual buttons of the CRMT_ THTMLB_BUTTON type. Transferred via the IV_CUSTOMBUTTONS parameter of the create_popup_2_confirm method. |

**Table 14.5**  Button Combinations

To be able to evaluate a user's selection, an event handler method needs to be available in the view controller to evaluate the query from the dialog box. The system publishes the event handler method to the dialog box by calling the SET_ON_CLOSE_EVENT method, which receives the view controller and name of the event handler as input parameters. Implement the call after the call of the `CREATE_POPUP_2_CONFIRM` method. The example that follows illustrates the use of the `POPUP_CLOSED` event handler:

```
call method m_popup_confirm->set_on_close_event
  exporting
    iv_view      = me
    iv_event_name = 'POPUP_CLOSED'.
```

Displaying a dialog box

The last step is to implement the statement for displaying the dialog box. This is done by calling the `OPEN` method, as illustrated in the following example:

```
m_popup_confirm->open( ).
```

Implementing the event handler

We will now take another look at the event handler, which is called `POPUP_CLOSED` in our example. The query results of the dialog box are evaluated using the `GET_FIRED_OUTBOUND_PLUG` method, which returns a result of the `STRING` type.

```
DATA lv_result TYPE string.
lv_result = m_popup_confirm->get_fired_outbound_plug( ).
```

If the dialog box is closed without the user using one of the buttons, the `GET_FIRED_OUTBOUND_PLUG` method returns an empty string. After the dialog box is closed, the `M_POPUP_CONFIRM` attribute should be cleared to release occupied memory resources.

### 14.4.2 Dialog Box for Displaying Views

We will now take a look at how you can implement the statements for calling a dialog box with variable content. This section uses an example to illustrate how you can display an interface view of an embedded UI component in a dialog box. Chapter 9, Section 9.6.4 discussed the component usage in detail. The example assumes that a component usage, `usageMyComponent`, for the ZMYCOMPONENT UI component is already available and that the name of the interface view is ZMYCOMPONENT/MAINWINDOW.

As you already know from Section 14.4.1, a dialog box is always started from a view. Consequently, you must first define a new attribute with the following properties in the implementation class of the view controller:

- ▶ Name:               M_POPUP
- ▶ Type:               Instance Attribute
- ▶ Visibility:         Public
- ▶ Type assignment:    Type Ref To
- ▶ Reference type:     IF_BSP_WD_POPUP

348

The system determines the instance of the dialog box by calling the CRE-ATE_POPUP method and storing it in the M_POPUP attribute. The CREATE_POPUP method receives parameters for the name of the view that should be displayed (IV_INTERFACE_VIEW_NAME), the name of the usage dependency (IV_USAGE_NAME), and the text of the heading (IV_TITLE). The method is called in a similar manner as a window of the specific UI component. An example is as follows:

```
m_popup = comp_controller->window_manager->create_popup(
  iv_interface_view_name = 'ZMyComponent/MainWindow'
  iv_usage_name = 'usageMyComponent'
  iv_title = 'Reuse sample dialog box '
).
```

To be able to identify that the user has closed the dialog box, an event handler method needs to be available in the view controller. This event handler method is processed by the framework after the dialog box has been closed. The system registers the event handler method by calling the SET_ON_CLOSE_EVENT method, which receives the view controller and name of the event handler as input parameters. Implement the call of the SET_ON_CLOSE_EVENT method after the call of the CREATE_POPUP method. The following is an example with the REUSED_POPUP_CLOSED transfer result:

```
call method m_popup->set_on_close_event
  exporting
    iv_view      = me
    iv_event_name = 'REUSED_POPUP_CLOSED'.
```

The dialog box is activated using the m_popup ->open( )statement.

The event handler, which is called REUSED_POPUP_CLOSED here, evaluates the outbound plug that was used to close the dialog box. For this purpose, the GET_FIRED_OUTBOUND_PLUG method is called. An example is as follows:

```
DATA lv_result TYPE string.
lv_result = m_popup->get_fired_outbound_plug( ).
```

As you know from Chapter 9, Section 9.6.4, the context of a UI component that is embedded in a dialog box is accessed either via a context node binding in the WD_USAGE_INITIALIZE method of the component controller or by calling the M_POPUP->GET_CONTEXT_NODE method.

You can define the window height and window width of a dialog box using the SET_WINDOW_WIDTH and SET_WINDOW_HEIGHT methods. After the dialog box is closed, the M_POPUP attribute should be cleared to release occupied memory resources.

## 14.5 Data Loss Dialog Box

If a user navigates to another work area during data input, you must check whether the user wants to save the specified entries because the data may otherwise be lost. For this purpose, the Web Client UI framework provides the *data loss dialog box* (see Figure 14.7). The user clicks on one of the three buttons in the data loss dialog box and thus defines how the system should handle the entered data.

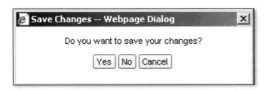

**Figure 14.7** Data Loss Dialog Box

Data loss scenarios The Web Client UI framework manages two possible data loss scenarios, which are initiated by navigation:

- If the work area is changed
- In the case of navigation via breadcrumbs (see Section 14.3)

The Web Client UI framework communicates with the active (visible) work area component to define whether the data loss dialog box should be displayed. Every work area component (that allows for data updates) must be able to let the Web Client UI framework know that data may be lost due to the navigation and that the data loss dialog box should be displayed. The work area component must also be able to process the query result (YES, NO, or CANCEL) of the data loss dialog box.

For an implementation, the controller class of a window or the overview page of a work area component must have an event handler and subscribe the static result, BEFORE_WORKAREA_CONTENT_CHANGE, of the CL_BSP_WD_VIEW_MANAGER class (see Figure 14.8).

> **Example in the SAP Standard Version**
>
> For an example of how you manage the data loss dialog box, refer to the BT116H_SRVO UI component in the SAP standard version. The ON_BE-FORE_WA_CONTENT_CHANGE event handler of the BEFORE_WORKAREA_CON-TENT_CHANGE event is implemented in the controller class of the MainWindow window.

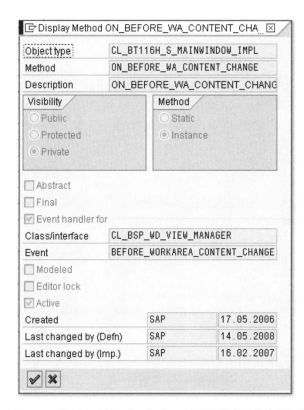

Figure 14.8  Event Handler for Event BEFORE_WORKAREA_CONTENT_CHANGE

You must manually create the event handler in the controller class. This process is not supported by a wizard. The event handler is usually activated in the `DO_VIEW_INIT_ON_ACTIVATION` method of the window controller using the following statement:

**Activating the event handler**

```
set handler on_before_wa_content_change activation abap_true.
```

To avoid incorrect runtime behavior, you have to deactivate the subscription with the

```
set handler on_before_wa_content_change activation abap_false.
```

statement when the work area component is hidden again. To do so, you can implement the statement in the `DO_CLEANUP_CONTEXT` method of the controller class, for example, so that the event handler is deactivated when the context is cleared from memory.

The `DATA_LOSS_HANDLER` event parameter provides a reference to the `IF_BSP_WD_DATA_LOSS_HANDLER` interface for the event handler. This interface

**Reference to the interface**

is required to set the callback methods for the buttons in the data loss dialog box (see Listing 10.3).

```
method on_before_wa_content_change.
  data_loss_handler->set_save_handler( me ).
  data_loss_handler->set_revert_handler( me ).
  data_loss_handler->set_cancel_handler( me ).
  data_loss_handler->trigger_data_loss_handling( ).
endmethod.
```

**Listing 14.4** Setting the Callback Methods for the Buttons in the Data Loss Dialog Box

Executing a callback method

This means that selecting a button in the data loss dialog box triggers an execution of a callback method. For this purpose, you must implement the IF_BSP_WD_EVENT_HANDLER~HANDLE_EVENT method of the IF_BSP_WD_EVENT_HANDLER interface in the controller class and evaluate the IV_EVENT_NAME parameter.

```
method if_bsp_wd_event_handler~handle_event.
  case iv_event_name.
    when if_bsp_wd_data_loss_handler=>save_event.
    ...
    when if_bsp_wd_data_loss_handler=>revert_event.
    ...
    when if_bsp_wd_data_loss_handler=>cancel_event.
    ...
  endcase.
endmethod.
```

**Listing 14.5** Callback Method with Result Evaluation

A callback call of SAVE and REVERT must return the ABAP_TRUE value with the rv_success = abap_true. statement in the event of success. If ABAP_FALSE is returned, the action that opened the data loss dialog box is canceled.

> **Note**
>
> To generate a data loss dialog box for the navigation within a UI component, you can call the RAISE EVENT data_loss_trigger. statement. You must first check, however, whether data has been updated. For a sample implementation, refer to the EH_ONCOPY event handler of the CL_BT116H_S_DETAILSEF_IMPL controller class.

## 14.6 Buttons

In CRM applications, buttons are used in different places:

- In the work area toolbar
- In the header area of assignment blocks
- In the header area of tables (see Chapter 10, Section 10.2.1)
- As a *one-click action* in columns of tables or hierarchy views (see Chapter 10, Section 10.2.2)
- As simple buttons in views

All of these buttons have in common that an event is triggered if the user clicks the button. This event needs to be processed by an event handler (see Chapter 9, Section 9.1.3) so that the system can trigger the function that is assigned to the button.

You have to create buttons manually by implementing interfaces or tags in a BSP page. This process is not supported by a wizard.

Creating buttons

### 14.6.1 Buttons in the Work Area Toolbar

Figure 14.9 shows buttons that are arranged in a work area toolbar at runtime. The SAVE and CANCEL buttons are visually separated using a *separator* (**❶**).

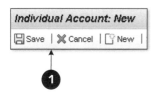

**Figure 14.9** Buttons in a Work Area Toolbar

You integrate the buttons with the work area toolbar of an overview page (see Chapter 10, Section 10.5) by implementing the IF_BSP_WD_TOOLBAR_CALLBACK~GET_BUTTONS and IF_BSP_WD_TOOLBAR_CALLBACK~GET_NUMBER_OF_VISIBLE_BUTTONS callback methods of the IF_BSP_WD_TOOLBAR_CALLBACK interface in the view controller of the overview page. This implementation requires redefining the methods in the view controller. You can redefine these methods in the Component Workbench at the TOOLBAR RELATED METHODS of the view controller, provided that the IF_BSP_WD_TOOLBAR_CALLBACK interface is implemented in the view controller (see Figure 14.10). This is always the case for overview pages.

> **Note**
>
> After you have redefined the IF_BSP_WD_TOOLBAR_CALLBACK~GET_BUT-
> TONS method of one of the views provided by SAP, the first statement of
> the redefined method should be the call of the IF_BSP_WD_TOOLBAR_
> CALLBACK~GET_BUTTONS method of the superclass. Otherwise, the buttons
> of the original implementation are not displayed.

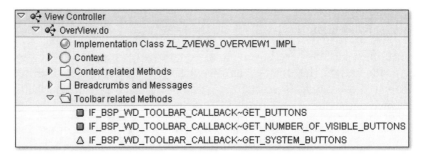

**Figure 14.10** Toolbar-Related Methods in the Component Workbench

**Rendering the work area toolbar** When the work area toolbar is rendered, the Web Client UI framework sequentially processes the GET_BUTTONS and GET_NUMBER_OF_VISIBLE_BUT-TONS callback methods. The GET_BUTTONS method provides a description table with buttons to the Web Client UI framework in the RT_BUTTONS parameter. To insert a button in the work area toolbar, you must add a row of the CRMT_THTMLB_BUTTON_EXT type to the description table in the GET_BUTTONS method. Listing 14.6 shows an example of how you can integrate a button, including the corresponding icon and the text EDIT, with the work area toolbar.

```
DATA ls_button TYPE CRMT_THTMLB_BUTTON_EXT.
ls_button-type = cl_thtmlb_util=>gc_icon_edit.
ls_button-on_click = '{CLICK_EVENT}'.
ls_button-enabled = abap_true.
ls_button-text = 'Edit'.
ls_button-page_id = me->component_id.
APPEND ls_button TO rt_buttons.
```

**Listing 14.6** Button in a Description Table

**Event handler** To respond to the onClick event {CLICK_EVENT} of the button, you need the corresponding event handler, which you must create in the view controller of the overview page.

It is important that you specify `me->component_id` to enable the Web Client UI framework to delegate the onClick event of the button to the event handler of the overview page. The `CL_THTMLB_UTIL` class contains certain constants for mapping icons for buttons. If you want to use a separator, you can use the `GC_SEPARATOR` constant of the `CL_THTMLB_UTIL` class.

The `RV_RESULT` parameter from the `GET_NUMBER_OF_VISIBLE_BUTTONS` method returns the number of buttons that should be displayed to the Web Client UI framework. If the number is less than the number of rows of the description table from the `GET_BUTTONS` method, the last button of the work area toolbar becomes a MORE button. At runtime, the user can then select the remaining, not directly displayed buttons in the action menu of the MORE button.

## 14.6.2 Buttons in Assignment Blocks

Unlike with displaying buttons in the work area toolbar, you do not have to implement an interface to display buttons in an assignment block (see Figure 14.11). Instead, you can use the `areaFrameSetter` tag of the THTMLB tag library to display buttons in the header area of an assignment block. You integrate the `areaFrameSetter` tag with the BSP page of the view that provides the content of the assignment block.

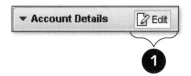

**Figure 14.11** Buttons in an Assignment Block

You must assign a description table of buttons of the `CRMT_THTMLB_BUTTON_T` type to the `toolbarButtons` attribute of the `areaFrameSetter` tag. You transfer the number of visible buttons to the `maxButtonNumber` attribute. If the number of buttons exceeds this value, the system displays a MORE button. At runtime, the user can then select the remaining, not directly displayed buttons in the action menu of the MORE button.

Listing 4.7 provides a sample implementation of a BSP page for the mapping of an EDIT button in the header area of an assignment block.

**Sample implementation**

```
<%@page language="abap" %>
<%@extension name="thtmlb" prefix="thtmlb" %>
<%
  DATA: ls_button type CRMT_THTMLB_BUTTON,
  lt_buttons type CRMT_THTMLB_BUTTON_T.
```

```
CLEAR ls_button.
ls_button-type = cl_thtmlb_util=>gc_icon_edit.
ls_button-on_click = '{CLICK_EVENT}'.
ls_button-enabled = 'X'.
ls_button-text = 'Edit'.
append ls_button to lt_buttons.
%>.
<thtmlb:areaFrameSetter toolbarButtons  = "<%= lt_buttons %>"
                        maxButtonNumber = "1" />
```

**Listing 14.7**  "Edit" Button in the Assignment Block

Event handler

To respond to the onClick event {CLICK_EVENT} of the button, you need the corresponding event handler (*see* the earlier text).

> **Note**
>
> The ABAP statements in the listing were provided only for illustration purposes. To ensure the transparency of a BSP page, you should not provide the ABAP statements in a BSP page, if possible. Instead, you can bind the attributes of the areaFrameSetter tag to the attributes of the view controller, for example, and outsource the statements to a controller method.

### 14.6.3  Tag THTMLB:Button

THTMLB:Button

If you want to map a button (*see* Figure 14.12) in a view, use the Button tag of the THTMLB tag library.

**Figure 14.12**  Button as THTMLB:Button

To map a CANCEL button in a view (*see* Figure 14.12), integrate the Button tag with the BSP page of a view with the id, type, onclick, and text attributes, as illustrated in the excerpt in Listing 14.8.

```
<thtmlb:button id      = "CANCEL"
type    = "<%=cl_thtmlb_util=>gc_icon_cancel %>"
onClick = "{CLICK_EVENT}"
   text =  "Cancel" />
```

**Listing 14.8**  Example of a Simple Button

Then, create an event handler in the view controller class to be able to respond to the onClick event {CLICK_EVENT}.

## 14.7 Internationalization

Globalization also affects software development. Today, virtually all professional applications are provided in multiple languages. This fact was the motivation for writing this section. Internationalization in software development is the capability of an application to map language-dependent texts within the application without having to adapt the program code of the application—it is therefore no longer necessary to provide a separate program version for each language.

Chapter 5, Section 5.1.1 already discussed the origin of language-dependent text for field labels. However, this description did not cover all screen elements. For example, you cannot edit button texts or work area titles (see Chapter 1, Section 1.3.2) with the UI Configuration Tool. Therefore, application developers must ensure language-dependent texts of buttons and work area titles. For this purpose, they are supported by the *online text repository* (OTR).

Language-dependent texts

### 14.7.1 Online Text Repository (OTR)

To design user interfaces for your web application, SAP provides OTR technology, which enables you to manage language-dependent texts in an SAP system. To create short and long texts and change them without modifications, use Transaction SOTR_EDIT.

The alias of the OTR text defines the unique name of the text. For structuring, OTR texts are assigned to packages. All texts that are stored in the OTR are output in the respective logon language at runtime. If the texts are not available in the logon language, they are displayed in the system language. In the OTR, defined texts are linked to the transport system and are available in a task list of the translation transaction (Transaction SE63) for translation. Each defined text should occur only once in a package.

Alias of the OTR text

The following example shows how you can determine a text with the MY_OTRTEXT_ALIAS alias of the MY_PACKAGE package from the OTR using a statement:

```
DATA: lv_my_text TYPE string.
lv_my_text = cl_wd_utilities=>get_otr_text_by_alias( ' MY_
PACKAGE/MY_OTRTEXT_ALIAS' ).
```

> **Tip**
>
> The texts are read from a buffer at runtime. This buffer is not automatically cleared during the translation process. However, you can manually clear the OTR buffer by entering "/$OTR" in the OK code field in the SAP GUI.

Within BSP pages, you can also use the following variant wherever text is used:

```
title  = "<%= otr( PACKAGE/ALIAS ) %>"
```

If you use links, you should use `otr_trim`,

```
link   = "<%=page->otr_trim( PACKAGE/ALIAS ) %>"
```

because `otr_trim` truncates blanks at the beginning and at the end.

Table 14.6 lists useful SAP Notes on the OTR.

| SAP Note | Short Text |
|---|---|
| 579365 | Modification of OTR Texts |
| 503346 | OTR: Incorrect text length |
| 448220 | OTR: Text is not determined/incorrect text is displayed |
| 575367 | Text changes are not transported |
| 855966 | Forbidden characters in the OTR alias |
| 802767 | OTR: Maintaining alias names in the customer namespace |
| 523055 | OTR: Making changes in non-original systems |

**Table 14.6**  Notes on the OTR

## 14.7.2  Defining Work Area Titles (Headings)

To define the text of a work area title (see Section 1.2.2) at runtime, redefine and implement the `IF_BSP_WD_HISTORY_STATE_DESCR~GET_STATE_DESCRIP-TION` method in the controller of a view that is displayed in the work area.

Assign a text to the `DESCRIPTION` parameter. This text can be determined from the OTR, for example (see Section 14.7.1).

> **Note**
>
> When creating work area titles, you have to adhere to certain conventions for various business objects in the SAP standard version (see Chapter 1, Section 1.2.2). To generate an overview for the work area title, the SAP standard version uses the following statement for business transactions, for example:
>
> ```
> cl_crm_uiu_bt_tools=>get_title_header( lr_entity ).
> ```

*Problems can never be solved with the same thinking that created them.*
— Albert Einstein

# 15    Tips and Tricks

This chapter provides practical and useful tips and tricks for troubleshooting as well as runtime analysis that have proven invaluable in our experience. A great deal of runtime information can be obtained from the application if you know where to look for it.

## 15.1    "View Hierarchy" Dialog Box

With CRM 2007 support package 5 (see also SAP Note 1248803), SAP introduced a VIEW HIERARCHY dialog box. The background for this new feature is that it is impossible to identify, at first glance, the UI components that comprise the active CRM application displayed at runtime in the web browser. However, it is essential to know the composition of an application (e.g., a UI component extension) for analysis purposes. Although the TECHNICAL DATA dialog box (see Section 5.1.3) allows you to determine certain details about the views and UI components used, the names of embedded UI components may in some cases remain a mystery if they do not display separate screen elements on the user interface and therefore cannot be accessed from the TECHNICAL DATA dialog box.

Runtime information

The VIEW HIERARCHY dialog box shows all windows, view sets, and views that form part of a work center page together with their UI components in the form of nodes in a hierarchy. This allows you to identify UI components that make up the technical structure of the work center page.

To call the VIEW HIERARCHY dialog box, use the key combination `Shift`+`Alt`+`F2` in the web browser. As an example, Figure 15.1 shows the ACCOUNTS work center page as a view hierarchy.

Calling the "View Hierarchy" dialog box

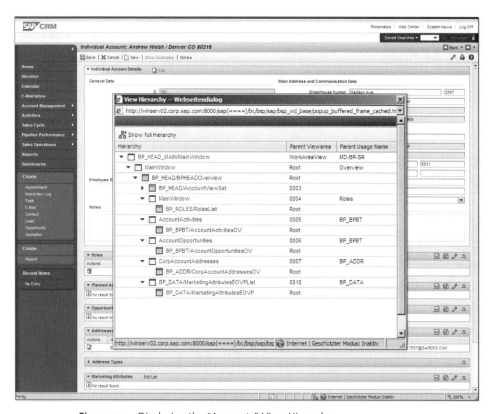

**Figure 15.1** Displaying the "Accounts" View Hierarchy

> **Note**
>
> To open this dialog box, you need DISPLAY authorization for the S_DEVELOP authorization object.

Link to the "Technical Data" dialog box

Each of the hierarchy nodes is displayed as a link. If you click on one of the nodes, the TECHNICAL DATA dialog box opens.

## 15.2 Where-Used List for UI Components

The where-used list function in the Component Workbench (Transaction BSP_WD_CMPWB) allows you to determine the other UI components in which a UI component is reused. To do this, call the UI component in display mode and click on the WHERE-USED LIST button ([Ctrl]+[⇧]+[F3]) on the workbench toolbar.

For example, the results of executing the where-used list function if you want to know the UI components in which the BT111H_OPPT UI component is used are shown in Figure 15.2.

---

**Usages of Component BT111H_OPPT (12 Hits)**

| Component | Component Usage |
|---|---|
| BP_HEAD_PHA_EXT | Opportunities |
| BP_PA_CHM | Opportunities |
| BP_PC_CHM | Opportunities |
| BP_PM_CHM | Opportunities |
| BT111H_OPPT | CUBTOpptOverview |
| BT111S_OPPT | CUBTOpportunity |
| CRMCMP_PPM | UCPPM_CRM_BT111H_OPPT_TTD |
| CRMCMP_PPM | UCPPM_CRM_BT111H_OPPT_CLD |
| CRMCMP_PPM | UCPPM_CRM_BT111H_OPPT_SPV |
| CRMCMP_PPM | UCPPM_CRM_BT111H_OPPT_PCR |
| PPM_PCR | UCBT_CRM_BT111H_OPPT |
| ZOPPORTUNITY | Overview |

**Figure 15.2** Where-Used List for the BT111H_OPPT Component

You can also use forward navigation to navigate from this list to any of the specified UI components.

## 15.3 Tips and Tricks for Troubleshooting

**Debugger**

A debugger is an essential troubleshooting tool used to execute ABAP programs line-by-line or section-by-section. It allows you to edit the contents of data objects and verify the flow logic of a program, for example. You can set one or more *breakpoints* in a program, and the debugger is then called when the ABAP runtime processor reaches these points. For the debugger to be called, an SAP GUI session must be open on the SAP NetWeaver Application Server.

**New ABAP debugger**

A new ABAP debugger was delivered with SAP Web AS 6.40. It is the standard debugger as of SAP NetWeaver 7.0. You can choose to use the classic debugger or the new debugger. In Transaction SE24, SE38, or SE80, select the menu option UTILITIES • SETTINGS and select one of the debuggers under DEBUGGING on the ABAP EDITOR tab.

You can set a breakpoint in an ABAP statement or in the source code of a BSP page. To do so, position the cursor in a line in an executable statement (see Figure 15.3) and click the SET EXTERNAL BREAKPOINT button on the toolbar.

```
Method                  EH_ONNAVIGATIONOP                                          Active
        1  ⊟ method eh_onnavigationop.
        2
        3       data lr_window type ref to cl_bsp_wd_window.
  🔵    4       lr_window = me->view_manager->get_window_controller( ).|
        5       lr_window->call_outbound_plug( 'START' ).
        6
        7
        8  └  endmethod.
```

**Figure 15.3**  Setting an External Breakpoint

### 15.3.1  External Debugging from the Running Application

Activating
debugging

The Component Workbench has a function for activating external debugging from the current application. In the workbench menu bar, choose DEBUG-GING • ACTIVATE (see Figure 15.4).

**Figure 15.4**  Functions for Activating and Deactivating Debugging

Stopping the
debugger at a
statement

During the next roundtrip, the debugger stops in the first statement of the DO_REQUEST method of the current view manager instance (class CL_BSP_WD_VIEW_MANAGER). To deactivate external debugging, select the DEACTIVATE menu option.

### 15.3.2  Conditional Breakpoints

Debugging an application is often a painstaking and time-consuming task. One reason for this is the call depth of methods and function modules. You frequently need to click many times to reach the point in the program that caused an error.

With CRM 2007 support package 4, SAP introduced the concept of conditional breakpoints (see also SAP Note 1225639). A conditional breakpoint is a predefined stop that can be activated from a CRM application. With conditional breakpoints, the debugger stops at a predefined point in the program if the condition defined in the application is met when an event occurs. For example, the debugger can be automatically shown as soon as a program exception occurs, a BOL component is loaded, or the navigation bar is used for navigation.

You define a conditional breakpoint in a special dialog box (see Figure 15.5), which you can open from the Web Client with the key combination $\boxed{\text{Alt}}$ + $\boxed{\text{F2}}$.

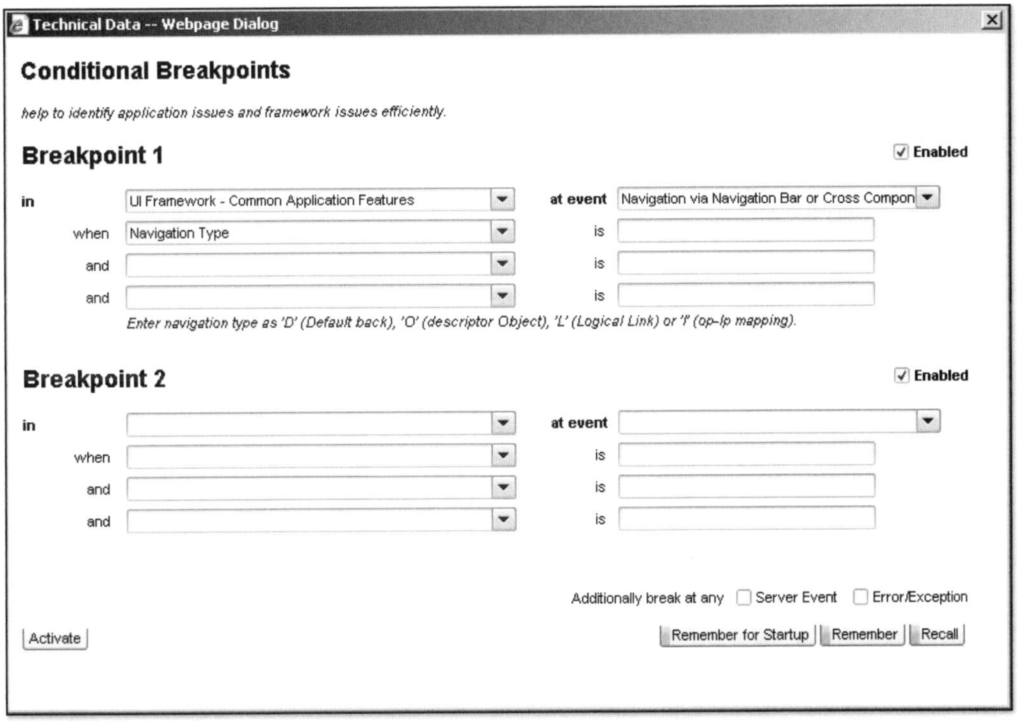

Defining a conditional breakpoint

**Figure 15.5**  Dialog Box for Conditional Breakpoints

For some events, a short explanatory text is also displayed for the possible values. In our example, the debugger stops at an ASSERT statement in the program code when the event occurs and if the predefined condition is met, that is, when the navigation bar is used for navigation (see Figure 15.6).

```
 98        ev_view_name       = lv_view_name
 99        ev_inbound_plug    = lv_inbound_plug
100        ev_target_id       = lv_target_id
101        ev_link_id         = lv_link_id
102        ev_object_type     = lv_object_type
103        ev_object_action   = lv_object_action.
104      lv_navigation_type = gc_navtype_default.
105  *    Navigation to default is a good time for a session restart
106        publish_before_context_change( ).
107  -  ENDIF.
108
109  *  Conditional Breakpoint
110     ASSERT ID crmuif_conditional_breakpoints
111        SUBKEY 'Application Frame - Navigation via Navigation Bar'
112        CONDITION navigation_assert(
113                     iv_navigation_type = lv_navigation_type
114                     iv_view_name       = lv_view_name
115                     iv_inbound_plug    = lv_inbound_plug
116                     iv_target_id       = lv_target_id
117                     iv_link_id         = lv_link_id
118                     iv_link_type       = lv_link_type
119                     iv_object_type     = lv_object_type
120                     iv_object_action   = lv_object_action
121                  ) = abap_true.                        "#EC NO
122
```

**Figure 15.6** Conditional Breakpoint at an ASSERT Statement

This means that you can continue parsing the program code or analyzing and manipulating variables as required.

Prerequisites    If you want to exploit the full potential of conditional breakpoints, the following prerequisites must be met:

▸ The CRMUIF_CONDITIONAL_BREAKPOINTS checkpoint group is activated in Transaction SAAB.

▸ External debugging is activated (see Section 15.3.1).

▸ The conditional breakpoint is activated in the application ($\boxed{\text{Alt}}$ + $\boxed{\text{F2}}$).

▸ The predefined event occurs and the condition is met. The debugger is started automatically.

### 15.3.3 Attributes and Values of BOL Entities at Runtime

If you want to analyze the content of the attributes of a BOL entity during a debugging operation, this analysis at first appears to present a number of problems because BOL entities exist in memory as object instances. Object instances initially appear more complex in the debugger than in simple internal tables, for example, due to their structure. However, there is a "golden thread" that will lead you directly to the attributes of a BOL entity. This section explains how to display these attributes with the new debugger.

If you have identified the variable in the program code that refers to the object instance of the BOL entity in the new debugger, this variable appears in the debugger as an object instance of the CL_CRM_BOL_ENTITY class, as shown in Figure 15.7.

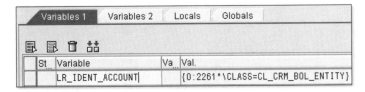

**Figure 15.7** Object Instance of a BOL Entity

At runtime, the object instance of the CL_CRM_BOL_ENTITY ABAP class with the CONTAINER_PROXY attribute contains a reference to a generic container object. The container object exists as an object instance of the CL_CRM_GENIL_CONTAINER_OBJECT ABAP class. Click on the CONTAINER_PROXY attribute in the debugger (see Figure 15.8).

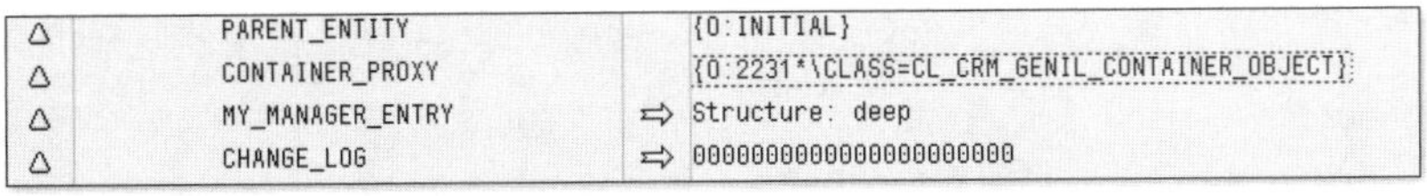

CONTAINER_ PROXY attribute

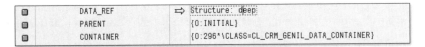

**Figure 15.8** Reference to a Container Object

The attributes of the object instance of the generic container object are then displayed in the debugger (see Figure 15.9). Click on the DATA_REF attribute, which refers to the header structure of the generic container object.

DATA_REF attribute

**Figure 15.9** DATA_REF – Reference to Header Structure

Three components in the field list of the DATA_REF attribute (see Figure 15.10) are particularly relevant. First, the OBJECT_NAME component indicates the name of the GenIL object. Second, the OBJECT_ID contains the unique key identifying the runtime instance of the GenIL object. Finally, the ATTRIBUTE_REF component refers to the attribute structure of the BOL entity, which you can also view in the GenIL model browser (see Chapter 12, Section 12.2.1). The attribute structure contains the runtime data of the BOL entity.

ATTRIBUTE_REF component

| Exp. | Component | Val. | Val. | | Ch | Technical Type |
|---|---|---|---|---|---|---|
| | OBJECT_NAME | | BTAdminH | | | C(30) |
| | OBJECT_ID | | FF0602010102800034313033006 | | | XString(77) |
| | IS_HANDLE | | | | 📎 | C(1) |
| | DELTA_FLAG | | | | 📎 | C(1) |
| | ATTR_REQUESTED | | | | 📎 | C(1) |
| | IS_QUERY_ROOT | | | | 📎 | C(1) |
| | ATTRIBUTE_REF | ⇒ | Structure: flat & not char | | | REF TO \TYPE=CRMST_ADMINH_BTIL |

**Figure 15.10** Reference to Object Attributes

Field list with runtime data

Click on the ATTRIBUTE_REF reference. This displays a field list that includes the runtime data of the BOL entity in the debugger. Figure 15.11 shows an extract from the field list for the BTAdminH BOL entity.

| Component | Val. | Val. | Ch | Technical Type |
|---|---|---|---|---|
| CLIENT | | 800 | 📎 | C(3) |
| GUID | | 0448BB2658DA7D478F4EDCBC9F | 📎 | X(16) |
| OBJECT_ID | | 0000011773 | 📎 | C(10) |
| PROCESS_TYPE | | TA | 📎 | C(4) |
| POSTING_DATE | | 20060405 | 📎 | D(8) |
| DESCRIPTION | | | 📎 | C(40) |
| DESCR_LANGUAGE | | D | 📎 | C(1) |
| LOGICAL_SYSTEM | | T90CLNT090 | 📎 | C(10) |
| CRM_RELEASE | | BBPCRM 400 | 📎 | C(10) |

**Figure 15.11** Attributes and Values of the BTAdminH BOL Entity (Extract)

> **Tip**
>
> You may encounter an object instance of a collection (see Section 13.2) during a debugging session and may want to know which entities are provided by this collection. It is therefore important to note that an object instance of a collection manages the ENTITY_LIST internal table, which contains the references to BOL entities.

## 15.3.4 Debugging BSP pages

Analyzing exceptions

You do not normally need to pay much attention to the technical BSP structure of the Web Client UI framework. However, exceptions occasionally occur in the display of a view for no immediately obvious reason. It is therefore useful to know that you can use the classic debugger to analyze the processing of a BSP page. If you set a breakpoint in a BSP page, the debugger stops when the page is rendered (see Figure 15.12, ❶).

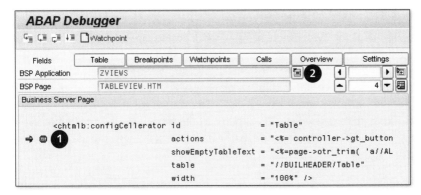

**Figure 15.12** BSP page in Debugging Mode

As discussed earlier, a BSP page is compiled in normal ABAP classes at run-time the first time it is accessed. To analyze the executable program code of the BSP in the debugger, click on the button to the right of the BSP application name (❷) to switch to source text mode in the debugger (see Figure 15.13).

**Source text mode**

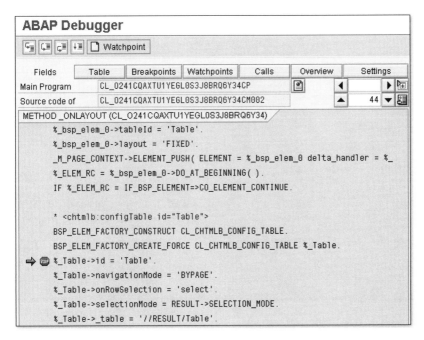

**Figure 15.13** Source Text Mode of a BSP

### 15.3.5 Message Sources

All layers of the Web Client UI framework are possible message sources. For example, function modules frequently generate messages to be displayed in the user interface from the API layer. We know, from experience, that it is not always easy to determine the precise origin of a message when troubleshooting. Knowledge of the various entry points for debugging may prove useful in such cases. Set a breakpoint at the entry points specified in Table 15.1. When processing a message, the debugger will then stop at one of these entry points.

| Entry point | Explanation |
| --- | --- |
| Function module<br>CRM_MESSAGE_COLLECT | The CRM_MESSAGE_COLLECT function module can be used as an entry point for messages that are generated from the OneOrder framework, for example. |
| Methods<br>ADD_MESSAGE<br>ADD_BAPI_MESSAGES<br>Class<br>CL_BSP_WD_MESSAGE_SERVICE | Methods of the CL_BSP_WD_MESSAGE_SERVICE class can be used as an entry point for messages generated in the CRM Web Client. |
| Methods<br>ADD_MESSAGE<br>ADD_BAPI_MESSAGES<br>Class<br>CL_CRM_GENIL_GLOBAL_MESS_CONT | Methods of the CL_CRM_GENIL_GLOBAL_MESS_CONT class can be used as an entry point for general (non-object-specific) messages from the GenIL. |
| Methods<br>ADD_MESSAGE<br>ADD_CURRENT_SY_MESSAGE<br>Class<br>CL_CRM_GENIL_SIMPLE_MESS_CONT | Methods of the CL_CRM_GENIL_SIMPLE_MESS_CONT class can be used as an entry point for object-specific messages from the GenIL. |
| Methods<br>ADD MESSAGES<br>Class<br>CL_CRM_GENIL_BAPI_MESS_CONT | Method ADD_MESSAGES of the CL_CRM_GENIL_BAPI_MESS_CONT class can be used as an entry point for object specific messages from GenIL. |

**Table 15.1** Entry Points – Message Generation

If the debugger stops at one of the entry points, you can trace the call sequence of the processed methods and function modules in the debugger call stack.

**Call sequence**

### 15.3.6 Analysis of the Navigation Queue

If you navigate within an application using, for example, the navigation bar or a link to other application areas, you can determine the navigation target at runtime. To do so, set a breakpoint at the first executable statement of the PROCESS_NAV_QUEUE method in the CL_BSP_WD_VIEW_MANAGER class.

When you navigate within the application, the debugger stops during processing of the PROCESS_NAV_QUEUE method. You can then analyze the NAV_QUEUE attribute of the CL_BSP_WD_VIEW_MANAGER class in the debugger (Figure 15.14).

> **Note**
>
> Alternatively, you can activate the debugger from the running application (see Section 15.3.1). After processing the DISPATCH_INPUT method in the view manager instance, you can evaluate the NAV_QUEUE attribute.

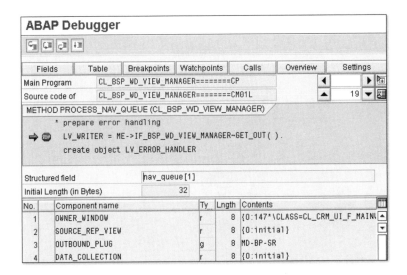

**Figure 15.14** NAV_QUEUE Attribute at Runtime in the Debugger

If you use the navigation bar for navigation, the name of the logical link of the navigation target is contained in the OUTBOUND_PLUG component. If you click on a link to navigate within an application, the OUTBOUND_PLUG component contains the name of the outbound plug that was "fired" to exit the current display.

The DATA_COLLECTION component may contain the instance of the collection that is passed to the navigation target (see Chapter 9, Section 9.1.4).

## 15.4 SAP Community

You will find additional tips and documentation on the *SAP Developer Network* (SDN). The SDN has over one million registered members and gives all participants in the SAP ecosystem—customers, partners, developers, and consultants—the opportunity to exchange information in the context of forums. You can register as a member of the SDN free of charge at *http://sdn.sap.com*.

SDN forums
After successful registration, you can ask questions or search for solutions in the SAP CRM 2007 forum, for example. Clicking on the FORUMS link brings you to a page showing all forums available on the SDN. These include a range of forums for CRM. To access the dedicated forum for SAP CRM 2007, select FORUMS • SAP CRM 2007.

In addition to the SAP CRM 2007 forum, there is also a forum devoted to BSP pages, the UI technology for the CRM Web Client.

*Practice should be the result of contemplation,*
*not the other way around.*
— Hermann Hesse; German-Swiss poet, novelist, and painter

# 16 Practical Examples

In this chapter, we will introduce practical examples for implementing a search page with subsequent navigation to an overview page. We will describe the creation of a form view or table view in exactly the same systematic way as the implementation of a dropdown list. The examples build upon each other; for instance, the first practical example begins with creating a UI component, whereas the last example illustrates integrating the UI component into the navigation bar. For space reasons, we had to omit implementation details. The practical examples are not complicated and offer sufficient potential for your own enhancements.

ABAP knowledge and experience of using the class builder are required. For the most part, we have also omitted details about software logistics such as transport requests of type workbench. You can decide whether you want to transport the objects or prefer to store them as local objects.

**ABAP knowledge**

## 16.1 Creating a UI Component

The objective of this practical example is to create a UI component called ZMY_COMPONENT. You will use this component as a container for all objects that you create in other practical examples.

As you can see in Figure 16.1, a UI component is created in the Component Workbench (Transaction BSP_WD_CMPWB).

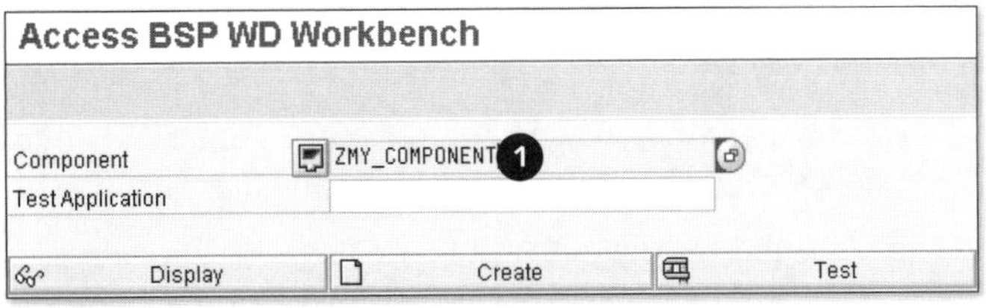

**Figure 16.1** Creating the ZMY_COMPONENT UI Component

Transaction BSP_
WD_CMBWB

1. Start Transaction BSP_WD_CMBWB and enter the name ZMY_COMPONENT in the COMPONENT (❶) field.

2. Click the CREATE button.

3. A dialog appears where you can enter a descriptive text for the UI component and assign the name of the window for the UI component. Copy the settings without making any changes. Confirm your entries by pressing the Enter key.

4. A dialog for assigning packages displays. Enter the name of the required package or save the UI component as a local object. Press the Enter key.

5. If you do not want to store the UI component as a local object, you may be required to perform an assignment to a transportable transport request of type workbench. Perform the assignment and confirm the dialog queries in each case using the Enter key.

## 16.2 Linking a UI Component to an Object Model

The object model is provided by the ALL (❶) component set and added to the MODELS node in the runtime repository editor.

Adding a model in
the runtime
repository editor

1. Open the ZMY_COMPONENT UI component.

2. Switch to the runtime repository editor.

3. Go to change mode by clicking the EDIT button in the runtime repository editor.

4. Select the ADD MODEL (❶) option in the MODELS node.

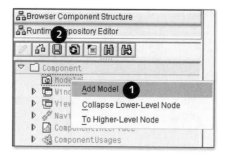

**Figure 16.2** Add Model Option

5. A dialog now appears where you can add a component set. Enter ALL in the COMPONENT SET field and confirm this entry by pressing the Enter key.

6. Click the SAVE (❷) button to save your settings.

## 16.3 Implementing a Search Page

The objective of this section is to create a search page for business partners. For the sake of simplicity, we will use an already existing dynamic search object in the ALL component set. The search page consists of two views that are organized in one view set. We will restrict ourselves to a SEARCH button and will not implement a RESET button. We will also show you how you can create a custom controller using the wizard. Other topics include creating a table view as a result list and creating a view set.

### 16.3.1 Creating a Custom Controller

1. Open the ZMY_COMPONENT UI component.

2. Select the CUSTOM CONTROLLER node in the component structure browser and select the CREATE option from the context menu.

*Creating a custom controller*

3. A wizard for creating a custom controller now appears. Click CONTINUE to continue.

4. Enter CUCOSEARCH in the NAME field and click CONTINUE.

5. In the third wizard step, you define model nodes. Enter BUILHEADER in the MODEL NODES (❶) and BOL ENTITY (❷) fields respectively, as shown in Figure 16.3.

*Adding model nodes*

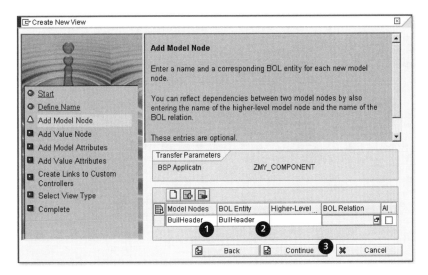

**Figure 16.3** Defining BuilHeader Model Nodes

6. Exit the wizard by clicking CONTINUE (❸) until you come to the last wizard step. Then, click COMPLETE to close the window with the wizard.

## 16.3.2 Creating a View for Entering Search Criteria

1. Open the ZMY_COMPONENT UI component.

Creating a view
2. Select the VIEWS node in the component structure browser and select the CREATE option from the context menu.

3. A wizard for creating a view now appears. Click CONTINUE to proceed.

4. In the second wizard step, enter SEARCHVIEW in the NAME field and click CONTINUE again.

5. In the third step, you define two model nodes. Enter the values shown in Figure 16.4 into the MODEL NODES (❶) and BOL ENTITY (❷) fields.

6. Click CONTINUE (❸) until you come to the CREATE LINKS TO CUSTOM CONTROLLERS step.

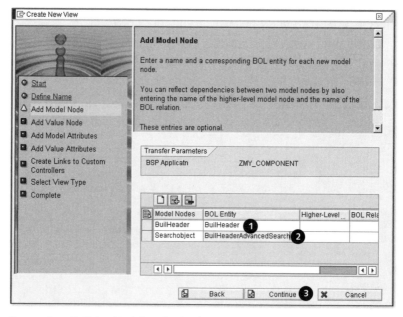

**Figure 16.4** Defining Model Nodes for a Dynamic Search Object

7. Now perform a context node binding to the BUILHEADER model node of the CUCOSEARCH custom controller by copying the settings (❶) from Figure 16.5. Then click CONTINUE (❷).

*Defining context node binding*

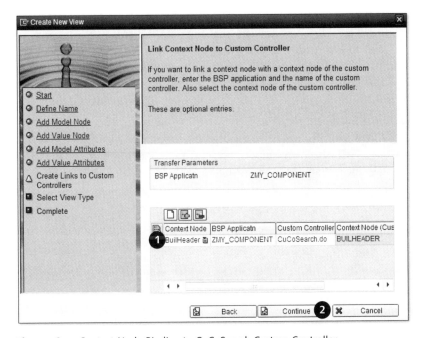

**Figure 16.5** Context Node Binding to CuCoSearch Custom Controller

8. In the second to last wizard step, you define the view type. Copy the EMPTY VIEW default setting, click the CONTINUE button, and exit the wizard by clicking the COMPLETE button.

*Defining a view type*

9. After the generation by the wizard, switch to the detailed overview of the SEARCHVIEW view in the Component Workbench. Double-click the implementation class of the SEARCHOBJECT model node in the context of the view controller. This takes you to the Class Builder.

10. In the Class Builder, you change the superclass from CL_BSP_WD_ CONTEXT_NODE to CL_BSP_WD_CONTEXT_NODE_ASP on the PROPERTIES tab by switching to change mode beforehand and clicking the CHANGE INHERITANCE button. Enter the CL_BSP_WD_CONTEXT_ NODE_ASP class in the INHERITED BY field and activate your changes. Then, return to the detailed overview of the SEARCHVIEW view.

*Changing an inheritance relationship*

11. The next thing you must do is change the inheritance relationship of the view controller superclass. Double-click the implementation class of the view controller to go to the class builder for displaying the ZL_ZMY_COMP_SEARCHVIEW_IMPL class. Switch to the PROPERTIES tab and double-click the entry in field superclass to go to the ZL_ZMY_COMP_SEARCHVIEW class. Activate change mode and change the inheritance relationship from CL_BSP_WD_VIEW_CONTROLLER to CL_BSP_WD_ADVSEARCH_CONTROLLER on the PROPERTIES tab. Click YES to confirm the dialog about receiving redefinitions. Then, activate the class. Finally, return to the detailed overview of the SEARCHVIEW view.

12. From the detailed overview, switch to the editor for editing the SEARCHVIEW.HTM BSP page. Now, the objective is to create a configurable search page. Activate change mode and replace the statements in the BSP page with the statements from Listing 12.1. Then, activate the BSP page.

```
<%@page language="abap" %>
<%@extension name="thtmlb" prefix="thtmlb" %>
<thtmlb:searchArea>
  <thtmlb:searchTagArea>
    <thtmlb:advancedSearch id = "AdvancedOrderSearch"
                fieldMetadata = "<%= controller->get_dquery_
definitions( ) %>"
                header         = "<%= searchobject->get_
param_struct_name( ) %>"
                fieldNames    = "<%= controller->get_
possible_fields( ) %>"
                values        = "//searchobject/parameters"
                maxHits       = "//searchobject/max_hits"
                ajaxDeltaHandling = "false"
                onEnter       = "SEARCH" />
  </thtmlb:searchTagArea>
  <thtmlb:searchButtonsArea>
    <thtmlb:button design  = "EMPHASIZED"
                id       = "SEARCH_BTN"
                onClick = "SEARCH"
                text     = "Search" />
  </thtmlb:searchButtonsArea>
</thtmlb:searchArea>
```

**Listing 16.1** Configurable Search Page

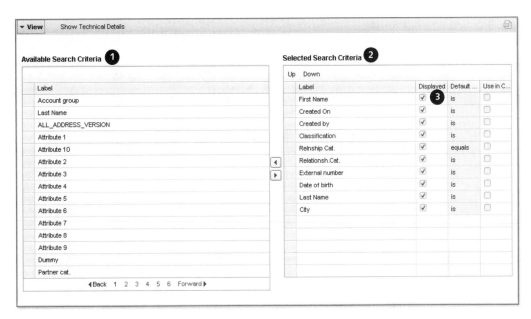

**Figure 16.6** UI Configuration Tool – Defining Search Criteria

13. Switch to the UI Configuration Tool and create a new default configu- ration by clicking the New Configuration button. Copy the default values by pressing the `Enter` key. If the UI Configuration Tool is not immediately available, start the Component Workbench again and try once more. In the UI Configuration Tool, copy a few criteria from the amount of available search criteria (❶) into the Selected Search Criteria (❷) area. Set the Displayed option for every selected search criterion (❸ in Figure 16.6). Then, save the configuration by clicking the Save button and switch to the detailed overview of the Search-View view.

*Creating a default configuration*

### 16.3.3 Creating an Event Handler

1. In the detailed overview of the SearchView view, select the Event Handler node (❶ in Figure 16.7) and select the Create option from the context menu.

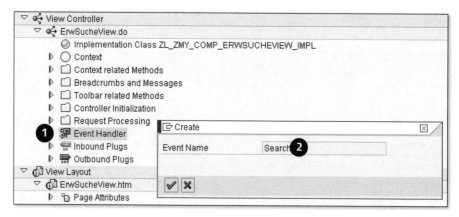

**Figure 16.7** Creating a Search Event Handler

Defining a SEARCH event

2. In the dialog that opens, enter SEARCH in the EVENT NAME field. Confirm this entry with the ⌈Enter⌋ key to create the event handler. Pay attention to the spelling of the event name—you must enter the event name entirely in upper-case letters.

Implementing an event handler

3. Then, double-click the EH_ONSEARCH event handler. This, in turn, takes you to the class builder. Switch to change mode and enter the statements from Listing 16.2 between the method definition.

```
data  l_qs  type ref to cl_crm_bol_dquery_service.
l_qs ?= me->typed_context->searchobject->collection_wrapper-
>get_current( ).
data  l_result type ref to if_bol_entity_col.
l_result = l_qs->get_query_result( ).
me->typed_context->builheader->collection_wrapper->set_
collection( l_result ).
```

**Listing 16.2** Event Handler for Starting a Search

4. Activate your changes in the class builder, and return to the detailed overview of the SEARCHVIEW view.

### 16.3.4 Displaying the Result List as a Table View

1. Open the ZMY_COMPONENT UI component.

2. Select the VIEWS node in the component structure browser and select the CREATE option from the context menu.

3. A wizard for creating a view appears. Click CONTINUE to proceed.

4. In the second wizard step, enter SearchResultView in the NAME field and then click CONTINUE again.

5. In the third wizard step, you define a model node of the BUILHEADER BOL entity. Enter the values shown in Figure 16.8 into the MODEL NODES (❶) and BOL ENTITY (❷) fields.

> Defining the BuilHeader model node

6. Click CONTINUE (❸) until you come to the CREATE LINKS TO CUSTOM CONTROLLERS step.

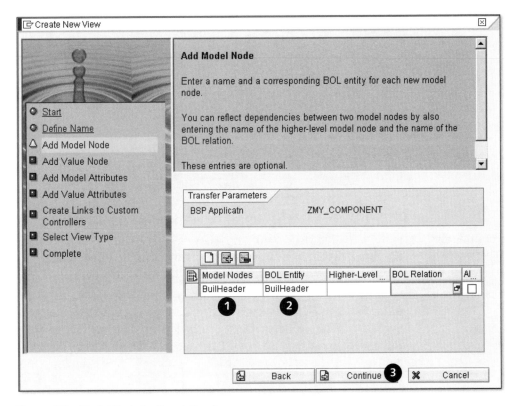

**Figure 16.8** Model Node for Search Result

7. Now, perform a context node binding to the BUILHEADER model node of the CUCOSEARCH custom controller by copying the settings (❶) from Figure 16.9. Then, click CONTINUE (❷).

> Creating a context node binding to the custom controller

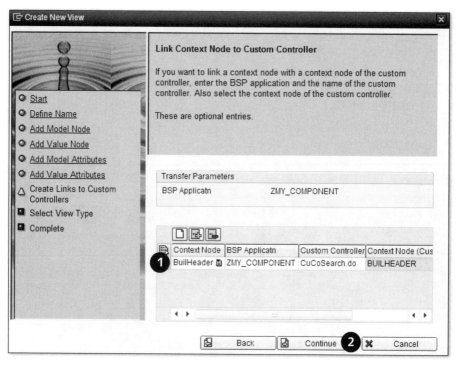

**Figure 16.9** Context Node Binding to the Custom Controller

Selecting the table view option

8. In the second to last wizard step, select the TABLE VIEW view type. Select the BUILHEADER entry from the CONTEXT NODE dropdown box. Click CONTINUE and exit the wizard by clicking the COMPLETE button.

Implementing a BSP page

9. In the detailed overview of the SEARCHRESULTVIEW view, switch to the editor for editing the SEARCHRESULTVIEW.HTM BSP page. Here, the objective is to create a configurable search table view. Activate change mode and replace the statements in the BSP page with the statements from Listing 16.3. Then, activate the BSP page.

```
<%@page language="abap" %>
<%@extension name="chtmlb" prefix="chtmlb" %>
<chtmlb:configCellerator
    id = "Table"
    table = "//builheader/Table"
    width = "100 %" />
```

**Listing 16.3** Defining a Configurable Table View

10. Switch to the UI Configuration Tool and create a new default configuration by clicking the NEW CONFIGURATION button. Copy the default values by pressing the ⏎ Enter key. If the UI Configuration Tool is not immediately available, start the Component Workbench again and try once more.

11. Click the SHOW TECHNICAL DETAILS button in the UI Configuration Tool. Then, copy the STRUCT.ACCOUNT_DESCRIPTION and STRUCT.BP_DESCRIPTION fields from the AVAILABLE FIELDS (❶ in Figure 16.10) area on the left into the DISPLAYED FIELDS (❷) area on the right. Confirm your changes by clicking the SAVE button.

*Implementing a configuration*

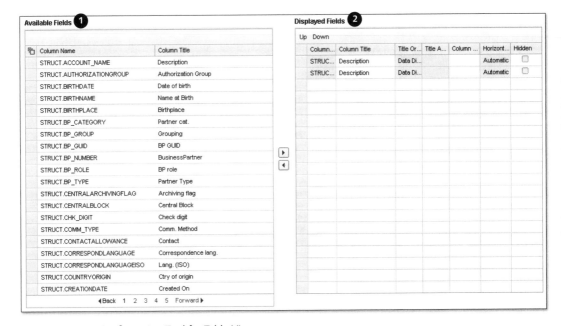

**Figure 16.10** UI Configuration Tool for Table View

## 16.3.5 Creating a View Set

1. Open the ZMY_COMPONENT UI component.

2. In the component structure browser, select the CREATE VIEW SET (❷ in Figure 16.11) option from the context menu in the VIEWS (❶) node.

*Creating a view set*

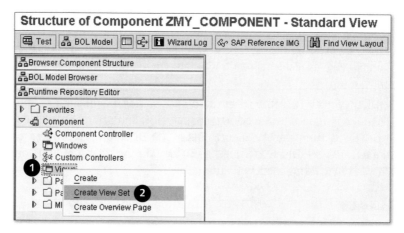

**Figure 16.11** Creating a View Set

3. A wizard for creating a view set appears. Click the CONTINUE button.

Defining a view
set name
4. Enter ADVSEARCHVIEWSET in the NAME field (❶ in Figure 16.12). In the fields for the grid size (❷), enter the value 2 into the LINES field and the value 1 into the COLUMNS field. Then, click the CONTINUE (❸) button.

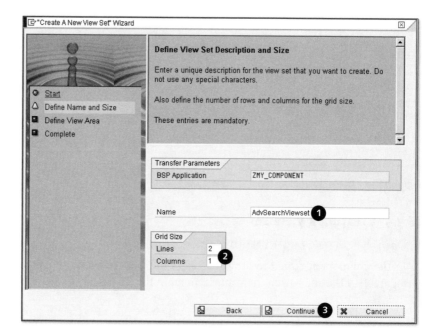

**Figure 16.12** Name and Size of a View Set

5. You will now define the view areas. Implement the settings (❶) for the view areas shown in Figure 16.13.

6. Click CONTINUE (❷) and exit the wizard by clicking the COMPLETE button.

Defining the view area

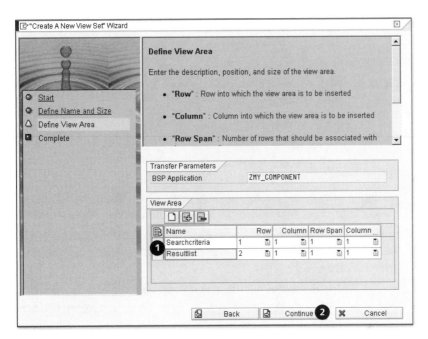

**Figure 16.13** Defining View Areas

7. Switch to the detailed overview of the ADVSEARCHVIEWSET view set, double-click the ADVSEARCHVIEWSET.HTM branch to open the ADVSEARCHVIEWSET.HTM BSP page, and activate change mode.

8. Replace the generated statements with the statements from Listing 16.4 and activate the BSP page.

```abap
<%@page language="abap" %>
<%@extension name="bsp" prefix="bsp" %>
<%@extension name="chtmlb" prefix="chtmlb" %>
<chtmlb:pageType type="SEARCH" >
  <thtmlb:searchFrame showSearchFields="TRUE"
      <thtmlb:searchCriteriaFrame>
  <bsp:call comp_id = "<%= controller->GET_VIEWAREA_CONTENT_
ID( 'Search criteria' ) %>"
           url     = "<%= controller->GET_VIEWAREA_CONTENT_
URL( 'Search criteria' ) %>" />
```

```
</thtmlb:searchCriteriaFrame>
<thtmlb:searchResultFrame>
<bsp:call comp_id = "<%= controller->GET_VIEWAREA_CONTENT_
ID( 'Result list' ) %>"
        url     = "<%= controller->GET_VIEWAREA_CONTENT_
URL( 'Result list' ) %>" />
    </thtmlb:searchResultFrame>
  </thtmlb:searchFrame>
</chtmlb:pageType>
```

**Listing 16.4**  View Set Statements for a Search Page

Assigning a view
to a view area

9.  Then, switch to the runtime repository editor. Activate change mode by clicking the EDIT button and open the VIEW SETS node. Select the SEARCH CRITERIA view area of the ZMY_COMPONENT/AdvSearch-ViewSet view set and select the ADD VIEW option from the context menu.

10. A dialog now opens. Select the AdvSearchView entry from the value help of the VIEW field and confirm the action with the [Enter] key.

11. Select the RESULT LIST view area of the ZMY_COMPONENT/ AdvSearchViewSet view set and select the ADD VIEW option from the context menu.

12. In the dialog that appears, select the AdvSearchView entry from the value help of the VIEW field and confirm the action again with the [Enter] key.

13. Use the SAVE button in the runtime repository editor to save your settings.

### 16.3.6  Assigning a View Set to a Window

1.  Open the ZMY_COMPONENT UI component.

2.  Then, switch to change mode in the runtime repository editor. Open the WINDOWS node and select the ZMY_COMPONENT/MAINWINDOW window.

3.  Select the ADD VIEW option from the context menu.

Assigning a view
set to a window

4.  In the dialog that opens, select the AdvSearchViewSet entry from the value help of the VIEW (❶) field and confirm the action with the [Enter] key (see Figure 16.14).

**Figure 16.14** Assigning a View Set to a Window

5. Use the SAVE button in the runtime repository editor to save your settings.

## 16.4    Implementing an Overview Page

The structure of an overview page is kept quite simple. It contains a form view and represents an interface view of an embedded UI component as an assignment block. Aside from its implementation, we will show you how to set up component usage and create a configurable form view. Other topics include creating a dropdown box and context node binding to the component controller.

### 16.4.1    Setting Up Component Usage

1. Open the ZMY_COMPONENT UI component.

2. Use the EDIT button in the runtime repository editor to activate change mode. Select the COMPONENTUSAGES node and select the ADD COMPONENT USAGE option from the context menu.

3. A dialog opens. Enter the values shown in Figure 16.15 in the input fields (❶ – ❸) of the dialog and confirm your entries with the ⌷Enter⌷ key.

Defining component usage

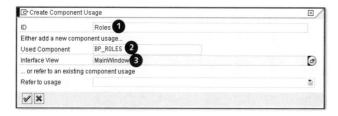

**Figure 16.15** Defining Component Usage

4. Use the SAVE button in the runtime repository editor to save your changes.

5. Confirm the next dialog that appears by pressing the ⎡Enter⎤ key.

6. Switch to the component structure browser and select the component controller.

Adding a context node in the component controller

7. Add a model node in the context in the detailed overview of the component controller. Select the CONTEXT NODE node and select the CREATE option in the context menu.

8. Click the CONTINUE button in the wizard to proceed.

9. In the second wizard step, define a model node. Enter the values in the input fields (❶ and ❷), as shown in Figure 16.16.

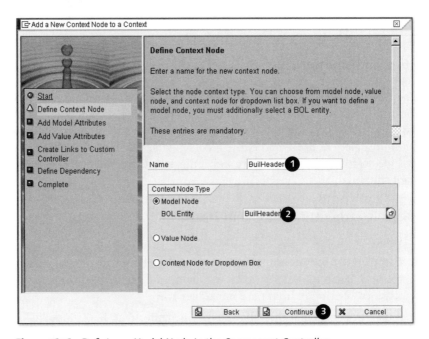

**Figure 16.16** Defining a Model Node in the Component Controller

10. Click the CONTINUE button (❸) until you come to the last wizard step and then exit the wizard by clicking the COMPLETE button.

11. After you generate the model node with the wizard, switch to the implementation class of the component controller by clicking the IMPLEMENTATION CLASS ZL_ZMY_COMP_BSPWDCOMPONEN_IMPL node in the detailed overview.

12. Switch to change mode in the class builder and redefine the WD_    Redefining the
    USAGE_INITIALIZE method by selecting it and clicking the REDEFINE    WD_USAGE_
    button. Enter the statements from Listing 16.5 in the method definition    INITIALIZE method
    of the WD_USAGE_INITIALIZE method.

```
case iv_usage->usage_name.
  when 'Rollen'.
    call method iv_usage->bind_context_node
      exporting
        iv_controller_type  = cl_bsp_wd_controller=>co_
type_component
        iv_name             = iv_usage->usage_name
        iv_target_node_name = 'BUILHEADER'
        iv_node_2_bind      = 'PARTNER'.
endcase.
```

**Listing 16.5**  Context Node Binding by Component Usage

13. Activate your changes to the implementation class of the component
    controller and return to the detailed overview.

## 16.4.2  Instantiating the View Group Context

The use of the BP_ROLES component makes it necessary to instantiate the
view group context in the MAINWINDOW window. If you do not do this, an
error message is issued at runtime.

1. Open the ZMY_COMPONENT UI component.

2. Select the MAINWINDOW window at the WINDOWS level in the component structure browser.

3. In the detailed overview of the MAINWINDOW window, double-click the
   implementation class of the window controller (❶ in Figure 16.17). This
   takes you to the class builder.

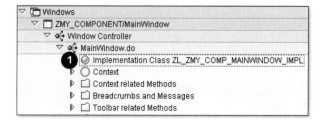

**Figure 16.17**  Implementation Class of the MainWindow Window

4. Redefine the SET_VIEW_GROUP_CONTEXT method by selecting it in the class builder and clicking the REDEFINE button.

5. Enter the statements from Listing 16.6 in the redefined SET_VIEW_GROUP_ CONTEXT method.

```
if iv_first_time = abap_true.
  if not me->view_group_context is bound.
    if iv_parent_context is initial.
      create object
      me->view_group_context type    cl_bsp_wd_view_group_
context.
    else.
      me->view_group_context = iv_parent_context.
    endif.
  endif.
endif.
```

**Listing 16.6** Instantiating the View Group Context

6. Activate your changes in the class builder and return to the detailed overview.

### 16.4.3 Creating and Configuring a Form View

1. Open the ZMY_COMPONENT UI component.

Creating a view

2. Select the VIEWS node in the component structure browser and select the CREATE option from the context menu.

3. A wizard for creating a view appears. Click CONTINUE to proceed.

4. In the second wizard step, enter FORMULARVIEW in the NAME field and then click CONTINUE.

Defining a model node

5. In the third step, define a model node called BUILHEADER. Enter the values from Figure 16.18 into the MODEL NODES (❶) and BOL ENTITY (❷) fields.

6. Click CONTINUE (❸) until you reach the SELECT VIEW TYPE step.

Selecting the "Empty View" option

7. Make sure that you activate the EMPTY VIEW option in the SELECT VIEW TYPE step. Click the CONTINUE button. Exit the wizard using the COMPLETE button.

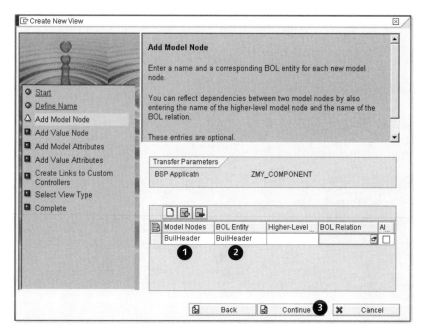

**Figure 16.18**  Defining Model Nodes for a Form View

8. After the generation by the wizard, switch to the detailed overview of the FORMULARVIEW view in the Component Workbench. There, open the editor for editing the FORMULARVIEW.HTM BSP page. Here, the objective is to create a configurable form view. Activate change mode and replace the statements in the BSP page with the statements from Listing 16.7. and Then, activate the BSP page.

*Implementing a BSP page*

```
<%@page language="abap" %>
<%@extension name="chtmlb" prefix="chtmlb" %>
<chtmlb:config xml   = "<%=
controller->configuration_descr->get_config_data( )
%>"
mode = "RUNTIME" />
```

**Listing 16.7**  Defining a Configurable View

9. Switch to the UI Configuration Tool and create a new default configuration by clicking the NEW CONFIGURATION button. Copy the default values by pressing the [Enter] key. If the UI Configuration Tool is not immediately available, start the Component Workbench again and try once more.

*Creating a configuration*

10. In the UI Configuration Tool, click the SHOW AVAILABLE FIELDS and SHOW TECHNICAL DETAILS buttons consecutively. Copy the following fields from the AVAILABLE FIELDS (❶) area on the left into the left panel (❷ in Figure 16.19):

▸ *//BuilHeader/Struct.bp_number*

▸ *//BuilHeader/Struct.account_description*

▸ *//BuilHeader/Struct.bp_description*

▸ *//BuilHeader/Struct.SEX*

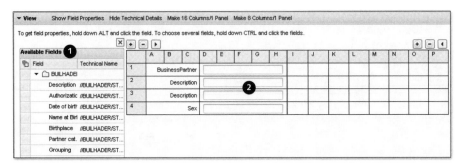

**Figure 16.19** UI Configuration Tool for Form View

Saving settings

11. Confirm your changes with the SAVE button and return to the detailed overview of the FORMULARVIEW view.

### 16.4.4 Creating a Context Node Binding to the Component Controller

1. Open the ZMY_COMPONENT UI component.

2. Double-click the FORMULARVIEW view in the component structure browser.

Defining context node binding to the component controller

3. In the detailed overview of the FORMULARVIEW view, double-click the ZL_ZMY_COMP_FORMULARVIEW_CTXT implementation class of the context. This takes you to the class builder.

4. Switch to change mode in the class builder and open the CREATE_BUILHEADER method for editing.

5. Enter the following statement as the last statement in the CREATE_BUILHEADER method:

```
owner->do_context_node_binding(
        iv_controller_type = cl_bsp_wd_controller=>co_type_
component
```

```
iv_target_node_name = 'BuilHeader'
iv_node_2_bind = builheader ).
```

6. Activate the ZL_ZMY_COMP_FORMULARVIEW_CTXT class and return to the detailed overview.

### 16.4.5 Creating and Configuring an Overview Page

1. Open the ZMY_COMPONENT UI component.

2. Select the VIEWS node in the component structure browser and select the CREATE OVERVIEW PAGE option from the context menu.

3. In the dialog that appears, enter OVERVIEW PAGE in the NAME field. Confirm your entries with the ⌈Enter⌉ key. The overview page is generated and subsequently available in the component structure browser.

4. Switch to the runtime repository editor and activate change mode.

5. Select the VIEW SETS node and select the ADD VIEW SET option in the context menu. In the dialog, choose the OVERVIEWPAGE entry (see Figure 16.20) for the VIEW (❶) field from the value help and confirm your selection with the ⌈Enter⌉ key.

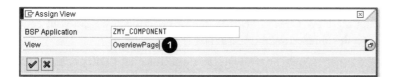

**Figure 16.20** Defining a View Set of an Overview Page

6. Now, select the OVERVIEWPAGE view set and select the ADD VIEW AREA option in the context menu. In the dialog, enter OVERVIEWPAGE in the ID field and confirm your entries with the ⌈Enter⌉ key.

    *Editing an overview page*

7. Then, select the OVERVIEWPAGE view area and select the ADD VIEW option in the context menu. Select the FORMULARVIEW view from the value help of the VIEW (❶) field in the dialog. Confirm your selection with the ⌈Enter⌉ key.

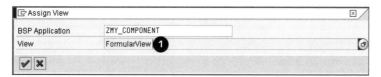

**Figure 16.21** Assigning a Form View to the Overview Page

8. Select the OVERVIEWPAGE view area again and select the ADD VIEW option in the context menu. Select the ROLES.MAINWINDOW interface view from the value help of the VIEW (❶) field in the dialog. Confirm your selection with the ⌜Enter⌟ key.

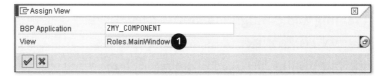

**Figure 16.22**  Assigning an Interface View to the Overview Page

Assigning an overview page to a window

9. Next, select the MAINWINDOW window in the runtime repository editor. Select the ADD VIEW option from the context menu. Select the OVERVIEW PAGE entry from the value help of the VIEW field in the dialog. Confirm your selection with the ⌜Enter⌟ key. This assigns the overview page to the main window of the UI component.

10. Use the SAVE button in the runtime repository editor to save your settings.

11. Switch to the component structure browser. With the UI Configuration Tool of the OVERVIEWPAGE view, create a new default configuration by clicking the NEW CONFIGURATION button. Use the ⌜Enter⌟ key to copy the default values shown in the dialog.

12. Copy the OVERVIEWPAGE default setting in the UI Configuration Tool and click CONTINUE.

Inserting assignment blocks

13. Insert all available assignment blocks (❶) into the DISPLAYED ASSIGNMENT BLOCKS (❷) area and implement the settings displayed in Figure 16.23.

14. Save your settings by clicking the SAVE button.

**Figure 16.23**  Configuring the Overview Page

### 16.4.6  Implementing a Dropdown Box

The objective of this practical example is to implement a dropdown box (see Figure 16.24) based on an input field of a configurable Form view. The dropdown box (❶) contains entries for selecting the gender of a business partner.

**Figure 16.24**  Dropdown Box

The example is kept very simple and has potential for optimizations such caching or implementation as a local class.

1. Open the class builder (Transaction SE24) and create a new ABAP class called ZCL_VALUE_HELP_SEX.

   *Creating an ABAP class*

2. Switch to the INTERFACES tab and add the IF_BSP_WD_VALUEHELP_PLDESCR interface. Then, change to the METHODS tab.

   *Adding an interface*

3. Click the IF_BSP_WD_VALUEHELP_PLDESCR~GET_SELECTION_TABLE method and implement the statements from Listing 16.8.

```
data: lt_domain_entries type standard table of dd07v.
call function 'DD_DOMVALUES_GET'
  exporting
    domname  = 'BU_SEXID'
    langu    = sy-langu
    text     = 'X'
  tables
    dd07v_tab = lt_domain_entries.
data: ls_sel_table type line of
bsp_wd_dropdown_table,
lt_sel_table type bsp_wd_dropdown_table.
field-symbols: <domain> type dd07v.
loop at lt_domain_entries assigning <domain>.
  ls_sel_table-key = <domain>-valpos.
  ls_sel_table-value = <domain>-ddtext.
  append ls_sel_table to lt_sel_table.
endloop.
rt_result = lt_sel_table.
```

**Listing 16.8**  Filling a Dropdown Box with Domain Values

Creating and
implementing a
constructor Save your settings and then return to the method overview in the class builder (Figure 16.25). Now, create the CONSTRUCTOR method (❶) by clicking the ☐Constructor button.

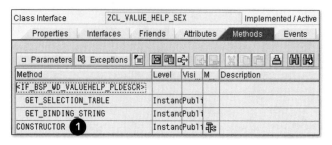

**Figure 16.25**  Methods Tab of the ZCL_VALUE_HELP_SEX Class

4. Insert the following statement in the constructor method:

```
me->if_bsp_wd_valuehelp_pldescr~source_type =
me->if_bsp_wd_valuehelp_pldescr~source_type_table.
```

5. Activate the ZCL_VALUE_HELP_SEX class.

6. Open the ZMY_COMPONENT UI component.

7. Double-click the FORMULARVIEW view to select it in the VIEWS node in the component structure browser.

Generating a
V getter method 8. In the detailed overview of the FORMULARVIEW view, open the ATTRIBUTES node of the BUILHEADER model node in the context of the view. Then, select the STRUCT.SEX attribute and select the GENERATE V GETTER option from the context menu.

9. Next, select the STRUCT.SEX attribute again and select the GENERATE P GETTER option from the context menu.

10. Double-click the GET_P_SEX P getter method. This takes you to the class builder. Switch to change mode and implement the following statement in the P getter method:

```
CASE iv_property.
    WHEN IF_BSP_WD_MODEL_SETTER_GETTER=>FP_FIELDTYPE.
        RV_VALUE =
            CL_BSP_DLC_VIEW_DESCRIPTOR=>FIELD_TYPE_PICKLIST.
ENDCASE.
```

11. Activate the changes and return to the detailed overview.

12. Double-click the GET_V_SEX V getter method. This takes you to the class builder. Switch to change mode and implement the following statement in the V getter method:

    Implementing the V getter method

```
create object rv_valuehelp_descriptor type zcl_value_help_
sex.
```

13. Activate the changes and return to the detailed overview.

## 16.5 Navigating with Navigational Links

This practical example is the implementation of navigation from a search page to an overview page based on navigational links. We will therefore show you the integration of a link into the search result list of a search page. You will use the link to start the navigation to the overview page. We will also cover creating inbound and outbound plugs and a navigational link.

### 16.5.1 Creating Inbound and Outbound Plugs

1. Open the ZMY_COMPONENT UI component.

2. Double-click the ADVSEARCHRESULTVIEW view in the component structure browser.

3. Select the INBOUND PLUGS node in the detailed overview of the ADVSEARCHRESULTVIEW view.

   Creating an inbound plug

4. Select the CREATE option in the context menu.

5. A dialog opens. Enter DEFAULT in the PLUG NAME field and confirm your entry with the ⌜Enter⌟ key. The inbound plug called IP_DEFAULT is subsequently generated.

6. Select the OUTBOUND PLUGS node in the detailed overview of the ADVSEARCHRESULTVIEW view.

7. Select the CREATE option in the context menu.

8. Another dialog opens. Enter TO_OVERVIEWPAGE in the PLUG NAME field and confirm your entry with the ⌜Enter⌟ key. The outbound plug called OP_TO_OVERVIEWPAGE is subsequently generated.

9. Double-click the generated OP_TO_OVERVIEWPAGE outbound plug. This takes you to the class builder. Switch to change mode, and insert the following statement in the OP_TO_OVERVIEWPAGE method:

   Implementing navigation

```
view_manager->navigate(
  source_rep_view  = rep_view
  outbound_plug    = 'TO_OVERVIEWPAGE'
  data_collection  = iv_data_collection ).
```

10. Activate your changes in the class builder and return to the detailed overview of the AdvSearchResultView view.

11. Double-click the OverviewPage view in the component structure browser.

12. Select the Inbound Plugs node in the detailed overview of the Over-viewpPage view.

13. Select the Create option from the context menu.

14. A dialog opens. Enter Default in the Plug Name field and confirm your entry with the [Enter] key. The inbound plug called IP_DEFAULT is generated.

### 16.5.2  Creating Navigational Links

1. Open the ZMY_COMPONENT UI component.

2. Switch to the runtime repository editor.

3. Switch to change mode by clicking the Edit button in the runtime repository editor.

Adding a navigational link
4. Select the Navigational Links node and select the Add Navigational Link option in the context menu.

5. In the dialog that opens, insert the entries displayed in Figure 16.26 (❶ – ❺). Confirm your entries with the [Enter] key.

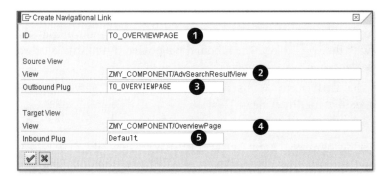

**Figure 16.26**  Defining a Navigational Link

6. Use the Save button in the runtime repository editor to save your settings.

### 16.5.3 Integrating a Link into the Result List

1. Open the ZMY_COMPONENT UI component.

2. Double-click the ADVSEARCHRESULTVIEW view in the component structure browser.

3. In the detailed overview of the ADVSEARCHRESULTVIEW view, select the STRUCT.ACCOUNT_DESCRIPTION attribute (**2**) in the BUILHEADER (**1**) context node and select the GENERATE P GETTER option from the context menu (**3** in Figure 16.27).

Generating a P getter method

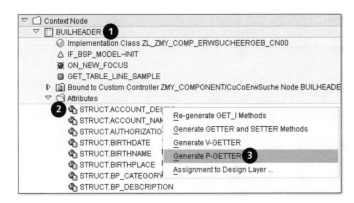

**Figure 16.27** Generating a P Getter for the ACCOUNT_DESCRIPTION Attribute

4. After you have generated the P getter method, open the STRUCT. ACCOUNT_DESCRIPTION node. Double-click the GET_P_ACCOUNT_ DESCRIPTION method. This takes you to the class builder.

5. Switch from there to change mode and insert the statements from Listing 16.9 in the method definition.

Implementing the P getter method

```
case iv_property.
  when if_bsp_wd_model_setter_getter=>fp_fieldtype.
    rv_value = cl_bsp_dlc_view_descriptor=>field_type_event_
link.
  when if_bsp_wd_model_setter_getter=>fp_onclick.
    rv_value = 'LINKCLICK'.
  when if_bsp_wd_model_setter_getter=>fp_tooltip.
endcase.
```

**Listing 16.9** Integrating a Link into the Result List

6. Activate your changes of the GET_P_ACCOUNT_DESCRIPTION method and return to the detailed overview of the ADVSEARCHRESULTVIEW view.

<table>
<tr><td>

Creating event
handlers for
LINKCLICK event

</td><td>

7. In the detailed overview of the ADVSEARCHRESULTVIEW view, select the EVENT HANDLER node and select the CREATE option from the context menu.

</td></tr>
</table>

8. A dialog appears. Enter LINKCLICK in the EVENT NAME field and confirm this entry with the ⌜Enter⌝ key to create the event handler.

9. Then, double-click the EH_ONLINKCLICK event handler in the EVENT HANDLER node of the detailed overview. This takes you to the class builder.

<table>
<tr><td>

Implementing an
event handler

</td><td>

10. Switch to change mode in the class builder and copy the statements from Listing 16.10 into the EH_ONLINKCLICK method definition.

</td></tr>
</table>

```
data lv_index type i.
cl_thtmlb_util=>get_event_info
( exporting iv_event = htmlb_event_ex
  importing ev_index = lv_index ).
check lv_index is not initial.
data lr_entity      type ref to if_bol_bo_property_access.
lr_entity ?= me->typed_context->builheader->collection_
wrapper->find( iv_index = lv_index ).
check lr_entity is bound.
data lr_collection  type ref to if_bol_bo_col.
create object lr_collection type cl_crm_bol_bo_col.
lr_collection->add( lr_entity ).
data lr_coco type ref to zl_zmy_comp_bspwdcomponen_impl.
lr_coco ?= me->comp_controller.
lr_coco->typed_context->builheader->collection_wrapper-
>add( lr_entity ).
call method me->op_to_overviewpage(
    iv_data_collection = lr_collection ).
```

**Listing 16.10** Starting Navigation to the Overview Page

11. Activate the class and return to the detailed overview.

## 16.6 Integrating the UI Component into the User Interface

The objective of this practical example is to integrate the ZMY_COMPONENT UI component in the form of a work center page as a link in the navigation bar. In this example, we assume that you already have your own navigation bar profile called ZSALESNAVPROFIL. We also show you how to define a window inbound plug and a window as an interface view.

### 16.6.1 Defining a Window Inbound Plug

1. Open the ZMY_COMPONENT UI component.

2. Double-click the MainWindow window in the Windows node in the component structure browser.

3. Select the Inbound Plugs node in the detailed overview of the Main-Window window.

   *Creating a window inbound plug*

4. Select the Create option from the context menu.

5. Enter SEARCH in the Plug Name field and confirm your entry with the Enter key.

### 16.6.2 Defining a Window as an Interface View

1. Open the ZMY_COMPONENT UI component.

2. Switch to the runtime repository editor and activate change mode by clicking the Edit button.

3. Select the ComponentInterface node and select the Add Interface View option from the context menu.

   *Adding an interface view*

4. A dialog appears. Select the ZMY_COMPONENT/MainWindow entry from the value help for the Assigned To Window field and confirm this with the Enter key.

5. Then, select the InboundPlugs subnode of the ZMY_COMPONENT/MainWindow interface view in the runtime repository editor.

6. Select the Add Inbound Plug option from the context menu.

7. A dialog appears. Select the Search entry from the value help for the I/O Plug field and confirm your selection with the Enter key.

8. Use the Save button in the runtime repository editor to save your settings.

### 16.6.3 Integrating into the Repository for Work Area Components

1. Start the SAP Implementation Guide (Transaction SPRO).

2. Start the Customer Relationship Management • UI Framework • Technical Role Definition • Define Repository for Work Area Components IMG activity.

3. Confirm the dialog containing the comment Caution, the Table is Cross-Client. with the Enter key.

4. Click the NEW ENTRIES button and copy the entries (❶) from Figure 16.28.

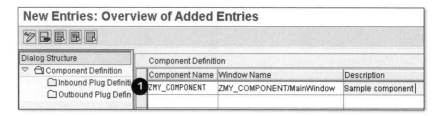

**Figure 16.28** Defining a Work Area Component

5. Select the line and double-click the DEFINITION FOR INBOUND PLUG node in the dialog structure.

*Defining an inbound plug for a work area component*

6. Click the NEW ENTRIES button and copy entries ❶ – ❹ from Figure 16.29.

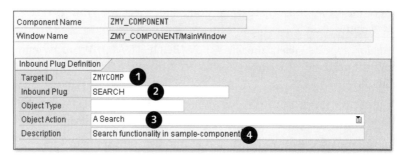

**Figure 16.29** Defining an Inbound Plug

7. Save your settings by clicking the SAVE button.

## 16.6.4 Defining a Logical Link and a Work Center Page

1. Start Transaction CRMC_UI_NBLINKS.

*Defining logical links*

2. Double-click the DEFINE LOGICAL LINKS node in the dialog structure and create a new entry by clicking the NEW ENTRIES button. Copy values ❶ – ❺ from Figure 16.30.

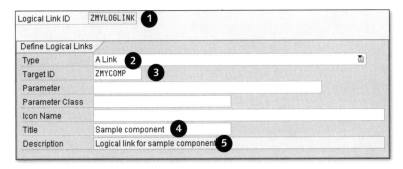

**Figure 16.30**  Defining a Logical Link

3. Save your settings again by clicking SAVE.

4. Double-click the DEFINE WORK CENTRE PAGE node in the dialog structure and create a new entry by clicking the NEW ENTRIES button. Copy values ❶ – ❹ from Figure 16.31.

*Defining a work center page*

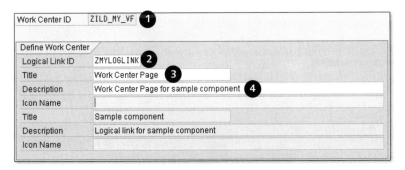

**Figure 16.31**  Defining a Work Center Page

5. Click the SAVE button.

6. Then, assign the work center page to the ZSALESNAVPROFIL navigation bar profile to make the page available as a link in the navigation bar.

*Assigning to a navigation bar profile*

*This chapter presents the base core competencies of CRM version 7.0. The individual areas of the Web Client are developed further on the basis of SAP CRM 2007. Increasing user-friendliness is a central goal of subsequent CRM versions.*

# 17    Outlook for CRM 7.0

Currently, the topic of customer relationship management is experiencing a boom. According to *Gartner*, in 2007 alone, the global demand of CRM applications increased by 23% (*http://www.itworld.com/saas/53453/gartner-crm-market-23-percent-07*) [February 13, 2009]. Nevertheless, there are still obstacles for the implementation of CRM applications. Factors such as user-friendly operation or logical structure of the CRM application should therefore be considered during the development of the software in the runtime repository editor so that the product becomes a success in real life.

SAP tackles this challenge with the new *CRM version 7.0*. On the basis of today's Web Client, the new release is expected to enter the pilot phase at the customer in the first half of 2009. For this reason, the main additional developments can be found in the enhanced, user-friendly operation of the user interface. Additional developments for version 7.0 focus on flexibility and intuitive usability for untypical software users whose work focuses on marketing and sales. Furthermore, additional new industry solutions will be provided and the areas *public sector* and *travel management,* including *loyalty management,* are newly integrated with the new release. The latest Internet standard Web 2.0 will also be supported. Its use not only provides additional fun for the end user, but also allows users to determine the creation and editing of content to a qualitative and quantitative extent, for example, by personalizing the user interface. In general, the *look and feel* of the user interface is further adapted to the interfaces known from the Internet. This enables end users to use the knowledge they have acquired in using the Internet for the new SAP CRM release 7.0.

**Based on SAP CRM 2007**

## 17.1 General, Non-Technical Outlook

At a glance   With CRM version 7.0, SAP continues its approach of a holistic and consistent structure of the user interface. Great importance is placed on enabling the users to customize their daily work environment to their specific requirements and flexibility and personalization in the structure of the user interface remain the main focus of development. The *BSP technology* provides the basis for this flexibility. The structure of the user interface for CRM version 7.0, however, is almost identical to Web Client CRM 2007 (❶ in Figure 17.1). The work area is enclosed by an L shape, including the header and navigation area. The header and navigation areas are still fixed to a large extent to ensure that the end user can always return to the starting point of the navigation.

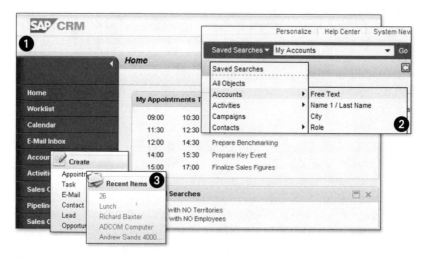

**Figure 17.1**   User Interface in CRM Version 7.0

New options in the header area   The known system links (PERSONALIZE, HELP CENTER, SYSTEM NEWS, AND LOGOFF) are still available in the header area and the information blocks FAVORITES and CRM FEED are new in the personalization area. CRM FEED provides access to personalized system content with any RSS feed readers. The Favorites information block enables you to integrate your favorite links to CRM applications, web sites, and widgets with the home page. In the header area of the user interface, the comprehensive search was improved (❷) through an enhancement with a TREX-based search. The search query now interlinks simple searches, expert searches, and saved searches. Consequently, the result list provides cross-application results that can be filtered according to the end user's specifications.

In the navigation area, it will be possible to integrate additional logos (❸ in Figure 17.1). You can then display *direct links* and *recent items*. This enables fast navigation in recently processed business objects. Each user can also personalize the number of business objects displayed and up to ten entries can be displayed in the navigation bar.

New options in the navigation area

The navigation sequence to the individual pages remains unchanged compared to version SAP CRM 2007. Known page types and their structure continue to be used and enhanced; pages will appear in a new, revised design (❶ in Figure 17.2). For example, the overview page will have a new optional *tile layout* as an alternative to the default one-column layout. Other options such as showing videos and a *smart value help* are also provided. Smart value help offers user-specific suggestions for input fields based on the last entries made by the user.

New options in the work area

There will also be many additional options to map graphical displays. The flexibility known from SAP CRM 2007—for example, the moving of information and assignment blocks—is kept and extended further. However, the new flexibility of version 7.0 becomes most obvious in the calendar (❸). Almost all combination options for personalizing the user interface are now possible for this page type (❷).

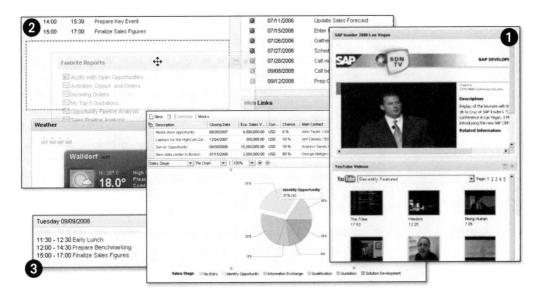

**Figure 17.2** Page Types in the Work Area

The SEARCH PAGE page type is still structured according to the pattern known from the search area and the result list. As of version 7.0, it is also possible to display the search result as an *overview*. Thus, the person who is performing a search can quickly obtain an overview of the entire search result. The new features of version 7.0 include the graphical display of results and the addition of brief information above the result list on the search page, with the system displaying the number of currently found results here. The flexible display of the message bar is also new. You can now place the message bar at other positions in the user interface using drag-and-drop. In general, improvement of the drag-and-drop functionality in the personalization and configuration tools is further advanced. Particularly, moving content both within and between them will be possible as of version 7.0.

> **Note**
>
> The user interface for SAP CRM version 7.0 will continue to be a Web Client user interface. There will be enhancements that increase the flexibility and user-friendliness of the user interface.

## 17.2 General, Technical Outlook

New options in the framework

SAP CRM version 7.0 will be delivered on the basis of *SAP NetWeaver 7.0 enhancement package 1*. This enables a greater decoupling of the UI framework. Up to and including SAP CRM 2007, the framework as a CRMUIF software component used to be an adapted *add-on* for the SAP_ABA 7.0 application basis. In particular, this resulted in a strong dependency on the basis of ABA support packages, which could only be imported using a suitable CRMUIF *conflict resolution transport* (CRT). As of version 7.0, the UI framework is an independent software component (WEBCUIF) based directly on the SAP_ABA 7.01 application and there will be no dependencies between the basis, the framework, and the CRM support packages. CRM version 7.0 is embedded in SAP Business Suite release 2009. The software component is now available throughout the suite and in particular in SAP ERP 6.0 EhP 4.

Revised application framework

The most striking feature of version 7.0 is the completely revised application framework; at the latest, this becomes obvious in the profile selection (see Figure 17.3).

In addition to making the design more appealing, *session handling* was also revised to a great extent. It is now possible to both implement a *browser refresh* and return to the last application using a real-time *browser back* after you have accidently exited the application, without losing the session. Furthermore, you can start a new CRM session in Microsoft Internet Explorer using the ⌈Ctrl⌉ + ⌈N⌉ key combination.

**Figure 17.3**  Example: New Selection of Business Roles

From a technical perspective, the comprehensive use of the design layer across the entire CRM application should also be mentioned. It enables a cross-view adaptation of the user interface such as *re-labeling* or *hiding of fields* in the standard. This increases the consistency of customer adaptations and greatly reduces the associated effort, particularly through the implementation of generic UI object types. The following text outlines additional innovations of version 7.0:

Design Layer

▶ **Implementation of a new application enhancement tool**
The tool will replace the EEWB and cooperate with the integrated UI Configuration Tool in most use cases.

Summary of innovations

▶ **Enhancement of the online analysis tools**
In addition to the field information dialog box (⌈F2⌉ key), you are provided with a system information and a view hierarchy dialog, as well as a simple performance monitor. The analysis of application behavior is supported by *conditional breakpoints*. Furthermore, it is possible to generate a support message directly from the field information dialog using *Solution Manager*.

▶ **New page type**
You are provided with a new framework support for developing task-based user inputs and the development of process-oriented user interfaces is supported by the implementation of a new page type. The development is analogous to overview pages but it offers additional options for process control (see Figure 17.4).

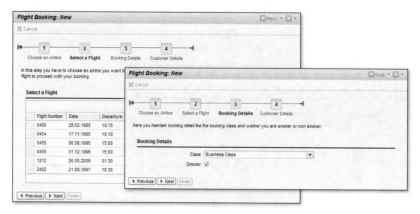

**Figure 17.4** New Page Type

Furthermore, it is worth mentioning that the Component Workbench was revised in version 7.0. You are now provided with a wizard for context node binding and a new wizard for generating value attributes, among other things. In addition, you can delete view, controller, and component enhancements in the Component Workbench as of version 7.0. Moreover, you will be able to use the Component Workbench for explicit component node enhancements and to create and delete enhancement sets. According to the product management, version 7.0 should provide a clear performance advantage, which becomes primarily apparent in the display of dialogs and tables.

**Application Enhancement Tool**

From a consultant's perspective and with a focus on customer-specific system adaptations, the new implementation of the integrated *Application Enhancement tool* (AET), which enables object enhancements in running applications, is relevant. The benefits of the AET include the following:

▶ Embedding in the web UI control logic at runtime

▶ Improvement of performance, usability, and software logistics

▶ Greater "coverage" than the EEWB regarding supported applications

▶ Homogeneity in all applications

▶ Integrated translation of texts

▶ More functionality in the reporting area

In particular, the missing metadata transport is fixed with the AET. Consequently, as of CRM version 7.0, the EEWB is only required for special cases (e.g., time-dependent customer tables for business partner). Nonetheless, you can still use the EEWB in parallel for enhancements in release SAP CRM 7.0 and in the subsequent releases.

# Appendices

# A    Glossary

| Abbreviation | Description |
|---|---|
| ActiveX | ActiveX refers to a software component model developed by Microsoft for active contents. ActiveX components enhance the component object model (*COM*) standards by Microsoft. |
| AJAX | AJAX (*asynchronous JavaScript and XML*) refers to a concept of asynchronous data transfer between a server and the browser; this data transfer enables you to carry out an HTTP request within an HTML page without having to completely refresh the page. |
| API | API (*application programming interface*) is a programming interface that provides a software system to other programs for connection to the system. An API defines the use of the interfaces at the source text level only. |
| BOR | BOR (*business object repository*) represents the central point of access to the SAP business object types including their BAPIs. Originally, the BOR was developed for the business workflow. Today, the BOR is not only used to store SAP business object types and their BAPIs but also for the ArchiveLink, message control, and other generic object services. |
| CSS | CSS (*cascading style sheets*) are a declarative style sheet language for structured documents. They are primarily used together with HTML and XML and specify how a specific content or area should be displayed. |
| Design object | The design object defines field settings that relate to the user interface and is assigned to multiple views that are used in the same business context. |
| Fat client | Fat client is a term from data processing: In a client-server architecture, the concepts *fat client*, *rich client*, or *smart client* are used for a client for which the actual processing of data is implemented directly in the client. In most cases, it also provides the graphical user interface. |
| Internet transaction server | The Internet transaction server (*ITS*) is used for displaying graphical application interfaces as HTML pages in the SAP environment. Through this, users only need a web browser instead of the SAP GUI. Both SAP's own and custom-developed applications can be operated via the ITS. |
| Object-based navigation | Object-based navigation (*OBN*) provides portal users an additional navigation option on the basis of business objects that come from production back-end systems and are not defined in the portal. |
| Payload | Payload (user data) is the data that is transported between two partners during a communication. It includes, for example, language, texts, characters, images, and sounds. |

| Abbreviation | Description |
|---|---|
| Presentation (view) | The presentation layer (MVC architecture pattern) is responsible for the presentation of the required data from the model and the acceptance of user interactions; however, it is not responsible for the further processing of data transferred by the user. |
| Singleton | The singleton is a design pattern used in a software development and belongs to the category of generation patterns. It prevents that more than one object is generated of a class. |
| Smalltalk | Smalltalk is a dynamic object-oriented programming language whose original version is untyped. It was developed by the XEROX PARC research center in the 1970s. |
| SOAP | SOAP (*simple object access protocol*) is a protocol you can use to exchange data between systems and implement remote procedure calls (RPCs). |
| Style sheet | Style sheets are a markup language in IT and comparable to a form template. |
| Thin client | Within data processing, a thin client refers to an application or a computer as an end device (*terminal*) of a network whose functional equipment is limited to input and output. |
| W3C | W3C (*world wide web consortium*) is a board for standardizing technologies that concern the world wide web. |
| Web 2.0 | The concept "Web 2.0" does not necessarily refer to specific technologies or innovations but rather to a changed use and perception of the Internet. The term was characterized by Dale Dougherty and Craig Cline in 2004. It did not become popular until Tim O'Reilly, owner of *O'Reilly Media*, published his article "What is Web 2.0" on September 30, 2005. |
| Widget | A widget (or applet) is a small computer program that is not operated as an independent application but is integrated with a graphical user interface or a web site. |
| WSDL | WSDL (*webservice description language*) defines an XML specification that is independent of platforms, programming languages, and protocols to describe network services (web services) for exchanging messages. |
| XDP | XDP (*XML data package*) is the file format in XML notation used by Adobe LiveCycle Designer. |
| XSL | XSL (*extensible stylesheet language*) is a family of languages to create layouts for XML documents. |
| XSLT | XSLT (*extensible stylesheet language transformation*) is a programming language for the transformation of XML documents. It is part of XSL and represents a complete language. |

# B    Bibliography

▶ Blumstein, R., Wardley, M. *Worldwide Marketing and Sales Automation Applications Software Forecast, 2003 – 2007: A New Look at 2002.* In: *IDC,* Study No. 29387 (2003).

▶ Buck-Emden, R., Zencke, P. *mySAP CRM: The Official Guidebook to SAP CRM 4.0.* SAP PRESS, 2003.

▶ Burton, J. *Maximizing Your SAP CRM Interaction Center.* SAP PRESS, 2008.

▶ Kirchler M, Manhart D., Unger J. *Service with SAP CRM.* SAP PRESS, 2008.

## Additional Sources

▶ **UI Guidelines for CRM Web Client User Interface**
*www.sapdesignguild.org/resources/CRM-UI-Guidelines-Customers.pdf* (February 13, 2009)

▶ **SAP Design Guide**
*Providing a Web-Like User Experience to Business Users – The New SAP CRM Web Client User Interface* by Martin Schrepp and Theo Held. *http://www.sapdesignguild.org/community/readers/reader_crm_web_client.asp* (February 13, 2009)

▶ **SAP Documentation**
You can find official SAP documentation on the topic of CRM under *http://help.sap.com* via the path SAP BUSINESS SUITE • SAP CUSTOMER RELATIONSHIP MANAGEMENT • SAP CRM 2007 (6.0) SP02 • APPLICATION HELP • SAP CUSTOMER RELATIONSHIP MANAGEMENT • COMPONENTS AND FUNCTIONS • BASIC FUNCTIONS • UI FRAMEWORK AND CONFIGURATION, or under *http://help.sap.com/saphelp_crm70/helpdata/en/34/6b69b1691b47a599052284e185f374/frameset.htm*

# C   The Authors

**Michael Füchsle** worked for several years as a development consultant and business process consultant for SAP Deutschland AG. As a ramp up coach, he gained in-depth knowledge of the Web Client UI Framework in CRM 2007 and CRM 7.0. Since the middle of 2009, Michael has been working as a freelancer on international projects. Michael can be reached at *michael@fuechsle.net*.

**Matthias E. Zierke** holds a degree in information management and a master degree in management and consulting. After international SAP projects for Siemens AG, he now works as a CRM consultant at SAP Deutschland AG both on a national and international scale.

# Index

## D

## E

## T

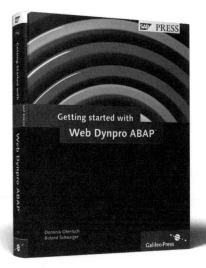

Explains architecture, basic principles, and real-life solutions

Provides step-by-step guidance on the first functional Web Dynpro application

Covers UI elements, standard components, and dynamic applications

Dominik Ofenloch, Roland Schwaiger

# Getting Started with Web Dynpro ABAP

Web Dynpro ABAP is the standard UI technology used by SAP for the development of web applications on SAP NetWeaver Application Server ABAP. This book makes it easier for developers with existing ABAP knowledge to become familiar with the component-based UI development environment, and lays the foundation for the creation of complex applications based on Web Dynpro ABAP. It discusses the functions and special features that are critical for you if you're a beginner, and is structured so that you can understand basic concepts.

approx. 480 pp., 69,95 Euro / US$ 69.95
ISBN 978-1-59229-311-7, Nov 2009

**>> www.sap-press.com**

The definitive SAP rules for ABAP development

Detailed examples of good and poor programming style

With numerous recommendations for everyday programming

Horst Keller, Wolf Hagen Thümmel

# Official ABAP Programming Guidelines

This book, the official SAP programming style guide, will show you how to maximize performance, readability, and stability in your ABAP programs.
Sorted by programming tasks, this book will provide you with guidelines on how to best fulfill each task. Starting with basic considerations about the use of comprehensive programming concepts, the book continues with formal criteria such as organizing your source code, and then concludes with descriptions of the various areas and tasks of ABAP development. Filled with real-life code examples, both good and bad, this book is a must-have guide for ABAP developers.

approx. 310 pp., 69,95 Euro / US$ 69.95
ISBN 978-1-59229-290-5, Oct 2009

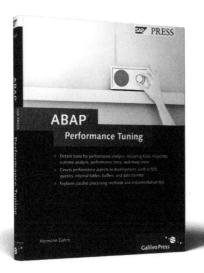

Tools for performance analysis: Code
Inspector, runtime analysis,
Performance Trace, and more

Performance aspects in development:
SQL queries, internal tables, buffer,
data transfer

Application design: general
performance and parallelization

Hermann Gahm

# ABAP Performance Tuning

This book for ABAP developers details best practices for ABAP
performance tuning. Covering the most critical performance-relevant
programming issues and performance monitoring tools, this book will
show you how to best analyze, tune, and implement your ABAP
programs.
Starting with a description of the client/server architecture, the book
moves on to discussing the different tools for analyzing performance.
Programming techniques are then analyzed in detail, based on numerous
real-life examples. This book will help you ensure that your ABAP
programs are tuned for best performance.

approx. 350 pp., 69,95 Euro / US$ 69.95
ISBN 978-1-59229-289-9, July 2009

All about fundamentals, technologies, and practical solutions

Covers the usage in online and offline scenarios

With examples of Adobe Document Services, Adobe LiveCycle De-signer, ISR Framework, Web Dynpro Integration and many more

Jürgen Hauser, Andreas Deutesfeld, Stephan Rehmann, Thomas Szücs, Philipp Thun

# SAP Interactive Forms by Adobe

The book adopts a classic structure: A general introduction explains what Interactive Forms are and how they are implemented. It then illustrates the creation of print and interactive forms by the usage of technology (Adobe Document Services), via tool (Adobe LiveCycle Designer) and interface call (Web Dynpro, web service). The level of complexity of the described approaches successively increases. According to the product idea, the book covers all topics comprehensively and holistically. Basic knowledge in the areas of ABAP and Web Dynpro are, however, taken for granted.

624 pp., 2009, 79,95 Euro / US$ 79.95
ISBN 978-1-59229-254-7

>> www.sap-press.com

**Interested in reading more?**

Please visit our Web site for all
new book releases from SAP PRESS.

**www.sap-press.com**